RESEARCH BUSINESS MARKETS

The IMRA Handbook of Business-to-Business Marketing Research

Edited by

Ken Sutherland

on behalf of

IMRA

KOGAN PAGE

First published in 1978 by
John Wiley & Sons as the
Manual of Industrial Marketing Research
edited by Allan Rawnsley

This edition first published by
Kogan Page in 1991.

Apart from any fair dealing for the purposes of research or private study, or criticism or review, as permitted under the Copyright, Designs and Patents Act, 1988, this publication may only be reproduced, stored or transmitted, in any form or by any means, with the prior permission in writing of the publishers, or in the case of reprographic reproduction in accordance with the terms of licences issued by the Copyright Licensing Agency. Enquiries concerning reproduction outside those terms should be sent to the publishers at the undermentioned address:

Kogan Page Limited
120 Pentonville Road
London N1 9JN

© Industrial Marketing Research Association, 1978, 1991

British Library Cataloguing in Publication Data

A CIP record for this book is available from the British Library.

ISBN 0 7494 0421 3

Typeset by DP Photosetting, Aylesbury, Bucks
Printed and bound in Great Britain by
Biddles Ltd., Guildford and Kings Lynn

Contents

Preface	9
Foreword	11
List of Contributors	15

PART I: INTRODUCTION   23

1. General Introduction – *Ken Sutherland*   25
2. Marketing and Marketing Research – *Andrew McIntosh*   29
3. The Scope of Business Marketing Research – *David Smith*   45

PART II: THE TECHNIQUES OF BUSINESS MARKETING RESEARCH   71

4. Preparing for a Business Marketing Research Project – *Johann Aucamp*   73
5. Desk Research – *Martin Stoll*   83
6. The Collection of Primary Data – *Christine Eborall*   95
7. Sample Design, Selection and Estimating – *Phyllis Macfarlane*   141

8.	The Skills of Interviewing – *Tony Lake*	163
9.	Questionnaire Use and Design – *Paul Hague*	177

PART III: ANALYSIS, INTERPRETATION AND PRESENTATION — 217

10.	Analysis and Interpretation of Quantitative Data – *Rick Moore*	219
11.	Analysis and Interpretation of Qualitative Data – *Nick Watkins*	237
12.	The Presentation of Survey Results – *John Wigzell*	253

PART IV: THE APPLICATIONS OF BUSINESS MARKETING RESEARCH — 287

13.	Product Market Size – *Tony Dent*	289
14.	Researching Competitors – *Conrad Brigden*	307
15.	Corporate Image – *Peter Hutton*	325
16.	New Product Development and Testing – *Ken Sutherland*	341
17.	Advertising Research – *Roy Haworth*	351
18.	The Role of Sales Forecasting in Business Planning – *Alan Wolfe*	359
19.	Acquisition Research – *Chris da Costa*	373

PART V: INTERNATIONAL RESEARCH — 393

20.	International Research – *Denis Pirie*	395

PART VI: THE MANAGEMENT OF BUSINESS MARKETING RESEARCH — 419

21.	The Management of Commissioned Research – *Keith Bailey*	421

Contents

22.	Personal and Corporate Organisation – *Ken Sutherland*	443

PART VII: APPENDICES   **453**

A.	IMRA – its Aims, Functions and Membership Grades	455
B.	Qualifications and Training in Business Marketing Research	459
C.	Summary of the Code of Conduct	461
D.	List of Information Sources	465
E.	Bibliography of Major Relevant Texts	467
F.	The Export Marketing Research Scheme	471
Index		474

Preface

Researching Business Markets – The IMRA Handbook is a complete guide to the techniques and applications of marketing research, as used in the business-to-business context. It is also, effectively, a second edition of the *Manual of Industrial Marketing Research*, first published by John Wiley in 1978 and edited by Allan Rawnsley. The change from 'Industrial' to 'Business' in the title is an indication of the broadening of the profession that has taken place in the intervening 12 years.

The 1978 edition was 'prepared under the auspices of the Industrial Marketing Research Association'. So, too, is the present Handbook, but now the input from the Association is even stronger – hence the inclusion of 'IMRA' in the title. The Association is the leading body in the UK representing those involved in business marketing research and, indeed, is one of the most important of such organisations in the world. This Handbook is intended to demonstrate and maintain that importance.

The present Handbook has been written by a group of authors, each expert in his or her selected field, and to these authors IMRA extends its warmest thanks. The Handbook has been edited under the auspices of the Publications Committee of IMRA, which is ultimately responsible for any errors of omission or commission – but it is hoped that these are few.

The Editor's task, apart from the initial planning of the Handbook, has largely been one of organising the various contributions to achieve some uniformity of layout, and to minimise duplication. No attempt has been made to change the style of the individual contributions, and it is hoped that the resultant variations in style will make the Handbook pleasantly readable. Some duplication of content does and must occur, however, partly because the reader has the right to expect

Researching Business Markets – The IMRA Handbook

completeness of coverage under any one heading without having to read the entire book.

The Handbook is intended as a source of information and instruction, to those who are new to business marketing research and to those who are expert in some of its techniques or applications. For the newcomer, it provides a complete introduction to the profession and its skills, and a sourcebook for the knowledge necessary to progress through any examinations in the subject. For the worker experienced in some aspects of business marketing, it provides the knowledge necessary to move successfully into other aspects. Even for someone expert in all fields, it is hoped that the Handbook will provide fresh insight into topics long considered familiar.

It is anticipated that equal value will be obtained from the Handbook by researchers in company marketing departments ('in-house' researchers) as by people working for those consultancies and agencies providing business marketing research services. While it is aimed primarily at the practitioner of business marketing research, the Handbook is also intended to be of value to business marketing personnel in general – especially those who commission, or who use the results of, such research.

To all these intended readers, IMRA commends this Handbook as a book to be in their possession and to be used to their benefit. Comments on it will be welcome; it is recognised that the world of business marketing research continues to change, and a third edition may be necessary in less than another 12 years.

K S Sutherland
Chairman
IMRA Publications Committee
February 1991

Foreword

Sir Monty Finniston, F Eng, FRS

Since the issue of the first IMRA Handbook some 12 years ago, the worlds of industry and of business to which it is linked have changed markedly, and both will change even more rapidly in the years to come. The present Handbook will last until the end of the century, but the third issue will differ from the second even more than this one does from the first. But do not wait until the turn of the century before making up your minds to buy this issue, since it is an up-to-date account of the state of the art which cannot be and has not been bettered by any other organisation or institution. Buy the volume now, since today the world at large and the industrial and business worlds in particular do not make decisions by the seat of their pants (firms which do, in time usually go bankrupt) but rather on information based on research, experience and practice, whether obtained in-house or through the independent externally-based professional and knowledgeable companies, many of whom are members of IMRA. This information is as fully relevant to the specific circumstances obtaining as can be, but above all the data and advice given are accurate and up to date.

The Handbook in its six Parts treats the many aspects of today's complex and complicated market research on matters industrial. It describes through its many experienced authors the techniques which have been employed, in the first place, in consumer research but which are now extended to business research, how the data obtained are analysed and interpreted, the conclusions to be drawn and what the future looks like from these conclusions, how international workers in the field differ from their British counterparts, the organisation of people in the various teams which engage in this work, in-house or independently and, what is most important but is rarely referred to, it has Appendices which detail what the reader should know, but which do not confuse. Incidentally, the reader does not have to plough through everything which is written, but can choose those matters which are of concern at the moment.

Why am I enthusiastic at the publication of this Handbook by the IMRA Publications Committee? It is for three main reasons. The first of these is that the economy of this country is not in good shape (and worsening) in comparison with our international rivals, who exploit the new technologies to their greater advantage and more quickly than we do. (Socially we all desire to see the standards of living of our population improved but this is wholly dependent on the continuing advance of our international industrial and business activities.) In achieving this desirable state of affairs, however, what has to be taken into account is not what is produced but what the market thinks it wants of the new or modified products. And what the market wants, which in many cases it is unclear of itself, has to be determined by the industrial or business research worker. Design, performance, cost, reliability, ease of maintenance or a mix of these and other features? The Japanese and Germans, to name but two economies, in their cars, ships, china, heaters, computers, television, radio, Walkmans and other products, consumer or capital, saw that the basic criteria which have been outlined above had to be met, if their manufacturing operations to produce these products were to be marketable and profitable. It is the business research worker who can help the investor to decide on action based on the facts of a properly designed inquiry.

Second, and this is a temporary but important feature of the future, is that this country enters the Single Market of Europe in January 1993. We will have to accommodate not only what we know now but also the differing views of our European partners. This will not be easy although I have every confidence, knowing the calibre of the people involved, that this hurdle will be surmounted to our ultimate advantage, but the sooner British industry starts to cultivate and work within the new régime, the better of course.

Finally I have left my third reason to the last because it is the easiest and nicest to write. I have been the President of IMRA for longer than

Foreword

the membership may care to remember; I have enjoyed the company of the membership, the discussions at Council meetings, but most of all the organisation's success, which all strove for, whatever their own interests. The Handbook proves that members are prepared to tell all they know to the betterment of the profession. As far as the book itself is concerned, may I take this opportunity (not always afforded to Presidents publicly) to thank the IMRA Publications Committee, without whose drive and persistence this Handbook might never have seen the light of day; the Editor, who saw the volume put to bed; the contributors, whose expertise is to be found under their names in the appropriate chapters; the officials of IMRA, without whose decision to publish, nothing would have been done and, last of all, to wish the Handbook all the commercial success it deserves – and that's a lot.

Editor's note. It is a sad fact that just two weeks after he wrote this foreword, Sir Monty died. He had served IMRA well as its President, and it is to be hoped that this Handbook may stand as a record of that service. To his memory it is dedicated.

List of Contributors

Johann Aucamp (Chapter 4). Johann is managing director of Aucamp Business Research Limited. He has more than 30 years' experience in consumer and industrial research. In 1973 he founded IFT Marketing Research as the company specialising in industrial/business-to-business research in the Gordon Simmons Research Group. He formed ABR in 1991 to specialise in research-based consultancy in international business-to-business markets, but remains a consultant with IFT. Main interests outside market research include photography, watching cricket and rugby, and a passionate love for good red and white Burgundy.

Keith Bailey (Chapter 21). Keith is a consultant in marketing research. He gained his initial grounding in market research in an academic environment. The research content of the International Marketing course at North Staffordshire Polytechnic convinced him that this was his calling, although he has never recovered his faith in postal surveys after personally addressing, stuffing and sealing 300 questionnaires only to receive six replies. He began his career with Metal Box Packaging, travelling Europe interviewing packaging users. He retains vivid memories of a blizzard in the Peloponese on his way to interview (with interpreter) a Greek olive packer. Having experienced the 'sharp end', he joined the Carbonless Papers Operations of The Wiggins Teape Group where he became market research manager. He managed projects throughout Europe regretting only that, of all the marketing managers he supported, he never persuaded his Portuguese colleague to undertake a project there. Keith joined Communication Research Limited in 1987, and there established, as director of CRL Business Research, a select team of specialist business researchers. With this experience as a supplier, he set up his own consultancy in 1990. He is an active member of IMRA's London Section, and serves on the MRS International Committee.

Conrad Brigden (Chapter 14). Conrad is manager of the Market Research Group for IBM UK. Following an earlier career in the RAF, Conrad joined IBM in 1966. After a period of time working as a programmer, as a systems analyst and as a salesman, he joined the Market Research Group where he has been for the past 18 years. He now manages the work of the Group, which involves the identification and planning of the research requirements for the Marketing, Manufacturing, and Development groups in IBM UK, and the coordination of research activities with its European and US Headquarters. In his spare time, Conrad pursues his interests in collecting antiquarian books, in gardening and in yachting – and is looking forward to the time when he can plan a voyage to sunnier climes.

Chris da Costa (Chapter 19). Chris is managing director of Corporate Information Limited. As one of the leading independent market research houses, the company is best known for its acquisition research. It does, however, also undertake research for corporate strategy, investment, and marketing decisions. The company serves both the commercial and manufacturing sectors, as well as the City, and is the only business marketing research company accepted into membership of the British Venture Capital Association. Before joining Corporate Information, Chris commenced his career in marketing by working for the advertising agency Ted Bates. His financial career started as a trainee with merchant bankers N M Rothschild & Sons; he later joined the research department of stockbrokers Savory Milln as an investment analyst. He then moved back into merchant banking and spent ten years with Hambros Bank. His major role was in corporate finance where he set up the Corporate Development Department, specialising in acquisition search and research. He is a member of the British Institute of Management, and a member of IMRA.

Tony Dent (Chapter 13). Tony is an independent computer, marketing and research consultant. He holds an MSc and has been engaged

List of Contributors

in industrial and business-to-business research since starting out as Company Statistician with the MIL Group in 1968. He has subsequently worked with many research and user organisations both in the UK and throughout the world. During this time he has been responsible for almost every kind of research information – qualitative and quantitative, internal and external. As a mathematics graduate, his primary area of interest has been the development of software to improve estimation procedures for market studies. More recently he has been engaged in tracking studies and modelling work.

Christine Eborall (Chapter 6). Christine is a freelance consultant, and was formerly Director of MRB International Ltd. She has 13 years' specialised experience of industrial and business-to-business survey research gained at two leading agencies: IFF Research and MRB International. She has worked on numerous large- and small-scale surveys, both domestic and international, involving the full range of data collection and sampling techniques. In 1989 she started her own consultancy, specialising in the design, analysis and interpretation of industrial and business-to-business surveys. She is a scientist by training, has an MSc in Information Science, is a full member of IMRA and the Market Research Society, and is strongly committed to maintaining the highest possible standards in the conduct of survey research.

Sir Monty Finniston, FEng, FRS (Preface). Sir Monty was President of IMRA for many years, and a good friend to the Association. Perhaps most widely known as the Chairman of British Steel during a stormy period of that company's existence, he had previously been Head of Harwell's Metallurgy Division. He produced the Finniston Report on the future of the Engineering Profession.

Paul Hague (Chapter 9). Paul is a Director of Business & Market Research plc. He graduated in 1969 from Durham University with a degree in Geography, and began his business life in the market research department of Dunlop in Manchester, developing there an immediate affinity for the job which has never waned. After a short time he moved to become Market Research Manager to a Manchester steel company, completing his baptism as an industrial market researcher. At the age of 25, long on ambition and short on experience, Paul established Business & Market Research in Stockport. He acknowledges that in those first few years he learned far more from his clients than they did from him. Notwithstanding this limitation, B&MR has grown to become one of the largest industrial market research consultancies in the UK with one-third of its work derived from overseas projects. Paul has written widely on market research subjects. He is the author of *The Industrial Market Research Handbook*, the joint author with Peter Jackson (his long-time business partner) of *Do Your Own Market Research* and *How To Do Marketing Research*, and is a co-editor of *A Handbook of Market Research Techniques*, all published by Kogan Page.

Roy Haworth (Chapter 17). Roy is market research manager for 3M (UK). He has been working in market research for over 20 years, both consumer and industrial. He began as a consumer researcher with the Littlewoods Company, a large chain store and mail order concern. After that he was market research manager with the Amalgamated Dental Company in London, and then a research consultant with IMACON AG, a research agency specialising in European research into electrical and electronics industries. For the past 12 years, he has been at 3M (UK), where he runs a small in-house department and has responsibilities for all the company's UK research. He has also been industrial research manager of 3M Europe for the past six years. He has given presentations for ESOMAR, is an active member of IMRA, and loves going to the movies.

Peter Hutton (Chapter 15). Peter is a director of MORI. He graduated in Social and Political Sciences from Cambridge University in 1974. As a director of MORI he has research specialisations in social and political, shareholder, and corporate communications research. He is author of *Survey Research for Managers* (Second Edition, Macmillan, 1990), and a chapter on 'Measuring Opinion' in the *Handbook of Financial Public Relations*, edited by Pat Bowman (Heinemann, 1989). He is a frequent speaker on research topics, a regular contributor to the PR Summer School, and a member of the Market Research Society (MRS), Social Research Association (SRA) and World Association of Public Opinion Research (WAPOR).

List of Contributors

Dr Tony Lake (Chapter 8). Tony is managing director, Management & Marketing Studies Ltd. He is a social and management psychologist with 20 years' experience of industrial marketing research, and specialises in 'difficult' interviews with scientific and technological experts, singly or in groups. Tony writes and presents programmes for BBC Radio 4, and is the author of eight books on different aspects of relationships, published in more than 20 countries.

Phyllis Macfarlane (Chapter 7). Phyllis is Managing Director of INDAL Business Research, the specialist business-to-business agency within the MAI Information Division. She has specialised throughout her career in the sampling and estimation problems presented by business markets, particularly the mass business markets such as telecommunications, reprographics and despatch. These markets require the application of large-scale random sample methods typical of consumer work, combined with the specialist sampling techniques necessary for classic industrial markets. This work has been undertaken regularly in the UK and Europe (and less frequently in Australasia, South East Asia, South Africa and Iran). It is probably fair to say that, in the main, the same old problems keep presenting themselves but fortunately the development of IT has meant that there have been new possibilities for solutions (and the opportunities for travel have always been appreciated).

Andrew McIntosh (Chapter 2). Andrew is deputy chairman of IFF Research Limited, the business-to-business market research and consultancy company which he founded in 1965. He was educated at Oxford and the Ohio State University, and his market research career has included posts at the Gallup Poll, Hoover, and GEC. He was chairman of the MRS in 1972/3, and has edited its quarterly journal. He has lectured on marketing and market research subjects in 17 countries over nearly 30 years. Publications include *Industry and Employment in the Inner City* (1979); *Employment Policy in the United Kingdom and the United States* (1980); *Women and Work* (1981), and many articles on the theory, practice and findings of survey research. Since 1983 he has also been chairman and principal shareholder of SVP United Kingdom Limited, the UK member of the SVP International network of business information companies. In public life he spent 20 years in local government, and was opposition leader on the Greater London Council. He was chairman of the Association for Neighbourhood Councils from 1974 to 1980, chairman of the Fabian Society from 1985 to 1986, and has been principal of the Working Men's College in London since 1988. He joined the House of Lords (as Lord McIntosh of Haringey) in 1983, and has been Labour spokesman on trade and industry, education and (since 1987) the environment, local government, housing, and planning.

Rick Moore (Chapter 10). Rick is a director of INDAL Business Research. He started his market research career at Dexion International in the halcyon days of the late 1960s, having graduated at Enfield College of Technology (now Middlesex Polytechnic) with one of the first Business Studies degrees to be awarded. From Dexion, which ran a modest-size in-house marketing research department, he moved to the International HQ of Rank Xerox to manage its programme of basic market measurement studies. Agency life began in 1974 when, as a director of the newly formed Denjon 'Group', Rick combined international market research with an increased involvement in data analysis. A move to INDAL Business Research in 1983 coincided with the development of the UK's largest specialist business-to-business full service agency, in which Rick has specialised in the area of quantitative research. In total, over 20 years at the grindstone during which time a promising young sportsman has become a Saturday and Sunday afternoon couch potato.

Denis Pirie (Chapter 20). Denis is a consultant in marketing research, specialising in international research. He has been closely involved in international industrial marketing research since 1973, and has undertaken research in 18 European and North American countries. Between 1978 and 1989 he spent a total of eight years as an export marketing research adviser to the DTI's Export Marketing Research Scheme, advising thousands of large and small UK companies. His wide experience also includes working as an in-house researcher, an in-company consultant, a freelance consultant and a lecturer helping to develop a distance-learning marketing-research teaching package. He is still an adviser to the DTI on export marketing research and is a Member of the Council of IMRA.

List of Contributors

Dr David Smith (Chapter 3). David is director of D V L Smith and Associates – an agency specialising in business-to-business research. His BA degree was followed by an MA and PhD from the Department of Occupational Psychology at Birkbeck College of the University of London. He is a former vice-chairman of the MRS and an examiner for the MRS Diploma, as well as being a full member of IMRA. He also lectures on a part-time basis at the London School of Economics. He is a graduate member of the British Psychological Society and has written a number of articles and papers on business research. His other interests include football, cricket, squash, windsurfing, sailing, long-distance running and the theatre.

Martin Stoll (Chapter 5). Martin is a partner in Chambers & Stoll, a consultancy specialising in business research. Martin has a particular interest in information research and has lectured and written widely on the subject. For IMRA, he has convened and lectured at seminars on desk research and online research.

Ken Sutherland (Editor, and Chapters 16 and 22). Ken is managing director of Northdoe Ltd, consultants in process engineering and industrial marketing research. A chemistry graduate of Kings College, London, he converted at once to chemical engineering and is a chartered chemical engineer. He has been engaged in marketing research in the chemical and process industries for over 12 years, but has also retained an interest in engineering consultancy. Ken is Chairman of IMRA's Publications Committee, is equally active in the Institution of Chemical Engineers (as an Honorary Secretary), and in the evenings, as Chairman of his local Branch of the CPRE, can be found saying 'No' to development of the countryside.

Nick Watkins (Chapter 11). Nick is a Director of INDAL Business Research. He started his market research career at Business Decisions Ltd, after graduating from Nottingham University with a Masters degree in Industrial Economics. Since then, he has worked at Remy Genton Data and INDAL Business Research, where he is currently the Director responsible for all qualitative work. In total, he has nearly 12 years of agency experience which has encompassed a wide variety of projects, all within the business-to-business sector. Outside working hours, most of Nick's time is taken up with trying to renovate his Edwardian house faster than his baby daughter can destroy it.

John Wigzell (Chapter 12). John is a consultant. He graduated from St Catharine's College, Cambridge, at about the time that the Wright Brothers were learning to fly, and did academic research, before joining a small marketing and research company. Seduced by the promise of greater involvement in marketing (and free luncheon vouchers), he joined Ogilvy and Mather, the advertising agency, where he helped to change the research function into a planning department. In 1980 he co-founded Phoenix Advertising and, when it had grown to reach the 'Top Agency List' in 1985, left to join the board of The Research Business. In 1989 he became a director of MaS, and in 1991 set up his own consultancy. He also runs marathons.

Alan Wolfe (Chapter 18). Alan is marketing services director of Primary Contact, a subsidiary of the Ogilvy Group, to which he is also a consultant on strategic marketing. He has had over 35 years' experience, working in a wide range of markets and marketing techniques. These have included market research as assistant to the research manager at Rowntree-Mackintosh, head of the research group at Ogilvy and Mather, and director of RSGB. He is Honorary Visiting Research Fellow at Bradford University, a full member of MRS and IMRA, and fellow of five other professional bodies.

Part I:
Introduction

As it is hoped that many readers of this Handbook will be relatively new to the practice of business marketing research, the book begins with some introductory chapters, setting the scene for what is to follow.

An introduction which describes the format of the Handbook is followed by an essay relating business marketing research to the broader field of marketing.

The subject is then expanded into a general description of the functions of business marketing research, each of which will be dealt with separately later in the Handbook. This review of the whole scope of the subject provides the new reader with that introduction necessary to permit the complete view.

1

General Introduction

Ken Sutherland

Researching Business Markets – The IMRA Handbook is designed for use at different levels of need. It is intended to be referred to in order to satisfy that need, rather than to be read as a whole from start to finish. Nevertheless, it is planned in what is intended to be a logical fashion, developing from the general to the specific – with more detail given in the more specific parts – and in as readable a style as possible, so that it can be read all at once should the reader so wish.

The Handbook begins with an introduction to marketing and the place within it of business marketing research. There follows a general review of the whole field of the practice of business marketing research. This review provides the necessary broad picture of the subject for a reader seeking such an introduction.

The practice of business marketing research involves a number of important techniques, each of which may be vital to the success of a particular research exercise. These techniques are discussed separately, and in detail, in Part II of the Handbook. Each topic is complete in itself, and may be studied in isolation as well as in the context of all the others.

The broad purpose of business marketing research is the acquisition of data – both quantitative and qualitative – upon which recommendations for action can be based and management decisions taken. The analysis, interpretation and presentation of research data is an

Researching Business Markets – The IMRA Handbook

important part of the marketing researcher's task, and this is covered in Part III of the Manual.

Business marketing research is used for a variety of purposes – not all connected with just the determination of a particular market size. These applications are explored in Part IV, which may be read as a whole to gain a view of the breadth of application, or by individual chapter for particular detail.

The techniques and applications of business marketing research are largely independent of the place where the work is done – either the base of the company seeking the information or the area in which the research is undertaken. Nevertheless, there are significant geographical differences, both in the availability of published information and in the attitudes of individuals to being questioned. The international aspects of research are thus important, and these are covered in Part V of the Handbook.

The bulk of the Handbook is concerned with the work of the business marketing researcher. Part VI looks in addition at the people involved in the whole activity – their management and organisation. It deals with the in-house department and the independent research company, as well as with the different activities of consultancies and fieldwork services.

The Handbook concludes with a number of informative appendices – about IMRA and about qualifications in business marketing research, as well as providing some supplementary details on information sources.

There is no denying that many, if not most, of the techniques of business marketing research originated in consumer research. The business side is now completely established in its own right – largely on the basis of the difference in the nature of the respondent to questions (a consumer on behalf of himself or, at most, his family; a business contact on behalf of a company or similar enterprise). Accordingly, the Editor has attempted to minimise the 'in consumer research we do it this way, but in business research that way' approach, and has allowed business marketing research to stand on its own. The reader interested in how consumer research is done should look elsewhere.

Finally, an acknowledgement that, even in a profession where a significant proportion of practitioners are female, the Editor has used the male pronoun throughout to avoid the cumbersome 'he or she'

General Introduction

construction. He pleads the inadequacy of the English language in not having, say, the third person pronominal usage of the French, and the choice of 'he' instead of 'she' on the grounds that it is only two-thirds the length (and, of course, just possibly only two-thirds as important).

2

Marketing and Marketing Research

Andrew McIntosh

The first contribution to this Handbook is intended to 'set the scene', by showing the subject in its context. The use of the word 'marketing' rather than 'market' in the title is no misprint – marketing is the whole field of satisfying customer needs, and marketing research provides the information upon which marketing decisions are taken.

Introduction

As we approach the end of the twentieth century, we look back on it as a period in which almost all aspects of human development – and the environment in which it takes place – have been subject not just to change but to accelerating change. Among the most conspicuous changes which have transformed our daily life are developments in transportation, in science and medicine, and in analytical power brought about by computing technology. The explosion of our capacity for self-destruction has made two world wars the most deadly in history, and seems now to have given us a somewhat fragile peace, promoted initially by fear of annihilation.

In our economic life, it took nearly 200 years for the developed world to learn that all the food needed for survival in temperate climates could be produced by 10 per cent, not 80 per cent of the population. In the second half of the twentieth century, it has taken barely 30 years for us to learn that all the manufactured goods we need – and we 'need' many more than we used to – can be produced by 20 per cent, not 50 per cent of the population. Without new forms of employment, therefore, we face the prospect of a majority without work in its traditional forms.

The agricultural revolution, and the second industrial revolution, have been achieved by technological advance, by mechanisation, and now by automation. This has speeded up the change brought about by the first industrial revolution, and the intensified division of labour which it caused: it is now almost unknown for the producer to meet his ultimate customer, as the artisan once did. Green and Tull[1] use the example of Paul Revere, the highly skilled silversmith (and horseman) of the time of the American Revolution, who made tankards, platters and teapots to the direct requirements of his customers and at a price agreed with them. The linearly descendant company, Revere Copper and Brass Inc, is isolated from its thousands of customers and must rely on other means of communication to learn what they want to buy, where they will go to buy it, and what price they are prepared to pay.

The discipline of marketing

Twentieth-century economies have developed solutions to the problem of communication between producer and consumer, and to the problem of technologically-induced labour productivity: the solutions are called *marketing*. New methods of production have brought with them the need for new methods of distribution, and new means of communication. Most of the ways in which we now transport raw materials to the point of manufacture, and distribute finished goods to the point of sale and then on to the point of consumption, are new to the twentieth century. So, too, are the marketing methods which are used by managers to make decisions about the formulation of the product, the method of distribution, the identification of consumers, the determination of price, and the means of communicating information and persuasion from producer to consumer. If marketing methods are new even for manufactured goods, they are more evidently new for the immense range of services which have acquired such a dominant role in twentieth-century economic life.

Marketing and Marketing Research

The discipline of marketing attempts to bridge the gap between the producer of goods or services, and the customer. Marketing decisions are essentially management decisions, taken about parts of management activity which are less under the direct control of the manager than are other management decisions, because they concern management's relationship with the customer. Marketing decisions, even more than most other management decisions, are taken under conditions of uncertainty where the manager is obliged to assess risks, and costs of failure, against the potential rewards of success.

The essence of marketing research

If decision making under conditions of uncertainty is the essence of the discipline of marketing, the acquisition of information to help the marketing manager to take such decisions in as rational a way as possible is the essence of *marketing research*. If marketing is the attempt to bridge the communications gap between producer and consumer, marketing research attempts to provide the feedback loop, to bridge the communications gap between consumer and producer.

This is the context in which we can usefully set out the components of a definition of marketing research, closely following the analysis of Green and Tull.[1] Their definition is that 'marketing research is the systematic and objective search for and analysis of information relevant to the identification and solution of any problem in the field of marketing'. An expansion of this definition will help to explain the characteristics of marketing research.

'Systematic' is an essential characteristic of research in any field of enquiry. It implies that the problem to be researched has been clearly defined so that the information sought, the methods to be used in obtaining it, and the analytical techniques to be employed are systematically laid out in advance. One major consequence of this is that the marketing research, like a scientific experiment, is capable of being replicated, to establish, at least, the reliability (in the statistical sense) of the findings.

'Objective' is another characteristic which marketing research has in common with scientific enquiry – though we do not claim that research dealing with probabilities in human behaviour can aspire to the full rigour of scientific experimentation, in which exogenous variables can be effectively controlled or excluded. The closest analogy to marketing research is probably economics; as Harold Laski said in a letter to Justice Holmes: 'economics is only scientific to the point that it is reverent in the presence of facts'.

Marketing research must be objective – in the sense that it does not presuppose any particular outcome – or it is worthless. A research project which fails to anticipate the possibility of the full spectrum of outcomes, however unpalatable, is positively dangerous, in that it offers spurious evidence rather than no evidence at all.

'Search for' reflects what all researchers know – that not all research works. The most carefully laid plan of the researcher to measure (before and after), experiment and control the effect of a given unit of marketing activity, can all too frequently be upset by outside factors: the product specification changes; competitors launch new products, or change their prices, or themselves take a new marketing initiative; the marketing department is so pleased with test market results that they go national early – or become so depressed that they cancel the project.

'Analysis' is perhaps an over-cautious element in the definition. Marketing researchers, who have established themselves in the confidence of marketing management, will of course analyse their findings; however, they will also expect, and be expected, to interpret them in the light of their knowledge of the market or of other comparable markets, and to make a positive contribution to the 'identification and solution' of marketing problems.

The core of the Green and Tull definition lies in the phrase 'identification and solution of any problem in the field of marketing'. Marketing research is not an academic discipline, though it draws on many academic disciplines; nor is it a suitable field of activity for those whose prime interest is in scientific discovery for its own sake.

Marketing research is applied research: it uses, or tries to use, existing knowledge to solve actual business problems. If research is properly conducted, and the researcher's skills are fully used, the identification of the problem is as important a contribution to the business as the conduct of the research itself.

Origins of the discipline of marketing research

The development of marketing research depended on the growth of survey research as an academic discipline, notably in sociology. Early sociological investigation, such as Booth's nineteenth-century investigations of social conditions in London, long preceded marketing research but operated without the benefit of the theory of probabilistic statistics.

Statistics, in its early use, is defined in the *Shorter Oxford English Dictionary* as 'that branch of political science dealing with the collection, classification and discussion of facts bearing on the condition of a state or community'. More recently, in the late nineteenth century, it came to mean 'the department of study that has for its object the collection and arrangement of numerical facts or data, whether relating to human affairs or to natural phenomena'.

The relationship to human affairs has respectable and ancient origins, as with Jewish and Roman censuses for the purposes of taxation and conscription – though David (II Samuel 24) called down a plague from heaven by carrying out a military census of the people of Israel. More recently, Anatole France considered the Chinese to be backward because of their lack of an effective census: *'Tant qu'ils ne seront pas comptés, ils ne compteront pas'*. (Until they're counted they don't count.)

The development of that branch of statistics concerned with sampling – which is the core discipline of survey research – owes as much, paradoxically, to agricultural research as to sociology: Frank Yates, author of the great *Sampling Methods for Censuses and Surveys*, was head of statistics at the Rothamsted Experimental Station, and head of statistics for the Ministry of Agriculture.

Sampling is a core discipline of survey research, and survey research is the core discipline of marketing research: but the strength and joy of marketing research as a business and a career is that it is not based on a single academic or professional discipline. Although a good proportion of the best marketing researchers have training in the social sciences, economics or business, many do not – and they appear none the worse for it. Sociologists, accountants, psychologists, engineers, linguists, economists, botanists, statisticians and musicians all find a home and earn a living in marketing research.

Business marketing research

In the broad sense in which it can be used, 'business' embraces all economic activity – the 'world of work'; in the title of this Handbook, however, and in the development of the trade of marketing research in recent years, 'business' has come to mean something rather more specific.

It is a curious feature of almost all writing about marketing research, over at least 50 years, that it is assumed that the most important – indeed, often the only – application of such research is in consumer markets.

This was historically true for many of the early years of marketing research, for very understandable reasons. Marketing first came to its present dominance, as we have seen, in product and service sectors where the distance between producer and customer was at its greatest. This was inevitably in mass consumer markets, where the sheer numbers of potential customers, individuals or households were beyond the reach of direct contact.

In consequence, marketing, sales, and advertising budgets for consumer products and services – the three were not always clearly separated – were, as they are now, very much larger than the budgets for products and services sold to businesses. As the cost of mistaken marketing decisions was correspondingly greater in consumer markets, the pressure to spend money on marketing research, seen as insurance against failure, also increased.

Thus, in the inter-war period, and the years after the second world war, research budgets broadly went where the money was. The biggest money, and that most capable of influence by research techniques as known at the time, was in above-the-line advertising. Marketing researchers were to be found mainly in advertising agencies, in publishing, on the staff of large advertisers of consumer products, and in the research agencies set up to serve their needs.

Two other strands were significant from the war period: public opinion polling, and research in the public sector. The former continues to be rather more significant in the public mind than it is in business terms; the latter largely reflected the fact that government, too, was responsible for substantial advertising budgets.

However, it has been within only the last 30 years that business marketing research has emerged as a significant element in marketing research, alongside consumer research and social research. Aubrey Wilson, one of the authors of the first text on the subject[2] was also the founder of the first specialist industrial marketing research company in Britain, in 1960.

'Industrial marketing research' as it was when I joined the Industrial Marketing Research Association in 1964, and set up in business in the discipline in 1965, reflected the structure of the business world at that time. Visiting Sheffield to start up a project on the potential market for spirally welded steel pipe (before North Sea gas transformed the market) I drove down the Don Valley, past miles of steelworks in a nineteenth-century setting. In 1990 they were being replaced by DIY warehouses and buildings for a student Olympiad.

Spirally welded steel pipe, sand and aggregates, power distribution equipment, high-pressure wire-reinforced hose, glass packaging, escalator cleaning machines, fire-resistant electric cable, reduction gears, power take-off on trucks: among my first year's projects were many classical 'industrial' marketing surveys. Yet, even in 1965, service industries, the financial sector, and communications industries were important sources of business: investment research, the cost of industrial training, personnel managers, translation services, hotel feasibility studies, the image of building and civil engineering contractors, the market for point-of-sale materials. High technology was already becoming a significant market area: electronic test equipment, a market model of the computer industry, Polaroid identification systems, electronic accounting machines.

What soon became apparent, despite the word 'industrial' in my company name, was that industry – in the classic sense of manufacturing industry – was only one part, and not necessarily the most important part, in the range of work we set out to do. The common element, which had no recognised name, was the fact that our respondents were buying the goods or services we researched, not with their own money but with the money of the companies or organisations for whom they worked.

That became our working definition of our sphere of activity. We came to call it by the unlovely name of 'research in non-domestic markets', but the subsequent use of the descriptor 'business marketing research' is clearly more satisfactory.

One important qualification must be made to the adoption of the title. Much valuable work by business marketing researchers is carried out on subjects, and for clients, where the use of the word 'business' can be confusing or too limiting. A substantial part of my own work has been for public bodies, government departments, academic institutions and research foundations, on such subjects as manpower and human resources policy, training, industrial relations, and policies to tackle the curse of unemployment. Although the research techniques are related closely to those in marketing research – enquiry among business respondents though in this case in their capacity as employers, trainers, or human resources managers – neither the clients nor the respondents would readily recognise the words 'marketing' or 'business' as describing the work.

In this type of work especially, research work shades into policy analysis, and the evaluation of public sector employment, and industrial and social programmes. The effective social researcher, like the effective marketing researcher, develops from being a survey technician to being a problem solver and a participant in management decisions.

The practice of business marketing research

Many of the practitioners of business marketing research would be surprised to learn that this is the name given to what they do: like Moliere's M Jourdain, who discovered that he had been speaking prose all his life.

It may be thought to be a positive advantage that practitioners of business marketing research do not – or certainly do not yet – have professional status. There are no examinations for entry, no required academic qualifications, no apprenticeship, no pupillage. Membership of professional bodies, at least at associate membership level, is available to all who express an interest and agree to be bound by a code of conduct.

Eclecticism in recruitment and qualification well suits the nature of the work of business marketing research. Marketing research is not a limited profession, and would suffer greatly if it attempted to ape the major professions. I hesitate to claim that marketing researchers are intrinsically nicer than civil engineers or lawyers or accountants. However, they certainly have more varied interests, and gain more in terms of the quality of their work if they live fully in the world and have a keen appreciation of aspects of society which may not seem to be directly relevant to their work.

This is particularly true of business marketing reseaerch, which has the good fortune to be less codified, and more exploratory, than other forms of marketing and research. Consumer marketing research, in contrast, has a venerable history, and has acquired a body of technique which does not, unfortunately, always encourage spontaneity or creativity.

Comparison between business and consumer research

Many of the products and services investigated in consumer surveys have been the subject of many, and frequently repeated, surveys. My first day's work in marketing research was to analyse a paired blind comparison taste test of instant coffee, which was at least the fiftieth in a series which had been started some years before. Any change in the questionnaire, the sampling method, the analysis, or the reporting would have been disastrous, and the results would have been incomprehensible. Indeed, the senior researcher in charge of the project was so familiar with the data, and the series of data, that she was able to spot my tyro's errors of calculation – this was before the days of computers – almost without reading a word or a table.

In contrast, in 25 years of working in business marketing research, I could count on the fingers of one hand the number of times I have been involved in a project which was not new, in terms of the product or service under investigation; the kind of people responsible for purchasing decisions, who had to be surveyed; the sampling method to be adopted; the form of the interview or the questionnaire to be used; the form and content of the report and recommendations. Most projects have been innovative in most or all of these ways. It is for this reason, above all, that business marketing research is more enjoyable, and often makes a more significant contribution to marketing decisions than does its big sister – consumer marketing research.

There are, of course, other significant differences between business and consumer marketing research. Business market researchers are commonly concerned with more complex and more expensive products and services than those sold to consumer markets. This is not to underestimate, for example, the complexity of the chemical formulation of toothpaste, or the engineering refinement in a domestic washing machine, or the subtlety of the process of communication and persuasion between advertisers and the individual consumers of their products, but most of the complexities, refinements, and subtleties are not apparent to the consumer and are only indirectly subject to the research process. The chemists, the engineers, and the creators of advertising face the challenge of interpreting research findings, and improving their products, in the light of indirect evidence about the nature of consumer demand.

In some ways this makes consumer research more intriguing; the implication for business marketing research, however, is that more explicit questioning is possible, and necessary, about complex and often expensive products and services. This, in turn, means that those who do the interviewing in business marketing research, whether they are the researchers themselves or executive interviewers, need considerably greater understanding than consumer interviewers of the market under investigation, as well as skills in reaching senior managers and discussing technical and financial issues with them.

A second major difference between business and consumer marketing research is the complexity of the purchasing process for products and services in business markets. Not that consumer purchasing decisions are simple, or that business purchasing decisions are rational, as some have claimed, but the sheer number of people involved in business purchasing decisions is inevitably greater than the individual, or the household, who buys consumer products or services.

The purchase of even a relatively simple engineering component will involve the product design department, manufacturing, quality control, marketing and possibly sales (if there is likely to be any effect on the final product specification), financial management (in control of budgets) and, inevitably, the purchasing function. In some companies the purchasing function is dominant; in some, engineering; in others, marketing and sales. The business marketing researcher must recognise and allow for such differences in power, and the fact that different

Marketing and Marketing Research

functions will have different roles at different stages in the purchasing process.

A high proportion of business marketing research projects, therefore, involves interviewing more than one respondent who may be involved in a single purchase decision; it is not enough to attempt to make one respondent speak on behalf of the whole company or organisation. Indeed, some of the most revealing insights in business marketing research arise when there is a conflict of testimony between different participants in the purchase process, in the same company.

A third important difference between consumer and business marketing research is the size of the respondent group, and therefore the scope of sampling required. The market for nuclear power stations, even after privatisation of electricity supply, is severely limited, and consumer sampling techniques are inappropriate. At the other extreme, telephones are used by all businesses, and the size of the business telephone market is significantly larger than the domestic telephone market. Business marketing research covers both these markets, and all gradations in between.

The change from 'industrial' to 'business'

Traditional industrial market research, in chemicals, engineering, and for many raw materials, tends to be in markets where the number of customers – and hence the number of interviews required – is relatively small. When IMRA was founded, in 1964, this type of industrial marketing research was dominant, and the contrast with consumer marketing research as practised by members of the Market Research Society was felt keenly. Many of the founding members of IMRA thought of industrial marketing research as a discipline in which most projects were carried out by individual researchers, usually employed by the manufacturing company and undertaking the research design, the interviewing, and the reporting on a one-person consultancy basis. Interviews were more likely, at least in theory, to be between technical equals, and the idea of industrial interviewing carried out by non-experts was anathema. It was even possible for leading founders of IMRA to claim that sampling had no place in industrial marketing research.

Researching Business Markets – The IMRA Handbook

The last 20 years have seen a significant expansion of business marketing research skills, prompted by the recognition that neither the consumer research model nor the one-person consultancy model was appropriate to tackle the growing demand for research in mass business markets. The most obvious example of such markets is in office products and information technology: typewriters, word processors, copiers, telephones, fax and computer systems. The scale of investment in these markets, and the lack of information on them – within living memory our international trade statistics measured computers by weight – prompted substantial investment in research, which in turn provided the thrust for developments in research techniques.

For the first time there was significant investment in the development of sampling frames of industrial and commercial establishments (as opposed to enterprises). Sampling theory was extended to recognise and measure the enormous benefits of stratification, especially by size, and of weighting, in surveys of business markets. The executive field force of interviewers who are not themselves researchers on the payroll but have the skill and experience to master complex briefs and the persistence and presence to interview senior managers, was another important development in business research.

Such developments made research accessible to many markets which had been established for much longer than information technology but had been neglected by the practitioners of consumer, and traditional industrial, marketing research. Products such as industrial and commercial cleaning materials, industrial fasteners, lighting and heating equipment; business services such as the post, couriers and messengers, information services, business travel, business financial services: all these and many more are examples of mass business markets, which have benefited from research techniques developed specifically for such markets.

The essence of this type of research is the application of the most rigorous procedures of consumer research – questionnaire design, sampling, interviewing, analysis – to the more complex technical and commercial issues raised by business markets. It complements effectively the older-established skills of industrial marketing research, to provide the subject matter of this Handbook.

Marketing and Marketing Research

Ethical standards in business marketing research

All survey researchers have a common interest in, and a need for, a code of conduct which protects the rights and interests of respondents and research sponsors. The Code of Conduct agreed jointly by the Industrial Marketing Research Association (IMRA) and the Market Research Society (MRS) is summarised in Appendix C, and individual practitioners who are members of these bodies are required to adhere to it. At research company level, the Association of Market Survey Organisations, which has in its membership all the largest companies carrying out survey research, has its own code of standards, which is compatible with the IMRA/MRS code, but stresses corporate responsibilities.

There is a strong element of enlightened self-interest in the existence of a code of conduct, in its proper drafting, in effective measures to secure compliance, and in wide publicity and recognition given to it. Survey research, after all, consists of asking questions, almost always of people who are not obliged to give answers or paid to do so.

For business market researchers, the case for an effective code is even stronger. Respondents on business surveys are normally people answering on behalf of their employing organisations, even if they are asked for personal opinions and their business experience. They are prepared to give up time which belongs to their employers, without payment, if they can be persuaded legitimately that a particular research project is justified.

For respondents to be so persuaded, two conditions must apply. First, the motivation behind the research must, at the very least, not be damaging to the interests of the respondents; ideally it would be to their advantage. Research among the competitors of a sponsor, which conceals the nature of the sponsor's interest, is clearly damaging to the respondents' interests; the concealment is unethical, even though some researchers argue that it is permissible to try for answers without volunteering information on the nature of the sponsor's interest, on the *caveat emptor* principle.

Second, respondents need to feel that they gain something from answering questions, and to justify devoting their time – their employers' time – to the research. They could gain simply from knowing what questions are being asked and therefore what subjects are of interest or concern to the sponsors of the research, who are likely to be in the customer/supplier relationship to them.

They could gain – and this is an element in business marketing research which is insufficiently appreciated – by being given the opportunity to talk about their business experience with someone who is not a colleague, a supplier or a customer. Most normal business discussion is constrained by the colleague/supplier/customer relationship: there are usually ulterior motives which affect and distort what is said and what it is safe to say without unintended effects.

The one-to-one marketing research interview, on the other hand, is confidential to the respondent and the researcher, and provides an opportunity for the respondent to let off steam, to say the things he could not say in normal working circumstances. We have had innumerable letters from business respondents thanking us for interviewing them, for the opportunity to talk freely and perhaps to influence the service provided by their suppliers, and sometimes for the clarification of business issues which can result from a well-thought-out interview.

There is, however, a danger for business marketing research when the interview is not well-thought-out, when it is boring or repetitive, when it is so full of rating scales or multiple-choice questions that respondents have no chance to express their own ideas in their own words, when the questions are inappropriate to the person being interviewed, or when the interviewer is clumsy or incompetent. There are some categories of business respondent – such as finance directors, investment analysts, or data processing managers – who are in short supply, and who have understandably short tempers if they think that their time is being wasted.

It is the utmost folly for business marketing researchers, as a result of insensitive or incompetent interviewing, to risk killing the goose that lays the golden egg by alienating the very respondents they depend on for their livelihood. This is one reason why the IMRA/MRS Code of Conduct contains, in addition to ethical rules, extensive sections on the good practice of marketing research and why 'researchers' who do not subscribe to the Code of Conduct, and implement it fully, damage the interests of their clients and of the whole profession of business marketing research.

The marketing researcher in business

The working life of business marketing researchers is devoted to solving problems – applying the techniques of systematic and objective enquiry and analysis to the marketing and management problems of the business community, and public policy-makers. It follows from this that researchers are not fulfilling their true potential if they remain only survey technicians, important though survey technique may be. Problem solving, using evidence from the outside environment, the marketplace, in which businesses operate, is a core business skill and should enable the business marketing researcher to contribute to management at the highest level.

Ludwig Erhard was the first marketing researcher to govern his country, as Chancellor of the Federal Republic of Germany. Who will be the first business marketing researcher to become chief executive of one of Britain's top 100 companies?

References

1. Paul E. Green and Donald S. Tull, (1966) *Research for Marketing Decisions* Prentice-Hall Inc, Englewood Cliffs, NJ.
2. Aubrey Wilson, (1973) *The Assessment of Industrial Markets* Associated Business Programmes, London.

3

The Scope of Business Marketing Research

David Smith

Business marketing research is a complex subject, multifaceted in both its techniques and its applications. This chapter is an attempt to illustrate the whole of the practice of business marketing research, so that the reader may gain a grasp of what business marketing researchers actually do. Each of the main techniques employed is expanded upon later in the Handbook, but this is intended to be a reasonably complete overview of the subject.

It concentrates on the very important issue of translating a business problem into a practical research exercise, and then shows how such an exercise may be undertaken.

Problem definition

Rarely are business problems presented in an accurate, comprehensive, concise and unambiguous way. Usually, the first stab at defining a problem for research – whether this be within the marketing department, by the market research function within a company, or by an external research organisation – provides only a rough starting point. In some cases, the initial attempt to get a fix on a problem may actually be wrong. For example, for very good reasons the initiator of the research may feel that a drop in sales is product-centred, where in fact it is more related to the performance of the sales force. Similarly, there could be ambiguities in the wording of the opening briefing document, as written by the initiator. In addition, some research briefs may pre-judge the issue; in other cases the initial presentation of the problem may show a blinkered understanding of its complexities.

Research briefs are often method led – that is, they present a problem intertwined with possible methods for its resolution. While suggestions on possible methods are welcomed, it becomes confusing if the method is inextricably woven into the problem. Finally, it is quite common for research briefs to mix, in the same list, research objectives, the decision outcomes that must follow from the research, and possible questions for the questionnaire. Such mixed lists of objectives, outcomes and questions need careful unravelling.

The stages of problem definition

There are many possible pitfalls, therefore, that can await a research study as it struggles into existence. It follows from this that the researcher must tackle the problem definition stage in a systematic way, aimed at minimising the chances of a complete misunderstanding. The problem definition step of a project involves the following stages.

Clarifying assumptions
It is important to clarify assumptions that are being made in the initial statement of the research problem (for example, do not just assume that the study excludes Northern Ireland – this should be checked).

Summarising the research problem
The starting point for any problem definition exercise is to provide a précis or summary of the initial problem. Here the aim is twofold: first, to cut out any unnecessary verbiage; second, to provide concrete examples of issues raised that will help those involved in the project to understand the key factors.

Delimiting the scope of the study
It is quite common for companies new to the concept of market

research to want to conduct a wide-ranging study that includes all aspects of the company's operation. In these situations, it is necessary to make sensible decisions about which elements fall naturally within one type of study and which should be addressed separately. The decision on how to delimit a study must be driven by marketing, not market research, issues.

Prioritising issues
After the decision is taken as to which aspects of the problem fall into which parts of the research programme, there is the question, within each aspect of the programme, of prioritising the research objectives. For example, if checks of customer awareness of a company are to be the central thrust of a proposed study, the sponsor should not be named at the beginning of the study on the grounds that this will contaminate subsequent awareness measures. However, this strategy could make certain respondents reluctant to provide information about the performance of existing suppliers, on the grounds that they do not know by whom the study is being sponsored (a compromise would be to release the name of the sponsor at the end of the interview). It is important to know where the priorities lie in research design: if awareness is the top priority then this will dominate other research design decisions, but if building up a profile of different companies' strengths and weaknesses is of most importance, certain sacrifices may have to be made on the awareness front.

Applying lateral thinking
During the definition stage, it is important to stand a problem on its head so as to look at it from different angles and perspectives. Not surprisingly, this shows very different parts of the whole problem.

Anticipating future research problems
At the main problem definition stage, it is important to think through the ensuing research process and anticipate all the issues that must be dealt with satisfactorily in order to complete the research programme. A good researcher is like a good chess player: he will always be one move ahead of the disaster that is lurking around the corner.

Refining the problem
It is helpful to locate problems in an analytical framework. This can

vary from simple concepts, such as the product life-cycle, to more sophisticated models. This may sound slightly pretentious, but it is extremely important to start seeing how a new problem might be fitted into the context of existing theories or patterns, as this might help to solve the problem.

The techniques of problem definition

There are a number of techniques available to the researcher at the problem definition stage. The researcher might consider undertaking several kinds of preliminary research and other activity in order to define and understand the problem successfully.

Internal interviews
In addition to any written brief, it is often helpful to hold internal discussions and, possibly, slightly more formal interviews with the initiators of the research programme.

Desk research
Desk research is an important starting point for most research studies. It is a term that refers to research conducted using existing sources of information on the topic under investigation. It is undertaken at this stage of problem definition in order to provide more information relevant to the problem and, indeed, to show if it has already been solved. The general principle of desk research is to start at one of the key libraries such as the City Business Library or the British Library Science Reference and Information Service. The starting point for an investigation should be a one-stop solution on the topic. For example, if you are studying sports sponsorship, a useful starting point would be the 1988 Mintel report on Sponsorship. This source would provide a sound overview plus a host of clues on sources of more detailed specialist information.

Expert opinion
It is often extremely helpful at the beginning of the definition process to talk to one or two key experts in that particular industry. For instance, if you are about to embark on a research study aimed at evaluating the potential for a new packaging exhibition, it would be

sensible to talk to a journalist who writes for one of the packaging trade magazines.

Observation
Observation is an under-used research method; on a number of projects it can be particularly productive. For example, while considering investigating the corporate image of a retail organisation, it would be sensible for the researcher to visit different retail outfits (preferably with a camera), to observe particular features of store layout.

Brainstorming
Brainstorming techniques can be helpful in providing a lateral perspective on the problem under investigatioin - here, there is a host of techniques. For example, there could be a group discussion with the project team: each member of the team, going round the table, could be asked to cite one possible problem with the proposed venture. The group could then brainstorm ways in which each of these problems might be resolved, each member being asked to provide a possible solution (however apparently outrageous) that does not duplicate a solution that has already been given in the session.

Some time has been spent on exploring methods of problem definition, but this is a vital stage in a research exercise. If the sponsor of the research is uncertain of the nature of the basic problem to be solved, the understanding of the researcher undertaking the task will never be clear and thus a less than perfect job will be done as far as the sponsor is concerned. It is essential that the researcher has a clear understanding of the sponsor's needs, and it is the sponsor's duty to ensure that he gets this understanding.

Qualitative research

Once the problem has been properly defined, the researcher - whether a member of the sponsor's staff, or on contract to the sponsor - can begin to explore it. He will need to begin with some qualitative research, in order to start to understand the broad characteristics of the market segment or phenomenon to be surveyed.

Definitions of qualitative research vary, but most researchers would agree that it has the following features.

- It tends to involve relatively few sources, a small sample of all the opinion that could be sought – there are no hard and fast definitions, but qualitative studies typically include up to 30 respondents.

- It tends to be response-, not question-orientated: that is, to a large extent the answer given by a respondent to a particular question determines the next question the qualitative researcher will ask; it does not ask respondents a predetermined list of questions.

- It normally aims to explore a respondent's view of the world; to achieve this, qualitative researchers adopt a fairly flexible approach at the data collection stage.

- It is concerned more with identifying the range of attitudes and behaviour on a particular issue, than with any attempt to provide measurements about the proportion of individuals (or companies) holding a certain view or behaving in a particular way.

- It often mixes the collection and analysis of data. That is not to say that the qualitative researcher is instantly analysing the data being collected but inevitably, as the fieldwork progresses, the qualitative researcher will start beginning to interpret the data he is collecting; patterns will begin to emerge that will give a focus to the later stages of research.

- It operates by what may be termed face validity, rather than a more precise statistical validity. With qualitative research, there is less emphasis on demonstrating that the evidence has been collected in a totally systematic way that is completely free from any form of bias, and it is sometimes said to be valid when it fits with one's prior knowledge about the issue under investigation.

The depth interview

There are numerous qualitative research techniques, which are discussed in greater detail in Part II of the Handbook. In order to gain an idea of the researcher's task in implementing a business marketing research project, it is necessary to look only at the two most common techniques, of which the first is the depth interview. This term is used to refer to face-to-face interviews, usually lasting a significant period of time, perhaps an hour or more. In some ways the term is slightly misleading, because it can imply an in-depth, psychologically orientated interview. This is not so in the majority of cases, however, which are usually just flexible, free-ranging, sympathetically conducted interviews, with little recourse to any psychologically based techniques. The interview is normally tape recorded, and subsequently transcribed prior to analysis. The interviewer follows a guideline covering the topics under investigation but, as indicated above, the interview is response-orientated and therefore the interviewer is not restricted to a predetermined set of questions.

The depth interview offers a number of advantages. First, the interviewer can keep track of the way an individual's behaviour is related to his attitude. For example, from a simple claim by a machine shop foreman that the most important consideration in selecting a particular oil is the extent to which the oil minimises skin problems for his operators, the interviewer could find out in a depth interview the extent to which this attitude is, in fact, related to any health and safety problems encountered at this respondent's plant in recent times.

Second, the depth interview is to be commended when exploring particularly sensitive issues. For instance, a study among businessmen who are running into difficulties with the credit limit on their plastic cards would perhaps lend itself to an individual airing, rather than discussion in a group.

Third, in the business setting the depth interview offers a number of practical and logistical advantages. It is often more straightforward to set up an individual interview than a group discussion. For example, it is probably easier to conduct a programme of individual interviews with architects, than attempting to gather together such a difficult-to-recruit group at one particular point in time.

The only major limitations with the depth interview are the time and resources involved in setting up a programme of interviews. In addition, of course, the individual interview does not have the interactive component of the group discussion. Another consideration is the type and quality of executive interviewers to be used, who must be experienced at this task. It should be pointed out that interviewing styles vary enormously; it is important to ensure that all executive interviewers are fully trained and briefed on the project.

Group discussions

The other main qualitative research method is the group discussion, which involves a group – typically of between eight and ten respondents – meeting for a session, usually of one-and-a-half to two hours. The group is normally led by a moderator who, following a guideline, will steer the discussion through a range of different topics. Usually the session is tape recorded, and on some occasions it may also be video recorded.

There are many variants of the group discussion method, including the extended group discussion that may last for four hours or more. There is also the reconvened group discussion, where individuals are asked to attend a number of group discussions over a period of weeks. However, for the most part, group discussions in the industrial context will consist of a one-off session. The strengths of the business research group discussion include:

- the provision of that interaction between group members which can spark new ideas;

- the provision of a setting in which respondents can listen to their colleagues' attitudes (this can be useful in encouraging respondents to reappraise their own position, and arrive at a more considered one);

- inclusion of the presentation of prototypes of equipment that could perhaps not be easily made available for an individual depth interview;

- the fact that it is an event that can be observed by clients (although it can be argued that this is a disadvantage rather than a benefit of the method in some cases).

The group discussion is not without limitations. Individuals within a group setting will often start displaying group behaviour. For example, respondents in a group may be more likely to focus on the environmental benefits of introducing unleaded petrol than to give vent to any concerns about whether or not the unleaded petrol lowers the performance of their own cars.

It must then be remembered that there will not always be the full interaction between group members that is claimed for the group discussion method. It is well known that certain individuals will withdraw in the group setting. In addition, groups can fall prey to opinion leaders; this is particularly problematic with the business group attended by managers who are experienced in taking control of meetings. To some extent it is possible to offset these problems by careful planning of the composition of each group, but it is not always possible to anticipate whether the tensions and conflicts of the group processes will be productive or counter-productive.

In the group setting it is difficult to check individual awareness and knowledge of different products or markets. Clearly, once the first individual has spoken it becomes impossible to check the awareness and knowledge of other members on an unprompted basis. It is also difficult to go round the group and ensure that a detailed picture of the relationship between an individual's attitudes and his behaviour is being built up.

Finally, as is the case with depth interviews, group interviewing or moderating styles will vary considerably. Some moderators will have a particularly tight, rigorous way of working; others will sacrifice a certain degree of rigour in order to build up rapport with the group. Clearly, there is no one right style; however, it is important to ensure that the moderator's style is compatible with the topic under investigation. For instance, the moderator required to explore a haulage contractor's views on different transport advertising treatments may need to be quite different from the moderator required to deal with an assessment of lighting cameramen's attitudes towards video technology.

Data collection methods

On certain research projects, the investigation need go no further than the qualitative research stage. However, a significant proportion (if not the majority) of such projects will require quantification. This leads us to the next stage of the research process: the choice of quantitative data collection methods to be used in its implementation.

There are numerous ways of collecting data and these are reviewed in considerable detail in Chapter 6. The main data collection methods are face-to-face interviewing, telephone interviews, and the use of self-completion questionnaires (which may be despatched through the post).

Face-to-face interviews

A face-to-face interview, as its name implies, occurs when the interviewer sits close to the respondent and asks questions in the absence of anyone else. There are a number of advantages to the face-to-face method:

- it is both powerful and flexible;
- it offers a strong visual element;
- it enables close control of the interview.

Power and flexibility

Face to face with a respondent, an interviewer can ensure full understanding by the respondent of what is being asked, and can adapt the interview to suit the respondent's personality. This method copes well with the complexity and nuances inherent in many interview situations, allowing the interviewer to unearth the range and depth of a respondent's feelings on particular issues. In addition, respondents like the method because it does justice to their knowledge and feelings on the subject under investigation.

The visual element

The fact that the interviewer can see the respondent confers a number of different advantages. First, the interviewer can note down observations about the respondent's work environment that can support the main data collection exercise. Second, the face-to-face interview enables the use of photographs or diagrams to illustrate concepts or ideas, and of course show-cards and rating scales can be used as part of the questioning technique. Admittedly the availability of fax, in conjunction with a telephone interview, offsets some of these advantages, but face-to-face interviews still offer certain benefits because material can be shown to respondents and their immediate reaction can be observed.

Third, the face-to-face interview allows the interviewer to respond to the eye movements, facial expression and body language of the respondent. Often, loss of eye contact, a wry smile or a shrug of the shoulders speak volumes. Moreover, from the interviewer's standpoint, non-verbal techniques such as an expectant glance or a muttered 'Mm?' can prove to be an extremely effective probing technique to encourage a respondent to give an answer or clarify or amplify a point.

Control
The face-to-face interview gives the researcher a control over the research often denied by other methods. First, unlike postal research and (to a lesser extent) telephone research, with the face-to-face method the interviewer can easily ensure that he is interviewing the appropriate sampled respondent (the problem in postal research is not usually perversity but over-helpfulness).

The second aspect of control concerns the release of information within the questionnaire itself. This is particularly important to market researchers, who often wish to ask respondents to name brands on an unaided basis before checking their awareness after prompting. Similarly, in assessing the image of an organisation it is often helpful to work from the general to the specific, starting by checking out attitudes towards widely known aspects of the company and then, when this has been safely documented, focusing on specific, less well publicised aspects that, if known, could well have contaminated replies to the previous, more general image questioning.

There are, of course, some limitations to the face-to-face interview method. It is considerably more expensive than an equivalent telephone interview, even of similar length, and it takes considerably longer to achieve, allowing for setting-up, travelling, and so on. What this means, of course, is that care must be taken in the planning of a research project to ensure that those interviews which can be done on the telephone are done that way, reserving face-to-face visits for those interviews that would benefit from the kind of advantages just described.

A more serious problem is that of interviewer bias, in that two interviewers asking the same question of the same respondent might easily obtain different answers. This is actually a limitation to any research method involving more than one interviewer, although it is rather more of a problem with face-to-face interviews than it is over the telephone. Recent methodological work has suggested that much interviewer variability is attributable to avoidable factors, and that the careful construction and piloting of questionnaires, the detailed briefing of interviewers, the preparation of interviewer instructions that provide clear definitions on terms within the questionnaire, rigorous supervision, and intelligent fieldwork planning, can go a long way to minimise the interviewer effect.

Telephone interviewing

The telephone is particularly appropriate for business-to-business research because respondents are comfortable with the telephone mode. It may be undertaken by the interviewer at home, or in a small office. It may be done by centralised telephone interviewing, with a bank of dialling bays within a survey organisation. Then there are computer-assisted telephone interviewing (CATI) systems, in which the interviewer has the questionnaire presented on a screen, and a keyboard for entering the respondent's replies (and the supervisor has the facility for both audio and visual supervision).

Among the advantages of all kinds of telephone interviewing are:

- Availability – virtually all businesses are accessible by telephone, and increasingly more by fax.

- Cost and speed – provided that the data being collected are suitable for telephone collection (which means a bias towards quantitative rather than qualitative responses).

- Access – the telephone allows the intelligent planning of interview appointments, and improves the chances of contacting busy respondents (this, of course, also concerns face-to-face interviews, where prior telephone calls are a vital part of a successful visit).

- Reduced clustering – geographical distance has a major effect on the cost of face-to-face interviews, so researchers tend to cluster

The Scope of Business Marketing Research

the interviews close to particular centres of easy travel; telephone interviewing is much less affected by distance, allowing easier research on national samples.

Additional benefits accrue from the use of a centralised telephone room with several interviewers at work in sound-proofed bays. These include:

- an increased efficiency in unclustered sampling;
- central supervision – the careful training, briefing and monitoring of interviewers necessary in reducing the interviewer effect are much more easily achieved in one central location;
- experimentation – experiments with question wording can be easily incorporated into the piloting of questionnaires, and any problems with the main survey can be quickly identified and rectified.

In addition to the above advantages of the telephone method, there are certain added benefits offered by CATI systems. First, some have computer-driven procedures for the dialling of telephone numbers. Second, the computer steers the interviewer through the various filters (or branches) of the questionnaire, so that an interviewer does not miss a question, or ask a question in the wrong order. In addition, more ambitious sequencing could be entertained in a way that could not be handled manually. With CATI systems, the supervisor can listen in to interviews and observe the entry of data on his own monitor; finally, the system provides for almost instant tabulation of results.

A major use of telephone interviewing is for quantitative data collection by means of pre-coded questionnaires. The telephone makes it easier to conduct before-and-after studies, and also lends itself to mixing with other data collection methods. For example, a short telephone interview, followed by more detailed questioning using a self-administered postal return questionnaire, can be an efficient and cost-effective design.

There are two major limitations to telephone interviewing, of which the first is the general inability to use visual aids. It is, of course, possible to fax visual material and show-cards to respondents about to be interviewed over the telephone, but with no guarantee that they will reach the respondent in time. On balance, the absence of visual aids remains a limitation to the telephone interview method. However, it should be pointed out that there is growing industry expertise in using alternative techniques to show-cards, such as unfolding questions – for example: 'I am going to read out a number of statements that other people have made. For each, I'd like you to tell me whether you agree or disagree'. Then, after each statement is read out, the interviewer is instructed to ask those who agreed, 'Do you agree a lot or a little?', and for those who disagreed the interviewer asks 'Do you disagree a lot or a little?'.

It is asserted that the quality of data collected over the telephone is less than that collected on a face-to-face basis, because it is more difficult for the interviewer to communicate interest to the respondent, check for attention, give encouragement, help the respondent to concentrate, and respond to non-verbal cues. Certainly there are some concerns about the quality of questions asked over the phone on an open-ended basis. However, the quality of telephone data should not be underestimated, because it can be argued that the absence of an interviewer and the relative anonymity of the telephone situation, normally considered likely to discourage respondents from relaxing and opening up, may actually encourage them to be more honest.

In business marketing research, the telephone is a powerful tool when used for those purposes for which it is best suited. It has been somewhat down-valued in the past, but it can now be acknowledged that in certain situations the telephone is not just a second-best alternative but a method capable of yielding better survey data than do other methods.

Self-administered questionnaires and postal research

Data collection that takes place without the presence of an interviewer is a technique that can be used extremely successfully. The questionnaire to be completed by the respondent could be postally despatched and returned, or personally delivered and collected, and then the researcher's main task is to ensure that it gets into the right hands.

Among the method's strengths are:

- Economy – there are often situations in which the budget does not

The Scope of Business Marketing Research

run to face-to-face or even telephone interviewing, and where a properly designed, postally-despatched questionnaire will be the most appropriate tool.

- Unclustered sampling – the distribution of questionnaires by post avoids the clustering inevitably associated with face-to-face interview surveys.
- Quality of the data – postal questionnaire respondents tend to give more valid (ie honest) answers, particularly on sensitive topics, than respondents in personal interviews (for example, postal respondents are more likely to admit that school and college careers were incomplete, to be more honest about their state of health, and so on).
- Quantity of data – self-administered questionnaires offer definite advantages in the collection of large amounts of detailed information, especially if it has to be obtained from different places or sources.
- Locality – data can be recorded close to the action under investigation (for example, by keeping a careful record of the different ways in which a machine is used throughout a typical day).
- Experimentation – it has the potential for experimenting with different elements within the research design, including the use of different incentives, reminders, colour of questionnaire, use of first- and second-class stamps, and even the despatch day.
- Central control – the administration of the survey can easily be concentrated in one location.

The postal research method can, of course, be used as part of a mix of research techniques, and can play an important part in an overall research design, but it does have its limitations:

- The right respondent – it is by no means sure that the sampled person will in fact fill in the questionnaire, and there is also the likelihood of intra-office collaboration in its completion.
- Lack of control – it must be assumed that the respondent will read

to the end of the questionnaire before beginning to answer, and this could limit certain lines of questioning.

- Limits on type of question – questions on self-administered questionnaires must be kept comparatively straightforward, and those requiring detailed definitions should be avoided if possible; it is, of course, inappropriate to use self-administered questionnaires to obtain measures of awareness; any filtering or branching of the questionnaire needs to be kept to a minimum; if open-ended questions are used, a comprehensive answer may be as much an indication of the respondent's fluency with the written word as of his strength of feeling on the particular issue; on certain questions (for example, type of occupation) respondents tend to give insufficient data for adequate classification.
- Length of questionnaire – as a general rule, good response rates tend to be associated with short questionnaires, because they are quick and easy to answer.

Questionnaire length is not the only factor affecting response rates, low levels of which are usually cited as the main argument against postal methods of research. In fact, good response rates are encouraged by a professional approach to the survey – a proper letter of introduction, a well-designed questionnaire – as much or more than just the length of the questionnaire. When studies are conducted among groups with some commitment to the research, and when the commitment is encouraged in the accompanying letter, postal methods can be very successful. However, when used in an inappropriate way the postal research method can be utterly disastrous. If responses to postal research fall below 60 per cent, the survey results will need careful interpretation; at much below this level the working hypothesis must be that the respondents are not typical of the overall population under investigation.

Sampling method

A well organised research survey, for which the best methods of data collection have been decided, must have a group of respondents from whom to gather the data. In some surveys, the whole group of interest to the survey may be small enough so that all may be contacted. In other cases (and more usually) some kind of sample must be selected from the group. An important part of the research process is, therefore, the method of sample design. In simple terms, there are two methods of drawing a sample from the whole group (or population) to be investigated: probability and non-probability sampling.

Probability sampling

Probability sampling (described in detail in Chapter 7) involves sampling in such a way that the probability of inclusion of an individual or firm in the sample is known, and so that statistical methods can be used to analyse the results of the survey. Probability sampling has statistical theory as its corner-stone: if probability methods have been used, it is possible to calculate the range of error surrounding a particular survey statistic, and state with what degree of confidence the survey result falls within this particular range. In order to provide this precision, the researcher must follow a number of stages that are often difficult to adhere to in practice.

First, the researcher must find or create a sampling frame, a list of all the units in the population under investigation. In business research it is difficult to identify a sampling frame that meets all the conditions of probability sampling: namely, that the list be up to date, have no omissions, be free from duplication, and be freely available to the researcher. If there is any shortfall with the sample frame then this is likely to introduce a sample bias, and this is a major problem in business research.

From this best-possible sampling frame, the researcher must select the appropriate units; however, with probability sampling, only the selected units are eligible for the study – substitutes may not be taken. Where a unit cannot subsequently be included, the interview would have to be declared as part of the non-response. It is generally accepted that the response rate target for a probability sample should be 65 per cent or more; if this percentage rate is not achieved, the attitudes and behaviour of those taking part in this study, or the data supplied by them, may not be typical of those unable to take part in the study.

Probability sampling places quite heavy demands on the research process in time and budget terms: first, identifying an appropriate sampling frame is not always easy, and second, at the fieldwork stage it can be difficult to achieve a 65 per cent response. For these reasons it is quite common for market researchers to use alternative sampling methods. The most common of these is quota sampling.

Quota sampling

In drawing a quota sample, the researcher must first obtain sufficient data about the population (or universe) under investigation in order to be able to describe it quite accurately. From this description, the researcher must identify the key characteristics of the population under investigation, and then set quotas for the interviewing team. The quota specification usually involves at least two, and often three or more, of the key characteristics and could be defined, for example, in terms of:

- geographical area
- type of company (preferably by Standard Industrial Classification (SIC) code)
- company size

and possibly even job function of the respondent (if more than one manager could have relevant views or data).

Given that the interviewers are successful in securing interviews with individuals up to their target quotas, it follows that the resultant sample will mirror that of the population that provided the basis of these quotas. This method of sampling is predicated on the notion that the haphazard procedures that interviewers follow in securing their quotas will approximate random probability procedures.

Inevitably, with quota sampling there will be a slight bias towards respondents who are available and predisposed towards interviews. This is in sharp contrast to the probability method, whereby a particular individual to be interviewed is chosen in a properly random fashion.

However, on a more positive note, various experimental studies have shown that quota sampling produces results that approximate the results that would have been obtained via the probability approach.

Thus, although quota sampling does not enjoy the rigorous theoretical underpinning of probability sampling, it does seem to work in practice.

Sample size determination

Once the sampling method is decided, the researcher must choose the size of the sample. Here there are five factors to be taken into account:

- the greater the required precision, the larger will be the necessary sample;
- the research survey design may have included stratification (which improves sampling efficiency) and clustering (which lowers sampling accuracy), and thereby affected the estimate of the standard error;
- it may be necessary to analyse the research results among different sub-groups – clearly, larger initial samples are required if they are to be divided into many different sub-groups, for subsequent analysis, by industry sector and so on;
- the available budget for the research study, and also the time available for conducting the interviews, will have an important effect on the sample size;
- rarely will the research evidence alone be used as a basis for decision making (the more the research evidence can be placed in a wider context of prior knowledge, the less pressure there is on the research and therefore the greater justification for smaller, rather than larger, samples).

In the final analysis, choice of sample size becomes a matter of judgement, which the researcher has to exercise, based on all the relevant evidence including, of course, the size of the population to be surveyed. Sometimes a 1 per cent sample may be enough to provide the required solution to the problem (remember that pre-election polls in the UK are based on a sample of about 0.005 per cent), and sometimes it may need a 30 per cent sample.

Data analysis options

The final research project decision centres on the type of analysis to be employed in interpreting the data. The two main options open to the researcher are:

- the conventional cross-tabulation approach, which involves correlating a particular survey statistic such as the number of litres of cutting oil purchased in the last four weeks, with various key survey parameters such as the size of the company and the type of machinery in use;

- multivariate analysis, which involves simultaneous inspection of all the attitude and behavioural measurements taken during the survey, to identify groups of companies that – across a range of characteristics – appear to be similar.

Data analysis methods are explored in greater detail in Part III, but they must be considered at the start of the project (to ensure that the resources will be there for them), and in questionnaire design (to ensure that data are collected in the best way for subsequent analysis).

Business marketing research in practice

Business marketing research must be carried out under a series of constraints:

- Cost – within what budget parameters must the research solution to the marketing problem be contained?

- Time – how much time is available to the researcher to work towards a solution to the marketing problem?

- Level of precision – what are the tolerance limits in terms of the precision of information required in the solution of the problem?

- Depth of understanding – how important is it to understand the motivations and complexities underlying behaviour, as opposed to the need simply to measure behaviour?

The Scope of Business Marketing Research

- Practicality – to what extent does the field in which the research will take place impose practical and/or ethical constraints, that will limit the opportunities for comprehensive research design?

These constraints will exercise the researcher's mind, but successful projects continue to be completed in spite of (or, perhaps, because of) them.

Perhaps the most helpful way of guiding readers through the business marketing research process is to look at some examples. There follows, for each example, the marketing problem together with the research design used to solve that particular problem.

Evaluating a slide video recorder

Background
A slide video recorder enables around 300 35mm slide images to be transferred to a small disk, such that they can be displayed on a piece of equipment the size of a video cassette recorder. The user would then have a durable, easy-to-store disk, providing random access to any one of the 300 images.

Research objectives
1. To determine the extent of interest in this product in the UK market.
2. To obtain reaction to the quality and efficiency of the equipment.
3. To identify the product benefits that should be featured in the promotion of the product.

Design constraints and considerations
A limited number of slide video recorders were available. This, coupled with the need for technicians to explain detailed technical points and operate the equipment, led to a decision to carry out the research at central locations, rather than having interviewers visit potential customers.

Overall design
Qualitative research, employing ten group discussions with potential users and five depth interviews with independent film producers, who

were seen as being particularly difficult to recruit to an industrial group.

Sampling design and procedures
The research was targeted on those likely to use the slide video product: business presenters, AV specialists and lecturers in educational establishments, advertising agencies, and independent film producers.

Approach to analysis
Transcripts of each group and depth interview were prepared prior to full content analysis.

Decisions taken as a result of research
Identification of benefits offered by the product, and identification of the application areas that should be given a marketing priority.

Cutting oils services

Background
An oil company wished to identify the range of technical and back-up services that they must offer in the market for cutting oils, in order to maintain a competitive advantage in what is becoming a price/commodity market.

Research objectives
1. To establish what competitive cutting oil suppliers are offering by way of technical services.
2. To identify which technical services are most likely to give the oil company a competitive advantage.

Design constraints and considerations
No sampling frame or customer list was available to provide a comprehensive picture of cutting oil usage by type and size of firm.

Overall design
Six depth interviews were conducted with machine shop foremen to understand the critical issues in the market. To identify key issues,

internal and external desk research and then a large-scale telephone interview survey were carried out.

Sampling design and procedure
The sample was divided into one half existing customers, drawn from the client's customer lists (stratified by type and volume of cutting oils used), and one half non-users selected from the Kompass/SIC categories to mirror the profile of the client's customers. Kompass was used because there was insufficient budget for a large-scale sampling operation, to identify this very diverse market for cutting oils. Kompass provided adequate representation, given the fact that the study was not about market measurement but about identifying attitudes towards technical back-up services.

Data collection method and procedures
Telephone interviews were conducted with respondents responsible for cutting oils. In some cases two interviews were conducted, where more than one respondent was involved in the decision process. The telephone was used because of the need for a large sample on a limited budget, that would allow cross-analysis by different industry subgroups.

Approach to analysis
The analysis was presented in terms of conventional aggregate cross-tabulations, but also in terms of case studies (drawing on the qualitative research), highlighting the way in which decisions are made within particular organisations.

Decisions taken as a result of research
The study identified the technical back-up services on which the client should most concentrate, in order to maintain and win a share from competitive cutting oils suppliers.

Aviation fuel supply

Background
If a supplier of road-fed aviation fuel fails to deliver fuel at the time contractually agreed, the airline can submit a claim for compensation

for any losses incurred such as putting up passengers at hotels, providing drinks and so on, which can become very expensive, with bills as high as £5,000. It is therefore essential that the ordering and delivery procedures for aviation fuel are efficient and smooth running.

Research objectives
1. To determine the proportion of aviation fuel customers who are receiving a first class service.
2. To identify specific ways in which the ordering and delivery procedures might be improved.

Design constraints and considerations
There were several individuals at some establishments with responsibility for deciding which aviation fuel suppliers to use.

Overall design
Six depth interviews were conducted with a mixture of people responsible for ordering and delivering aviation fuel at six airports/aerodromes/establishments where aircraft are tested etc. This was followed by a face-to-face interview survey.

Sampling design and procedures
There were around 60 establishments receiving aviation fuel by road. From client lists, supplemented by telephone calls to check on the exact status of establishments, it was possible to identify the establishments that ordered aviation fuel. All of these establishments were included in the study. This decision was taken given the small size of the overall population and the budget available.

Data collection method and procedures
The qualitative research identified the fact that different respondents were responsible for ordering, delivery and quality control, and that it would be sensible to have a master questionnaire for each establishment with different respondents completing each section. It was felt that it was easier to administer the master questionnaire by sending out an interviewer to each establishment to collect the information on a face-to-face basis. It might have been possible to collect information

The Scope of Business Marketing Research

over the telephone, but the budget was available and the sample was sufficiently small to warrant a face-to-face approach.

Approach to analysis
The analysis was similar to the previous cutting oils example, with a combination of conventional cross analysis and the presentation of different case studies to reflect the different airport/aircraft establishment scenarios.

Decisions taken as a result of research
The study identified specific improvements that could be made to the ordering procedures, and also to the delivery routing arrangements.

Evaluation of an exhibition

Background
Four local authorities joined together to run a trade and industry exhibition, with the specific aim of improving the sales of local firms, thereby helping to reduce the high level of unemployment.

Research objectives
To determine whether the £100,000 subsidy of the trade and industry exhibition should be continued the following year, or whether the money should be given in the form of direct grants to individual companies rather than working indirectly through the provision of a business-generating trade and industry exhibition.

Design constraints and considerations
Limited budget and the need to find out how sales were generated after the exhibition.

Overall design
A mixture of desk research, qualitative research, telephone survey and face-to-face interviews with all people involved with the exhibition.

Sampling design and procedures
The critical issue was to identify all those involved whose view was relevant to the evaluation. Lists of people in several categories were

identified, and appropriate samples drawn, with the maximum sample being drawn within each category given the budget available. The final sample structure was as follows:

- Exhibitors
- Visitors
- Council personnel
- Exhibition organisers and
- VIPs attending the exhibition.

Data collection method and procedures
The data collection pattern included face-to-face interviewing, telephone research, and a postal study.

Approach to analysis
The analysis involved drawing together in an elective way the evidence collected from the above.

Decisions taken as a result of research
The study showed that the exhibition did work to increase employment in the area.

Part II:
The Techniques of Business Marketing Research

The primary task of business marketing research is the gathering of data in response to a specific need to solve a marketing problem. These data may be matters of fact, usually numerical in character, or matters of personal opinion; their collection involves a number of techniques which are the subject of this part of the Handbook.

These techniques run from the precise definition of the problem to be solved, through the planning and organisation of the collection process, to the actual gathering tasks:

- *of published data, or*
- *of data available only from contact with individuals.*

The skills involved in gathering include the ability to develop appropriate samples, from a large population of potential contacts; the ability to carry out interviews, by telephone or by direct personal contact; and the design of the list of questions to be answered, by whatever means are deemed appropriate.

The six Chapters of Part II explore these techniques and personal skills in full detail. The one significant aspect that is not covered is the basic knowledge of statistics necessary to complete the sampling and analysis process. The reader, if not already in possession of this knowledge, is referred to the texts on statistics listed in Appendix E.

4

Preparing for a Business Marketing Research Project

Johann Aucamp

Before the actual work involved in doing a job of business marketing research is described, it is necessary to look at the preparatory stages – the definition of the task. This is so whether the research is to be done in-house or on behalf of a client by an independent consultancy or fieldwork agency. Because any research project could be expensive in terms of both money and time, it would therefore be better to have no information at all than to have poor or wrong information.

The brief

Marketing research is only undertaken in order to solve a problem. It is therefore essential to know what the real problem is, and clearly to understand the necessary depth and direction of the investigation. Without a clear but also realistic brief, it can be very difficult or even impossible to satisfy the sponsor of the research. (For the in-house situation, the sponsor is the appropriate part of the company management; otherwise it is the client commissioning the work.)

It is definitely the responsibility of the researcher to ascertain the sponsor's exact requirements. In doing so, answers must be obtained to questions such as the following.

- Is that really the problem?
- Is that really what the sponsor wants?
- Is that the best way of answering the question?

The researcher should understand clearly the background to the problem and the proposed survey. Only then can he ensure that, to the best of his ability, the research will be correctly executed. Only then can he successfully avoid:

- wasting effort in seeking unobtainable information;
- wasting time on obtaining irrelevant information or unnecessary details;
- taking the wrong direction and producing an excellent report which is irrelevant to the original problems.

The means by which all this is achieved is a properly prepared research brief. Ideally, the brief should be a written statement from the sponsor of the research, clearly stating the problem and the questions to be answered. Frequently, however, the sponsor supplies a fairly general statement such as: 'We have a problem with our sales in such-and-such a region. What can we do?' In this case, after discussion with the sponsor, the researcher should prepare a statement himself and submit it to the sponsor for approval.

The ideal brief should be concise, but at the same time it should leave no misunderstanding on the actual work required. It should include:

- background information,
- definition of terms,
- technical specifications and explanations,
- information required,
- special factors,
- timing.

These topics are amplified in the following paragraphs.

Preparing for a Research Project

Background information

The amount and detail of the background information included in the brief depends entirely on the nature of the study, and only a few general rules can be made. As a minimum, the background information should cover points such as:

1. the nature of the sponsor's business, in so far as it is necessary, to explain the purpose of the research;
2. why the study is being undertaken;
3. what action is dependent on the results of the survey;
4. what relevant information is already available.

The last of these is particularly important; obviously the sponsor is not going to appreciate having his money spent on producing information he already knows. It follows, of course, that the sponsor should play his part and disclose exactly what is available, and especially reveal what interviewing has already been done and whether formally or informally. It is most irritating to a respondent to be re-interviewed, or even to be approached about a subject on which he has already granted an interview.

Definition of terms

One of the major errors in interviewing is to assume that respondents understand the technical terms used by the interviewer, as supplied by the sponsor. Frequently these are jargon, well understood by the sponsor and everybody else in his company but not necessarily by outsiders. By using these terms, however, the interviewer could meet a number of problems, for example:

- in an anonymous study, it may become obvious who the sponsor is, if too many of these technical terms are used;
- customers buying from the sponsor's competitors could interpret the terms in a totally different way from those who buy from the sponsor;
- if the respondent does not understand these terms, the results of the interview may be valueless.

It is therefore essential that all such terms are clearly explained in the brief but avoided, as far as possible, in any interview.

Technical specifications and explanations

A considerable amount of business marketing research involves technical matters, and in order to be able to conduct the interview intelligently it is vital that an interviewer understands those which are relevant to his research. Any respondent who recognises that the interviewer does not know what he is talking about will soon stop the interview.

The interviewer's technical knowledge of the subject of the research does not have to be encyclopaedic, but it must be good enough for the interviewer to recognise the value of any supplementary comments made by the respondent, and to pursue them as necessary.

Information required

Most types of information can be divided into the essential, the useful but not so essential, and the interesting but superfluous. In any brief, it is very important that the sponsor clearly differentiates between the essential, the desirable, and the merely interesting information. This enables the researcher to spend the greater part of his time finding answers to questions in the first and second categories rather than to those in the third. As the respondent is frequently a busy executive, giving up valuable time, this is essential.

Obviously it is vital that the scope of the research be explained in the brief – the geographical areas to be covered, any limitations on the nature and size of respondent companies, and the range of products or services to be included in any questioning. The researcher should not be left to guess at this information, even if the basic definition of the problem may have tried to make it clear. In particular, the business sectors to be explored should be defined, preferably in some standard form, such as by means of SIC code numbers.

A third point concerns the depth and degree of accuracy of the information required. Some examples of the kind of difficulties arising are:

- whether the sponsor requires an indication of market size within

Preparing for a Research Project

a fairly wide bracket, say, 5,000 to 10,000 tons, or whether he requires very accurate definition, such as 5.1–5.2 thousand tons;

- whether he needs the names of the top five or ten companies operating in the field, or the names of all the companies operating, and how much detail he requires about these companies;
- whether approximate rates of growth are sufficient or if the research must provide detailed sector analysis, with precise rates of change in each industry or user sector.

Frequently, far too much effort is spent on unnecessary accuracy in terms of market size, leaving too few resources to establish how to tackle the market.

Special factors

For reasons which may be well understood by the researcher, the sponsoring company may wish to be anonymous or to disguise its interest in one way or another. This is frequently the case when new product development research is mounted or when company image research is done. It is essential that points such as these are indicated very clearly in the brief, since this could considerably affect how the approach to the respondent is made.

Timing

In many cases the results of a research exercise must be known by a certain date, to enable a decision to be made at the right time. In cases such as these, one day late could be disastrous. In other cases, such as advertising research, the actual fieldwork must take place before or after a certain event such as the appearance of a new advertisement in the press. Important points like these should be mentioned in the brief, which should indicate clearly when the research can begin and when, if fieldwork is involved, it must stop. The brief must also indicate, very clearly, when the actual report is required.

The proposal

The brief is the formal statement of the information needs of the sponsor. The resultant terms of reference, or proposal, are the researcher's commitment and his statement of what he proposes to do and how he proposes to do it. To a large extent this involves turning a brief into a working document, covering at least the following points:

- a restatement of the objectives – in most cases taken straight from the brief;
- how the results of the research will be used;
- what specific questions are to be answered;
- the industrial sectors to be covered or excluded;
- the geographic areas to be covered or excluded;
- the size range of companies or organisations to be covered or excluded;
- the research techniques to be employed, including sampling and interviewing;
- any special considerations;
- the timing in detail, including warnings about how delays in vital decisions will affect the deadline;
- the cost.

These elements would be included in a proposal by an in-house researcher, or by an external researcher bidding for the work. In the latter case the cost would appear as a price, probably accompanied by an acceptance validity clause and the terms under which the fees would be remitted. A bidder would probably also include some reference to the personnel to be involved in the work.

The research task

As will be explained at greater length elsewhere in this Handbook, marketing research can be divided into two basic parts: desk research and field research. These must both be considered very carefully at the proposal stage.

Preparing for a Research Project

Desk research

Desk research consists of the use of secondary sources – sources of already published information. Good desk research is as much an art as good field research, and many projects can in fact be completed by desk research only.

It is surprising how much information can sometimes be obtained, not only from outside desk sources but also from the sponsor company's own internal sources. No research project should be begun without thorough desk research to find out what is already available, so that unnecessary duplication of information gathering can be avoided.

Field research

Once every available secondary source has been scanned, the researcher can analyse which questions have been answered and decide which other questions need to be answered through field research. In writing a proposal, a researcher must make an intelligent guess at the amount of field research necessary, by a sensible interpretation of the sponsor's brief.

Whether such field research is conducted by in-house employees or by outside consultants, or by a field force of outside industrial interviewers, and whether this fieldwork is conducted by post, by telephone, or by personal interviews, depends on the nature of the problem, on the sponsor's resources, and on his wish to remain independent of the research task.

Whenever a project is planned, every single method should be considered and consciously accepted or rejected.

Costing a research project

As can be expected, there are different costing systems within research just as there are within industry. For a company's own research department two of the major cost elements are salaries and general overheads. How the overheads are calculated and allocated depends to a large extent on each company's own accounting system.

Should a project be carried out by in-house researchers, the main cost elements to be taken into consideration are:

- staff costs (which would, to a large extent, be represented by the time spent on a particular project – different companies will have different views on whether time is allocated to a specific project or just counted as a general overhead);
- subcontracted field costs (if any);
- travelling expenses;
- telephone expenses;
- data processing such as coding, data entry, analysis of results;
- administrative costs, which consist of stationery, printing, postage etc, spent specifically on that job;
- clerical, including secretarial, editing, coding, and general processing costs of the project.

When a specific project is put out to an external marketing research company, the costing from a sponsor's point of view becomes rather more straightforward. The cost now consists of the basic time element of project supervision, plus the amount of money paid to the external marketing research company for undertaking the project.

How then does a market research services company work out the cost of a proposal? Essentially there are three basic elements to bear in mind, which are:

- the direct, job-related costs;
- overheads (both salary related and non-salary related);
- profit.

The direct job-related costs are largely made up of the money paid to interviewers for carrying out the research, including travelling expenses. To these must be added other direct costs, such as:

- telephone costs;
- stationery, printing, postage;
- editing, coding;

Preparing for a Research Project

- data processing – which could be done by an outside DP bureau or by an internal DP department.

How overheads are calculated differs a great deal from company to company. In some agencies, very accurate job time sheets are kept calculating how much time every person at every level is spending on each job. In other agencies only time spent by researchers is measured.

However overheads are allocated to jobs, in costing a proposal it is important to take account of:

- the time of researchers and consultants allocated to the job;
- the time of other staff;
- the time of administrative staff such as secretaries, typists and printers;
- rent, rates, lighting, cleaning and so on.

Marketing research companies are in business to make a profit. How this is calculated depends on the company's costing system, but it must be included in the cost.

Who should carry out the research?

It was mentioned earlier that the research could be carried out either by the internal research department of the sponsoring company or by an outside company (whether a one-man consultant or a market research agency).

How is this choice made? Generally, research departments in research user companies have become smaller during the last five years and they can only carry out relatively small projects – desk research, and perhaps a handful of interviews. Should fieldwork be carried out by internal departments, the IMRA Code of Conduct on confidentiality has to be observed as strictly as if the research had been carried out by an outside company. Whether or not the in-house researcher discloses for whom he works, he has to state either that he will disclose information as given to his company or that the answers will be treated confidentially (and then ensure that this is done). There is no half-way house.

One argument in favour of in-house researchers carrying out the fieldwork is 'their superior understanding' of technical problems. A strong counter-argument is that in-house researchers are too close to the problem to be independent. Most often, the choice of an outside company is made because of the availability of special skills – in interviewing, for example, or in the technical knowledge of a consultant.

Control of the project

Whether a project is a small two-week project or a long project lasting months, whether it involves one city or ten countries, whether it has one person working on it or a hundred, it is essential to set up a thorough control system. This control system must allow for one main controller of the project, who should be responsible for answering queries, referring queries to other sources if necessary, timing and so on.

In a very small project it is probably sufficient to arrange for a weekly progress check, and a system of bearing the ultimate deadline in mind throughout. In large projects, it is advisable to have a much more organised project control system. This should start with a detailed list of dates when various decisions have to be made. In order to do this thoroughly, it is sometimes far better to put it down graphically in the form of a critical path analysis. On this chart – where traditionally one starts by working backwards, commencing with the due date of the report – various potential bottlenecks can be isolated. In addition, whenever a particular stage is beginning to fall behind, one can immediately see what effect this would have on other stages and, in turn, on the ultimate deadline. Needless to say, there is absolutely no need whatsoever to construct a complicated control system if nobody is going to look at it. Therefore an essential part of any control system is appointing a person who checks regularly that everything is in order.

5

Desk Research

Martin Stoll

The first, and usually vital, business marketing technique to be explored is that of desk research. After a brief introduction noting the rapid changes in desk research sources, this Chapter suggests an efficient approach to desk research. It then discusses where to look for the information and takes a look at the broad categories of information sources available. It ends with a consideration of some of the future trends in desk research.

Introduction

Desk research involves the basic skills of searching published information sources, such as books and periodicals. As this is a skill that most researchers acquired at school or college, it can often seem boring or too simple to bother with. In fact it is an exciting area, which is ignored at a researcher's peril. Some of the biggest changes in marketing research that have taken place between the publication of the first and second editions of this Handbook are probably to be found in the area of desk research.

While the number of reports and periodicals being published has increased each year, the most important change has come from the development of computerised databases. This development has markedly changed the research options available to someone looking for market information. The growth of this 'online' information has been dramatic. In 1979 there were only 400 databases, most of them indexes and abstracts of scientific periodicals. Ten years later, in 1989, there were 4,062 databases, many of them aimed specifically at business users.

For the most part, the information from online databases has to be paid for on a fairly direct use basis. This can make online sources seem expensive, though in reality the option may often be cheaper than alternatives. For example, it may be cheaper for an executive to spend half an hour in the office searching online, than to spend half a day out of the office travelling to and using a library.

This focus on the cost of information is a relatively new concern among market researchers. It has at least two important consequences. The first is that, in some measure, it enhances the perceived value of desk research. Information that is paid for is frequently seen as having more value than information that comes free. A consequence of this is that corporations have had to budget more, and more directly, for information resources.

Second, the fact that information can be charged for has resulted in the growth of specialist information services, which charge clients for carrying out desk research. This means that researchers have more choice about whether to do desk research themselves or whether to farm parts or all of it out to specialists.

A suggested approach to desk research

Whoever does the desk research, nearly every piece of market research starts with some form of it and a good few go no further. Since the greater part of market research is usually taken up with fieldwork, there is often a temptation to skip the desk research, but it is a temptation that should be resisted. Desk research is cheap and fast to do; field research is costly and usually runs into weeks to carry out. Even if the desk research does not save the need for fieldwork, it will ensure that the fieldwork asks the right people the right questions.

The key question to be answered by desk research is: 'Has anyone else done the research already?' If the answer is 'Yes' and the research

Desk Research

is accessible, it will almost always make sense to start there.

There are no hard and fast rules for desk research, but the following approach is suggested as one that has proved useful to many researchers.

Start simple with the one-stop reference book

The less a researcher knows about a topic, the more important it is to start with a short general overview before plunging into the detail. The best place to start is in the office, not the library. There are a number of useful one-stop reference books which have a little data on a lot of markets in them. There are, of course, reference books for individual industries, and again these are the right place from which to start any desk research.

Good examples of one-stop reference books are the UK Advertising Association's *Marketing Pocket Book*, which gives a lot of basic data about consumer markets, or the US Department of Commerce's annual *Industrial Outlook*, which gives useful summaries for almost every major industrial sector, or Elsevier's two-volume *Yearbook of World Electronics Data*, as an example of a single industry sector source.

Look in-house

If the basic information cannot be found on the researcher's own shelves, it may well be sitting on someone else's shelves, or in their filing cabinet, in the same organisation. Obviously a lot will depend on the size of the organisation, but even if it is not large enough to have its own library it is surprising what sort of information may be available. It is very common for one manager to buy a market research report or to subscribe to a useful journal without telling anyone else. The larger the organisation, the more time a researcher should spend searching in-house – it is bound to be in there somewhere – and the search should not just be for research reports.

Review articles in newspapers or magazines are an ideal starting point. A number of newspapers, such as the *Financial Times*, publish regular supplements on particular industries. Most trade magazines, especially US ones, also publish an overall review of their markets at the beginning or end of the year.

Try a trade association

If nothing is found in-house, it is usually worth contacting a trade association before heading off to a library or going online. To find out which trade association to contact requires reference to a directory of trade associations. This should be part of any market researcher's basic library holding, but can usually be found in a local library. This need not entail a visit – many local libraries are quite happy to give details of a trade association over the phone.

Trade associations vary considerably in the amount of information they collect and provide. Some have libraries and information services and actively collect and disseminate information. Others do not collect market data at all.

Unfortunately for market researchers, some trade associations and professional bodies make information available only to their members; even so, it always makes sense to contact trade associations at an early stage. With some, the desk research may not need to go any further; with others, the enquiry may still generate a list of more helpful contacts or sources for further research.

Libraries

Once in-house resources and trade associations have been covered, it is time to start looking in libraries. When choosing a library, it is again worth asking a simple question: 'Is there a library with a specialist collection on the subject of interest?' This can be easily checked by consulting a published directory of specialist libraries, or by asking the librarian at a local reference library. Many of these specialist libraries are housed in professional or trade associations, and some are kept as part of public or academic libraries.

If there is no specialist library in reach, there are usually good business reference libraries close by. In the UK, most large cities have good collections. In the US, business schools and universities are often the best starting point. Major cities tend to have the best libraries. In London, there is the British Library's Science Reference Library, the Department of Enterprise's Export Marketing Intelligence Centre (EMIC, formerly SMIL) and the City Business Library. In Washington

Desk Research

there is the Library of Congress, and in New York there is the New York Public Library.

Some of the best libraries in particular market sectors are private libraries in corporations. In the UK, it is sometimes possible to access the holdings of such libraries through membership of a 'library cooperative'. These are usually managed by local authorities, so can be very active in some parts of the country and non-existent in others. It is worth asking at the nearest major county or city reference library whether there is an active library cooperative locally.

Finally, if a researcher has a particular problem locating a particular periodical, it is worth considering using the British Library Document Supply Centre. The Centre, based at Boston Spa in West Yorkshire, provides books or copies of articles from any periodical in its extensive holdings. The service, which is used by subscribers all round the world, is very fast. To use the service, a researcher needs to register and to buy a pack of pre-paid request forms. As many public and academic libraries around the world are registered users, a researcher with a single request may be better advised to use their services.

Online services

An alternative to visiting libraries is searching online. Online services give access to published information from all over the world. This can be the full text of the *New York Times* or the *Financial Times*, summaries of reports in papers and periodicals, or economic statistics. Searching online eliminates the frustrations of finding a reference to a particular topic in an index but failing to find a copy of the periodical in the library. But the strength of online information does not lie just in its coverage; it is also to be found in the flexible way in which it can be accessed.

As online services become more user friendly, and as their coverage grows, they are clearly a resource that market researchers must understand, even if they do not use them directly themselves.

Online advantages

The advantage of online searching is that it offers instant access to an enormous number of sources without moving out of the office. A researcher can carry out searches in a matter of minutes, which would take hours or even days to carry out in a library. As the search is usually taking place on a computer, the information can be directly down-loaded on to the computer for editing or direct use in a report or, say, in Lotus 1-2-3 format, for analysis on a spreadsheet.

As with relational databases, such as DBase, online databases can be searched in a variety of ways. For example, they can be searched using standardised codes or abbreviations, but they can also carry out 'free text' searching, where the user asks for every occurrence of a particular word or words. In addition, online offers the power of Boolean logic, so that, for example, a user could specify that he wanted all articles from a certain database about 'Market Research in the US' *and/or* 'Desk Research' *but not* 'Consumer Research'.

Disadvantages

The disadvantages of online are partly a question of cost and partly the usual frustrations of using computers. On the cost side, a pound or a dollar a minute is a fairly normal charge, so with telephone line charges on top it is easy to spend a lot of money in a fairly short time. On the computing side, although online searching is getting easier, most users still have to master a variety of different command languages.

Hardware

Most people today access online information using a personal computer and a modem. The information may be available from more than one online source and in more than one form. For example, a number of useful databases can be accessed through electronic mail systems such as Telecom Gold or MCI Mail. In the UK, a considerable amount of information is also available on Prestel Viewdata system. Most commonly, though, online information is accessed via an online 'host': for example Dialog, Pergamon Infoline, or Datastar.

Each host has a large mainframe computer which holds a large number of databases. These databases come from a variety of sources, such as publishers and learned societies, but the host usually tries to standardise the commands used to operate the various databases.

Desk Research

Even so, there are usually differences between databases on the same host and there are always differences between commands on different hosts. This is being overcome by the introduction of more user-friendly 'front-end' software, which is intended to allow a user to use a single command language to address different databases and different hosts.

Software

In principle, it is possible to search online with fairly limited communications software. In practice, for someone who is going to do a lot of online searching, it is a help to have more sophisticated software. There are now a number of software packages which will store and dial telephone numbers, give user identification at the appropriate moment and can also store 'search strategies' (the set of commands for a search). Details of where to go for further information on software for online searching are provided in a later section of this Chapter.

Using online

Online searching is probably best used at the beginning or the end of a desk research exercise. It can be an excellent way of checking out a new subject in a hurry, and it can also be a useful way of checking that the researcher has not overlooked something about a topic. Budget constraints may determine how it is used.

If money is a constraint, then this may also determine who actually does the search. Searching online is quite a specialist skill and the whole online scene is changing very fast. This means that it is difficult to do online searching on a casual, infrequent basis. Probably searching once a week is the minimum frequency for someone to keep his hand in.

For this reason, in many research departments one person, often an information professional, is assigned the job of doing all the online searching. Another approach often adopted is to use an external agency – either the host or a commercial information service – to carry out a company's entire online searches. This may seem to add cost to a costly process, but in fact it can save money. Information professionals waste less time and make fewer false starts because they are usually very experienced at searching and they know the best databases to use and the most appropriate search strategies.

Sources for sources

Although it is a rapidly changing situation, which will probably be out of date before this Handbook is published, some reference to what sources are available must be given here, if only to provide a key to the future pattern.

Market research reports

Desk research is about using other people's research labours, and a researcher should always check the availability of market research reports at an early stage. There are a number of different sources of market research reports, but the two most comprehensive sources are the US publication *Findex* and the British *MSI Marketing Surveys Index*. Both are large, both try to be global in their coverage and both are available online.

There are two kinds of market research report – those that are too expensive for libraries to buy, and the rest. If a library does not have a report, it is possible to ask the publisher for a press release, which often contains useful information. Of course, it may make sense to buy the report itself instead of duplicating the research.

General press

An online search will detail what the major newspapers and periodicals said about a particular topic. A press cutting service, such as McCarthy's in the UK, will do the same. Failing that, a researcher will have to look in an index and then look in the appropriate newspaper or journal. The major newspapers are often indexed separately, but they are also covered in general indexes, such as *Predicast's F&S Index*, or in specialist indexes such as the British Technology Index or the American publication *Business Periodicals Index*. These indexes usually include a small abstract which can serve as a good guide to whether or not an article is worth chasing up.

Desk Research

Trade press

The most comprehensive listing of periodicals of all kinds is *Ulrich's International Periodicals*, but there are also less comprehensive listings of general and trade press publications, such as *Willing's Press Guide* and *Benn's Media Directory* in the UK. Some libraries publish lists of their own holdings, which can help to identify the important periodicals. For example, the Baker Library at Harvard Business School or London's City Business Library publish details of their periodical and newspapers holdings.

Statistics

It is best to start with the government's own summary of its statistics, the *Annual Abstract of Statistics*. If that does not give enough information, in the UK the government also publishes a *Guide to Official Statistics*, which gives details of all the statistics that the government publishes. The government publishing offices – the GPO in the US and HMSO in the UK – also publish listings of statistics in publication. With some perseverance it is possible to get hold of similar listings for UN, OECD, and Eurostat publications. Finally, most government departments or agencies do not publish all the statistics that they collect and many of these statistics are available on request. It takes some research to find where the knowledge is held, but the effort is often well worth while.

Company information

Dun & Bradstreet produces directories listing companies both in the US and in Europe. In the UK and Europe the other main source of information is the Kompass series of directories. For more detailed information about companies, there are a number of online databases, including Datastream for US and non-US companies, ICC in the UK, Dafsa in France, Hoppenstedt in Germany and so on. In the UK, there are also the Extel cards covering a number of private companies as well as public, while Kompass and Dun & Bradstreet information is also online.

Information about private companies is dependent ultimately on legal reporting requirements. In the UK, annual reports for all private and public companies are available from Companies House in London, Cardiff or Edinburgh for payment of a charge, currently £2.75 per company. In the US, reports for public companies are available direct from the companies or in fiche collections.

Online

The major source of information about online databases worldwide is the *Directory of Online Databases* from Cuadra Associates Inc.

Most major online hosts run courses on getting started online, as do a number of other organisations such as Aslib, the British Library and IMRA in the UK, or the ALA and AMA in the United States. These bodies are probably also the best starting point for someone looking for advice on some of the other online issues, such as choice of software. There are now also a number of annual online conferences and trade shows for regular users.

The future

The direction that desk research will take in the near future is strongly linked to developments in computers and, in particular, in the use for storing information of new storage media - notably CD-ROM and videodisk. While the number of databases and the number of online users is growing, other ways of storing information are beginning to be used commercially: of these, CD-ROM (Compact Disk Read Only Memory) is the best established. One CD-ROM disk, similar to an audio compact disk, has the capacity to store the equivalent of a few large books. For example, 12 volumes of Kompass for most of the countries of Western Europe, are now available - the UK File covering 162,000 companies, and the European File with 280,000.

Accessed via a personal computer, CD-ROM eliminates the need for telephone links and, unlike online, it carries no usage charge. Like a book, the more you use it the better value it represents. But unlike a book, it can be searched in myriad ways and can be used to generate mailing lists and addresses on labels as well as for information.

One drawback of CD-ROM, against online, apart from its initial cost (the Kompass disks cost £4,000 and £2,200 respectively) is

Desk Research

topicality. Like the printed word, it is out of date when it is produced and may quickly get too far out of date. Here, though, the possibility of using WORM disks (Write Once, Read Many times) opens up the possibility of CD disks that can be updated hourly or daily via a telephone link.

The other pointer to the future is the use of videodisk as a storage medium which allows the storage of visual as well as textual information. One commercial example currently available is the complete set of US patent files on videodisk available from Pergamon.

Thus, while the principles of desk research will remain the same, over the next decade the practice of desk research is likely to continue changing, with the computer very much at the heart of the change.

6

The Collection of Primary Data

Christine Eborall

The main activity in business marketing research is the acquisition of field data, either as numerical information or as personal statements. Its importance is recognised by the fact that four Chapters of the Handbook are devoted to it, of which this is the first.

Introduction

The purpose of this Chapter is to review the methods of collecting primary data that are currently in use in business marketing research surveys, to assess their relative strengths and shortcomings, and to indicate the types of research to which they are best suited. The main methods reviewed are face-to-face (personal) interviewing, telephone interviewing, postal (mail) and self-completion questionnaires, and observational techniques.

At the end of the Chapter there is a review of certain special techniques, which employ one or more of the above methods and which have some relevance to business research. The techniques reviewed are panels, group discussions (focus groups), hall tests, clinics and other central location methods, and the use of omnibus surveys in business research.

Face-to-face (personal) interviewing

A face-to-face or personal interview is one in which interviewer and respondent are in direct face-to-face contact. It is widely considered to be the classical method of interviewing, and is probably the most demanding in terms of execution. It is the basis for a number of special techniques, notably those used in qualitative research.

Current usage

Face-to-face interviewing is probably the most versatile of the data collection methods, and has many applications in business marketing research. It is used for all types of questionnaire, from the highly structured through to the unstructured topic guide. It is used in various situations: at the respondent's place of work, at his home, at central locations which respondents have been invited to attend, at conferences, exhibitions and airports, or even on planes and trains. Virtually all respondents can be reached by this method and, while more frequently conducted on a one-to-one basis, the face-to-face approach is also the basis of the group discussion technique, described later in this Chapter.

Face-to-face interviewing in the business context is not often used in isolation, except when sampling at particular places (exhibitions, airports and the like). It is usually preceded by some form of telephone contact, which is not only necessary to arrange a convenient time for the interview, but is also needed for the preliminary screening of samples and to identify the most appropriate respondents. Telephone interviewing may also be used to follow up a face-to-face meeting, to collect supplementary information not available at the time or for further clarification of any point. Validation of face-to-face interviews (to check that they genuinely took place) is frequently conducted by telephone too. Finally, a short series of face-to-face interviews may be necessary to determine the parameters for a larger telephone interview survey.

The face-to-face approach is also frequently used in conjunction with self-completion methods. Sometimes a face-to-face interview has a self-completion element in it, or a self-completion questionnaire may

The Collection of Primary Data

be sent in advance of, or left behind after, a face-to-face interview. An extreme version of this is the so-called computer-assisted personal interviewing (CAPI) technique; this is really a self-completion method, since the respondent himself completes the questionnaire on a computer, with the interviewer present only for initial training and guidance.

Strengths of face-to-face interviews

Data collection by personal interviewing has a number of very significant advantages over other methods, and these advantages are concerned mainly with the *quality* of the data collected.

Respondents can be encouraged to give much fuller responses in a face-to-face situation than is possible with other methods. There are several reasons for this:

- the interviewer can give encouragement in the form of the wide range of prompts and probes which can be deployed in a face-to-face situation;
- the interviewer can observe the respondent's behaviour and reactions, and react accordingly – moreover, such observations can contribute to the interpretation of the data;
- face-to-face interviews are generally conducted at a slower pace then, for example, telephone ones and, even though business interviews are almost always conducted under some degree of time pressure, there is usually time for respondents to gather their thoughts, and therefore to give considered responses;
- respondents are also likely, barring interruptions, to give the interview their undivided attention, whereas with a telephone interview in particular they may be trying to do something else at the same time.

Research conducted on behalf of the Market Research Development Fund (MRDF)[2] in 1984–5 corroborated previous studies in finding that respondents in face-to-face interviews gave more responses to open and unprompted questions than did those in telephone interviews. This was attributed to the faster pace and difficulty of probing in telephone interviewing. The MRDF survey, which is discussed later in connection with telephone interviewing, also demonstrated a clear preference for face-to-face interviewing among the survey respondents. The reasons given were to do with its being 'reassuring to know who you're talking to' and the telephone's being 'too impersonal'. Face-to-face respondents also needed less reassurance about the reasons for the research, and the uses to which the information was to be put, than did the telephone respondents. Despite the fact that these survey respondents were representative of the entire UK population, rather than just the business one, it seems probable that the finding is applicable to both although the greater use of the telephone for business purposes makes it a more familiar, and hence less impersonal, means of communication for business respondents.

Face-to-face interviewing therefore encourages respondents to give considered responses, which they feel will be appreciated as such and which they feel confident about divulging. Reassurance about the use of the information, which can be most easily given in a face-to-face situation, is also supported by the use of the Interviewer Card, which is usable only in this method of data collection (although a validation service for telephone interviewing is operated by the Market Research Society).

There is also the consideration that the face-to-face interview is better able to take account of the enormous variation that can occur among businesses than can a less flexible method. Interviews can generally be tape-recorded so that all details are retained; respondents may in any case be prepared to give to a receptive interviewer explanations of 'how' and 'why' that they would not make over the telephone or on a self-completion questionnaire. It is also possible that more senior respondents in particular may be prepared to participate in research only if they feel that due weight is being given to their responses at a face-to-face interview, and would therefore not respond to a telephone interview or a self-completion questionnaire.

The issue of which is the most appropriate method for collecting information of a confidential or sensitive nature is not straightforward. Much depends on the nature of the information itself: whether it is commercially sensitive, or something that respondents might personally feel sensitive or embarrassed about. The face-to-face interview, supported perhaps by an advance letter of authorisation

The Collection of Primary Data

and explanation, is probably the most suitable method in commercially sensitive situations, since it offers the greatest opportunity for reassurance and attention to detail. However, subjects that are more personally sensitive, admittedly more common in consumer than in business research, are often better handled by telephone interview (which is more impersonal), or by various self-completion techniques where confidentiality of response can be maintained (such as, for example, the computer-assisted approach[11] or those developed for researching AIDS[6]). This can sometimes be appropriate for junior staff who, if interviewed at work, may be inhibited by being in a shared office and observed or overheard by their colleagues.

The issues discussed above show that the amount of information that can be collected at a face-to-face interview can be very great. This is not only because information can be collected in depth, but also because the duration of the interview can be greater than for other methods. Interviews conducted at the place of work normally last for an average of 40 minutes and a maximum of 60 minutes, but others can be much shorter (eg at exhibitions), or longer if outside the workplace or for real in-depth exploration.

Questionnaires that are unavoidably lengthy or boring for respondents (and some of the information that marketing management needs can be very tedious) are also best administered face-to-face for another reason. This is because of the variety of questioning methods and visual aids that can be employed. Both can enhance the quality of data collected. The use of show-cards to convey – in words or graphics – detailed information, instructions and rating scales, and as an *aide-mémoire* to respondents, is generally regarded as making the interview easier and more varied, although the MRDF study[2] showed that many verbal prompts can be successfully administered by telephone, provided that sufficient attention is paid to questionnaire design. There are some techniques involving respondent participation (eg sorting techniques) that can only be administered face-to-face. Likewise there are a number of research problems where it is essential that respondents are present to see, hear, examine, try out or even taste and smell: these include many types of advertising test, product concept and product tests, and readership studies. Clearly all these involve a major element of face-to-face interviewing.

The ability to observe a respondent's behaviour during face-to-face interviewing has already been mentioned, and feedback on this can be very useful in interpreting the research findings. Likewise, observations of a respondent's workplace, made during an interview visit, can provide an opportunity to collect or check on information, such as makes and types of equipment installed or products in use, and can also provide insights. The conditions under which the respondent works, the number of interruptions, the presence of other people and the type and nature of the site itself may all be relevant.

Face-to-face interviewing shortcomings

It goes without saying that there are drawbacks to face-to-face interviewing, and the first two are entirely predictable: cost and time. Face-to-face interviewing is usually the most expensive method of collecting data, because of the interviewer's fees and the travelling time and costs involved. The cases when this may not be so are those when the respondents come to the interviewers, such as central locations, conferences, exhibitions, ports and airports. In terms of value for money, face-to-face interviewing may compare very favourably with other methods; in absolute terms the comparison is less favourable, particularly when compared with telephone interviewing.

Face-to-face interviewing also compares unfavourably with telephone interviewing (although not usually with postal surveys) on another parameter: timescale. It almost always takes longer to conduct a programme of face-to-face interviews than the equivalent number of telephone ones. This is not only because the interviews tend to be longer, but also because the need to travel usually means that fewer can be conducted per day; additionally, delays are often caused by respondents not being available for immediate appointments. The only exception, again, are situations where the respondents come to the interviewers.

It often happens that cost and time considerations eliminate face-to-face interviewing from a research design even before the information required, and the best way to obtain it, has been properly considered. This is putting the cart before the horse, and can force the use of an alternative method (frequently telephone interviewing) in inappropriate circumstances and with potentially damaging consequences.

Another drawback of face-to-face interviewing is that it offers

The Collection of Primary Data

greater opportunity for interviewer bias, compared with other data collection methods. This may seem strange in a method which lends itself to high quality data collection, but it is this very characteristic which allows bias to come in. This is because so much depends on how interviews are conducted by the individual interviewers, who for the most part work independently. There can be wide variation in the extent and nature of prompting and probing, in the level of detail recorded, in alertness for unexpected or additional information that may turn out to be important, in the ability to cope with information that does not fit in with the structure of the questionnaire, in the conveying of reassurance and confidence to the respondent, and so on. Any business marketing researcher who has inspected quantities of completed questionnaires will have found that they range from the comprehensively covered, with the back of every page written on, to the occasionally distressingly inadequate (normally needing follow-up by telephone). Thorough interviewer training can reduce but not eliminate the problem. It is neither possible nor desirable to achieve a completely systematic approach, so there is always some variation and bias in the quality of the data collected at face-to-face interviews by more than one interviewer. Interviewer bias is reduced in situations where it can be controlled centrally, as in telephone interviewing units, or where the respondent administers a large part of the interview himself (as with CAPI).

A final problem with face-to-face interviewing is sample clustering: the concentration of the achieved sample in a limited number of geographical areas, so that the whole country is not covered (or, perhaps, the more rural parts within the areas sampled). This is because it is not a practical proposition to train and maintain a nationwide business research field-force when most of the interviewing is, by definition, concentrated in areas where the number of businesses is greatest. The United States, where distances are much greater than in Europe, provides a significant example of this difficulty.

Sample clustering may not be a problem in markets that have mass-market tendencies, since there are often other factors that explain more of the variance between individual units than does their geographical location. Thus, for example, differences between small businesses are more likely to be because of their relative size, sophistication and type of business activity, than whether they are in an urban or a rural environment. It can, on the other hand, be a serious problem in markets where the universe is limited and some key units are away from the urban areas: power stations, oil refineries, large printing plants and so on. Omitting such large units from the sample could well bias the findings, yet covering them by face-to-face interview can present practical difficulties and have cost implications. Likewise a deliberately clustered sample, such as a survey in a particular region or in a limited number of central locations, can present similar difficulties, by increasing the cost of travel.

Guidelines for the use of personal interviews

Face-to-face interviews are thus particularly appropriate for research designs that involve the following:

- the physical presence of respondents to see, hear, examine or try out, as in many kinds of advertising research, product and product concept tests, and readership studies;
- the sampling of respondents when at particular places, such as conferences, exhibitions, ports, on aeroplanes or in trains;
- investigating a subject in depth, such as highly technical or other complex subjects, preliminary investigations and market intelligence studies;
- seeking commercially sensitive information;
- questionnaires that are unavoidably lengthy and/or boring;
- interviewing very senior respondents.

They are less appropriate for designs that involve:

- completion in a very short timescale;
- questionnaires that are short and fairly straightforward;
- business in rural or inaccessible areas being an essential part of the sample;
- restricted budgets (but this constraint should not be allowed to override the fundamental requirements of the research design).

The Collection of Primary Data

Telephone interviewing

A telephone interview is one in which interviewer and respondent communicate by telephone, and therefore without direct face-to-face contact. Telephone interviewing can be conducted from one central location, or from multiple locations such as interviewers' homes. Centralised interviewing can lend itself to the use of computer-assisted telephone interviewing (CATI) systems, now in widespread use.

Interviews administered by means of videoconferencing equipment, still in its infancy in the UK, share some of the characteristics with many of the advantages of telephone interviewing, and so have been included in this section.

Current usage

Telephone interviewing is probably the most frequently used method of data collection in business marketing research. Since virtually all businesses are on the telephone, just about complete coverage of business units – but not necessarily of all business respondents – can theoretically be achieved by this method, although in practice many very small businesses, in the UK at least, are difficult to sample because they do not have a business telephone line and are therefore not listed in business directories.

The only types of business respondent who cannot be effectively reached are those who are inaccessible to the telephone or those whose work takes them away from it. Thus shop-floor workers, miners, construction workers, drivers and sales representatives are among the more difficult groups to interview by this method, although the availability of car phones is improving the accessibility to some of them.

Although usually used for one-to-one interviewing, it is also possible to conduct interviews and discussions with several respondents at once, using videoconferencing or teleconferencing equipment.

As well as being a major data collection method in its own right, telephone interviewing is also often used for preliminary screening, ie to build up a sampling frame which can then be further investigated.

It is equally widely used to make appointments for personal or telephone interviews to be conducted subsequently. It can be used in conjunction with any other method as a way of making initial contact, and as a subsequent follow-up to supply missing information, clarify any uncertainties and, indeed, to check that the original interview took place (much back-checking in business research is conducted by telephone). Numerous combinations of telephone and face-to-face interviewing, telephone interviewing with self-completion questionnaire, and telephone interviewing with pre-mailed questionnaire (the 'phone–mail–phone' approach, particularly popular in the USA) are possible, offering great versatility in use.

Strengths of telephone interviewing

The advantages of telephone interviewing tend to be the weaknesses of face-to-face interviewing, and vice versa although not exclusively so. Telephone interviewing is probably the speediest method of data collection available at present. This is because no travelling is involved, interview lengths are generally short and the interview process is concentrated and fairly resistant to interruption, thus maximising the number of interviews per day that can be conducted.

This gives rise to a number of advantages. The main consequence is that surveys based on telephone interviewing are much more quickly completed than their face-to-face or postal equivalents. The fieldwork for a small, straightforward business survey can be completed in a few days, whereas a matter of weeks is required for surveys of similar size by either of the other main methods. The total survey time can be reduced even further by the use of CATI systems, in which the previously separate data entry and tabulation set-up stages are largely integrated. Such capabilities have allowed researchers to be much more responsive to the information needs of their marketing clients (although this should not lead to abandoning all attempts at forward planning of information requirements).

The speed with which telephone interviewing can be conducted also means that it is particularly appropriate both for preliminary screening of samples and for identifying the correct respondent(s). These two activities, often interrelated, are essential in business research. Inadequate sampling frames mean that it is invariably necessary to check on

The Collection of Primary Data

an establishment's qualifications for inclusion in a sample. Business activity, number of employees, presence of particular equipment, and use of certain services are all examples of criteria that may be used to determine this qualification. This kind of screening can be done as a separate sample-building exercise or as an immediate preliminary to the main interview, but in either case it is the speed with which large numbers of such screenings can be conducted that makes telephone interviewing the undisputed choice for such purposes. Likewise, identifying the correct respondents is also most quickly and accurately done by telephone: the need to transfer from respondent to respondent until the most appropriate ones are identified particularly lends itself to this approach.

Because of its ability to maximise the number of interviews completed per day, telephone interviewing is a relatively inexpensive method of data collection. In business research it almost always costs less than the face-to-face equivalent, and on a cost-per-interview basis it may frequently be found to be less expensive than the postal equivalent. The cost factor can be a very powerful argument for telephone interviewing, but it should not be allowed to override other considerations.

The ability to conduct telephone interviews from one central location leads to a further series of advantages (most of which, however, do not apply in decentralised situations). These advantages are mainly to do with research quality. The interviewers can all be briefed at the same time, and their work can be monitored throughout the interviewing. Problems can be dealt with quickly, and solutions and procedural changes quickly disseminated, so that all the interviewers work in as similar a way as possible, thus reducing interviewer bias. Likewise, changes or additions to the questionnaire, resulting from last-minute thoughts or from early findings, perhaps from an initial pilot phase, can quickly be made. CATI systems bring even greater control and flexibility in these areas and, although currently suitable only for simpler questionnaires with few grids or open-ended questions, their automatic routeing and checking procedures can lead to greater accuracy and ease in administering interviews. These advantages do not, however, mean that centralised telephone interviewing is automatically superior to decentralised methods. Lack of local knowledge and pressures on interviewer recruitment and training are factors that can lead to loss of quality.

The almost complete coverage of a large population of contacts that can be achieved by telephone interviewing is an advantage that is not unique to this method. Compared with face-to-face interviewing, however, telephone interviewing in business research does offer the real possibility of unclustered (ie widely geographically dispersed) samples. This factor, which can be even more efficiently achieved by postal methods, is particularly important when dealing with businesses that are inaccessible by their nature (eg offshore oil rigs) or samples where the largest units tend to be outside main metropolitan areas, and whose omission from the sample could cause bias. These are much easier to cover by telephone or postally than face-to-face, and this is one reason for the widespread use of these methods (often in combination) in the USA, where distances are much greater than in Europe. Telephone interviewing can be conducted over a very wide area. Multicountry business research by telephone is increasingly commonplace, while small-scale studies, where there are a few key respondents widely distributed over the country, can also be conducted by telephone, thus saving travelling time and cost.

Conversely, it may also be efficient to use the telephone for samples that are heavily concentrated in one or just a few areas, where it would be difficult to put sufficient face-to-face interviewers in the field.

The familiarity of the telephone as a business communication tool is another advantage – not so much over the other data collection methods but as being particularly appropriate for use in a business, as opposed to a private, context. Apart from the near-complete population coverage discussed above, this is probably the one factor that has accounted for the much more rapid take-up of this method in business than in consumer research. In general, research respondents are accustomed to making business communications by telephone, and may often be more forthcoming and need less probing than would be the case if contacted at home.

A final advantage of telephone interviewing is its immediacy. People in business rarely ignore a ringing telephone, whereas they may keep a visitor waiting, and delay a written response. Immediacy can be a two-edged sword, in that the telephone can be felt to be irritatingly intrusive, but it means that the method particularly lends itself to making initial contacts and screening interviews, to making appointments for subsequent face-to-face or telephone interviews, and to conducting interviews at a prearranged time or on particular days. Some types of advertising research require the coincidental or day-after interview approach, and a research call can also be timed precisely to follow other occasions, such as conference visits, business travel and so on. Linked to this is the ability to use telephone interviewing to contact respondents who work outside normal working hours.

Shortcomings of telephone interviewing

Telephone interviewing does have a number of drawbacks, many of which are the reverse side of the considerable advantages discussed above. These drawbacks should be taken into account in any research design, not least because some of them are to do with the quality of the information collected.

The MRDF-sponsored research,[2] already mentioned, confirmed a clear tendency for respondents to give fewer responses to open and unprompted questions over the telephone compared to a face-to-face interview. The MRDF research was consumer-orientated, but since the underlying reasons were thought probably to be the faster pace at which telephone interviews are conducted, and the difficulty of probing when there is no eye contact, it seems likely that the finding is also applicable to business research – although to a lesser degree because of the more widespread use and familiarity of the telephone as a communication tool. This is not to say that unstructured, discursive business interviews cannot be carried out by telephone; they can be and frequently are, but in the context of conventional, fairly structured research interviews, the limited depth of response must be recognised.

A closely associated problem is the limited length of a telephone interview. Business respondents are frequently unwilling to devote much time to such interviews, especially if they are unplanned rather than prearranged interruptions to their work. Consequently, appointments to interview are often arranged in advance. A maximum of 20 minutes is often regarded as a rule of thumb for UK respondents, but this varies in other countries and in any case is also greatly dependent upon the subject matter of the interview and the position of the respondent. A discursive interview with an industry specialist can take an hour or more, but senior managers may be unwilling to discuss readership habits and advertising recall for more than ten minutes. It is therefore often the case that there is a limit to the amount of information that can be collected by telephone interview.

It also follows that telephone interviews are often conducted under time pressure, and this can lead to shortcomings with regard to quality. As already indicated, there is pressure on the interviewer to keep the interview moving, and probing is difficult to achieve; there is no eye contact, and pauses sound awkward. Respondents may feel inhibited from thinking, and pressurised into giving glib answers. Interviewers may feel pressurised to over-prompt or lead in their anxiety to save respondents from the embarrassment of silence, and to get through the interview in time and without the respondent hanging up. The pressure of time may also deter respondents from taking even more time to look something up, check on makes of equipment, or consult colleagues. There is a widely recognised tendency for respondents to over-estimate numerical information, which becomes even more pronounced in telephone interviews. Time pressure combined with lack of face-to-face contact may also make it difficult for both parties to establish a rapport, and make for impatience and irritation from respondents when confronted with questions they feel are irrelevant or unclear.

In telephone interviewing mishearing can also occur, caused by poor telephone reception, background noise, rapid speech or mumbling. No doubt this can be a problem for respondents as well as interviewers, and pressure of time and embarrassment can deter requests to 'say it again'. Indeed, a common cause of failure to establish a rapport with respondents is when interviewers have difficulty in hearing the responses given. Numerical information can cause particular difficulties: tens can be difficult to distinguish from teens when said (50 or 15?) and some equipment model numbers provide wonderful opportunities for mishearing (81/20 can become AT1/20, 45 can become 4T5 and so on).

There is thus not only a limit to the amount of information that can be collected by a telephone interview, but its quality may also be limited. These are both factors that must be considered at the research design stage, and also in the questionnaire design. The undoubted attractions of telephone interviewing in business research have given

The Collection of Primary Data

rise to the use of excessively long, and poorly designed, questionnaires which do not make best use of the method and may, indeed, be giving telephone research a bad name.

A further drawback of telephone interviewing, which also impacts on questionnaire design, is the inability to use visual aids or stimuli. This means that the method is usually unsuitable for research involving the evaluation of advertisements or products (although these can be sent in advance). It also means that it is difficult to use multiple choice and other forms of questioning, which are dependent on the inspection of written statements or instructions. However, many types of question normally involving the use of show-cards can successfully be administered by telephone, provided that attention is paid to questionnaire design. Thus, for example, the 'unfolding' approach can be used for rating scales and so on, although different patterns of response may be obtained from a read-out as opposed to a show-card approach, as has been demonstrated by, among others, the MRDF research.[2]

The lack of face-to-face contact in telephone interviewing also means that there is no opportunity to see the respondent or the establishment interviewed. This can mean, for example, that exact details of equipment or products in use cannot be checked by an interviewer, for which there is often the opportunity after a personal visit. Likewise, there is no visual impression of the respondent – how he reacted to the interview, the environment in which he was working – or of the site itself. A 'feel' for this can often be helpful in gaining a full understanding of the research findings.

A final drawback to telephone interviewing, and by no means a minor one, is that it may lead to lowered response rates. While the MRDF survey[2] demonstrated in a consumer research context that UK response rates to telephone interviews were unfavourable compared with the response rates to face-to-face interviews, no such comparison has been made in a business research context. Although it is more difficult to distinguish the two, since many face-to-face interviews are preceded by telephone screening, it seems likely that the situation is similar.

There are many reasons why respondents refuse to participate in telephone interviews. A preference for, and greater confidence in, face-to-face interviewing is one of them. The MRDF survey found evidence of this among consumers, and it has also been demonstrated more recently in connection with opinion polling.[10] Poor quality interviewing, because of high interviewer turnover and rushed training in central telephone units, may be contributory factors here.

In business research the disruption of respondents' work is another major cause of refusal. Over-interviewing in certain sectors is another. Yet another cause may be the suspicion that the interview may take longer than the interviewer says it will. A study conducted by Aucamp[1] among DP managers found complaints that 'interviews are frequently too long, and often they are much longer than the interviewer indicated when making the appointment'. While this applied to both telephone and face-to-face interviews, there is growing concern that the misuse of the telephone for excessively long interviews (not to mention the deception of respondents, which contravenes the MRS/IMRA Code of Conduct) may lead to major problems with non-response, and hence deterioration in the quality of this otherwise excellent method of data collection.

A final reason for non-response is the suspicion that the call may be a sales pitch in disguise, rather than a genuine research interview. Clearly, in telephone interviews the safeguard of the Interviewer Card cannot apply and the current MRS-operated validation service for telephone interviewing is not as comprehensive a safeguard.

The increase in telephone selling, now dignified by the name 'telemarketing', is causing concern among many business researchers. The practice is not compatible with market research, since by definition respondent confidentiality is not maintained: names are passed on to the sales force. Yet the similarity of skills needed for telephone interviewing and telemarketing, and the cost of installing large computerised telephone units, make telemarketing an attracting source of additional revenue to research companies and the sugging ('selling under the guise of . . .') 'survey' is still a common opening gambit in telemarketing. If the two activities should appear indistinguishable there are fears that response rates may further deteriorate, that increasing pressure may be put on business researchers by their sales colleagues to divulge respondent names, and that restrictive legislation may be introduced to curb telemarketing, which would also make telephone interviewing much more difficult to conduct.

The Collection of Primary Data

Guidelines for the use of telephone interviewing

It has already been stated that the advantages and disadvantages of face-to-face and telephone interviewing are, to a large extent, mirror images. So, therefore, are the guidelines, but they are well worth repeating. Thus, telephone interviewing is particularly appropriate for research designs that involve the following:

- sample screening, respondent identification and appointment making;
- completion in a very short timescale;
- questionnaires that are short and fairly straightforward – although longer and more complex interviews can also be conducted, particularly if in conjunction with other methods (such as self-completion) or with the use of post or fax to send material in advance;
- subjects that may be personally sensitive or embarrassing;
- covering businesses in rural or inaccessible areas, or those that are heavily concentrated in a few areas only;
- back-checking, or obtaining supplementary information from an earlier interview;
- interviewing people who work outside normal working hours;
- restricted budgets (but this should not be allowed to override the fundamental requirements of the research design).

They are less appropriate for designs that involve:

- long interviews;
- investigating subjects in depth;
- questionnaires that are complicated, need visual aids or have many open-ended questions;
- the physical presence of respondents to see, hear, examine or try out;
- interviewing very senior respondents.

The use of postal and self-completion questionnaires

The postal (mail) survey is one whereby questionnaires are sent by post to potential respondents and returned, after completion, by the same method. The questionnaire is therefore for self-completion by respondents, since there is no interviewer to administer the questions and record the responses.

Postal surveys are, in fact, just one of a number of techniques involving data collection by self-completion questionnaire. Others involve: the distribution of questionnaires to 'captive audiences' such as employees, passengers, or conference and exhibition attenders; the insertion of questionnaires into magazines and journals; their incorporation into the packaging of, or documentation accompanying, finished products. Also included here is the self-completion of computer-administered questionnaires by the CAPI system. Many of the issues discussed in this section are relevant both to postal questionnaires and to self-completion questionnaires in general, and so the two will be distinguished only when necessary.

The problems of questionnaire design for different purposes are explored at length in Chapter 9, and so coverage of this topic here is no more than is necessary to assist in understanding this present method of data collection.

Current usage

In business research, postal questionnaires are generally used to survey specialised populations such as customers, potential customers, dealers and distributors, readers of relevant publications, members of relevant organisations and employees. They are less commonly used to survey businesses in general, for reasons which are explained in subsequent paragraphs. As well as for 'one-off' enquiries, they are also used for continuous studies, whereby regular enquiries are made of the same respondents.

In a straightforward business research postal survey, questionnaires are mailed to a sample of the population, or to the entire population if it is of limited size, to be returned by the same method. However, the postal questionnaire is nowadays often used in conjunction with other methods of data collection, principally telephone or face-to-face interviewing. Numerous combinations can be used: initial contact by telephone followed by postal despatch and return; postal despatch followed by personal collection and checking; postal despatch after which responses are collected by telephone interview; telephone contact followed by postal despatch and then telephone interview and so on. Additionally, the sample can be segmented and different methods used as appropriate to take advantage of the strengths and shortcomings of each approach.

Newer methods of sending the questionnaires and collecting the data are also in use; questionnaires may now be sent by fax and even returned by the same method, or they may be sent by post in diskette form, or transmitted over a telephone line. All of these will become more widespread in the future.

Postal surveys are perhaps less widely used in business research than in the past, because of the increasing cheapness and efficiency of telephone interviewing. However, because no interviewers are involved, postal surveys can be set up and administered by a very small number of staff; this is a continuing attraction, especially for in-house researchers.

Strengths of postal surveys

Postal and self-completion methods of data collection have a number of attractions when compared with the other methods available; they also have a number of marked weaknesses. As already indicated, one of the most attractive features of the postal method is that it is relatively easy and inexpensive to set up and administer. There are no interviewer or field administration costs, while the use of modern word processing and data processing means that the entire survey (from design through to analysis) can be handled by only one or two people, and the other costs (printing, stationery, postage) are relatively low. However, this can sometimes be merely a superficial attraction; the real cost of the survey should be expressed in terms of the effective response, ie the number of questionnaires returned at least partly completed. This, of course, can only be calculated at the close of the survey, but when it is, it may be found that the comparison with other methods of data collection, notably telephone interviewing, is not as favourable to postal methods as might have been thought at the outset (in terms both of the number of interviews achieved and of the quality of the information obtained).

There are a number of aspects of self-completion questionnaires which, in comparison with other methods, can improve the quality of the answers obtained from respondents. Respondents may be encouraged to make more thoughtful and considered responses than might be made under the time pressure of an interview, particularly a telephone one. Postal survey respondents may also take the trouble to consult other people, look up documents, or go and find out about details of equipment in use, which they may be less keen to do during an interview. For this reason, questionnaires involving the collection of detailed factual information may sometimes be sent in advance of an interview, or left or sent afterwards, for respondents to complete at their convenience.

With all self-completion surveys, no interviewers are involved in the data collection and hence there is no interviewer bias - ie no opportunity for differences in the way the questions are asked, the prompts and probes are administered, or the responses are interpreted and recorded. Likewise, the absence of an interviewer may encourage respondents to be more honest in their answers with no attendant embarrassment, loss of face, or any of the other pressures that can arise in person-to-person contact. It also means that there is very little opportunity for cheating in data collection which can, regrettably, occur with face-to-face and decentralised telephone interviewing. All these factors may improve response quality.

A further advantage of self-completion questionnaires, when administered by computer (CAPI) is that they can be customised to individual respondents; this, together with the inclusion of error-checking routines, can lead to greater accuracy in data collection, particularly with complex questionnaires.[11] Though shared with CATI, this advantage is, however, of little relevance to other types of self-completion study.

Another way in which postal surveys may enhance the fullness and frankness of respondents' replies is by their potential for anonymity which can, if desired, be made very evident by omitting any reference to respondents' names and addresses and by having no identification numbers on questionnaires. This can be very reassuring to respond-

The Collection of Primary Data

ents, although it may present administrative difficulties with regard to the assessment of non-response and the administration of reminders and incentives.

A last way in which postal questionnaires can improve the quality of response is when clear and comprehensive visual aids are enclosed. Whitley[12] advocates the postal method for concept and advertising testing, with the extensive use of visual aids that this involves. Because of the above-mentioned lessening in time pressure accompanying the completion of most postal questionnaires, respondents may be prepared to spend time studying quite complex (albeit clear) visual aids, with a consequently improved quality of response.

Under certain circumstances speed of response can be an advantage of self-completion. People read questions more quickly than they can be spoken and so can respond more rapidly to written questions than to those administered by an interviewer, especially if the act of responding is a short one in terms of time. In addition, the words of the question remain in front of them and act as a prompt while they give their answer. This is a recognised advantage when using self-completion questions as part of a face-to-face interview, although it has little relevance in a postal context.

A final advantage of postal surveys (although not necessarily of other types of survey involving self-completion methods) is that the sample can be unclustered. The postal approach means that geographical dispersion is easy to achieve at no extra cost, which is not the case for face-to-face or even telephone interviewing. It follows that out-of-town areas as well as urban ones can be sampled with equal ease. It also means that the postal as well as the telephone approach can be used as a method of collecting data from far-flung businesses. On an international scale, therefore, the relatively low costs may make it particularly attractive.

Conversely, postal surveys, as with telephone interviews, can also be used for samples that are heavily concentrated in one or more geographical areas, where it would be difficult to deploy sufficient face-to-face interviewers.

Postal survey shortcomings

The problem of non-response is always cited as the most serious limitation of postal surveys, and indeed of most other types of self-completion survey. In the future the problem may be even more widespread. The problem is a serious one because the people in the sample who did not respond to the survey may be significantly different in regard to the survey topic from those who did respond. Thus, the survey results, based as they are on the respondents alone, could at best be a slightly biased and at worst a grossly distorted view of the whole sample.

Methods of data collection which involve personal contact usually yield some clues about the reasons for non-response. 'Purchasing done by Head Office', 'too busy', 'not allowed to participate in surveys', 'on holiday', 'company closed down' and so on, are usually reported back by interviewers and can be taken into account in assessing bias brought about by non-response, but with postal surveys there is rarely any feedback at all and so there are few clues to the non-respondents.

The results of a postal survey should be measured in terms of both the overall response or return rate, and the effective response rate. The overall response rate is the proportion of the total number distributed from which any feedback is received; it therefore includes items returned by the Post Office undelivered, blank or refused returns and any response in the form of letters and telephone calls, as well as completed questionnaires. The effective response rate is the proportion of the total distributed that is returned at least partly completed. Sometimes the usable response rate is also distinguished; this is the proportion of the total number distributed that is usable for analysis purposes, and therefore excludes any returned questionnaires rejected as insufficiently complete or erroneous.

Each of these measures is a survey finding in its own right and should be treated as one. It can be subjected to examination, discussion and interpretion in the light of the other findings:

- If, for example, the gap between the overall response or return rate and the effective response is wide, what does this mean?
- What are the implications if the usable response is substantially short of the effective response?
- (the major question) Has non-response caused the survey findings to be skewed? (Have, for example, most of the small businesses replied and none of the large ones? Have most of the users replied

The Collection of Primary Data

and none of the non-users? Understanding this situation is crucial to understanding the survey findings.)

There are some occasions when non-response can be a positive finding, and others when it can be demonstrated that non-response has not substantially affected the survey findings. However, there are also occasions when the researcher is tempted to ignore the whole issue or sweep it under the carpet. This is not only irresponsible but can be downright misleading. The MRS/IMRA Code of Conduct requires that response rates should be stated.

A secondary problem associated with non-response is that, if the response is poor, the cost per completed questionnaire may turn out to be as high as, or higher than, the equivalent (but pre-selected and controlled) sample interviewed by telephone or face-to-face.

The non-response issue is the reason why so much of the literature on postal surveys is devoted to appraising methods of boosting response rates, and a summary of these methods can be found in the next section.

Another drawback to postal surveys is the time lag that occurs between the initial mailing and the receipt of sufficient questionnaires for analysis. This lag may be only a matter of weeks for a short, straightforward questionnaire, but can be months or even years for a more complex one. International mailing is, of course, a further delaying factor. Regular users of postal surveys are sometimes in a position to demonstrate that early returns may be sufficiently representative of the total response to be usable after a minimal time lag. Cooper[3] showed this in connection with audience research at BBC External Services. In other cases, however, the time lags involved may mean that the postal method has to be rejected at the outset of business research projects.

The sending of questionnaires by fax can be a partial solution to this problem, having, as it does, the characteristic of immediacy; it can, however, present additional difficulties, eg with legibility, and also with cost to respondents especially if the questionnaires are to be returned in the same way. Reverse-charge fax systems, which at the time of writing are just coming on to the market, may help here.

Lack of personal contact can also be a drawback of self-completion methods. While the absence of an interviewer may improve some aspects of response as discussed above, the inability to use prompts and probes means that the response has to be taken at face value. There is no opportunity to expand on incomplete answers or clarify unclear or ambiguous ones, except by using another method (eg telephone follow-up). Likewise, there is no opportunity to correct routeing or other errors that respondents may have made in self-administering the questionnaire (which therefore calls for the utmost clarity in questionnaire design).

Another consequence of lack of personal contact is the lack of involvement in the survey that respondents may feel. The self-completion approach is not one that recognises the significance of individual respondents, or encourages them to think that their responses are uniquely important rather than just one of many. This is especially relevant to business research, where survey populations are often quite small but the range of individual responses may be very great, and key respondents may feel that their views merit a full discussion at an interview rather than an apparently more constrained and superficial self-completion approach.

Another point to be borne in mind when designing self-completion questionnaires is that respondents can read through all the questions before answering any of them. This can be a drawback, since respondents' answers to earlier questions may be conditioned by their knowledge of the later ones. In particular, certain standard techniques, such as spontaneous and prompted awareness and recall, certain image assessments and any techniques which involve things being done in a particular sequence, cannot be undertaken by self-completion.

A final drawback with self-completion questionnaires is not knowing who completed them. Even if the survey is not anonymous, respondents may not identify themselves or their positions, so that often it is difficult to assess the reliability of their response.

Maximising response to postal surveys in the business context

There are a number of techniques that may be used to increase the postal survey response rate. These include optimum selection of the addressee and encouraging a response from those who were actually addressed.

The Collection of Primary Data

Mailing lists
One of the chief response limiting factors in business research postal surveys, and one that is frequently given insufficient attention, is the quality of the mailing lists used for sampling.

It is noticeable that among the most enthusiastic advocates of postal surveys are researchers in organisations where the maintenance of mailing lists is an important part of the business in its own right. This includes companies that sell goods by mail order, as well as banks, credit card companies, publishers of subscription magazines and so on. In such organisations the 'mailing list' is not just one of names and addresses – it is a database which may contain other personal details, details of all recent transactions and dealings (including responses to previous surveys) and more. Possession of this database enables such researchers not only to segment their market and target individual postal surveys more appropriately, but also to know a fair amount about the non-respondents. Comparison of the profiles of the non-respondents with those of the respondents can, in conjunction with the survey findings, shed sufficient light on the non-response element for the whole picture to be seen (and can lead, in time, to the ability to obtain valid results from a small 'hard core' of respondents).

Clearly, postal surveys are a very valuable business research tool under such circumstances. Furthermore, they may have the additional merit of replicating the selling method, as Whitley[12] has pointed out in connection with the *Reader's Digest*. This situation is comparable with another that is not uncommon: using one or more magazine mailing lists for a postal survey.

On the face of it this seems an attractive approach, especially if the magazines are key specialist ones whose readers are likely to include much of the population to be surveyed. Microprocessor designers, corrosion engineers, and other small, professional populations, particularly lend themselves to this approach, and it is often easier to obtain mailing lists from publishers than membership lists from the relevant professional bodies.

However, such mailing lists may have flaws. They may not be up-to-date, so that the person (if named) or the company to whom the publication is addressed is not there any more. There may be incorrect addresses, so that the publication does not reach the intended person, or even the company. There may be duplication of recipients or companies within the list. The addressee may be merely a job title such as 'The Purchasing Manager', which may not exist, or may exist severally, at the location. Or the recipient may be a librarian, information officer or other person who distributes the publication to others, or leaves it available for passing readers to peruse.

Some of these problems may be less widespread in mailing lists based on subscriptions than in those that are not (although central receipt and distribution by librarians remains a difficulty). But it is evident that, if unchecked, they can have a devastating effect on apparent response rates, simply because a proportion of the mailing never reaches the intended recipients.

A further problem with such mailing lists is that they may themselves be biased. Not only may they not cover the entire population to be surveyed, but the proportion of the population that is covered may not be representative of the whole. The latter problem is even more widespread in lists which have been compiled from reply-paid return cards in magazines or product documentation, or from some other initiative by respondents, such as sales enquiries or competition entries.

The quality of the mailing list is therefore of critical importance in postal survey work, and must be the subject of extremely close scrutiny at the very beginning of any proposed survey:

- To what extent do the proposed lists cover the population to be surveyed?
- How representative are they of this population?
- From what sources have the lists been compiled?
- If from handwritten sources, how accurately have the names and addresses been recorded?
- How complete are the addresses?
- Do they have postcodes?
- How much information is held about each addressee?
- Does the list include names, job titles or both?
- Is it possible to identify and exclude inappropriate addressees (librarians and the like)?

The Collection of Primary Data

- Is the list updated?
- If so, how and how often is this done?
- Are the addressees listed in any particular order?
- If so, should this be taken into account in planning the sampling method to use?

These are the kinds of question that should be asked and answered, so that the researcher can make an accurate assessment of the shortcomings of the proposed lists, and plan accordingly.

If it becomes evident that a considerable amount of time and effort is required to produce mailing lists of acceptable quality, consideration should be given to the long-term cost-effectiveness of the operation. Is there any point, for example, in conducting an elaborate telephone screening exercise to identify target respondents precisely, and then leaving the list, after the survey, unused for several years? Mailing lists must be maintained constantly if they are to retain their usefulness, and one of the chief ways of doing this is to use them and incorporate the feedback. Postal surveys are at their most valuable when conducted regularly and where there is commitment to constant feedback and updating of the mailing list database. As indicated earlier, this is most likely to occur in organisations in which the maintenance of mailing lists forms an essential part of the business. In cases where this is not so, and where it seems unlikely that such a commitment will be made, the merits and drawbacks of postal surveys should be weighed carefully against those of other methods of data collection.

Other methods of maximising response
There are many other techniques that can help to enhance response rates to postal surveys; most have at some time been the subject of controlled experiments, mostly among consumers, to measure their effects on response rates. However, there is no magic formula and the appropriateness of each technique has to be considered for each survey. If time and budget permit, there is plenty of room for experiment.

Questionnaire length, content and clarity are among the most important factors affecting response rates. Respondents are much more likely to complete a short, interesting questionnaire than a long and boring or irrelevant one. Clarity and lack of ambiguity in layout, and in question wording, make the questionnaire less onerous to complete (and also maximise the quality of response, as discussed in the preceding section). Like all questionnaires, self-completion questionnaires should be carefully tested out at the design stage on a pilot sample, if necessary by conducting face-to-face discussions with those who completed them out of this sample, about areas of difficulty, ambiguity and so on.

An explanation of the reasons for conducting the research is also important in encouraging respondent participation. This is usually conveyed in a covering letter, together with information about for whom the research is being done. While it may not in all cases be desirable to disclose the identity of the client, respondents should be told as much as possible about by whom, and in what way, the information they supply will be used. (At this point it is worth noting that if the client's name is disclosed, the questionnaire and covering letter should be checked by other people in the client company who may be in contact with the target respondents, such as sales staff.)

In some cases, protecting respondents' individual identity can encourage response, especially when the survey is being conducted directly by a client rather than by means of a third party. However, this can make for difficulties in conducting other parts of the survey: issuing reminder letters, administering some types of incentive, and assessing non-response characteristics.

Making initial ('foot in the door') contact by telephone can boost response rates substantially, and in the business research context is particularly advisable when some screening of the mailing list is needed, such as when the list does not adequately identify the target respondents or when the questionnaire is relevant only to some of them. Personal placement of self-completion questionnaires can also be done.

Standard of presentation is a further factor affecting response rates – 'eye appeal' is important. An uncluttered and attractively laid-out letter and questionnaire, on good quality paper and with judicious use of coloured paper or print, all have a part to play. Personalised, individually 'typed' letters are easily produced on modern word-processing equipment. Whether the outer envelope is stamped or

The Collection of Primary Data

franked probably has little relevance in the business context, not least because respondents may not open their own mail. The inclusion of a correctly sized business reply-paid envelope is usually good practice for UK surveys; internationally it is difficult to offer a professional reply-paid service, although the Royal Mail's new International Business Reply service may improve this situation.

The subject of incentives is a controversial one. In the business context, monetary or any other incentives of more than nominal value are generally regarded as unethical, and many companies do not allow their employees to accept them. The choice usually lies between a 'blanket' incentive enclosed with every mailing, and a 'response' incentive awarded only on receipt of a completed questionnaire. The 'blanket' incentive is usually a token gift (although US researchers favour dollar bills); 'response' incentives can include postable gifts, various lottery-type prizes, a summary of the findings of the survey or donations to charities of the respondent's choice. The charity donation is attractive in several ways, but it is administratively important to restrict the choice in the number of charities and to obtain their permission first.

Reminder mailings and follow-up telephone calls or visits can also boost the initial response, sometimes substantially. Plotting the response each day shows when it begins to fall off, and therefore when the optimum time for reminders has arrived. It is usual for the reminder mailing to include another copy of the questionnaire in case the first has been mislaid, and a covering letter pressing for its completion. Telephone reminders can be used for key non-respondents (and sometimes the questionnaire can be completed over the telephone, or sent by fax). This is a more costly approach, but essential if the sample contains some units that are known to be important such as very large users or opinion leaders.

How to deal with non-response

As with other types of survey, it is incumbent upon the researcher to make some assessment of the extent of bias that may be due to the lack of response. This can be particularly difficult with postal surveys, for the reasons discussed earlier. Telephone follow-up of a sample of non-respondents (if identifiable) can be used to investigate the reasons for their non-response and the extent to which they differ from the respondents. Comparison of the data from the initial response with that generated by reminders (mailed or telephone) can also help to distinguish the characteristics of the non-respondents. The inclusion of relevant classification data in the questionnaire enables the profile of the respondent sample to be compared with data from other surveys or published sources, and weighted accordingly. In the longer term, the compilation of survey findings into databases and the use of data fusion techniques may offer a solution.

Guidelines for use of postal surveys

Postal and self-completion questionnaires are particularly appropriate for research designs that involve the following:

- sampling from a database or other source which contains sufficient information to assess non-response characteristics;
- sampling 'captive' audiences such as conference visitors, air travellers and employees;
- subjects that have a high level of interest, are sensitive, or require information to be sought by the respondent before replying;
- subjects that can be narrowly and clearly defined, and which do not require much open-ended questioning;
- geographically dispersed samples, including international ones.

They are less appropriate for designs that involve:

- investigating subjects in depth;
- questions that have to be administered in a particular order;
- completion in a short timescale (usually);
- interviewing very senior respondents.

Observational techniques

In contrast to the three previous methods, data collection by observation requires no direct participation by respondents. Instead, data are collected by observation of people, objects or records, by manual or mechanical means. It is usually visual information that is collected but sound, particularly voice, can also be important.

Current usage

Some major continuous consumer surveys are based on observational techniques, but the method is much less used in the business context. Perhaps this is because the business environment is felt to be too diverse and complex compared with the domestic one, or because there are few business activities that lend themselves to an observational approach. There are certainly too few companies with a desire for continuous observational data to make viable in a business context the large-scale data collecting operations that flourish in consumer markets.

Nevertheless, there are opportunities to use observational techniques in business research although, as Hague[4] has pointed out, they are so little used in their own right that each usage occasion is often unique. They can be used on their own but are probably more frequently used in conjunction with other methods, particularly face-to-face interviews and self-completion questionnaires. In such cases they may not even be recognised as observational. The recording of respondents' sex in telephone interviews, the checking of makes and models of equipment by going to inspect them, and the noting of the way respondents react to questions are all done by observation, but are usually taken to be part of the main data collection method.

In their own right, observational techniques are used mainly for the collection of numerical information (how many of a particular occasion or thing) and behavioural information (how people behave in particular circumstances). In the latter case, the provisions of the MRS/IMRA Code of Conduct must be followed.

Strengths and shortcomings of observational techniques

The main advantage of the observation method is that it can be used for the systematic recording of large quantities of information that it would be impossible to collect by any other method. This is the principle behind audit-based surveys. As well as price and stock checks, the observation method can be used for inventories of equipment installed, counts of invoices or other records, enumeration of establishments, traffic counts and so on. This can give very precise information, provided, of course, that the recording is accurate and that the underlying sampling approach has been carefully followed.

Another advantage of observation is that it can be used to record what really happens, as opposed to what respondents may think or say happens. Information can be collected about how pieces of equipment are actually used in practice, or about how people work or deal with customers. Much has been learned about how to improve photocopier design by observing how people actually use photocopiers, and Hague[4] cites an example of how observation identified the types of information that transport and distribution managers take for granted in their work. Observational studies of this type require a highly systematic approach.

A third advantage of observation is that because no interviews are involved it can be an inexpensive way of obtaining large amounts of information. Much depends, however, on the availability of the information, the number of observers needed and the length of time involved.

Observation alone has limitations as a data collection technique because it does not explain the reasons behind the observations: why certain records are absent, why a particular machine is used as it is, or why people behave in a certain way. Other methods of data collection, used in conjunction with observation, are needed to complete the picture.

One of the drawbacks that can occur in using this technique is bias created by a lack of objectivity in making observations. Different people notice different things, and filter out what they regard as unnecessary information. It follows that observers have to be trained to be objective, and that a very systematic approach to recording observations has to be adopted, to ensure that bias does not occur. Photographs can also be used to record information.

Bias can also arise because being observed can make people behave atypically, and it is therefore better if the observation can be conducted as inconspicuously as possible. However, the people under observation must be made aware of what is happening, unless they are in a situation where they can reasonably expect to be observed, such as in

The Collection of Primary Data

shops or at exhibitions.

A final drawback to using observational techniques is that it can be difficult to obtain access to the data sources, particularly if they are people or records. Much time and effort may have to be invested in obtaining permission and cooperation from everyone concerned – more than might be necessary for interviews alone.

Guidelines for the use of observational techniques

There are plenty of opportunities for the creative use of observation in business research and the following are merely initial suggestions, based mostly on personal and colleagues' experience:

- enumeration of many things: vehicles or people at particular points, stock inventories, counts of equipment installed, numbers of establishments in a given area (the latter being essential for systematic sampling of businesses in countries where there are no data on the business population);
- price and merchandising checks from displays or price lists (although trade discounting needs to be borne in mind);
- 'dustbin' checks of discarded packaging or used products which, over time, can provide estimates of usage volumes;
- inspecting test products after trials;
- observation of people at work to show how equipment is used, how information flows, how decisions are made, and so on;
- visits to exhibitions for market overviews.

Special techniques

In this section the value and the pitfalls of four special data collecting techniques are reviewed. The four techniques are: panels; group discussions (focus groups); hall tests, clinics and other central location methods; omnibus surveys.

Panels

A panel is a sample which is surveyed more than once in the same context. The information collected may either cover the same topics each time, so as to provide a continuous measurement or tracking, or cover different topics on different occasions. In this latter case, the panel provides a pre-recruited sample of known specification, of which multiple enquiries can be made. Aucamp[1] has advocated this type of panel as one way to reduce respondent over-interviewing and non-response, which in some business sectors is a cause for serious concern.

All the methods of data collection reviewed in the preceding sections can be used, singly or in combination, to survey panels. Thus there can be panels where data collection is by face-to-face interview; telephone panels, mail panels and panels based on observational techniques; panels where face-to-face and telephone interviewing, or telephone and mail are alternated, where self-completion diaries are kept, or where observational methods are combined with face-to-face interviews. Panel samples can be large or small, the timescale can be long-term or short-term, and the research can be quantitative or qualitative in nature. The respondents in a series of reconvened group discussions constitute a panel, as do those who keep a self-completion diary for a time or who participate in regular interviews or audits. In Britain many of the major continuous surveys of consumer products and services are based on panel methodology, including the Nielsen Retail Index and national television audience measurement for the Broadcasters' Audience Research Board (BARB).

The most frequent reason for starting a panel is to obtain trend data: a series of measurements taken at intervals over a period of time. From this information, change can be both observed and predicted. Panel data provide more information than the equivalent measurements taken from matched samples, because change at the level of the individual respondent or business unit, as well as at the total sample level, can be monitored. Thus, for example, individual brand switches or changes of procedure can be recorded on a case-by-case basis. This is valuable information in its own right, as well as in helping to explain the total change observed.

Panel data are also more accurate than the information deriving from matched samples, in so far as the sampling error associated with taking the subsequent samples is removed. This gives panels an additional attraction for business research, simply because it is often very difficult to achieve sample matching, sometimes because the relevant universe is so small that matched samples of adequate size cannot be created. There are, for example, limited numbers of production directors of aircraft manufacturing companies, or of specialist buyers in grocery multiples, and attempting to survey them at intervals becomes a panel almost by default. Another and greater problem with matching samples in business research arises because of the enormous variation that can occur between superficially similar businesses. This means that valid matches are very difficult to make, even if the relevant key variables can be defined (itself no easy task). A panel offers at least a partial solution to these problems.

Panels can also offer improved efficiency and quality of data collection. This is partly because, after initial agreement to participate, there is little need for further explanation and reassurance of respondents at subsequent contacts – a mutual trust and confidence develops and one can proceed directly to the task in hand. It is also because, when the same topics are covered or the same methodology is used at each contact, respondents quickly learn what is required of them; they become 'experts'. Indeed, some researchers, such as Schlackman[8], have argued that short-term panels involving a series of group discussions with expert respondents are much more efficient than conventional group discussions in getting through individuals' defensive and protective barriers to the real feelings beneath.

The chief drawbacks of panels are the two problem areas most often mentioned when any potential panel is under discussion. These are conditioning and wearout (the latter being sometimes rather morbidly referred to as mortality). Conditioning is the change in panel respondents' behaviour and attitudes brought about by virtue of their being part of the panel: by becoming experts they may also become atypical. This is generally less of a problem in business research than it is in the consumer context, since it is unlikely that a business will change its pattern of routine purchasing, for instance, simply because it is participating in a panel that is monitoring such purchases. However, changes in individuals' behaviour, attitudes and perceptions probably occur as much in the business as in the consumer context, so there is always the possibility of bias when using a panel to measure variables of this kind. Thus, for example, being on a panel may cause a respondent to give greater consideration to alternative products or suppliers, to read about topics he has been questioned on, or to be more alert to advertising. The conventional approach to limiting the effects of this bias is to operate the panel for a short time only, or to have a 'rolling' panel whereby each panel member participates for a short time and is then replaced by a matching new one. The frequency of data collection is also a factor in the extent to which conditioning occurs.

A fair degree of 'roll' may also be needed in a panel because of wearout, which is the loss of panel members due to non-cooperation. These losses should be replaced with matching new members although, as discussed above, achieving matched samples in business research can present great difficulties. A better solution may be to plan for losses at the beginning and recruit a larger sample than necessary, so that the final sample will be the required size and structure. This approach, however, still leaves the problem of non-response bias which is discussed in connection with self-completion surveys; ie how representative of the total sample is the part that responds? This difficulty with sample matching is probably one of the main reasons why panel techniques are relatively little used in business research, in contrast to the situation in consumer, medical and agricultural research where established panels exist.

Group discussions (focus groups)

The group discussion, or focus group, is a technique whereby a small group of respondents, guided by a leader (known as a moderator), discuss a subject in some depth. The technique is one of the two normally used in qualitative research, the other being the individual depth interview. There are no hard-and-fast rules about the number of respondents per group, although eight is often regarded as the optimum, 11 or 12 as the absolute maximum, and between three and five as a 'mini-group'. Audio and sometimes video recordings of the discussion are made, and subsequently analysed. The limited number of respondents, their relative unrepresentativeness, and the discursive way in which the topic is explored all mean that group discussion

The Collection of Primary Data

findings are essentially qualitative in nature, and that it is foolish to attempt to draw any quantitative conclusions from them. Needless to say, there are those who will attempt to do this.

Group discussions are almost always conducted face-to-face, although there have been some attempts to conduct them by telephone, using teleconferencing facilities. In the future videoconferencing equipment may be sufficiently widely available to be used in this way. At present, however, there are many occasions in business research when it is logistically impossible to bring together in one central location all the target respondents, from widely scattered workplaces, and so individual depth interviews have to be employed instead.

The key characteristic of the group discussion, and the one that distinguishes it from the individual depth interview, is that respondents interact with each other as well as with the group moderator. This effect, termed group dynamics, means that a much wider range of stimuli are brought into play than in an individual interview, which in turn augments the range and scope of the information collected.

The combined effects of group dynamics, the skills of the moderator, and the various projective and enabling techiques that can and should be used to help overcome respondents' limited powers of self-expression, can together get past superficial reactions and through to underlying perceptions, attitudes and motivations. Uncovering these is the chief purpose of a group discussion. The technique is therefore particularly suited to investigating subjects in depth. It can be used for obtaining a full understanding of a particular topic before embarking on a quantitative survey, to understand the considerations and problems involved in the choice and the use of particular products or services, to explore reactions to new product concepts, to uncover responses to advertisements at various stages of development, and to build up pictures of respondents' deep-seated and often emotional reactions to particular companies and the products and services that they market. It is also very valuable for generating new ideas and creative thinking – respondents in a group can be stimulated into mental leaps which are difficult if not impossible to achieve at an individual interview level.

Most qualitative researchers feel that group dynamics make a major contribution to the group discussion technique, and that to treat a group discussion just as an occasion to conduct depth interviews on a number of respondents simultaneously is to miss major opportunities. Nevertheless, group discussions in business research sometimes end up in this way, for reasons that are suggested below.

In business research it is often the case that the issues under discussion can only be explained by reference to the current situation: what procedures are used, what equipment is installed, what tasks are done by whom, what alternatives were considered, and so on. However, since businesses vary so much in their operations and procedures, most of the group discussion time can be taken up by monologues from the respondents, each describing in some detail the way things are done at his company. This issue is one of the reasons why group discussions in business research sometimes end up being conducted like multiple-depth interviews. The chance of this occurring is something that the business researcher should consider carefully when evaluating the information being sought. If much of it is detailed but basically factual, collecting it by group discussion alone is probably inefficient. Better alternatives may be to switch to individual depth interviews completely, or to collect the factual information beforehand, either at separate earlier interviews or via self-completion questionnaires which respondents complete before the discussion starts. This is also a way of collecting sensitive information which respondents may not wish to discuss in front of others, such as company future plans and competitive knowledge.

Another reason why business research group discussions sometimes end up as multiple-depth interviews is because the discussion programme (or guide) has been overloaded. Such is the time, effort and money required to convene groups of business respondents, especially senior ones, that it is tempting to 'pump' them on every possible aspect of the topic(s) under discussion. It is important to avoid this if there is to be full discussion of the key issues, and consequently the discussion guide should be a list of topics for exploration rather than a long list of questions that must be answered.

Successful group discussions with business respondents can be quite difficult to achieve, and in some respects group discussions have much in common with the other types of central location interviewing reviewed in the next section. The recruitment can be particularly demanding; ensuring that sufficient members of the required target

The Collection of Primary Data

group actually turn up at the appropriate time and place is no easy task, and usually requires substantial over-recruiting and the use of incentives. It is important, too, that the group be balanced, with the respondents all being of similar rank or status, and being either all involved in the subject under discussion to a similar extent, or with a broad mix of experience. The location for the sessions must also be carefully selected; purpose-built discussion studios are still rare in the UK (although common in the US), and hotels and other public premises are often used. There is one school of thought, however, which suggests that for some types of investigation a relaxed domestic environment may release respondents from conventional business thinking more easily than a business-style meeting place.

Another vital factor in achieving success with a business group discussion lies in the skill and experience of the group moderator. Business respondents are generally accustomed to being in meetings and so do not often need much persuading to participate in the discussion. They can usually express themselves – in business terms – with reasonable competence. However, since business respondents usually disclose both their job titles and the name of the company for which they work (even if given the opportunity not to), all kinds of status and peer group pressures come into play right at the start of the session. It is sometimes difficult to prevent one respondent taking over the management of the meeting or to prevent the others from feeling inferior to someone who appears to have superior status or superior knowledge, or experience of the subject under discussion. Issues like these, although they occur in consumer groups, are probably more common in business ones; it takes a skilled moderator to manage the discussion well (and to interpret the findings afterwards).

Group discussions are often observed, or viewed, by other researchers and sometimes by clients. This can be done actually in the group discussion room (on view or screened off) or remotely via video link or one-way mirror. The MRS/IMRA Code of Conduct states that respondents must be informed of, and give their consent to, such viewing before the start of the discussion, and must also be informed of the true identity of the viewers although in practice clients are often introduced as 'colleagues'. In business research especially, viewing often occurs because there is a wish to allow as many people as possible to benefit from the rare opportunity of seeing and hearing information coming directly from respondents whose convening has cost much time and money. However, Robson and Wardle[7] have demonstrated that a number of adverse effects can arise from such viewing. One such effect that can be of significance is the withholding of extremely negative views, especially about a client's product or service, if the client is thought or known to be observing. These and other effects should be taken into account when considering whether to view, or whether not to view but to listen later to a tape recording of the discussion.

Another issue with regard to viewing, and one which is confined to business research, is the contravention of the fundamentally important respondent confidentiality clauses of the MRS/IMRA Code of Conduct. As indicated above, respondents usually disclose their job titles and the names of their employers at the beginning of the session, even if told they need not. This is probably because of wanting to know to whom they are speaking, as well as to establish status within the group. However, a major difficulty arises if clients are viewing, since they are then aware of who the respondents are. This can provide very useful information, and there is little that can be done to prevent this being further disseminated within the client company. As yet the Code of Conduct provides no guidance on how to deal with this situation.

Hall tests, clinics and other central location methods

Hall tests, clinics and central location interviewing are various names used to describe the technique whereby all the respondents are invited to come to a particular place to be interviewed, rather than being interviewed at their workplaces, homes or elsewhere. The place selected for conducting the interviews must necessarily be centrally positioned so that the respondents can get to it easily, and in the early days of UK consumer research church halls were often used – hence the name 'hall test'. The technique is frequently used to diagnose what is wrong with a new product or design, and this presumably is how the name 'clinic' came into use. Group discussions, described in the preceding section, are a specialised form of central location interviewing.

Nowadays a wide range of types of central location can be used

The Collection of Primary Data

although, in business research, hotels and purpose-built studios or laboratories are often the most suitable. Likewise, a wide range of data collection techniques can be employed. Face-to-face interviewing is almost always involved, but can be supplemented by self-completion questioning and by observation. Telephone interviewing is nearly always involved too, since in business research respondents are often, although not always, pre-recruited (ie contacted beforehand and invited to attend for interview at specified times). This is most often done by telephone.

Apart from group discussions, the main reason for conducting interviews at a central location is when respondents' physical presence is necessary to see, hear, examine or try out something. In the business context this can be one or more pieces of working equipment or machinery, prototypes, models or mock-ups of such equipment, or a series of concepts or advertisements in graphic form or on video. In each case it is easier to bring the respondents to the object than to take it to them. This may be because there is a shortage of supply (there is only one mock-up, working prototype or set of concept boards), because the object in question is not easily transportable (such as a car, commercial vehicle, or piece of office equipment), because it needs to be installed or viewed in special surroundings or with special equipment that is not widely available (such as professional format video equipment), or because it has to be demonstrated by specially trained personnel who are scarce or available for only a limited period (such as complex machinery or computers).

Another reason for conducting interviews at a central location is when the interviews are to be administered by computer (CAPI). A few years ago, when computers were less portable and robust then they are now, it was sometimes easier to bring the respondents to the computers than to take the computers to the respondents. However, the advent of truly portable, lap-top computers has enabled this kind of interviewing to be conducted at respondents' premises, thus obviating the need for a central location approach.

As indicated above, the main advantage of a central location technique is that it brings respondents into direct contact with the object(s) under study. Thus it is, to some extent, an experimental simulation of the actual marketing process, be it advertising or promotion, sales demonstration, price comparison, or usage while on trial. This is the reason why the technique is often used for various types of simulated test marketing. Competitive products or advertisements can also be tested alongside the experimental one(s). Respondents are then asked to assess the test object(s) and, if appropriate, to compare them with competitive ones or with what they currently use.

The results of this kind of experiment can give very valuable early warning of the strengths and the faults in any new product, design or advertising campaign, with consequently major potential impact on the new product itself and the pricing, promotional and marketing strategies that accompany it. There are some manufacturers who never launch a new product without first thoroughly testing its market acceptability, while there are others who never research market acceptability before a launch. In circumstances where the launch costs are relatively high, this is unwise; the cost of conducting some experimental central location interviewing ought in such circumstances to be regarded as an insurance policy against the more substantial losses of a failed launch.

The main problems associated with central location interviewing in business research are logistical. Much careful advance planning is required to ensure that everything is properly organised and functions correctly when respondents arrived. Hague's organisational chart[4] for an industrial clinic shows the amount of advance preparation needed. The recruitment aspect can also be very demanding; it is necessary to ensure that sufficient respondents actually turn up, and at the appointed intervals rather than all at once. Over-recruiting is always necessary, sometimes to a considerable extent, and incentives are frequently used. These are usually given in a form other than monetary since many companies do not allow their employees to accept such gifts, although for the legal, medical and other professions cash payments are made.

Needless to say, it is essential that it be made clear to respondents that they are participating in a market research study rather than a sales pitch. The distinction can sometimes be rather hard to maintain, particularly in situations where a piece of equipment has to be demonstrated by a member of the client's own technical or sales staff rather than by an independent researcher. In such cases the researcher must monitor the demonstrations closely, and take a firm line if they become too sales-orientated. It is difficult to control this, however, particularly when interested respondents start asking questions and an informal dialogue begins.

Omnibus surveys

Omnibus surveys are surveys on which clients can buy questionnaire space and where a variety of different subjects are therefore covered on the same questionnaire. The survey costs are shared among the clients in proportion to the amount of questioning each takes up, and each receives the results from his own questions only, plus classification questions that are common to all. Omnibus surveys are conducted at regular intervals and, in the UK, most of them are advertised each month in the *MRS Newsletter*.

There is a very wide range of consumer omnibus services, but at the time of writing there are only three business omnibus services operating in the UK. These are the two Business Line surveys of small (less than 50 employee) establishments and of larger ones, and the Key Directors omnibus of large companies. In each of these the data collection is by telephone interview.

Omnibus surveys usually offer a considerably faster turnaround than tailor-made surveys, because most of the survey design and management is already pre-set. This can be a great advantage. However, the individual questionnaires usually have to be short, since above a certain length it is generally more cost-effective to conduct a tailor-made survey. They also usually have to be straightforward, with no complicated questions, routeing or stimuli, since there is usually little opportunity for individual interviewer briefing in depth, and unusual requirements can slow down the routine management of these surveys. Both of these factors can be drawbacks to this technique.

Both consumer and business omnibuses can be useful tools for the business researcher. Since a fair proportion of all-adult omnibus respondents are in employment, they therefore form a sample of the working population from which information about this aspect of their lives can be sought. This can be used as an approach to market sizing for products and equipment which are fairly widely used: the stationery and writing equipment, the towels, soap and hand cleansers and the protective clothing that are issued at work, and also for commercial and industrial catering products. Care needs to be taken, however, because people at home often find it difficult to remember what they use at work, and are highly unreliable if more detailed information, such as make or type, is required. This therefore makes segmenting the market a difficult task.

It can also be difficult to convert the resultant information on numbers of people using, to data about numbers of items used or establishments using, which are usually more relevant measures of size in industrial and business markets. The sample itself over-represents large employers since they employ more people, and under-represents the small ones; thus, converting to a measure of establishments using can be problematic. A further difficulty arises with equipment that is shared among several users, such as various types of office equipment. This and other potential problems are well described in a paper by Smith,[9] which is essential reading for anyone contemplating market sizing by this approach.

Consumer omnibus surveys can be used to research both the working population in general, and particular types of workers such as supervisory and managerial staff. Various kinds of usage, attitude and image research can be conducted in this way, and sometimes an in-home rather than an at-work interview can be an advantage, especially for junior staff who may fear being overheard at work. It is often the case, however, that the research requires a more specific sample than can easily be both identified and interviewed by this means. In such circumstances the omnibus can be used to identify these samples, which are often small minorities, for subsequent re-contacting and interview later on. This approach can, for instance, be used for business travellers, lease or hire car drivers and such like; it may require several waves of omnibus surveys to achieve a sufficiently large sample. This approach also means that representative samples can be accumulated at intervals, which can be important if there is a need to track (ie monitor certain measures over time).

In business omnibus surveys the survey unit is the establishment or company and the respondents are interviewed at their place of work. These omnibuses can therefore be used for usage and attitude studies, image studies and particularly for tracking over time such things as advertising awareness and recall, usage and purchasing trends. They can also be used for compiling minority samples for subsequent interview in the same way as can their consumer counterparts.

However, unlike the consumer services, none of the business omnibus services currently available is representative of the UK business population as a whole; each covers only a segment of it. Therefore, by definition, they can only be used for research where it is appropriate that these sectors should be covered. This partial coverage also means that they cannot be used for total market sizing or market penetration studies. It is therefore most important that the coverage of each service is clearly understood, both when considering using it and when interpreting the results. The development of business omnibus services in the UK was reviewed in 1988 by Nathan.[5]

References

1. J. Aucamp, *Whither Business-to-Business Research*, 40th ESOMAR Marketing Research Congress, Montreux, 1987.
2. *Comparing Telephone and Face-to-Face Interviews*, Proceedings of a Market Research Development Fund Seminar, London. 1985.
3. A. J. Cooper, *Use of Postal Questionnaire Measures in International Research: Some Tentative Conclusions*, EMAC/ESOMAR Symposium on Methodological Advances in Marketing Research Theory and Practice, Copenhagen, 1984.
4. P. N. Hague, *The Industrial Market Research Handbook*, second edition, Kogan Page, 1987.
5. L. Nathan, *The Emergence of Business Omnibus Services*, ESOMAR Seminar on Business to Business Research, Brussels, 1988.
6. S. J. Orton and J. A. Samuels, *What We have Learned from Researching AIDS*, 40th ESOMAR Marketing Research Congress, Montreux, 1987.
7. S. Robson and J. Wardle, 'Who's watching whom? A study of the effects of observers on group discussions', *Journal of the Market Research Society*, Volume 30, No 3, 1988.
8. W. Schlackman, 'A discussion of the use of sensitivity panels in market research', *Journal of the Market Research Society*, Volume 26, No 3, 1984.
9. E. Smith, *A Novel Solution to a Business Research Challenge*, Proceedings

of the 31st Annual Conference of the Market Research Society, Brighton, 1988.
10. N. Sparrow, 'Telephone or face-to-face polls – which are better?' *Market Research Society Newsletter,* March 1988.
11. L. Van Doorn and T. Hess, *New Research Possibilities by Computerized Personal Interviewing,* 41st ESOMAR Marketing Research Congress, Lisbon, 1988.
12. E. W. Whitley, 'The case for postal research', *Journal of the Market Research Society,* Volume 27, No 1, 1985.

7

Sample Design, Selection and Estimating

Phyllis Macfarlane

Normally it is not possible to contact all those companies or individuals whose information or opinions are relevant to a particular research study, and some kind of sample must be selected from the total. The sample should be as representative of the whole as possible, and its selection is an important skill. This skill is the subject of this Chapter, together with the conversion of the sample data to the size of a total market.

Sample design for business markets

A *universe* is the statistical term used to cover all the units which make up the market to be covered by a market research study. (The term 'population' is also used in a similar context and, to all intents and purposes, the two terms are the same.)

Business universes range from the very small, to markets larger than major consumer markets. For example, the number of companies who might buy helicopters, or computers costing over a million pounds, can probably be counted in terms of hundreds if not tens, whereas the market for office equipment comprises over a million and a half business establishments, and the market for business telephone calls consists of almost the whole working population.

This Chapter is about sample selection for business markets which comprise at least a thousand potential units (users or buyers), for which statistical methods of selection and analysis are applicable. It is not concerned with sampling very small specialised markets, since this is obviously a matter for straightforward common sense. Such small markets are frequently surveyed as a whole, and 'sampling' in these cases has no relevance.

Sample design has just one aim: to select a small group of units from among a much larger group in order to be as representative as possible of that larger group, so that by testing the small group (or *sample*) for whatever reason, the results can be applied to a larger group by relatively simple multiplicative techniques. The reason for testing the sample is decided by the problem in the survey being undertaken – to determine opinions, or to evaluate a continuous variable (ie how many has each unit obtained, or used, or made of some object or service), or an attribute (ie does each unit have or not have, do or not do something).

The essence of good sample design is that the researcher should understand both the problem and the intended universe well enough to be able to design the sample in terms of its various characteristics as outlined in this Chapter. If that understanding is not there, no amount of comment on good sample design will achieve one.

Sampling characteristics of business markets

The approach necessary to achieve a representative sample of a business market is determined by the characteristics of such markets. These include:

- the wide variability among business markets (for example, the relative spending powers of companies of different sizes vary enormously);

- the usual lack of published data on a particular business market, on which to base sample design or to use for grossing up (so that a preliminary estimate may have to be made before the sample can be properly designed);

Sample Design, Selection and Estimating

- the difficulty of quota design, because a typical unit is not readily identifiable (for example, a unit may be defined as a company with 5 to 9 employees, in the business services sector – leaving very uncertain the definition of 'business services', and allowing an introduction of an unwanted bias).

Because of all these factors there is a great need for adherence to strict sampling procedures. In business research the risk of unrepresentative samples is high.

As the sampling exercise is going to involve statistical analysis, it is important to realise that such analysis has an inherent error, measured by statistical deviations and confidence limits. However, it is a characteristic of business marketing research that another error – bias, or systematic error – features strongly in many surveys and quite often at a scale to overwhelm any statistical analysis error. Care must be exercised always to minimise the chance of such error, and frequent reference to bias and its causes will feature in this Chapter. (Unlike statistical error, systematic error does not decrease as the sample size is increased.)

The final precision of any research survey involving sampling will be a combination of statistical and systematic error, and the required degree of precision should be established by discussion with the client before any detailed sample design is begun.

Defining the business universe to be covered

The business universe to be covered by a research study is the totality of the units which are identified as being of interest to the study. Since, eventually, this universe has to be defined in terms of the individuals to be interviewed, the definition of the respondent is frequently a good starting point for universe identification.

The survey designer should thus ask the following questions at the start:

- Who is to be interviewed? This should be defined carefully in terms of job titles and levels of responsibility; if the definition includes professional qualifications it may automatically lead to a suitable sample frame, such as architects or consultant physicians, but more usually the definition leads to the next stage:

- Where are these individuals likely to be found? This should lead to a definition of likely companies or establishments.
- What level of information is required from these individuals? In the simplest case, only the individual's opinion or usage is required, but more frequently he is asked to give data about his company, establishment or department; it should be very clear to interviewer and interviewee what level of data is required, otherwise fundamental errors can be made in data collection and sometimes it may be necessary to speak to several respondents to collect all the information required about the unit to be covered.

It is very important to define all these issues precisely and it is generally helpful to make lists of inclusions and exclusions. Some typical examples are listed in Table 7.1, together with some pertinent questions of definition in each case.

Identifying a suitable sample frame

A *sample frame* is a list of all the units in the defined universe. Such lists can be derived from a number of sources, such as:

- telephone directories,
- business directories,
- specialist direct mail lists,
- public sector listings,
- association membership lists,
- client lists.

Telephone directories, including *Yellow Pages*, and business or classified directories can be very useful. The main problems are that:

1. the classifications (business activity) do not equate to SIC codes;
2. they may be incomplete (in some countries entries have to be paid for);
3. there may well be duplication among classifications within the same directory, and between regional directories (the unduplicated master files should be used wherever possible).

Sample Design, Selection and Estimating

Table 7.1. *Examples of universe definitions*

Initial Definition	Relevant Queries
1. All architects	– Professionally qualified only? – Only *practising* architects? – Are architects in the public sector included? – Are architects employed by (non-architectural) organisations included? – Are data required about the architect himself or the practice/local authority/company?
2. All firms with 50 or more employees	– Companies or establishments? – Is the public sector included? – Are only full-time employees included?
3. All companies acquiring a microcomputer in the last six months	– Is it the decision maker or the user who is required? – How is 'microcomputer' defined? – Establishment or company? – What if decision taken at another site, eg headquarters?
4. All businesses	– Companies or establishments? – Public sector included? – With one or more full-time employees? – VAT registered? – With a business telephone line?

There is rarely any information available other than the classification, so only very simple sample designs can be employed.

Business directories available in the UK include Kompass, and Dun & Bradstreet's *Marketing File* or *Key British Enterprises*. These tend to be company and head office biased, rather than giving complete lists of establishments, and only larger companies tend to be represented.

There are frequently biases towards manufacturing rather than service companies in such directories. They should not be used if strict random sample designs are required, but they are useful to boost coverage of larger units.

Specialist direct mail lists are becoming more common and are improving in quality. The researcher should be very careful to evaluate them thoroughly before use. Potential problems are duplication and the inclusion of unsuitable companies.

For the public sector, listings such as the *Municipal Year Book*, the *Hospitals and Health Services Year Book*, and the *Education Year Book* are all invaluable sources.

Association and institution membership lists are, in reality, a form of specialist directory but are mentioned separately because of their unique problems. Professional bodies' lists are the most accurate, provided that all the eligible universe is obliged to have a professional qualification. All other such lists are likely to contain significant unmeasurable biases. Samples from such lists should be treated as representative of association members only – they cannot be assumed to be representative of a whole industry.

Client lists are of two kinds:

1. Customer lists. These should be reasonably accurate – but beware those compiled by salesmen specifically for the survey; they are likely to be inaccurate and biased (computerised records are generally correct, but may give invoicing points rather than actual customers' addresses and so may not be as efficient as they first appear).
2. Prospect lists. These should be avoided unless salesmen's behaviour or something similar is under investigation; they are very rarely representative of anything.

A frequent use of client lists is for 'cancellations' or 'losses' research, and again this can be full of pitfalls. Apparent losses can simply be a change of contract or upgrades and, again, screening for true losses can make the contacting procedure inefficient.

Evaluating a potential sample frame

Some of the problems which can be encountered have already been

Sample Design, Selection and Estimating

mentioned. It is, however, useful to have a checklist of factors for evaluating a potential frame, even if there are no alternatives.

Is it complete? Any weak areas or omissions should be identified. Many sample frames are over-complete in that they contain ineligible units. This means that an expensive screening exercise must be undertaken to identify the required sample.

Are the units defined in the way required? The screening questions should take account of *all* the potential problems.

Are any units duplicated on the list? Duplication causes irritation to both interviewers and respondent if units are selected twice. Also it can be a source of significant problems with universe estimation and market measurement – particularly if there is any correlation between duplication and ownership or usage of the product. Lists should be de-duplicated before sampling.

What information is available for each unit? Useful information ranges from telephone numbers to SIC codes and size information (number of employees, turnover etc). Size indications are particularly important for sample stratification.

How up-to-date is the file? If the file is very out-of-date then it is probably useless. If only a little out-of-date then the screening exercise must be used to measure the extent. Decisions as to whether to pursue movers must be taken. More importantly, newly established units will be excluded, which may introduce bias if the survey is about banking, new product acquisition, or rapidly developing industrial sectors such as biotechnology.

Is the file available and in what formats? Some lists are available to subscribers only. The format can make considerable differences to the ease of sample selection.

Is it easy to use for sampling purposes? Alphabetical lists are difficult to use if geographically clustered samples are required. Lists which are not centralised, such as rating lists, are also not 'user friendly'.

Since the possession of the best possible sample frame is necessary before sample selection is begun, the need to review any potential sample frame in terms of the above questions is essential. The screening process should include:

- careful examination of all entries for missing elements – it is a rare directory that is accurate and complete in every entry (this requires the use of telephone directory enquiries for missing numbers and telephone contact to complete incomplete addresses);

- a review of the list by someone familiar with the industry or service sector, to give a view on apparent completeness and up-to-dateness;

- a random telephone check on suitability (still in business, eligible, and so on).

Clearly the larger and more general the list, the more difficult such a screening exercise becomes – and for the largest (such as a telephone directory) one just has to rely on the reputation of the compiler.

A further, and occasionally vital purpose of a screening exercise comes when the researcher's knowledge of the universe, and hence of the characteristics of the sample frame, is less than it should be. This lack of knowledge may prevent a proper design, or result in a faulty one, and the screening process can then be used as a pre-test of the universe to establish those key characteristics (in particular, its stratification) necessary for proper design.

Once the potential frames have been evaluated it may be necessary to review the universe to be covered since, if a perfect sample frame cannot be found or made, it is better to redefine the universe in terms of the list available than to misrepresent it through the use of a biased or incomplete sample frame. For example, if the universe is defined as 'all businesses' and the only list available is *Yellow Pages*, it is better to redefine the universe as 'all businesses with a business telephone line' and accept that some small businesses will be excluded, rather than maintain the fiction that the complete universe is covered.

Sample selection

Once a suitable sample frame has been identified, the next task is to select the required sample. There are a number of points to be considered in this process.

Sample Design, Selection and Estimating

Single-stage versus multi-stage sample designs

The first decision is whether to use a single- or multi-stage design. Single-stage sampling is where the final sample is selected directly (in a single stage) from a sample frame. Multi-stage sampling involves initial selection of sample points (generally geographical areas), and then the actual addresses sampled as clustered in the sample points. Multi-stage sampling is unavoidable for obvious economic reasons when face-to-face interviewing is necessary, but the increased use of telephone interviewing means that single-stage designs are perfectly feasible. (The further problem of selecting individuals within an establishment, where several are eligible, is dealt with later in this Chapter.)

For business markets, single-stage sampling is particularly advantageous from a statistical point of view in that it gives a more representative sample. Towns are very different in their industrial activity structure, and their use as sample points can have a marked effect on the results. For example, a very successful dealer in one town can mean that the local share of a particular make is very high, whereas in another location, where the make is sold by a less successful dealer, market share might be relatively low. Also, the distribution network for a product may be very patchy, and choosing one location rather than another can significantly affect penetration and other market estimates.

Stratification

Stratification is a method generally employed to ensure that a sample be as representative of all its components as possible. It means splitting the universe into sub-groups (or strata) which are reasonably homogeneous, and selecting random samples from each stratum. Almost all sample designs employ regional stratification to ensure a regionally representative sample. In business markets there is frequently the major problem that some eligible units are of greater interest to the research than others, and therefore some strata may need to be proportionally oversampled. In general, it is the larger establishments or companies, which are larger consumers of products, that need to be oversampled. Sometimes, however, there are special groups (such as copy bureaux or commercial printers in the reprographics market) which need special treatment, and this is achieved by sampling specific sub-groups separately.

It is very important to stratify the sample as much as possible. It is often difficult to do this prior to sampling because the sample frame does not contain relevant information. Sometimes it can be beneficial to select a larger sample than required, to post-stratify (through screening, or judgement), and reduce the sample for the groups of lower interest. This will increase sample efficiency. Post-sample stratification can also assist in identifying biased response rates at the analysis stage.

Quota sampling

In business market research, quota sampling (ie the selection of units according to a range of categories) presents some difficulties, and interviewers should never be left to identify eligible units themselves. In business market research the term is used when a control is required on the sample structure, which cannot be implemented at the sampling stage. For example, it might be required that a sample comprises 50 per cent of client customers and 50 per cent competitive customers. The interviewer is instructed to interview both, as they are found, up to a certain sample size for each. Once that sample size is reached then further eligible units are not interviewed – they are 'out of quota'.

The method can be used when the structure of the market is known and data are available for weighting and estimation. It is *not* appropriate for any form of market measurement study, when used just by itself, because of the marked bias inherent in the method – especially if quotas in different market segments are then given to different interviewers.

Sample size

Theoretically the sample size should be determined by the required precision levels on the variable being measured. However, in practice, market research studies very seldom measure only one variable. Frequently the research is trying to estimate several variables with

Sample Design, Selection and Estimating

very different distributions. Thus, a study of the usage and attitudes to parcels carriers may be required to measure everything from very occasional use of international courier services, to mail order despatch, or a copier market measurement study will produce data at three levels:

1. copier penetration of establishments,
2. installed base of copiers,
3. total copy volume,

and also the recent market for copiers (shipments).

The statistical theorist would require different designs and sample sizes for each variable. In practice a compromise must be found, and it is generally in terms of the sample base required for analysis or estimation. Therefore, to recommend a sample size the following factors should be considered.

- What is the smallest number of products to be analysed separately (and what is their incidence)? If it is required to produce market estimates of individual models with relatively low incidence then large sample sizes are required.

- What is the smallest data table base required? The sample may be of farms with more than 250 acres, but if it is actually required to produce tables based on all tractors acquired in the last 12 months then a reasonable base is needed for this table.

- What is a reasonable sample size for each stratum of the universe? Consideration must be given to the fact that the data for each stratum must stand alone – how many interviews would then be necessary? (Note the weight and grossing-up factor for the stratum – is that acceptable?)

The final consideration in sample size selection is, of course, budgetary. However, it is much better to understand in the planning stages what the limitations of the data will be, than to have expectations disappointed at the analysis stage.

Screening for eligibility

It is frequently the case that the best sample frame identified is over-complete: that is, although it includes all the units required, it includes many others as well. Hence the initial sample must be screened to find eligible units, as well as for accuracy and completeness. The following points should be noted:

- If the screening criteria are complex, ensure that the correct respondent is spoken to (receptionists and switchboard operators are unlikely to have accurate information).
- If one of the objectives of the study is to measure the size of the eligible market, accurate response and contact records must be maintained for analysis.
- Where the actual incidence of eligibility is very low (less than one in ten) interviewers can fail to recruit the eligible units found through sheer boredom.

The researcher should be sure to select a screen sample which is sufficiently large to yield the required number of eligible contacts (if it is too small then the sampling exercise must be repeated). On the other hand, it should not be too large so that significant numbers are left uncontacted.

Selecting the sample

Given a well understood universe, a thoroughly evaluated sample frame, any necessary stratification, guidance on quotas, and then the appropriate sizes of sample specified, it is now possible to select the sample from each segment of the sample frame. This must be done by random choice, of course, in order to permit proper analysis of the results.

The procedure is relatively simple: the units in each segment in the frame are given a unique number in a sequence of numbers particular to that segment, a random number within that sequence is generated, and the corresponding unit is withdrawn from the segment and placed in the sample. This process – of random number generation and matching – is repeated until the sample is full. Random numbers may be drawn from tables of such numbers, or generated by one of the computer programs now available for the purpose.

Sample Design, Selection and Estimating

Response rates

A well designed sample can be ruined by poor or biased response rates. Unfortunately some business-to-business markets are severely over-researched and high response rates are becoming harder to achieve. Three of the most difficult populations are:

1. telecommunications managers,
2. data processing managers,
3. finance directors of major companies.

Also, some geographical areas demonstrate consistently lower response rates – London is the prime example in the UK.

Time and economic pressures also play a part. It takes a longer fieldwork period to achieve high response rates, and it costs money to have supervisors follow-up refusals on a consistent basis. Buyers of market research should be aware that insisting on fast turnaround can be detrimental to the research results – respondents who are readily available may be different from those who are more difficult to contact, and therefore the 'fast turnaround' can lead to a biased sample. The importance of good response rates cannot be over-stressed.

In any case the response rates should be monitored in as much detail as possible. Data on regional counts and within-sample strata are particularly relevant. Any bias identified should be corrected, by weighting, at the analysis stage.

It must be remembered that there is a difference between non-response, as just discussed, and variable response. If the same person is asked the same question twice in succession there is a high chance that the responses will vary, especially if the answer is a qualitative one but sometimes even if it is numerical fact. The chance for such variability should be allowed for in any questionnaire analysis, but it does also add to the systematic error.

Selecting individuals from those eligible

It is sometimes the case that an establishment contains several eligible individuals, such as:

- potential readers of a computing magazine,
- business car drivers,
- microcomputer users,
- international telephone callers.

The problem arises as to how to select an individual to be interviewed.

In theory a list of all eligible individuals should be constructed and a sample of one or more drawn at random. This sample should then be contacted.

In practice, collecting long lists of names in businesses is difficult. Senior respondents do not want their employees' time wasted. More junior respondents are afraid of giving names of senior management in case of repercussions. In any case, it is difficult to ensure that all eligible individuals are named and not just the most important or heavy users, which could cause sample bias.

Where usage is common, such as with business telephone users, it is worth considering interviewing at the respondent's home address rather than sampling at work-place level. However, where the study is covering a subject such as computer work-station usage, this method can cause problems of over-claiming, and potential estimation problems where several employees use the same machine.

Sampling through enumeration is therefore unavoidable in most cases and should be done as professionally as possible. Care must be taken not simply to interview the most available person, since this could be the source of considerable bias.

The business researcher should also remember that the possibility of selection of an individual varies according to the number of eligible individuals at the workplace. Corrective weighting is required at the analysis stage.

Weighting and estimation

Data derived from a survey are intended to be used to represent a whole universe. They must be manipulated so as to make this representation as correct as possible, allowing for all the inherent errors in selection and analysis.

Sample Design, Selection and Estimating

Why weight data?

The necessary manipulation of data in market size estimation involves two separate components, which need to be understood as different concepts:

- weighting is the correction of imbalances in the sample;
- grossing-up is the conversion of data from a balanced, representative sample to the total market estimates for the whole universe.

Imbalances can be introduced into samples either deliberately, through differential sampling of sample strata, or accidentally, through achieving differential response rates. The data must be weighted to correct either of these imbalances before totals can be derived.

The correction of differential response rates is extremely important where market size estimates are required. In these cases it is advisable to computerise the non-effective records, including all sample information, interviewer number, and reasons for non-response, coded in as much detail as possible. The response data can then be analysed by interviewer, region, and sample strata – all variables available in fact. Biased response rates can be identified and corrected and so, essentially, the effective sample is targeted to the issued eligible sample.

In general, poorer response rates are obtained for both very large and very small establishments, and for certain industries such as finance. There is also usually some interviewer variation which needs to be corrected if the regional balance is to be maintained. High response rates make the weighting process very much easier and, in fact, ensure unbiased estimates.

Two examples of weighting are described in what follows. The first is an example of deliberate differential sampling, and is illustrated in Table 7.2. Three equal-sized samples were issued for each of the three strata, with large sites relatively oversampled (1 in 40 compared with 1 in 1,000 for small sites). The response rate was uniform, with a 60 per cent response.

In order to look at the total data the sample must be weighted to represent the true proportions in the universe, as is shown in the lower half of Table 7.2. Thus, the 1–9 employee records are given a weight factor of 2.42, whereas the 100+ employee records are given a weight factor of 0.097. It is necessary to do this to achieve a correct

Table 7.2. Deliberate differential sampling

(a) Sample size						
Number of employees	Universe		Issued sample		Effective sample	
	No	%	No	%	No	%
1–9	1,000,000	81	1,000	33	600	33
10–99	200,000	16	1,000	33	600	33
100+	40,000	3	1,000	33	600	33
Total	1,240,000	100	3,000	100	1,800	100

(b) Weighting factors				
Number of employees	Effective sample	True proportions in universe		Weight factor
		%	No	
1–9	600	81	1,452	2.420
10–99	600	16	290	0.483
100+	600	3	58	0.097
Total	1,800	100	1,800	

balance in the sample. In most cases data are then grossed-up to give market size estimates; this process is explained later in this section.

The second example deals with the effect of biased response rates and the importance of weighting in this case. It is illustrated in Table 7.3, which shows the response achieved from an issued sample of 100 addresses. The survey was concerned with measuring a market, and full interviews were to be conducted with establishments who were eligible. Short interviews were conducted with ineligible establishments. It is frequently the case in market size measurement that respondents who do not form part of the market, or for whom it is

Sample Design, Selection and Estimating

Table 7.3. *The effect of biased response rates*

Total addresses issued	100
No contact	10
Refused: Total	20
Eligible	2
Ineligible	14
Not known	4
Effective: Total	70
Eligible	50
Ineligible	20

very insignificant, are less willing to take part, or even to complete a short interview. So, in Table 7.3, a high proportion of refusals were in fact ineligible (interviewers were instructed to find out about eligibility if they possibly could).

The question is 'What is the level of eligibility in the market?' If no account is taken of non-response, the simple answer is that 71 per cent of establishments are eligible since, of effective contacts, 50 out of 70 were eligible. However, there is a known bias in the response, because non-response was analysed and there were 86 contacts altogether where eligibility was determined, for which the rate of eligibility was 52 out of 86; that is, 60 per cent – a very different answer from the first one.

Market size estimation (grossing-up)

Once the data are weighted (ie all imbalances in the sample are corrected) then grossing-up to the universe total is a straightforward matter. In the example of Table 7.2, it is a case of multiplying every weighted sample by 1,240,000 divided by the sample size 1,800 (ie by 688.9).

In grossing-up, it is important to note that:

- results should always be grossed to the universe contained in the sample frame employed (it cannot be assumed that the sample is representative of anything apart from that universe);

- the universe should always be reviewed in the light of the response data obtained from the sample (if there were high levels of no contact, out of business etc, the universe will need to be revised, using this information).

In the example of Table 7.3, it might be assumed that the 10 'no contacts' are not part of the universe, and therefore the total universe estimate for the cell must be reduced by 10 per cent. This decision can only be taken using experience and judgement, and knowledge of the sample frame employed.

Statistical outliers

In business research it is sometimes necessary to measure very variable data, for example:

- telecoms expenditure; or
- establishment copy volume; or
- letters and parcels despatched;

and it is generally the survey objective to gross these data to universe levels to give market size estimates.

Sometimes a single record can dominate the data and completely upset the estimates. These are referred to as 'statistical outliers'. They are either:

- extremely large units with moderate weight factors, or
- small units with higher-than-average data, but with large weight factors.

It is imperative, first of all, to check that the apparent 'rogue' data have been collected and recorded correctly. It is always useful to have interviewers double check and confirm unusually high data, and it is always worthwhile to check that no clerical errors have been made.

Once the data are confirmed, the main option is to adjust either the weighting or the grossing-up factor, to diminish the impact of these outliers. In the case of very large units the weighting factor can be adjusted to 1.0, or thereabouts, on the principle that the record is unique.

Sample Design, Selection and Estimating

The case of units with above-average data and a high weight factor is more difficult. It is recommended generally that no record should be allowed to account for more than 10 times the expected average, and the weight factor on the record should be adjusted to give this result. So, if in a sample of 100, it is expected that each record should account for an 'average' of 1 per cent of the market, no record should therefore be allowed to account for more than 10 per cent.

Incomplete data

It is not always possible to obtain answers to every question and 'not stated' values can cause considerable problems in making good market size estimates – particularly since inevitably they are biased.

The only real solution is to allocate averages to those not stating, but the averages must be appropriate to the situation. Variables which are correlated with the value to be estimated should be sought and averages allocated within values of these variables.

For example, if the variable to be measured is machine monthly copy volume for copiers, then the best predictor is machine speed (in copies per minute). However, it is also the case that in larger establishments copiers tend to do higher copy volumes. A suitable matrix for the allocation of volumes to not-stated machines would therefore be machine speed by number of employees or number of white collar workers.

The danger of ignoring 'no answers' is illustrated in Table 7.4. The simplest analysis would multiply the average for all those stating (46 per week) by the total number eligible (99,700), to give an estimated total of 4.6 million. Calculating within each employee size band, however, gives a better estimate of 5.9 million, because of the bias in the response rate – larger sites having lower response rates. (Thus, in the 100–499 employee size group, the average weekly value based on those stating is 100. So, assuming that those not stated also have an average of 100, a total of 11,000 × 100 = 1.1 million is given, compared with 7,500 × 100 = 0.75 million based only on those stating.)

Correction of errors

If the market estimates derived from a properly conducted and

Table 7.4. *Allowing for non-answers*

Category	Number of employees				Total
	1–19	20–99	100–499	500+	
All eligible establishments	55,000	31,000	11,000	2,700	99,700
All establishments stating weekly value	49,000 (89%)	24,000 (77%)	7,500 (68%)	1,350 (50%)	81,850 (82%)
Average weekly value per establishment stating	10	50	100	1,000	46
Total per week (millions) based on those stating	0.49	1.20	0.75	1.35	3.79
Corrected total (millions/week)	0.55	1.55	1.10	2.70	5.90

analysed study are challenged, it is sensible to check first the source of the data with which they are being compared, as it may not be very authoritative. Manufacturers' estimates of total market size can be wrong, for the following reasons:

- data based on cumulative sales figures, taking no account of disposals, machines in stock etc, will give high installed-base figures;
- the data may have been based on hearsay;
- the data were based on another (incorrectly grossed-up) market survey.

However, if the source does appear to be authoritative, then the survey methodology must be reviewed, examining the following factors:

Sample Design, Selection and Estimating

1. Underestimation of the market, which can be caused by:
   - incomplete sample frame (whether there is any crucial sector that has been omitted);
   - incomplete data (whether the data were collected for the whole of the specified unit, or whether it is possible that some were missed);
   - biased response rate (whether there are any sectors with very high refusal rates – they may be high users).

2. Overestimation of the market, which is more common. The following should be investigated:
   - Are any very large weight factors distorting the data?
   - Duplication – were there duplicates in the sample frame?
   - Are the duplicated establishments more likely to possess the equipment in question?
   - Biased sample selection – was the sampling random or was some subtle bias employed to reject establishments which 'looked' as if they might not qualify?
   - Biased response rate (which could possibly cause overestimation, but is more likely to produce underestimates).

If bias is suspected, then it is important to try to establish the nature of the bias, so that it can be properly identified:

- Is the total market estimate about right?
- What about the relative market shares of manufacturers?
- Are larger machines relatively overestimated or the smaller ones?

The researcher should look at the data carefully, particularly the effect of the weighting; it ought to be possible to work out where things may have gone wrong.

Many market research practitioners are nervous about weighting and grossing-up; they think there is some mystique about it and that they might get it wrong. In reality, it is basically common sense. If there are a good sample and reasonable response rates, and the weighting and grossing-up take account of the sample design and response analysis, the results should be correct.

8

The Skills of Interviewing

Tony Lake

Even though interviewing someone is just talking to that person, there is a great deal more to it than just talk. This Chapter is devoted to a description of the characteristics of interviews, and how to talk to the required purpose. Although framed around the face-to-face interview, much of the advice applies equally to interviews over the telephone.

Introduction

Sometimes the printed word on paper, or on the computer screen, can give you the information you want for a research project. More often you have to engage people in conversation to obtain it. All the many ways you can do this are covered by the term 'interview'. Because an interview is a kind of conversation, a useful way to understand the techniques involved in it is by recognising that all conversations have some kind of structure.

Length

The first component of the structure of an interview is length – the time it takes. Within this dimension, interviews have a beginning, a middle and an end, each with its own distinct set of objectives and associated rituals. For example, the objective of the beginning phase might be to introduce yourself, set the agenda, and spell out some ground rules such as whether or not the information will be confidential and how long the interview will take. There will almost certainly be a greeting ritual, such as a spoken greeting or a handshake. At the end, you might wish to set up further meetings, or discuss the action to be taken as a result of the conversation. You will probably wish to thank the respondent, shake hands again and say goodbye. In the middle part you may want to ask particular kinds of questions, or explore issues of a general nature or perhaps of a specific character. In our culture this part has no set rituals.

In planning an interview, it helps to work out not only how long you want it to last, but also how long you expect to spend on each of the three parts. For example, if you know the respondent well, you can shorten the beginning and the ending. If you have never met him, particularly if you are using the telephone instead of working face-to-face, the beginning will tend to take more time, and the length of the ending will reflect how well you get on together during the middle part. You might also have to allow extra time for possible interruptions, and on the telephone you might not even know these are happening.

Also you need to plan how to begin the conversation, how you want to end it, and what you want to do in the middle. Many people find they have problems due to lack of planning, and even among those who do plan, some of us are temperamentally inclined to have problems with beginnings and endings, perhaps out of an excessive need to be polite. If you are like this, take account of it in your planning by allocating extra time. Of course, a well planned interview can still come adrift when the respondent wants to explore the issues you raise in the middle in ways you had not anticipated or did not want.

Width

All conversations have not only length but also width: they can be wide-ranging or narrow. What we mean by width, therefore, is the number of topics covered in the middle and at the end. For example, in the middle of a wide-ranging conversation you might discuss a dozen

The Skills of Interviewing

topics, while in a narrow one you would concentrate on maybe two or three. At the end of a wide conversation you might summarise only a narrow part of the spectrum covered.

You need always to decide in advance how wide you want the interview to be. The usual way of exploring a topic in an interview is by asking questions – although this is not the only way – and the best way to plan the width is to write down your questions and then sort them into topics (unless, of course, you have already been given them in a questionnaire). Once you have done this, make up your mind which topics are the most important.

By the way, always use this opportunity to check whether your questions really give you the key information you are looking for in respect of each topic. Then ruthlessly throw out the questions that do not.

In principle, it is best to have too few topics rather than too many. This is because if you have too many there will only be time for a few questions calling for one-word answers, and respondents who are treated in this way feel a bit controlled, and rather used. You might just as well take a postal survey questionnaire and read it out – doing this over the phone or face-to-face is not much fun for either of you, and no good at all if you want qualitative data. Also, if you have too many topics you can more easily make mistakes remembering, recording or transcribing the answers.

You also need to link the topics in a logical way which your respondent can understand. Nothing is more irritating, if you are a respondent, than the grasshopper-mind effect created by having to switch from topic to topic and back again, at the whim of a controlling interviewer who will not let you use your own logic. Irritated respondents give less information, and it is less reliable when you get it.

It is the sign of a very good interviewer that he knows which topics to concentrate on, and which parts of each topic are important, but does not prepare the actual questions in advance. The questions are improvised during the interview to suit the respondent's personality. Also, the topics are linked together in a flexible way so that they can be taken in any order with which the respondent feels happy. This helps to make the interview feel like a confidential chat with somebody, who is really interesting to talk to, and at the end it will be the interviewee who does the thanking. Of course, it takes planning and practice to work this way but it is well worth the investment, particularly in qualitative research or in research as part of consultancy, where the respondents may feel threatened or unwilling to trust you.

Depth

Finally, every conversation has depth: it may be shallow or deep. There are two ways of defining depth. One way is to regard it as the amount of technical detail given by the speaker. For example, you might look 'in depth' at the finances of a company associated with a particular market, and this would mean going into great detail on how the money is spent. The second way is to see depth as psychological or emotional depth. In this sense 'deep' topics are those which cannot be explored without deep feelings being expressed. When people talk about such topics they are 'self-disclosing', and there is a certain risk attached to self-disclosure. For example, they might thereby make themselves vulnerable to being judged morally by the listener, or they might stir up painful feelings. So we can define this kind of depth as the risk to the speaker of self-disclosure.

The terms 'in-depth interview' or 'depth interview' are often used to refer to techniques of interviewing designed to elicit information about the way somebody thinks or feels. Psychologists who work in the tradition founded by Freud believe that all of us suppress threatening feelings, so we are completely unaware we have them yet we may still be profoundly influenced by them. Such feelings are said to be 'unconscious', or are described as being part of the 'unconscious mind'. If a researcher wants to study the irrational ways in which people respond to products, he might use special techniques to convert this unconscious material into a form which can be studied (called 'projective' or 'enabling' techniques). One way, for example, is to ask people to draw pictures of their fantasies after watching a television commercial. The pictures are then analysed by the researcher so that guesses can be made about the hidden feelings that the respondents have about the product. It is not usual for these guesses to be reported to the respondents as part of the study, but they may be used as the starting point for a new advertising campaign. Another such tech-

The Skills of Interviewing

nique is the use of pre-prepared drawings of a scene connected with the topic, in which a person is drawn with an empty 'thought balloon' above his head, and the respondent is asked to fill in an appropriate thought.

More usually, depth in an interview deals not so much with unconscious material as with opinions and feelings which the respondent is well aware of, but which are only revealed to people whom he can trust. Thus, you might need to build up a trusting relationship with the respondent before he will give an honest opinion about some of the topics you raise. Examples are: questions about commercially confidential material; opinions about people in power in an organisation; matters regarded by the respondent as personal, such as his age, marital history, income, or personal hygiene.

Depth needs care

You need to think carefully about depth – whether this is depth of technical detail or psychological depth – in the planning stage before the interview. Generally speaking, the answers you get to shallow questions tend to be more homogeneous, and to deeper questions more heterogeneous or idiosyncratic; that is to say, we are all much more alike in our shallower feelings, and rather more different from one another in respect of our deeper feelings. The result is that, if you want consistency in your data for statistical reasons, you are more likely to get it with shallow questions than with deep ones, and this is appropriate in large-sample, quantitative study. On the other hand, deeper questions give a wide spectrum of personal opinions, which are harder to analyse using statistics, and this is appropriate to small-sample, qualitative research. It is usually easier to generalise about shallow things than deep things.

Another reason for thinking in advance about the depth you want is that anything other than the shallowest of answers means that you need to build a trusting relationship with the respondent. The deeper you want to go the more you have to establish trust, and this can take time. Often it is enough to say that the results will be treated as confidential and nobody will be identified personally, provided you mean what you say and sound convincing when you say it – but this does not always work.

In management consultancy research, for example, you might be part of a team looking at ways of restructuring a company, with the implication that redundancies or redeployment could follow as a direct result of your activities. Getting people to tell you what they really think under such circumstances can be difficult. Here you will need to set your own personal needs to one side and listen to the other person seeing the world as he sees it, accepting without reservation all the feelings that go with this. In effect, you listen in the way a counsellor or psychotherapist would. What is more, because of confidentiality you cannot repeat what you have been told without the respondent's permission. However, you can make up your own mind what is really happening, and then design more formal research projects which test this out by other, less deep interviews.

Techniques for depth interviews

Working in depth research requires specialised techniques which you cannot expect to learn overnight. Nevertheless, winning the trust of your respondent should be a first objective in all interviews, even the shallowest. A lot of it is simple courtesy, such as making an appointment before you conduct the interview, then turning up on time; dressing to fit the part; being considerate towards the respondent's support staff; waiting to be invited to sit before doing so; getting on with the interview when the respondent is a busy manager, instead of making lots of small-talk; getting out without fuss when you have finished the job and so on. Do not always accept the cup of coffee that is offered out of good manners – decide whether it will be added work for a secretary, whether it will interrupt the start of the interview, or whether you want the sound of a rattling cup just at the critical moment on that tape recorder which you brought with you.

Make a good impression from the start – remember, you only get one chance to make a first impression. Leave a good impression behind you when you go, or maybe one of your fellow researchers will one day curse you for giving your profession a bad name.

Managing the interview

We have seen so far that every interview has structure – a certain

The Skills of Interviewing

length, breadth and depth, and that within each of these dimensions there are structural considerations to be taken account of at the planning stage. It may be possible to hold good interviews without previous planning but this can only happen by chance, and even the best interview, like the most brilliant presentation, would have been even better if it had been planned in advance. Yet it has to be said also that planning can reduce spontaneity, if you become a slave to your plan instead of being its master.

So make your plan, but make it in order to free yourself from the obvious mistakes, rather than to determine every detail of the interview. Pilot it, too – try it out on a few friends. Once the interview is under way, your plan should be a guide to how you manage the interview, and no more than that. It should give you flexibility, allow you to use your creativity, and release you from worry so that you can be spontaneous in the way you put your questions.

The fact is that every interview has to be managed, and this is your responsibility as the researcher. This means that you are in charge of the duration and the timing, the topics and keeping the respondent to the point, the depth and the trust. You are the relationship builder. You cannot fairly blame the respondent if the relationship is a bad one at the end of the interview.

Managing the start

However you might feel when you arrive, try to look confident and businesslike. When you meet somebody for the first time, be careful to start with positive things to say. For example, however bad the journey, do not be tempted to describe its horrors even if asked. Be careful about handshakes – no 'wet fish', and no juggling with that file cover, briefcase, tape recorder, umbrella and plastic bag of shopping to get your hand free for the executive grasp. Make eye contact very early on, and smile – but do these things and then look around to show you are ready to start.

Sometimes you will need an ice-breaker – something to say which reduces tension and starts the rapport. It does not matter how banal this is, and the best ones give your respondent a chance to reply. For example, ask how his day has gone so far. As soon as you have heard the answer, get down to business. Never self-denigrate, for example, by saying you hope he does not mind seeing you and sounding as though he has good grounds to. If you try to go in with a hearty manner and a merry quip on your lips, you deserve a cup of tepid coffee laced with arsenic – especially on a Monday.

Taking notes makes free-flowing conversation impossible. The respondent slows down to dictation speed, frames every remark grammatically and then checks your spelling. Your options are either to remember everything for periods of 15 minutes and excuse yourself at the end of each period and then write it all down in the toilet, or to record it on tape to be transcribed or summarised later. The former method can evoke great sympathy from your respondent but requires abnormal stamina on your part. The latter is infinitely less artificial and more acceptable socially.

So, at an early stage remind your respondent that you said you would be recording the interview when you phoned to make the appointment. Do not ask for permission all over again, just set it up and get on with the interview. If he objects, explain the Code of Conduct and try to persuade him to agree. If there looks like being a hassle, leave it there switched off, get the respondent's confidence and ask again later. If you still do not get permission, you may have to try the 'excuse-me' method outlined above. So find out where the toilets are, first.

Right at the start, look around at the person's office. See where you want to sit, and hover there, or ask if this is all right, while you boldly pick up a chair and place it where you want to sit. You need to be not much more than six feet away, facing the respondent, and doing this across the corner of a desk is preferable to doing it across the width of the desk. If you act boldly at the start, there will be no protest even from the most powerful managers. They expect you to know your job and get on with it.

Keep a checklist in your head of what you need to say to get the interview under way, such as: the purpose of the research, who you represent, that you will be sending a short summary of the results, that it will take so many minutes, and that (if this is true) the material will be confidential. Try not to make this sound like a speech. If you need some personal details, get them out of the way quickly and use a calm voice to help settle you both down. In a qualitative interview, ask a good open question and sit back and listen.

The Skills of Interviewing

Managing the middle

An open question is defined as one that cannot be answered with either 'Yes' or 'No'. It makes people think. You can tell they are doing this by watching their eyes, which break off from eye contact and appear to wander round the room. In fact, the eye movements are connected with an internal search for information, and generally if they go up this means a visual search, to the side an audial search, or if they go down, a search into feelings. Open questions are very useful to start an interview because they take the pressure off you, and you can relax a bit while the other person is thinking. They are also essential to elicit qualitative information.

Managing the middle is really about managing the width and depth of the interview. You can get the person to expand on a point and stay on the same topic by requesting, 'Tell me more about that', or some variant of these words such as, 'Could you give me an example of that?' If you have specific questions, use these techniques to set them up so that they sound natural. Shifting to a new topic is done by making a slight pause and then asking a question.

Of course, you might sometimes need to get the respondent away from a topic he seems obsessed by. It is comparatively rare, and the best way to do it is just to interrupt and say, 'I'd like to interrupt you there and ask about *x* instead.' Then ask the question that changes the topic. Do not worry about the apparent impoliteness on your part. Politeness is mandatory at the beginning of an interview and at the end. In the middle it is only optional.

You may have heard of prompts and probes. The best way to prompt somebody into talking about a topic is the one-word question. Choose the appropriate word and put a question into your voice: 'Advertisements?' 'Expenses?' Or make a statement which the respondent can either accept or correct for you, such as, 'You're a regular user of galvanised gaskets' or, 'All your salesmen speak Esperanto.' Try to avoid beginning a question with 'do you . . .' or 'don't you . . .' unless you want a 'Yes' or 'No' in response. And try to avoid asking 'why' questions such as, 'Why shouldn't you ask "why" questions?'

Probes are an old-fashioned way of increasing the depth of the interview. The modern way is to ask the respondent about feelings and then follow up with a question on facts. For example, 'How do you feel about the way things are going in your business?' Then, after the response, 'What exactly is happening?' Give people space to feel safe about discussing difficult issues, instead of opening up the respondent. Leave that to the surgeons.

It is very important to increase warmth every time you want to increase depth. This acknowledges the risk to the speaker posed by your questions, and reassures him about safety. Use friendly and warm eye contact, smile gently and sincerely, or move very slightly closer. Lower your voice a bit too. Give the respondent a body-language caress. If really necessary, switch off the tape recorder and memorise the answer.

Pauses by the respondent during an interview should be accepted and used, not rejected and interrupted by you. Listen attentively and wait for more material during pauses, and you will usually be rewarded by extra information of more significance than that which preceded the pause. This is because people pause in order to decide whether to tell you more. If you interrupt, you make up their minds for them but not in your favour.

Oddly enough, this is also true on the telephone. There is a myth that people are less tolerant of pauses on the phone than face to face. In fact, if you get the person's trust by starting well on the phone, acceptable pause lengths are no different from those used in face-to-face speech. You do not have to rush in to fill them, and you could lose out by doing so.

To listen well is probably the most important skill that an interviewer can acquire. It is not easy to do, and it may require great restraint not to rush on to the next topic.

Inexperienced interviewers are sometimes so worried about the next question that they stop listening to the last answer. If this applies to you, have your key questions written out on a small file card, and keep it where you can see it. Then stop worrying – you can always look at the card near the end of the interview, say you need to check you have covered everything, and if you have missed out an important question simply read it out.

Before you reach the ending phase, it helps to ask if there is anything the respondent wants to add which will correct any wrong impressions he might have given you. Then switch off the tape recorder and pause for a few moments to see if anything else is added. Only then move to the end phase.

Managing the end

The purpose of this phase is to get out politely, without having to go back for anything and without being late for your next appointment. Using the minimum of fuss, thank the respondent, ask if you can phone again should you need to, hand over any fee or incentive with a smile, pick up your tape recorder and leave.

One of the characteristics of conversation is that during it, people produce synchronised body movements. Each gesture from one is answered by a movement or gesture from the other. When the conversation ends, this synchrony is disrupted, signalling the end of shared time, shared space and joint activity. If you cannot get away, it is usually because you cannot disrupt this synchrony. Usually the reason is that you do not want to appear impolite.

Getting out efficiently can only be accomplished by ending body motion synchrony, so if you have difficulties you have to risk seeming discourteous. Turn your back to pick something up. Pause for a long time in response to a question while moving through the door, then answer it at the moment of going through. Look out of the window, not at the clinging respondent. The adhesive handshake is broken by placing your other hand on top of the respondent's wrist, squeezing the wrist, and letting your grasped hand go limp; then let go of the wrist, retrieve both hands and turn away. Let the respondent have the last word, even if this is an unanswered question. If all this sounds difficult, then practise these techniques with a friend.

Setting up the interview

Of course, all that has gone before assumes that you have been able to set up the interview. This can be a problem too. For example, you need to be sure you have the right person – the decision maker you need for the project to be valid. Do this by phone, checking directly with the target person, not with the 'temp' who answers the phone. If you get the wrong person, carefully note down that one's name, and ask who is the right person. Then ring the right one, saying that Mr So-and-so said you were to talk to him. Never rely on job titles as a guide without checking. The 'Office Manager' of one famous consultancy firm is the title they give to their managing director.

Be very careful to record appointments when you make them and, if there is more than a three-week gap between making them and holding them, ring up a few days in advance to remind your respondent. Even with phone interviews it pays to make an appointment in advice: 'When can I ring you back for a 15-minute interview by phone?' If you want to use stimulus material, fax this the day before and check that it has been received when you phone for the interview.

Gate-keepers are people whose job it is to filter callers so that only the priority ones get through. They have a difficult job, and often respond helpfully if you acknowledge this when you phone. Do not try to break them, only to bend them. If they are very busy, ask when you can call back. Never expect them to call you back.

Sometimes setting up interviews can be harder than doing them, such as when they are all big powerful experts and you are only a shy little researcher. If you find you keep putting off making that call, ask for help rather than get hopelessly behind in your schedule.

Also, watch your case load. Nobody can do six face-to-face interviews of any quality in a day and remain either sane or sober. Allow adequate travel time in your planning too, and time for parking the car. It pays to ask about parking when you make the appointment. In many companies, car park attendants are more powerful than the directors, so be sure you have permission in advance.

The quality of the interview

It is worth asking yourself every time why you are doing the interview, and it is even more worth while to ask why the respondent is doing it. The first question can help you to remember never to do unnecessary interviews. If you can get what you want any other way, use it. Interviews are the most time-consuming and expensive way to get information.

What makes them worth while is that when people answer questions they add all sorts of data about themselves, their companies,

The Skills of Interviewing

the context in which they work, and the underlying attitudes they have towards markets. This cannot be gleaned from cold facts on printed pages. So why do they tell you these things?

Respondents give interviews for a variety of reasons. They might be curious about you, your company, your survey. They might be bored and have nothing else to do. They probably want to find out what you have already found out or will discover later. They might like the sound of your voice and want to meet you. But the most important reason that they agree to see you is that you can give them something quite precious – time and space and a good excuse for talking about their work and getting it into a new perspective. Managers get very little time to sit back and think aloud for themselves. You can give them this, and they can use it to make sense of what they are doing.

The quality of face-to-face and telephone interviews is dependent on this summing up and making sense. If the process does not happen, you will get a poor quality interview. If you can make it happen by being on the side of the respondents and helping them intelligently to explore the issues, you will obtain high quality information that can go far beyond the basic purpose of the study. What is more, they will feel warm and generous towards you, and look forward to being interviewed again.

9
Questionnaire Use and Design
Paul Hague

In business marketing research, interviews are almost always conducted with someone who is buying or specifying a product for someone else – a company or organisation. Putting oneself in the mind of the industrial buyer, in order to design sensible questions, is made difficult by the wide range of responses that are possible. A survey on steel bar usage will have to cope with the respondent who requires just a few metres per year through to one who may buy hundreds of tons.

This Chapter considers the role of the questionnaire in business marketing research. It shows how to write effective questions and how to design questionnaires for telephone, visit and self-completion.

The role of the questionnaire

It is useful to begin by looking at the overall role of the questionnaire in business marketing research. Quesionnaires have four functions:

1. they are intended to *draw accurate information* from the respondent – perhaps their most important function;
2. they provide a *structure* which ensures that an interview flows smoothly, and so is successful in drawing out the required information;
3. they are a means of *recording* information;

4. they provide a system from which information can be obtained for *analysis*.

Questionnaires provide structure to an interview and so make life easier for all concerned. The interviewer has an *aide-mémoire* which a well-thought-out reminder of all the questions to ask. The respondent enjoys the benefit of a logical sequence of questions which leads him through the interview. When all the interviewing is complete, data from the questionnaires can easily be transferred on to analysis paper or a computer for analysis.

Thus the questionnaire guides the interview, and acts as a means of recording and collecting together a number of responses for analysis. It provides a standard form on which facts, comments and attitudes can be recorded. In this way, patterns of response can be established, when tens or sometimes hundreds of interviews are carried out. It would be difficult to make sense of 100 free-ranging discussions, which have been written up, each in its own individual manner. Questionnaires are especially important when interviews are carried out by more than one person, as they ensure that each interview is conducted in the same consistent way.

A record of an interview is essential as, without it, points could be forgotten or distorted. Sometimes researchers claim that they do not need to take notes in an interview, arguing that they are able to commit the key issues to memory. In practice, people who are truly capable of accurately memorising a discussion of up to an hour, which may cover hundreds of points of specific information, are few and far between.

Equally, interviews could be recorded on tape, and this is a *bona fide* and excellent means of capturing data. Nevertheless, tapes have their disadvantages. They can break down and they run out. In certain circumstances they inhibit the response, and they are time-consuming to listen to and to interpret after the event. Besides, even when a tape is used, a questionnaire is also needed to *guide* the discussion.

The characteristics of business research questionnaires

The sizes of interview programmes can vary widely in business

Questionnaire Use and Design

research, and the scale or variability of possible responses is also very wide. It would actually be more correct to describe some business marketing research interviews as *discussions*. The researcher who designs the questionnaire is very often the interviewer, and therefore answers that do not seem quite right can be challenged. The researcher is quickly made aware if questions are not fully understood, in which case they can be rephrased. Indeed, such is the flexibility in most business interviews that questions can be modified to meet the special circumstances of the company that is being interviewed, especially in smaller samples. If these adjustments were not to take place, the interview would seem wooden and the respondent would be less willing to cooperate.

Of course, there are business marketing research surveys which involve hundreds of interviews. In these circumstances a team of interviewers are employed to work on the project and the study requires a much more rigid questionnaire structure. Interviewers do not then have the discretion to change questions even if they think the occasion demands it.

Thus there are three factors which characterise a business research interview:

1. the role of the respondent;
2. the variability in the types of businesses covered;
3. the range in the numbers of interviews required in a business survey.

The role of the respondent in business interviews

Respondents in business usually hold a specific title and position. They are buyers, works managers, managing directors, technical managers and the like. They have clearly defined duties and responsibilities in the company in which they work. They have a knowledge of their company, its attitudes and work practices, that may stretch beyond the responsibilities of their department. For example, if information is being sought on the consumption of cleaning chemicals within a company, a suitable estimate may be obtained from the buyer, the works manager or the maintenance manager.

Managers in business tend to be quite analytical about their company and its requirements and, because the company is the focus of conversation at work, most managers have a broad knowledge of how it operates and what its plans are. This is not to say that all managers in industry are equally knowledgeable, or that a researcher will be able to obtain all his answers from one person in a company. People in business may not even be prepared to give the answers to a marketing research interviewer. Confidentiality, cussedness, ignorance or a lapse of memory may be restraining factors. It is to be expected that there will always be a significant level of refusals or 'don't know' responses in a business-to-business survey.

In business research, the focus of interest is the company. The inability of a works manager to answer a question on the prices paid for glass bottles may demand that the researcher also speaks to the buyer. This may mean reserving certain questions in a questionnaire for different respondents, or it could demand more than one questionnaire.

In business-to-business surveys, it is important that respondents fully understand a question; although one would normally avoid the use of jargon, meanings may actually be made clearer by the use of jargon or technical terms. Sometimes the researcher needs to be prepared to use different expressions to be more meaningful to the respondent (inches for some, centimetres for others).

The important requirement – that the researcher should have, from the outset, at least some knowledge of the subject that is being researched – is the reason that the interview often becomes a discussion. The researcher needs to maintain flexibility in this discussion to accommodate the wide variances in each respondent's needs.

The variability in business-to-business interviews

Business marketing research is heavily influenced by the wide variations that exist in business markets. For example, there are obvious differences between companies that make chemicals and those that assemble toys, and yet they both buy the services of electrical contractors. Any survey of electrical contractors would need to take account of the different types of end user of the service.

Companies differ in size as well as nature. The man-and-boy

Questionnaire Use and Design

operation exists side by side with establishments employing thousands of people. A survey of office stationery consumption, among a cross-section of different sizes of company, would need a questionnaire which could cope with responses from a sole proprietor as well as those from centralised buyers.

The size of business interview programmes

It is not unusual in some business markets for a researcher to collect data by speaking to only a handful of people. A manufacturer of rolling mills, or a supplier of car paint lines, addresses only a few companies and probably knows each and every one of them very well. Equally, the buyers of rolling mills and paint lines are so familiar with the suppliers that any survey would usually require the disclosure of the research sponsor in order to obtain cooperation.

Other business surveys can be very large. In contrast to the example of the small number of rolling mill buyers, there are thousands of buyers of commercial vehicles. Depending on the objectives of the research, a survey could involve hundreds of interviews with the market segmented by, say, geographical region, size of fleet, and type of vehicles operated. Even so, a survey of more than 500 respondents is large in business-to-business surveys and a more typical quantitative study would have up to 200 interviews. In a study of 200 companies the design of the questionnaire and the control over the interviewing is difficult enough.

The types of business research questionnaire

A reasonably useful method of classifying questionnaires has three main types:
1. structured questionnaires – in which the questioning and the layout of the questionnaire is rigid;
2. semi-structured questionnaires – where the interviewer has some latitude in the order and way in which questions are asked, or where some of the questions are rigid in their structure and some are open-ended;

3. unstructured questionnaires – which are a checklist of questions giving the interviewer complete freedom as to the way the questions are asked and in what order.

Structured questionnaires

Structured questionnaires in many respects make an interviewer's job easier. The structured questionnaire contains all the wording which the interviewer requires. It instructs with 'routeings' showing which questions the interviewer should skip in the event of a certain answer. Usually, pre-coded answers are provided so that all the interviewer has to do is tick a bracket or a box, or circle a number against the response that is given. In theory, anyone could pick up a structured questionnaire, ask the questions and record the answers.

Table 9.1 shows an example of a few questions which formed part of a structured questionnaire, administered by telephone, that was targeted at chemists on behalf of a pharmaceutical wholesaler (the words in capitals are instructions to the interviewer).

The limitations of structured questionnaires stem from their rigidity and this gives rise to the widespread use of semi-structured versions in which the interviewer has more latitude.

Despite the inflexibility of structured questionnaires, they are useful to the business marketing researcher who has to carry out a large-scale interviewing programme. Whenever there is the need to interview 100 or so respondents, the interviewing will be carried out by a team of people. With a structured quesetionnaire the questions are all asked in the same way and therefore the answers are as free from interviewer bias as possible. In very large-scale industrial surveys, which involve many hundreds of interviews, structured questionnaires remove the practical problem of coding and classifying hundreds of different answers. For example, it is normal in structured interviewing to present a range of different answers to respondents as alternatives from which they can choose rather than leaving them free to give any answer.

A well-thought-out questionnaire, especially if it has been piloted, will enable hundreds of smooth, well-ordered interviews to be carried out. The interviewer's job is made easier because the asking and recording of the questions is straightforward. The respondent finds it

Questionnaire Use and Design

Table 9.1. *Structured questions*

2a. What is the name of the pharmaceutical wholesaler that you use most as a supplier to your shop? TICK UNDER (a)

2b. And what about the pharmaceutical wholesaler that is second in importance as a supplier to your shop? TICK UNDER (b)

	(a)	(b)
Ayrton Saunders	( )	( )
Butlers	( )	( )
Daniels (Richard)	( )	( )
Foster (George)	( )	( )
Harris (Philip)	( )	( )
Hills	( )	( )
Macarthy	( )	( )
Mawdsley-Brooks	( )	( )
Rowlands	( )	( )
Sants Pharmac.	( )	( )
SOT/Barclay	( )	( )
UniChem	( )	( )
Vestric	( )	( )
None	( )	( )

Others (specify) _____

3. Would you tell me how you selected your **first line** pharmaceutical wholesaler? DO NOT PROMPT

Previous experience	( )
UniChem share scheme	( )
Managed shop (told where to buy)	( )
Supplier has good ordering service	( )
They kept calling on me	( )
Have always dealt with them	( )
They have good service	( )
They have good product range	( )
They understand our business	( )
They helped me out in a fix	( )

    Other (specify) _____

4. Would you consider the following factors and tell me which *three* are most important to you in selecting your **first line** pharmaceutical wholesaler? ROTATE THE ORDER

Fast service when you need it	( )
Reliable service	( )
Wide range of ethical products	( )
Wide range of counter products	( )
Easy ordering via modem	( )
Competitive terms	( )
Independent ownership	( )
Cheerful/friendly company	( )
UniChem share scheme	( )
Always dealt with them – no reason	( )

easier because the order and sequence of the questions is logical, and multiple-choice answers alleviate the need to think up creative responses.

As well as being used in surveys of large numbers of companies, structured questionnaires are suited to surveys which measure responses. For example, in an image survey a structured question would ensure that every respondent gives the answer within the same limits, and it would facilitate any follow-up exercise at a later date that may be required to obtain 'tracking' of the responses (ie their variation with passing time).

The following question, of this kind, was used in the same telephone survey of chemists as that of Table 9.1 to find out their attitudes to pharmaceutical wholesalers.

> I would like you now to think about five pharmaceutical wholesalers. Would you first of all think about Hills and tell me what you think about their *product range* where 1 is the lowest score and 5 is the highest (score 6 for don't know). REPEAT FOR Vestric, Fosters, Mawdsley's and UniChem.
>
> | Score | Hills | Vestric | Fosters | Mawdsley's | UniChem |
> |---|---|---|---|---|---|
> | 1 | ( ) | ( ) | ( ) | ( ) | ( ) |
> | 2 | ( ) | ( ) | ( ) | ( ) | ( ) |
> | 3 | ( ) | ( ) | ( ) | ( ) | ( ) |
> | 4 | ( ) | ( ) | ( ) | ( ) | ( ) |
> | 5 | ( ) | ( ) | ( ) | ( ) | ( ) |
> | 6 | ( ) | ( ) | ( ) | ( ) | ( ) |

Semi-structured questionnaires

Semi-structured questionnaires give the interviewer more latitude in questioning. A semi-structured questionnaire has fewer pre-coded answers, leaving the respondent free to reply in his own words. The interviewer is allowed, and encouraged, to probe responses and so add clarity to what was said. If a respondent said he bought a product because he thought it was good quality, the interviewer would ask what was meant by 'good quality'. Equally, if a respondent was asked to name manufacturers of a product, the answer would normally be followed by a probe to find out if any more manufacturers are known. Questions may require the respondent to explain why he does something, in which case it may be necessary to ask a supplementary probe about one aspect of the answer, such as 'What do you mean by that?'.

Thus, a semi-structured questionnaire gives the interviewer the framework of questions to ask, but it also encourages the exploration of responses. In turn, the respondent is left free to express some views in his own words. The questions in Table 9.2 are taken from a semi-structured questionnaire which was used to guide 100 visit interviews with companies that use electrical contractors.

It should be noted that this classification covers those questionnaires which are a combination of fully structured and semi-structured questions, as well as those in which all the questions have a degree of latitude.

Semi-structured questionnaires are the most common type used in business marketing research. The wide range of different types and sizes of company that are encountered usually makes structured questionnaires too limiting. It is almost impossible to design a questionnaire on, say, the subject of cleaning chemicals used in commercial kitchens which is appropriate to the central buyer at Trust House Forte and the proprietor who runs the local Red Lion public house and restaurant. Forcing answers into response categories which suit the researcher is a frustration to the respondent and the true answer may not be flushed out.

For example, a structured question may read:

> I would like to read out a list of factors that you could consider important when choosing a supplier of . . . . Would you tell me which is most important in guiding your selection of supplier? (RANK 1). Which is second most important? (RANK 2).
>
> | ROTATE ORDER OF LIST | RANK |
> |---|---|
> | Delivery within a week | ____ |
> | Delivery on the date promised | ____ |
> | At least 25 per cent discount | ____ |
> | The reliability of the products | ____ |
> | Credit of 90 days | ____ |

Researching Business Markets – The IMRA Handbook

Table 9.2. *Semi-structured questions*

Q2a. I am particularly interested in the things that motivate you to select one electrical contractor in preference to another. What is it that you look for more than anything else when making your choice?

_____

_____

Q2b. IF PRICE NOT MENTIONED IN Q2a ASK: What about price? How important is this?

_____

_____

Q2c. IF NO MENTION OF QUALITY IN Q2a ASK: And what about the reputation of the company?

_____

_____

Q2d. IF NO MENTION OF TECHNICAL ABILITY IN Q2a ASK: What importance do you attach to the technical ability of the electrical contractor – to undertake technically difficult jobs?

_____

_____

Q2e. IF NO MENTION OF DESIGN CAPABILITY IN Q2a ASK: And what about the ability of the contractor to work on control circuit designs, plc designs and the like?

_____

_____

Q3. Would you ever select a company that you have never used before? *Probe*: What would motivate you to do so?

_____

_____

Questionnaire Use and Design

An analysis of the results may show that reliability is the key requirement, because it is ranked first more often than any other response. However, the researcher is left uncertain as to whether the respondent is tolerant of a certain level of unreliability or none at all. Is he saying that products are generally unreliable and therefore he is motivated to choose those that are most reliable, or is he saying that he will only choose zero defect products? It is unclear whether his concern about reliability is for a short period (which in industrial terms may be for one to three years) or if he requires reliability for many years. An open-ended question which asked simply 'Tell me the important considerations when you are choosing a supplier', followed by probing, would be more likely to give the true reasons for selection.

Questions with pre-coded answers and those which are left open-ended are not mutually exclusive. Frequently a semi-structured questionnaire would ask an open-ended question first and then follow it with one that was pre-coded. This type of questioning enables the researcher to obtain the unbiased and free response, as well as achieving a quantitative measure.

Unstructured questionnaires

Unstructured questionnaires are sometimes called discussion guides, topic guides, or checklists. Unlike structured and semi-structured questionnaires, they are not used as a form on which to write the answers during the interview. Instead they act as an *aide-mémoire* to the researcher of the points that he would like to discuss. The responses are then either written down on a pad or taped for subsequent transcription.

Whereas the structured questionnaire is rigid, the unstructured questionnaire is totally flexible. The order and precise working of questions are decided during the interview to suit the nature of the respondent's business. In Table 9.3 there is an example of a checklist of questions used in a group discussion to determine electricians' attitudes to protective sprays and fillers.

Unstructured questionnaires are used where the interviewer wants to explore a subject in depth. The boundaries of the discussion may not be known and so the interview is often exploratory. Unstructured interviews are used:

Table 9.3. *Unstructured questions*

Attitudes to Protective Sprays and Fillers

Introduce the reason for the study.

INTRODUCTION

In what type of work do the respondents specialise? What type of work do they enjoy?

How important is industrial work to them? What type of person is suited to this type of work?

What special skills are required to do industrial work as opposed to domestic electrical contracting?

What are the hallmarks of a well finished job? How important is this nowadays?

What annoys electricians when they have to follow a job some time after somebody else? PROBE: messy work; nuts and bolts seized up; joints not been left safe?

SPRAYS

What types of aerosol sprays do electricians carry in their bags? What are they used for? PROBE: are they ever used to **protect** equipment, eg nuts, bolts and terminations from corrosion and from water ingress?

Who buys these sprays? Who requests their purchase? What is the attitude of the management to their purchase? PROBE: are they seen as an unnecessary expense by management?

What brands of sprays are used? Why?

How many cans of WD-40 or equivalent are used per electrician per annum?

What are attitudes to a special silicone spray that protects a job – say, a distribution panel or other electrical enclosure? PROBE: what is known about silicone? What are its strengths and weaknesses?

(and so on)

Questionnaire Use and Design

- to find out from users of products or services how things are done and how they could be done better;
- to find out from users why they buy from certain companies and what would induce a change of supplier;
- to find out from those who have an overview of a market what they know about the market size, the shares of suppliers, trends and so on.

Unstructured interviews can be used in any application where a structured or semi-structured interview is used, except that they would be administered to only a handful of people and would give much more depth. Unstructured interviewing is not used in mass interviewing programmes, because it is difficult to control and analyse when there are more than about 20 respondents. Some or all of the interviews may be carried out by the researcher who wrote the questionnaire. It is very difficult to analyse the copious notes which are generated by large numbers of this type of interview.

The unstructured interview is usually carried out during a visit to a company as this permits probing in depth. However, it is often also used to guide telephone interviews, though the list of questions that can be covered is, in this case, necessarily restricted. Finally, the unstructured questionnaire is used as a guide by a moderator in a group discussion.

A classification of question types

It has been shown how questionnaires can be classified according to their type – so too can the questions be classified within the questionnaires. Marketing researchers recognise three types of question:

1. questions that show what people do – in the context of a business-to-business survey this may be how much they buy, how frequently they buy etc (these are *behavioural* questions);
2. questions that show people's attitudes to things – their image of products or companies, why they buy in a particular way etc (these are *attitudinal* questions);

3. questions that show how one company differs from another (these are *classification* questions).

An understanding of the different types of question is fundamental to designing questions for a questionnaire.

Behavioural questions

Behavioural questions produce answers to queries as to what a person or company does:

- how often it buys a product;
- how much it buys at the present;
- how much it expects to buy in the future;
- when it buys;
- who it buys from;
- what it uses the products for;
- who makes the buying decision or writes the specification;
- what role each person plays in the buying decision.

Behavioural questions should lead to factual answers. In one respect they are easy to ask, for if the respondent is knowledgeable and co-operative the questions are easy to answer. Most buyers will be able to say how much of a product they buy. Complications arise with respondents who may lack the whole picture, or where information is divided among different people. For example, to ask an architect what type of bricks he specifies may be straightforward. Finding out the value of the bricks he specified in the last 12 months may be more difficult, and asking him to estimate the value of the brick purchases for the whole practice may encourage a wild guess.

Good behavioural questions must be sensible and relevant to the respondent. It is better to ask a motor factor how many clutches he buys in a month than in a year, because a month is the timescale within which most factors work.

Behavioural questions can be asked in open-ended fashion or within ranges. Respondents usually feel more comfortable giving an answer

Questionnaire Use and Design

between prescribed limits than having to give free response. In a survey on smoke detectors, where interviews were carried out with buyers in major retail stores, the pilot question was as follows:

> Would you tell me how many smoke detectors you bought over the last twelve months? I am only interested in an approximation.

There were many refusals to the question. When it was changed so that the interviewer could ask for the purchases within ranges, the response rate was much higher. Respondents felt less inhibited giving their purchases between quite large limits, and yet this was a sufficiently accurate response within the objectives of the study:

> Would you say that the number of smoke detectors you have purchased over the last twelve months was (READ OUT RESPONSES):
>
> None   ( )
> Less than 5,000   ( )
> 5,000 to 20,000   ( )
> 20,000 to 50,000   ( )
> 50,000 to 100,000   ( )
> Over 100,000 (specify approximate number).................

Attitudinal questions

Attitudinal questions give insights into people's opinions on a company or a product. They show views on a subject and why those views are held. Behavioural questions help to quantify aspects of a market; attitudinal questions show how to improve a company's position in a market. Typically, attitudinal questions cover subjects such as:

- What do you think of a supplier?
- Why do you hold these views on this supplier?
- What do suppliers do well?
- What do suppliers do badly?
- How could suppliers improve?

In a similar vein, attitudinal questions give answers concerning the acceptability or otherwise of a new product.

As with behavioural questions, those which explore attitudes can be open-ended or closed. For example:

What do you think of Volvo trucks in terms of their reliability?

or the question could be asked in such a way that some *measurement* is obtained, as to the reliability of Volvo trucks:

What score would you give Volvo trucks in terms of their reliability on a scale from 1 to 5, where 1 is very unreliable and 5 is very reliable? (SCORE 6 FOR DON'T KNOW.)

(It is usual in questions which involve a scale to give the respondent a card on which the scale is spelt out in full. The scale can be any number of points but it is usually 5 or 10.)

Classification questions

Classification quesetions give information to the researcher that helps to construct a profile on the type of company or respondent that has answered. This information is useful for combining certain types of companies together so that their behaviour and attitudes can be compared and contrasted.

Examples of ways in which business marketing researchers classify companies are:

- according to whether they buy a product or service, or not;
- according to whether or not they have had experience of a product;
- by the size of the purchases of a product or service;
- by number of employees;
- by the industry in which it is positioned (the Standard Industrial Classification);
- by the region in which the company is located (eg Scotland, the North, the Midlands, the South).

There are many more ways in which a company can be classified and, indeed, behavioural and attitudinal questions can be used for classification purposes. A survey carried out on behalf of accountants may analyse the findings according to the frequency with which companies are in contact with their accountant for whatever reason. The 'frequency of contact' question is behavioural in nature, but it is useful in a classification capacity.

Classification questions are frequently positioned at the front of a questionnaire because the researcher needs to screen out companies that are ineligible for interviewing:

> Before I begin, can I check that your company uses double-sided adhesive tape. (IF NO, THANK AND CLOSE. IF YES, ASK Q1.)

Classification questions are also often located at the end of the questionnaire where they may be introduced thus:

> Just a few questions now to help me classify the answers you have given me. How many people work at your establishment, both staff and works combined?
>
> | | |
> |---|---|
> | Less than 25 | ( ) |
> | 25–100 | ( ) |
> | 101–250 | ( ) |
> | 251–500 | ( ) |
> | Over 500 | ( ) |
>
> (NOTE TO INTERVIEWER: CODE INDUSTRIAL CLASSIFICATION AND REGION)
>
> | | |
> |---|---|
> | Manufacturing | ( ) |
> | Government/local authority | ( ) |
> | Distribution | ( ) |
> | Other services | ( ) |
> | North | ( ) |
> | Midlands | ( ) |
> | South | ( ) |

These classifications are simply by way of example, and interviewers would need a thorough briefing to ensure that they fully understood definitions such as 'other services' or the boundaries of the North, Midlands and South geographical regions, within the context of the particular research project.

Principles of questionnaire design

The basic types of questionnaire, and the classes of question that they contain, have now been described. The next stage is to look at the more detailed aspects of questionnaire design.

The effect of the interview medium

Once the decision has been taken as to how the information is going to be collected – whether by telephone, personal visit or self-completion – some of the main elements of questionnaire design fall into place. Each method demands special care in the types of question which are used, and these are discussed in more detail in later sections of this Chapter. For now, the simple rules are:

- Telephone interviews:
  - keep questions simple;
  - keep the questionnaire short (15 minutes maximum);
  - no visual prompting is possible, so verbal clarity is essential.
- Personal visit (face-to-face interviews):
  - make the interview interesting;
  - build in open-ended questions to explore the subject;
  - be prepared to be flexible to meet the special needs of the respondent.
- Self-completion (or postal):
  - make the questions clear – there is no opportunity for seeking clarification at a later stage;
  - make the questions visually attractive;
  - make completion easy from the respondent's point of view.

Keeping the respondent in mind

A questionnaire has to work. It has to be successful in taking the respondent smoothly through the interview in such a way that he is helped in providing accurate answers to the questions. Too often questionnaires do not work because the researcher has failed to see the questions from the point of view of the respondent. Bad question-

Questionnaire Use and Design

naires are those where the designer has thought about what he wants out of the survey, but not thought about the ability of the respondent to give it. This leads to questions which are too long, which are unintelligible (at least to the respondent) and which are too complicated.

The first principle of questionnaire design, therefore, is to ask, 'What are *all* the possible answers that I can think of to this question?'.

Keeping the objectives in mind

In business marketing research, there are often a number of research approaches used to achieve the overall objective – desk research, interviews with people holding an overview, interviews with distributors, interviews with end-users etc. There will, of course, be an overall goal for the study as a whole. However, the researcher should think about the subsidiary objectives of each of the component parts of the study that involve fieldwork and interviewing. If end-users are to be interviewed, what information is being sought from them? If distributors are to be interviewed as well, what is hoped to be learned from them? The subsidiary goals of these fieldwork programmes should be listed.

For example, a foreign manufacturer of storage heaters wanted to enter the UK market by selling his products to builders, especially those who might use them in refurbished buildings. After discussions with the researcher, it was decided to use the telephone to collect the data and to carry out interviews with 100 builders across the country. The specific subjects that were to be covered in the telephone survey were listed by the researcher and the client and they included the following:

- the proportion of builders who installed storage heaters in the last year;
- how many storage heaters are required by those builders who do specify them;
- the types of buildings in which the storage heaters are used;
- the people who make the decision to specify storage heaters;

Researching Business Markets – The IMRA Handbook

Table 9.4. *Questionnaire based on survey objectives*

ASK TO SPEAK TO PERSON RESPONSIBLE FOR SPECIFYING HEATING EQUIPMENT IN BUILDING/RENOVATION PROJECTS

Good morning/afternoon. My name is .... from Business & Market Research in Manchester. I am working on a survey of the electric storage heater market and I would like to ask you a few questions on this subject. It will only take a few minutes. Can you help me?

Q1 During the last year have you specified electric storage heaters in any of your new building or renovation projects? CIRCLE RESPONSE
    Yes   1
    No   2   *Close*

Q2 How many electric storage heaters were fitted in these projects in the last year? PROMPT

1 to 25	1	251/500	5
26/50	2	501/750	6
51/100	3	751/1000	7
101/250	4	1000+	8

Q3A What factors led you to specify this type of heating rather than other methods such as gas central heating? Anything else?

_____

Q3B And who influenced you to specify electric storage heaters? Anybody else?

Q3C In what ways did they influence you?

_____

Q4A In what types of building have you specified electric storage heaters? READ AND PROMPT FROM LIST BELOW
Q4B ASK IF MORE THAN ONE CATEGORY Of all the electric storage heaters you specified in the last year, what proportion were in new private homes? READ OUT AND ASK FOR EACH CATEGORY

Category	Q4A	Q4B
NEW HOMES		
Private	1	____%
Housing Association	2	____%
Public Sector	3	____%
REFURBISHMENT		
Private	4	____%
Housing Association	5	____%
Public Sector	6	____%
NON DOMESTIC		
New	7	____%
Refurbishment	8	____%

Questionnaire Use and Design

- the factors that lead to the specification of storage heaters rather than some other method of heating.

Once the objectives were listed, the researcher was able to compose specific questions. In some cases, decisions had to be made as to whether a question should be open-ended (to cater for responses which could cover a wide area, and which could not be anticipated), or closed (where a response could be anticipated, so that by building it into the questionnaire it was a help to both the interviewer and the coding process).

Some of the questions which emanated from the above listing of subjects are given in Table 9.4 (as is customary, instructions to the interviewer are given in capitals).

Getting the question style right

The researcher has two important choices to make as each individual question is being created:

- Will it be open-ended or closed?
- If it is closed, will it be single or multiple choice?

Open-ended questions are used where the response possibilities are wide-ranging, so much so that an attempt to pre-empt them could be limiting to the survey. For example, if the complete list of applications for flexible couplings is not known (nor is it likely to be) it may be better to leave the question open-ended:

> Which products does your company make that incorporate flexible couplings?

That is not to say that a closed question (ie one with pre-coded answers) must be read out to the respondent. The answers may be there for the convenience of the interviewer. For example:

> How is the flexible coupling attached to the shaft? DO NOT PROMPT
> Taperlock ( )
> Tapershaft ( )
> Parallel shaft/keyway ( )

On a large interviewing project, pre-coded questions can lead to greater efficiency. However, it is important to take care that the pre-codes do not mask the true meaning of the response. In the following question on liquid roofing systems:

> In which sectors do you consider it appropriate to specify liquid roofing systems? MULTI-RESPONSE
> Private house building ( )
> Public house building ( )
> Industrial ( )
> Commercial ( )
> Public sector ( )

a respondent may give a highly qualified answer, saying that these systems are most suited to large flat roofs, which in his experience are mainly found in industry. However, he may go on to say that there are circumstances, such as flat roofs on schools and hospitals, where the system can be appropriate. In recording this answer, the interviewer would place a tick in both the 'industrial' and the 'public sector' boxes and the nuance of the response would be lost.

Some closed questions are single-response and some are multi-response. It may be helpful to the interviewer to have an instruction on the questionnaire flagging the occasions where a multi-response is permitted (as in the above example). In a single-response question it is essential to accept just one answer. Typical of a single-response closed question is a five point scale:

> Having seen the new flexible coupling, and without any commitment to buying it, how suitable or unsuitable would it be for your company's needs? SHOW CARD WITH SCALE
> Very suitable ( )
> Quite suitable ( )
> Neither suitable nor unsuitable ( )
> Not very suitable ( )
> Not suitable at all ( )

Bearing the method of analysis in mind

The style of questions will, in part, be determined by the method of data analysis that is to be used. If only half a dozen interviews are

Questionnaire Use and Design

carried out and each is in depth, the analysis will probably involve the researcher in reading the written notes taken during the interview and then using these to build a qualitative report.

Where there are 20 or more interviews it is normal for some form of quantification of response to take place. With a small number such as this it is normal to build up a tabulation of all the responses in columns on analysis paper or a computer spread-sheet. By a glance over the analysis, responses that are exceptional can be seen to stand out and a total view can quickly be gained by summing the columns. Weighting can easily be applied if the results are on a spread-sheet. When semi-structured interviews are analysed on a spread-sheet it is not necessary to make special provisions in the design of the questionnaire.

In larger-scale interviewing programmes, the results will most probably be analysed by computer, using software designed for the purpose. The software accepts single or multi-code responses and allows the researcher to filter and cross-analyse the results by any selection of questions.

It is necessary that the researcher who designs the questionnaire is familiar with the analysis package which will be used. For example, the following information may be required from a respondent:

What proportion of the products that you buy are sourced from:

	%
Builders merchants	_____
DIY sheds	_____
Other distributors	_____
Direct off manufacturer	_____
Total	100

Most computerised analysis programmes would cope better with answers to this question if it were laid out thus:

What proportion of the products that you buy are sourced from:

	0%	1–10%	11–40%	41–65%	66–99%	100%
Builders merchants	( )	( )	( )	( )	( )	( )
DIY sheds	( )	( )	( )	( )	( )	( )
Other distributors	( )	( )	( )	( )	( )	( )
Direct off manufacturer	( )	( )	( )	( )	( )	( )

Researching Business Markets – The IMRA Handbook

Although this layout is more suited to computer analysis, it limits the data since they are forced into ranges. In most studies this is acceptable – even desirable for the respondent as he does not have to be specific – and any calculations can be carried out in the mid-point value of the range.

Responses are usually marked on the questionnaire with a tick in a bracket or a box. When these responses are fed into the computer they are read as a number, and for this reason researchers sometimes provide a number to circle rather than a box to tick. The only other consideration the researcher should give to a question of this type is the facility to code the inevitable refusal or 'don't know' response. A final column (or two if the 'don't know' and the refusals are to be recorded separately) is usually necessary:

What proportion of the products that you buy are sourced from:

	0%	1-10%	11-40%	41-65%	66-99%	100%	DK	Refused
Builders merchants	( )	( )	( )	( )	( )	( )	( )	( )
DIY sheds	( )	( )	( )	( )	( )	( )	( )	( )
Other distributors	( )	( )	( )	( )	( )	( )	( )	( )
Direct off manufacturer	( )	( )	( )	( )	( )	( )	( )	( )

Getting the words right

As has been emphasised, business research interviewing is usually more of a discussion than a rigid interview. However, this does not mean that business questionnaires can allow ambiguous or confusing questions. Good research comes from asking the right questions of the right people. The researcher must avoid words which are:

- jargon or shorthand which may not be understood by the respondent (eg SIC, GDP, purchasing criteria, marque);

- sophisticated or uncommon words (eg salient, rancour, synergy);

- ambiguous words (eg usually, moderate, ordinary).

Questions must be constructed in such a way that they are meaningful to the respondent. The meaning of the question could still be lost because of:

Questionnaire Use and Design

- length – a very long question could lose the respondent part way through;
- bias – the presentation of the question could influence the answer (thus: 'Do you think that the company has a poor record for its service?');
- complexity – if multiple ideas are introduced the meaning could become confused (thus: 'When you buy both aluminium *and* steel strip, do you use a different supplier?');
- conflicting questions – in trying to make a question clearer the result can become confusing (thus: 'Do you care what brand you buy, or would you buy any brand?');
- too many meaningful words – questions should be simple (and not like: 'What motivates and inspires you in the selection or specification or a new supplier?').

Getting the layout right

The questionnaire should ensure the smooth flow of the interview. It needs to ease the respondent into answering the questions and lead him towards difficult and more sensitive issues. Typically, a questionnaire begins with a question that helps the interviewer to understand the nature of the company and at the same time engages the respondent:

Can I start by asking you for how many years you've sold artificial roof slates?
    Less than 2 years   ( )
    2–5 years   ( )
    More than 5 years   ( )
and why did you decide to start selling artificial roof slates in the first place?

As the respondent gets into his stride and the information begins to flow, the questions should be steered towards the more difficult subjects. These may well be questions which aim to find out the names of suppliers, the shares held by suppliers, the prices which are paid, and the amounts of products or services which are purchased. Where the sensitivity of such questions is great, they should be located at the end of the questionnaire. In this way the interviewer has a reasonable chance of success, as the respondent has become conditioned to answering and, at the very worst, an abandoned interview at this late stage would have yielded some answers.

Checking questions

Very often in business marketing research the subject is complex. With the best will in the world it may be difficult to design *simple* questions. Furthermore, some questions may be absolutely critical to the whole project. It is easy in the heat of the interview to mis-report and add an extra few noughts to the quantity of product bought. The figure 15 can sound like 50 over the telephone.

It is advisable, therefore, to include a number of check questions at critical points. These may be straightforward probes: 'Can I just check on that figure you gave me? Did you say ...?', or they could be questions designed to give the same answer but asked in a different way. For example, a builder may be asked about the total number of window frames he installs in a year while a later question could ask how many of the frames were softwood, hardwood, plastic, steel or aluminium. The addition of the volumes of the different types of frame should, of course, produce the overall figure that was given earlier.

Piloting questionnaires

In large quantitative marketing research studies it is important to 'pilot' the questionnaire (to test it on a small, reasonably representative sample of respondents). It is very important to get the questions right in business marketing research questionnaires, especially where a few hundred highly structured ones are to be carried out. However, for the business marketing researcher, piloting the questions to make sure that they are right can be a continuous process and not a special exercise. It is unusual to waste interviews in business marketing research – every one counts. For example, if after an interview programme has started it is determined that a question needs changing, it would be quite normal to go back to the early respondents and run through the modifications with them.

The best way of testing a questionnaire is for the researcher who designed it to administer the first few interviews. Misunderstandings, problems with the flow, difficult-to-answer questions and better ways of asking them can become glaringly apparent within the first half-dozen interviews.

The use of computers in questionnaire design

It may be of some comfort to the novice marketing researcher to know that it is quite normal to draft and re-draft questionnaires. To design the perfect questionnaire at a first sitting is seldom possible, and the final product will almost certainly contain compromises.

The drafting process can be made easier by computers. Word processing packages allow the researcher easily to insert or copy questions, and move them around the document. Repetitious actions such as drawing brackets, boxes, or phrases can be undertaken with a couple of key strokes.

An alternative to the word processor is proprietary software for questionnaire design and analysis. 'Marquis' software, from System Makers of Stockport, combines both questionnaire design and analysis functions. Each question is designed with prompts that ask if it is open-ended or closed and, if closed, the researcher is asked to say if the response will be single or multiple choice. Questions can be copied and moved, in which case the question and routeing numbers are automatically altered. The questionnaire is presented in a neat formatted structure so that the researcher does not need to be concerned with tabs and margins as is necessary when using a typewriter or word processor. (There are other packages available to help in questionnaire construction and, of course, in data analysis but 'Marquis' is the only one at present that can do both.)

Pitfalls of questionnaire design

In business marketing research there is no such thing as the perfect questionnaire. The variability of response is so great that there are sure to be some respondents who find difficulty in relating to the question. However, there are a number of common pitfalls that the researcher should aim to avoid.

- *Length.* There is a temptation to include as many questions as possible in a questionnaire on the grounds that the greatest cost is getting hold of the respondent in the first place. This leads to lengthy questionnaires that alienate respondents and yield questionable data because the respondent tires as the interview drags on. The ideal length of the three different types of questionnaire covered in this Chapter are:
  - telephone interviews: 5 to 15 minutes;
  - personal visit interviews: half an hour to two hours;
  - self-completion: four sides of A4 (say, 20 to 30 questions).

- *Leading questions.* Researchers must be objective and so must be their questions. A question that leads a respondent towards an answer is loaded and the answer cannot be trusted. When lists of companies (or factors influencing the buying decision) are read out to respondents, it is good practice to rotate them so that there is no bias favouring those that are mentioned first.

- *Inconsiderate questions.* Questions that ask too much of a respondent should be avoided. In most situations it would not be reasonable to expect a respondent to remember which companies he dealt with 10 years ago. Similarly, it would not be considerate to read out a long list of factors and then ask the respondent to rank or rate them – his power of recall would be taxed to the limit, and the quality of the response would be suspect.

- *Questions which miss the mark.* Questions should be as crisp and clear as possible. Those that are too broad could miss the mark. For example, a question that asked which journals are read may lead to the inclusion of those that cover personal interest and hobbies, and the trade magazines of actual interest may not be mentioned.

- *Poor layout or sequence.* Questions that follow a confusing or illogical order will lose the respondent. Complicated routeing may lose the interviewer or at least cause disruptions in the flow of the questioning which break the respondent's concentration.

Questionnaire Use and Design

- *Language and jargon.* It is perfectly acceptable to use everyday speech in questionnaires – indeed, they are less stilted as a result. Because questions are spoken, it is better to design conversational questionnaires rather than those that are elegant examples of the written word. However, complex and unusual words and jargon must be avoided (except where, as mentioned earlier, jargon terms are known to be 'common currency', and so help with comprehension).

Special issues associated with telephone questionnaires

In this Chapter it has been shown how questionnaires can be classified according to whether they are structured, semi-structured or unstructured. All these types of questionnaires can be administered over the telephone but care is required to cope with the limitations of this research medium.

With very few exceptions, business respondents are within access of a telephone. Interviews carried out by telephone save time and cost when compared with face-to-face interviews. They are by far the most common research method used in business marketing research whether as a simple 'dipstick' survey or as the backbone of a major study.

The telephone is a barrier to communication. The eye contact and gesticulation which are part of everyday speech are clearly not possible. It is also a very immediate tool, demanding a continuous smooth flow of words and considerable clarity in communication. The questionnaires that are used for telephone interviews need to be constructed very carefully.

Designing telephone questionnaires

A number of rules must be applied to the construction of telephone questionnaires:

- they must have a short, hard-working introduction that quickly communicates the purpose of the study and explains what is required. The aim should be to engage the respondent in the first question as soon as possible: 'Good morning/afternoon. This is . . .

from Business and Marketing Research in Manchester. I am carrying out a survey on products which you buy for concrete reinforcement. My questions will only take a few minutes and I wondered if you could help me. Can I check that you are the person who decides what makes of concrete reinforcement you use?'.

- It can be good practice to offer the respondent a benefit for helping in the study, no matter how tenuous: 'Your answers will be built into a nationwide study aimed at improving the standards of products and service in the supply of reinforcement products'.

- There may also be the need to make it clear that answers will be treated in confidence: 'Naturally, anything you say will be treated in confidence and will not be identified with you personally'.

- Questions should be short and clear – long and complicated questions are to be avoided.

- The first questions in the questionnaire should be used to 'qualify' the respondent and his company, by asking about the nature of its business or the way in which the product is used. This will help the interviewer by providing a better understanding of the company (if the question is simple and straightforward, the respondent will be eased into his task and become more likely to answer the difficult questions which come later).

Types of questions suited to telephone questionnaires

Simple questions that demand simple answers are most suited to telephone interviewing. Straight factual questions to which the respondent can quickly give a response are ideal. These tend to be behavioural questions:

- 'Do you buy . . . . ?'
- 'Approximately how many do you buy?'
- 'Who do you buy them from?'

If an attitudinal question is to be asked, it should be kept simple. It is perfectly acceptable to ask 'Why', although the interviewer must be prepared to probe constantly to find out if there is anything else. This

Questionnaire Use and Design

is necessary because the telephone encourages the respondent to keep the answer to a minimum, and yet there may be other responses that need teasing out.

In telephone questionnaires, consideration should be given to using scores to obtain answers to attitudinal questions. After just a little explanation, the respondent can quickly run through a number of supplementary questions. For example:

> I would like you to think about a number of factors that could influence your choice of suppliers. After I have read out the factor, could you tell me how important it is by giving it a score out of 5 where 5 is very important and 1 is not very important? First would you give AVAILABILITY a score out of 5? REPEAT QUESTION FOR:
> - PRICE
> - QUALITY OF BUILD
> - GUARANTEE
> - SIZE OF PRODUCT RANGE

Types of question not suited to telephone questionnaires

Questions that are not suited to telephone interviewing are those that are difficult to ask or to answer, those that are lengthy and those that are complicated. Any question that requires the interviewer to use a visual aid is clearly not suited to a telephone interview.

It is possible that the researcher could rethink a question to make it suitable for the telephone. For example, in a face-to-face interview respondents may be asked to describe their future buying patterns. This 'projective' style of questioning is more difficult on the telephone, and so the researcher may try to uncover future buying trends with a series of simpler questions:

> Imagine that your current purchases of . . . are equal to an index of 100 now. What do you think the index would be in 1995? Why do you say that?

Briefing notes for telephone interviews

Very often, telephone interviews are carried out by someone other than the person who designed the questionnaire. Instructions to the interviewer then need to be extremely clear. In the text of the questionnaire it is normal to highlight the instructions by the use of capital letters or emboldening.

Interviewers need to be personally briefed on the content of the questionnaire and how it should be administered. It is sometimes good practice to leave the interviewer with a short typed note (one or two pages at the most) which explains the background to the study. The note should cover:

- why the research is being carried out;
- a description of the product, the market or anything else that will help to make the interviewer fully conversant with the market;
- who is to be interviewed (both the type of company and the position of the respondent);
- how many times to phone back;
- questions which need special care, either when they are asked or when the answer is being recorded.

This last item is a reminder to the researcher to insert a check question if experience shows that the answers prove to be difficult to hear or understand.

Special issues associated with face-to-face questionnaires

Face-to-face interviewing has traditionally been the cornerstone of business marketing research, despite losing out to telephone interviewing on cost grounds over the last few years. There is no substitute for speaking to the respondent personally if time and cost will allow.

Very often face-to-face interviews in business marketing research are reserved for uncovering depth – providing more flesh on a subject. They may support some other research technique such as telephone interviewing. In such cases the interviews tend to be semi-structured or unstructured and they may be few in number. They are likely to be with specially selected companies or respondents whose businesses could be very different. Here, greater latitude exists on how the questions are asked. Indeed, some face-to-face interviews are so

Questionnaire Use and Design

flexible that they require the researcher to take 'seat of the pants' initiatives with probes and extra questions that are not on the discussion guide. Clearly, this type of interviewing requires considerable experience.

Designing face-to-face questionnaires

There are fewer rules in the designing of face-to-face interview questionnaires, because the interview situation is more flexible. Any trouble with the understanding of the question can be resolved in the interview itself. The interviewer can return to earlier questions and check on their meaning – perhaps prompted to do so by the answer to a later question.

Some suggestions, rather than rules, for the designing of visit questionnaires are as follows:

- Make the questions engaging (this will be necessary in order to maintain the interest of the respondent for what could be an hour or more);
- Try to get inside the mind of the respondent with questions which ask why and how;
- Include many probes – to find out if there is anything else that can be said, even after a lengthy answer;
- Pace the questionnaire (more time can be spent exploring the background of the subject and getting to know the respondent than is available on the telephone – it should be used to warm the respondent up ready for the tricky questions which come later).

Types of question suited to face-to-face questionnaires

At the onset of a face-to-face interview, when the researcher has completed the introductions, it is useful to pose a general and open-ended question. This could be:

> I would appreciate some background on your company to help me to understand your answers. Would you tell me how your company has developed over the years?

or

Tell me, how is business right now?

The considerable expense of face-to-face interviews means that they must be worthwhile. This is not to say that questions should be asked for the sake of it, but there is no point in carrying out a visit interview if the questions could be asked more quickly and with less fuss over the telephone.

In order to be worth while, face-to-face interview questionnaires must be probing. They must seek to find out how and why respondents act in the way they do. For this reason many questions in such a questionnaire begin: 'Could you explain . . .'. Responses tend to be recorded freely rather than pushed into pre-coded categories.

The use of visual aids in face-to-face interviews

Face-to-face interviews provide an ideal opportunity for using visual aids. Examples of such tools are:

- a simple sketch to illustrate a point (made by either the interviewer or the respondent);
- gauging the reaction to a new product;
- showing 'story boards' or 'scamps' of proposed adverts;
- using pictures and diagrams of products and situations as stimuli to the discussion.

Visual aids are a great focus. They bring the mind of the respondent on to the sample product, an advertisement or a diagram. Since they eliminate confusion by acting as a definition, they are to be encouraged wherever possible.

If a five-point scale is used in a visit interview question, a card can be given to the respondent for use when answering the question. All that would be on the card would be the words of the scale with a number against each line, thus:

1 Very likely
2 Quite likely

3   Neither likely nor unlikely
4   Not very likely
5   Not likely at all.

If the respondent is unable to provide an answer on any point from 1 to 5 because he does not know, the response would be recorded as 6. However, this option is not presented on the card as it could encourage a 'don't know' response.

Certain types of scale questions are better self-completed by the respondent rather than administered. After a short explanation, the respondent can look down the scales and rapidly tick off the answers, thus avoiding the tedium of repeatedly being asked each question and having to call out the answers.

Types of question not suited to face-to-face questionnaires

It will be necessary to ask some simple dichotomous (ie 'Yes' or 'No') or pre-coded questions in the visit interview, but these should not dominate. Too many questions which ask the respondent for an answer on a five-point scale will soon begin to jar. They are not likely to maintain the respondent's interest in an interview which it is hoped will last at least half an hour (less than that and it hardly justifies a visit). Also, it is a waste of an opportunity when probing questions could be asked.

Special issues associated with postal/self-completion questionnaires

Fifteen to twenty years ago, in the formative days of business marketing research and before junk mail had become prolific, researchers could anticipate response rates of 30 per cent or more from postal surveys. Today, the same survey may yield less than a 10 per cent response. A researcher who uses postal questionnaires cannot leave anything to chance. The questionnaire must be clear, precise and invite action.

Factors affecting the response rates to postal questionnaires

Before some of the actual questionnaire design points are considered, it is important to look at how the response rates to postal questionnaires are affected by different personal and design factors.

- *The interest factor.* The factor that influences the response rate of a postal questionnaire, more than anything else, is the interest that the respondent has in the subject. A postal survey aimed at people who have just bought a new truck will generate a high response because they are interested in the vehicle. If the same respondent received a questionnaire asking about the type of pen he uses, the response would be minimal because the subject is unlikely to be of vital interest to him. This fundamental point means that researchers should avoid using postal surveys except when the respondent is likely to be highly motivated to answer.

- *The incentive.* A respondent does not want to feel that his efforts in completing the questionnaire are a waste of time. It is important, therefore, that a strong cover letter be written that explains the purpose of the study and convinces the recipient that his reply matters. If possible the respondent should be given some benefit. This could be the intangible promise of better products or service, or a tangible gift. When the survey is of a small number of key players in a market, the offer of a summary of the findings may encourage the response.

- *The layout.* The questionnaire must be orderly and logical. More than ever there is a need to begin with easy questions – questions that involve simple ticking of boxes – and move later on to those that require more thought. Ideally, the questionnaire should be typeset (or desk-top published) and litho printed. A professionally produced questionnaire will lift the response. (As always there are exceptions; a questionnaire that looked as if it was designed specifically for the recipient by rattling it out on an old typewriter, has been known to yield a high response.) Instructions must be clear – there is no chance of providing any further explanation as to what is really meant by a question. There must be adequate

Questionnaire Use and Design

room to answer questions, especially any that allow a free response.

- *The convenience factor.* It has been emphasised that the successful self-completion questionnaire must be easy to complete. This means that questions with pre-coded answers should be used wherever possible. All the respondent should be asked to do is tick a box. Everything should also be done to make it easy for the respondent to reply. The enclosure of a stamped addressed envelope, or at least a business reply envelope, will raise the response by the odd percentage point.

Designing cover letters for postal questionnaires

The cover letter that accompanies the questionnaire is as important as the questionnaire itself. Unless there is absolute certainty about the name and position of the respondent, it is better to address the letter to a functional title such as 'The Production Manager' or 'The Glass Bottle Buyer'.

The rules that should be applied to the writing of a good cover letter are as follows:

- Explain what the survey is about and why the respondent has been selected.
- As with telephone interviewing, give the respondent a reason for wanting to complete the questionnaire – offer him a benefit of one kind or another.
- Give clear instructions as to what should be done – how to fill in the questionnaire, how to send it back.
- Give an assurance that completing the questionnaire is easy.
- Try to give an element of urgency to the completion and return.
- If it is possible to do so, give an assurance that replies will be confidential.
- Thank the respondent.

An example of a typical letter is given in Figure 9.1.

> The Metal Castings Buyer
> Longlife Tools Ltd
> The Industrial Estate   (Date)
>
> Dear Sir
>
> I am writing to seek your help in a study that I am carrying out of the metal castings market in the UK. Buyers of metal castings from selected companies throughout the country are being asked to take just a few minutes to say how they think suppliers could improve their products and services. Longlife Tools was chosen within the sample and your reply is important to the reliability of the study.
>
> You will see on the enclosed questionnaire that the questions are simple to complete, in the main requiring just a tick in a box. It will not be necessary for you to refer to your files to give the answers.
>
> I have left a space for your company name on the questionnaire as I would like to keep track of the replies. You have my assurance, however, that the answers you give will be totally confidential and no follow-up sales will take place as a result of your help.
>
> My timetable is tight and I need to complete the analysis of the replies by the end of the month. I would be extremely grateful if you could return the completed questionnaire to me straight away. As you will see, a pre-paid envelope is enclosed to speed your reply.
>
> In anticipation, may I thank you for your help.
>
> Yours sincerely
>
>
> Paul Hague

Figure 9.1. *Covering letter for questionnaire*

Types of question suited to postal questionnaires

It has been explained that self-completion questionnaires should be easy to fill in. This means pre-coded answers to questions wherever possible. Dichotomous questions, which need just a 'Yes' or 'No' answer, are the easiest of all to fill in. Scale questions are highly applicable to self-completion questionnaires, because they can be completed quickly by ticking boxes.

Questionnaire Use and Design

The researcher needs to know a great deal about a market to design a workable self-completion questionnaire. This knowledge is required to build in all the pre-codes for the answers. It would not be possible to construct the following question without some previous knowledge of who makes pipe lagging products. (The question is about as complicated as is possible in a self-completion questionnaire.)

Which of the companies listed below would you say has the widest range of pipe lagging products? (TICK ONE COMPANY ONLY IN COLUMN A). And which company has the smallest range? (TICK ONE COMPANY ONLY IN COLUMN B).

	Column A Widest range	Column B Smallest range
Jiffy	( )	( )
Climatube	( )	( )
Jetlag	( )	( )
Tublite	( )	( )
Armaflex	( )	( )
Insultube	( )	( )

Types of question not suited to postal questionnaires

Open-ended questions do not yield a good response in a self-completion questionnaire. Questions that ask for free-ranging explanations get inadequate (and often illegible) answers such as 'because it is good', 'we have always bought it', 'it does its job', and so on. There is no opportunity to probe to find out why it is good, why they always buy it, or in what way it does its job.

Nor is it possible to ask complicated questions in a self-completion questionnaire. A question that asks a builders' merchant for a detailed breakdown of his purchases of pipe lagging products over the last year will not be answered. The researcher stands some chance if pre-coded answers are given and the respondent only needs to complete the question between approximate ranges:

Finally, about how much did your branch spend on all types of pipe lagging last year?
    Under £1,000   ( )

£1,000 to £20,000   ( )
£20,000 to £50,000   ( )
Over £50,000   ( )

In a self-completion questionnaire it is not possible to disclose information piece by piece, as in a telephone or visit interview, because it is not administered and there is no control. It has to be assumed that some respondents will read ahead and therefore become aware of forthcoming questions. In an administered questionnaire the name of the sponsor is often given towards the end, sometimes with special questions to find out what is thought of the company. Such unveiling cannot be used as a self-completion questionnaire.

Complicated routeing must be avoided in postal surveys. Skipping questions creates confusion and leads to errors in completion.

Part III: Analysis, Interpretation and Presentation

The collection of data, quantitative or qualitative, is but the first stage – albeit a major one – in a business marketing research project. Once collected, the data must be analysed so as to provide the greatest possible value from them and the results of such analysis then presented to the sponsor of the research (client or in-house management), in a clear and thorough manner. This presentation must enable the sponsor to take whatever action was implicit in the original request for research.

Part III of the Handbook covers the methods of analysis of data, dealing separately with quantitative and qualitative information. It is completed with a review of the best ways in which to present the results of a survey.

10

Analysis and Interpretation of Quantitative Data

Rick Moore

The production of quantitative data, ie survey information in the form of numerical responses, or precisely coded responses, is a large part of the data acquisition stage of business marketing research. The analysis of such data should be straightforward, but does actually involve definite skills, as outlined in this Chapter.

Introduction

Because of their sequential positions in the overall survey process (it being normal to complete the analysis phase before interpretation), it is logical that the analysis and interpretation of quantitative data are discussed and described in the same part of this Handbook. However, they are, in fact, two quite distinct aspects of the survey process, and require separate treatment within the Chapter.

The analysis of quantitative data, whether by manual or computer methods, lends itself essentially to the employment of a whole range of techniques, basically arithmetical in nature. The interpretation of quantitative data, however, while retaining a significant element of the arithmetical, and increasingly the statistical in terms of the techniques employed, also requires a degree of judgemental skill. Analysis is a scientific, systematic process, while interpretation is something of an art, based on scientific input, market or product knowledge, and creative instinct. Ideally, the interpreter needs to understand the wider perspective against which the findings of the analysis can be evaluated and reported.

Analysis

The analysis of quantitative data involves their accumulation from a series of bits of information on a number of questionnaires, possibly a very large number, into a logical array, from which their pattern can be observed. It is an essentially simple process:

If it's on the questionnaire and it has been properly coded, there is absolutely no reason why it cannot be analysed.

Right from the start

A number of techniques, approaches, methods and styles exist for the analysis of quantitative data. The more widely used will be described in due course. It is appropriate at this stage, however, to position the 'analysis phase' within the context of the survey process as a whole. If data are gathered in the right way, then the analytical process can be made very much more easy.

Conventionally, the sequence of research survey activities runs along the lines of:

1. project definition, covering the question to be answered;
2. sample design, including size, structure, sample frames, selection criteria;
3. questionnaire design and development, piloting, modifications;
4. data collection (by the most appropriate medium – postal, telephone or face-to-face);
5. data preparation, editing, coding, cleaning;
6. analysis;
7. reporting.

(As here, there will frequently be no references to interpretation, which then becomes either an adjunct to analysis or a preface to reporting.)

The above sequence is hard to fault as a survey process. It facilitates the carrying out of certain activities in parallel, with others overlapped,

Analysis and Interpretation of Quantitative Data

in order to minimise the total project duration. For obvious reasons, analysis is positioned towards the end, on the principle that you cannot carry out any analysis until you have data. However, adherence to the survey process order tends to have a detrimental effect on the importance of the analysis specification. Frequently it is not discussed in earnest until the survey is under way. There is a tendency for it to arise under the 'what to do next' heading. It may be given insufficient consideration and, as a result, early recall of the key issues to be investigated may have been diluted. This is quite improper since the analysis requirement is frequently one of the first items for consideration in the marketing information process. If it can be assumed that quantitative survey data, following analysis and interpretation, form a vital input to the marketing information process, then logically the analysis specification should be of crucial concern to the marketing function.

As the marketing information requirement is the driving force behind the majority of marketing research undertakings, it follows that the key requirement, analysed data, should appear in some specific form in the research brief, so that the whole research team knows what it is looking to produce. Too frequently, the convention of preparing a statement of research objectives disguises what the end-user really wants in terms of analysed data.

Thus, the typical objective:

> To measure the current level of awareness (spontaneous, prompted and overall) for Blogg's products, by size of establishment and region

might, with advantage, be supplied in the research brief in the form of the blank table into which the analysed data would slot (as above).

The fewer translations and back-translations that there are between research brief and results, the more accurate will be the end product. Equally, if the marketing information function makes specific requests for hard numbers to complete marketing and business planning processes, the personnel should be persuaded to draw up blank tables and these (in preference, or at least in addition, to verbal objectives) should become an essential element of the research brief and the subsequent proposal and quotation, and should be a primary consideration rather than an incidental one.

Table 10.1. Specimen tabulation

	Establishment size			Region		
Awareness%	1-9	10-99	100+	South	Mids	North
Spontaneous Prompted Total						

The practice of specifying the analysis requirements (or, better still, the data required) early in the process has benefits for virtually every other element of the survey. Sample design, particularly sample size and structure, and the setting of quota controls, can be enhanced if the detailed data requirement is known in advance. (In an ideal world, which market research is not, the levels of error acceptable on any survey estimate should also be specified.)

Questionnaire design is a skilled art, but all too often it involves the art of squeezing 60 questions in the time originally set aside for only 40. Even the rigorous exercising of criteria based on 'need to know', rather than 'it would be nice to know', still contains an element of subjectivity. Replace this by a basic data requirement and it can be more forcibly argued that, if a question is not in the original requirement, it can only be added if the marketing or business plan will accommodate it.

Finally, data coding and editing are too frequently carried out without sufficient knowledge of the end data requirements. This can lead to a disproportionate amount of effort being wasted preparing data to a level of detail not ultimately required, such as coding-out makes and models of equipment when only make details are to be analysed.

Analysis techniques

The essential feature of analysis is the conversion of an unsorted mass of data into an orderly array, a tabulation, on a sheet of paper or on a computer screen. Nowadays the majority of quantitative data analysis

Analysis and Interpretation of Quantitative Data

in business marketing research is carried out by computer. There are several tabulation software packages available; there is a proliferation of computer bureaux specialising in survey analysis; most of the medium and larger full-service market research agencies have their own in-house data processing operations. Although this part of the Chapter is written as for computerised analysis, it is equally applicable to 'hand-powered' methods.

The simplest, and most frequently used, form of analysis is the two-dimensional tabulation (table or matrix – referred to in the remainder of this Chapter as a 'tab'). This has three main elements:

- base (the main data collection category);
- stub (the side or vertical axis subject);
- banner (the cross, top or horizontal axis subject).

As can be seen from Table 10.1, such tabs have a major advantage – their sheer simplicity. In addition to base, stub and banner, the

Table 10.2. *A typical analysis tabulation*

Table W
Q1A Does respondent personally use product
By number of employees
Base: All respondents

Col %

		Number of employees				
	Total	Up to 25	26–99	100–199	200–499	500+
Total	505	249	131	44	33	48
Use product?						
Yes	374	213	91	28	18	24
	74%	86%	69%	64%	55%	50%
No	131	36	40	16	15	24
	26%	14%	31%	36%	45%	50%

example contains a title and a note as to the method of percentaging. In this latter case ('Col %' = percentages of column totals) there are two further options: row percentages, and percentaging on overall total, such that each cell of the table is percentaged on the total base figure. The stub is normally the fundamental issue of the question asked, and the banner gives the breakdown by category, which may have just one set of divisions, or perhaps two or more different kinds of category (such as size and nature).

The category chosen for the banner, the 'standard break', is defined

Table 10.3. *Tabulation with filter*

Table X
Q2A Level of satisfaction with product
By number of employees
Base: All respondents using product

Col %

	Total	Up to 25	26–99	100–199	200–499	500+
Number of employees						
Total	374	213	91	28	18	24
Satisfaction rating						
Very satisfied (5)	123	65	29	10	7	12
	33%	31%	31%	36%	40%	54%
Quite satisfied (4)	112	56	43	2	5	6
	30%	26%	47%	7%	28%	25%
Neutral (3)	23	10	6	3	2	2
	6%	5%	7%	11%	11%	8%
Not very satisfied (2)	78	54	10	8	3	3
	21%	25%	11%	29%	17%	13%
Not at all satisfied (1)	38	28	3	5	1	1
	10%	13%	3%	18%	6%	4%
Mean score	3.5	3.4	3.9	3.1	3.5	4.0

Analysis and Interpretation of Quantitative Data

in the second line of the title ('number of employees'), and its divisions are those used in the questionnaire.

A somewhat more complicated tab introduces a filter, together with a mean score (which invariably helps in interpreting rating scales). An example is shown in Table 10.2.

There is some difference of opinion as to what constitutes a base and what a filter. Primarily a base is a unit of measure such as a respondent or an establishment, an item of equipment, an expenditure, a tonnage, an area or whatever. In other words it defines the units upon which the table is based. In Table 10.1, it is respondents.

A filter, on the other hand, is more properly deemed to be a subset of a base as demonstrated in Table 10.2 which is filtered on to a base of 'all respondents using the product'.

In addition to the definitions already used to describe the computer-generated table, there are a number of other terms in common usage:

- Tab Spec/Analysis Spec: the formal specification of tabulations or the analysis method to instruct the analyst as to what is needed ('the data requirement'),

- Edit Spec: the specification of manual and/or computer-based editing instructions, to ensure logic and consistency of data,

- Report Edit: an edit which lists all records which fail an edit check, in serial number order, reporting the reason for the failure (this enables records to be investigated and 'corrected' on a questionnaire by questionnaire basis),

- Force Edit: a set of instructions which summarily deals with errors arising, by treating each individual type of error in the same way.

Writing the tab specs

The instructions to the analyst must be simple and clear, so that the product of the analysis is unambiguous and lends itself to easy interpretation.

The simple approach
It is certainly true that tab specs have been written on the back of an envelope, and here is one that would just about fit:

Researching Business Markets - The IMRA Handbook

Base: all respondents
No filters
QA - N × STD BK
Unwtd
STD BK = size/activity/region

This specification tells the analyst that all N questions on the

Table 10.4. *Result of a simple tab spec*

Table Y
Q3 Banks with which accounts held
By number of employees and industry
Base: All respondents

Col %

		Number of employees				Industry		
	Total	1-25	26-50	51-100	More than 100	Manu	Dist	Service
Total	108	29	22	28	29	60	28	20
Barclays	28	9	6	7	6	16	8	4
	26%	31%	27%	25%	21%	27%	29%	20%
Lloyds	16	5	1	5	5	6	6	4
	15%	17%	5%	18%	17%	10%	21%	20%
Midland	19	4	5	3	7	11	2	6
	18%	14%	23%	11%	24%	18%	7%	30%
Natwest	26	7	7	5	7	16	8	2
	24%	24%	32%	18%	24%	27%	29%	10%
Other	23	6	1	9	7	10	7	6
	22%	20%	5%	32%	24%	16%	25%	30%
Refused	7	2	3	1	1	4	1	2
	7%	7%	14%	4%	3%	7%	4%	10%

Key:
Manu = manufacture
Dist = distribution

Analysis and Interpretation of Quantitative Data

questionnaire will be analysed, categorised in each case by the standard break (STD BK). All the tables (one for each question) will be based on all respondents, the assumption being that all N questions were asked of all respondents, and the data will be unweighted (Unwtd).

A typical table, for just one question of a series, from a tab spec like that is shown in Table 10.3, deriving from the question:

Q3 With which of the following banks does your company have an account?

Such a tabulation, other than analysing each response by the standard break (which will identify any differences according to establishment size and industry), is essentially a simple analysis of the questions themselves. It ignores the possible impact of one part of the standard break on another, or of one question on another.

Cross-tabbing questions
If it is now assumed that the questions may have a bearing on each other, clearly some kind of more detailed analysis in the form of question-by-question cross-tabs is required.

For instance, there may be two questions such as:

Q4a What make of photocopier did you choose on this occasion? (with three specified makes and 'other'), and

Q4b What was your main reason for purchasing this make? (with three specified reasons and 'other').

Using the simple approach to analyse the response to each question separately, the analysis of Q4a may be revealing, but the same analysis of Q4b would not contribute much, given that the whole purpose of Q4b was to relate the responses to the make selected at Q4a.

A much more useful analysis is given by cross-tabbing the two questions, using one in the stub and one in the banner, as shown in Table 10.4. Purchase price now appears to be the dominant purchasing factor for Make C, and reliability that for Make A.

Use of filters
The next level of 'sophistication' is to apply filters to the base for the tabulation. A distinction should be made between filtering a table

Table 10.5. *Cross-tabbing*

Table Z Q4b Main reason for purchasing make By Q4a Make of photocopier chosen Base: All respondents					Col %
	Total	Make A	Make B	Make C	Other
Total	108	29	22	28	29
Purchase Price	57 53%	4 14%	11 50%	21 75%	21 72%
Reliability	27 25%	18 62%	6 27%	2 7%	1 3%
Specific Features	23 21%	7 24%	5 23%	4 14%	7 24%
Other	1 1%	– –%	– –%	1 4%	– –%

because only that group of respondents were asked that question ('basing out'), and filtering a table in order to introduce a third dimension, based on responses to a totally different question.

An example of basing-out can be seen from the two related questions:

Q7a Have you ever used a next-day delivery service? ('Yes' or 'No'), and

Q7b Which service did you use? (four named companies)

The resultant tab spec would then cover:

Q7b Next day delivery services used, by size and activity.
Base = All respondents using next-day delivery services (Q7a).

Analysis and Interpretation of Quantitative Data

Those respondents not using such a service ('No' to Q7a) are thus filtered out of the analysis.

As an example of the three-dimensional analysis, add to Q7a/Q7b as above, the earlier: 'Q3 With which of the following banks does your company have an account?' This would lead to a tab spec including:

Q7b Next-day delivery services used, by size and activity.
Base = All respondents using next-day delivery services (Q7a) *and* having an account with Barclays Bank (Q3).

The needs of marketing information
The mechanical process of table specification can be applied, even for a long questionnaire. It can be argued that it is sound practice, and lends itself jointly to researcher development and the provision of comprehensive analyses. However, it is also totally questionnaire-driven, as opposed to having been generated from a marketing information standpoint. Too many tab specs are prepared using the systematic build-up approach just described, with the researcher laboriously working through the questionnaire, question by question. This is really only one step removed from the dreaded: 'I want everything analysed in terms of everything else'.

This over-detailed analysis does not have to be the case if the full data requirement is known from the outset. If information-driven analysis is now examined, it can be seen how the function of the questionnaire becomes merely that of a vehicle, which provides the means for fulfilling the marketing information needs. (It should be noted, of course, that if the questionnaire is written with the needs of analysis and of the user of the information firmly in mind, then the questionnaire-driven approach, as just described, may be perfectly satisfactory.)

As an example of this more general approach, let us assume that the marketing function has the following data requirements:

to measure the current levels of awareness, penetration, market share of installed base, share of annual shipments,

and that comparative performance by market segment is required. It follows that the required information would be given by the following tabulations, in each case in terms of total, and by market segment.

A Number of establishments in eligible universe

B Number of estabs aware of brand
   % of A (= level of awareness)

C Number of estabs using product
   % of A (= level of generic usage)

D Number of estabs using brand
   % of A (= level of brand usage = penetration)
   % of B (= level of brand usage amongst those aware)
   % of C (= level of penetration in user establishments)

E Number of products in use (installed base)
   Average number per user (EvC)

F Number of brand in use
   % of E (= brand share)
   Average number per user (FvD)

G Number of estabs acquiring product in last 12 months (shipments)
   % of A (= market activity)
   % of C (= user activity)
   (Difference between above = new business activity)

H Number of estabs acquiring brand in last 12 months
   % of A, C, D (= market, user and customer activity)
   % of G (= share of activity)

I Number of products acquired in last 12 months
   Average number per acquirer (IvG)

J Number of brand acquired in last 12 months
   % of I = share of shipments
   Average number per user (JvH)

Defining the market segments to produce the banner would normally involve the straightforward specification of conventional classification or demographic variables, such as establishment size, industry (SIC Code), or geographical region. The key, of course, is to choose variables which will maximise any differences in performance that might exist. These may relate to internally-held marketing information such as Major Account versus National Sales versus Dealer Network; or they may be the function of an additional item of information collected in the survey, such as satisfaction with supplier, level of marketing activity of suppliers, or value of recent purchase.

In fact, the search for discriminating variables and the specification of tables which provide an analytical tool for management make up the fundamental task of the researcher. Whether it be implemented by the 'bottom up' step-by-step analysis of the questionnaire sequentially, or by the 'top-down' summary approach to the information requirement, is not ultimately important, but the quality and the utility value of the analysis are paramount. For business marketing research to be successful, it must have the prerequisite of satisfying the needs of marketing management. It must be viewed as an integral part of marketing and business planning, and not as an isolated or only partially related event. The tools of the trade are available, but it needs a skilful and informed researcher to use them to their full potential.

Interpretation

Even after the efficient (and, it is hoped, creative and fruitful) implementation of the analysis specification, the job is only partially complete – the creative part is still to come. As stated at the outset, interpretation is something of an art and it could be argued that artists are born, not bred. This, however, is to suggest that the quality of interpretation cannot be improved through training and experience. As this Chapter aims to show, it most definitely can be.

Interpretation is that phase of a research project in which the assembled and analysed data are converted into images, verbal or visual, which can easily be conveyed to those end-users of the project's results, anxious to use them as the basis for decision. The researcher must look at the original research brief, put himself in the position of the end-user, ask all the appropriate questions, and then extract the answers from the analysis.

The methodical approach

To match the two basic approaches to analysis – bottom-up and top-down - there are parallels in the area of interpretation. The bottom-up approach requires that each computer table, or at least each of those worthy of being reported, is provided with a short narrative comment. The advantages of this method include ensuring that virtually every table, and hence every question, is reported. It does, however, tend to produce a lengthy report, in questionnaire order, with insufficient linking and cross-reference. There is probably an excess of the trivial, a lot of explaining of what is very obvious - putting into words what the basic numbers are shouting out - and it almost certainly necessitates a management summary, which is about all that gets any proper attention.

Faced with the task of reporting on trends in product awareness between two points in time, the researcher commences with a set of 'bottom-up' tabulations from the two relevant surveys, as shown in Table 10.5. (These are clearly fictitious, since they indicate an identical sample distribution. Matched samples are an obvious prerequisite for tracking studies, but the ability to match perfectly is rarely achieved.)

Traditionally, the interpreting researcher (not wanting to get involved in data merging, or waiting for the data processing department to produce time-series analysis) would then create additional tables for producing in the report along the following lines, with associated narratives.

1. *Awareness of makes of product - overall situation*

	1989	1990	% Change
Total	108	108	
	%	%	
Make A	41	31	-24
Make B	15	16	+7
Make C	22	35	+59

In 1989 just over four in ten respondents (41 per cent) were aware of Make A and this has now fallen to only three in ten (31 per cent), a drop of 24 per cent. On the other hand, awareness of Make C has increased by nearly 60 per cent, from a base of just over one in five respondents to just over one in three. (This probably reflects the success of the major TV campaign etc.) The situation for Make B is unchanged.

Analysis and Interpretation of Quantitative Data

Table 10.6. *Changes with time*

A1. Product awareness 1989
Q4A Awareness of Makes of Product
By number of employees and industry
Base: All respondents

Col %

		Number of employees				Industry		
	Total	1–25	26–50	51–100	More than 100	Manu	Dist	Service
Total	108	22	28	28	30	60	28	20
Make A	44	6	11	13	14	31	9	4
	41%	27%	39%	46%	47%	52%	32%	20%
Make B	16	2	5	5	4	10	3	3
	15%	9%	18%	18%	13%	17%	11%	15%
Make C	24	8	6	5	5	10	6	8
	22%	36%	21%	18%	17%	17%	21%	40%

A2. Product awareness 1990
Q4A Awareness of Makes of Product
By number of employees and industry
Base: All respondents

Col %

		Number of employees				Industry		
	Total	1–25	26–50	51–100	More than 100	Manu	Dist	Service
Total	108	22	28	28	30	60	28	20
Make A	34	5	9	10	10	25	7	2
	31%	23%	32%	36%	33%	42%	25%	10%
Make B	17	3	4	5	5	9	4	4
	16%	14%	14%	18%	17%	15%	14%	20%
Make C	38	10	8	8	10	19	8	11
	35%	45%	29%	29%	33%	32%	29%	55%

Key:
Manu = manufacture
Dist = distribution

Researching Business Markets – The IMRA Handbook

Awareness of Product A
1989 Vs. 1990

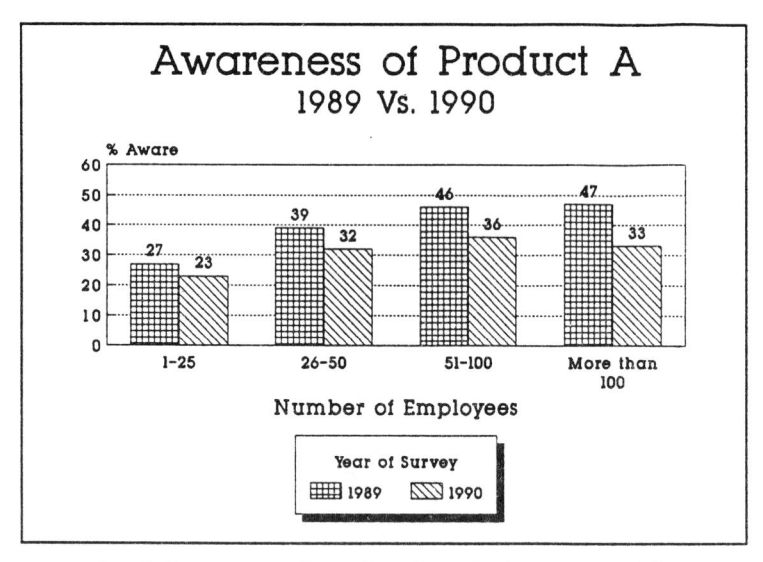

% Aware by Number of Employees:
- 1-25: 27 (1989), 23 (1990)
- 26-50: 39 (1989), 32 (1990)
- 51-100: 46 (1989), 36 (1990)
- More than 100: 47 (1989), 33 (1990)

Awareness has fallen across all size bands with the greater differences occuring in the larger establishment bands.

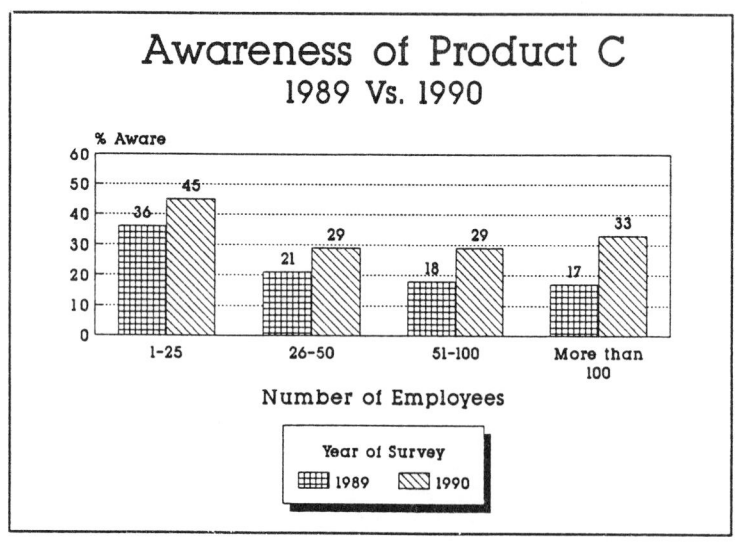

Awareness of Product C
1989 Vs. 1990

% Aware by Number of Employees:
- 1-25: 36 (1989), 45 (1990)
- 26-50: 21 (1989), 29 (1990)
- 51-100: 18 (1989), 29 (1990)
- More than 100: 17 (1989), 33 (1990)

Awareness has increased in line with size of establishment reflecting the direction of advertising and marketing activities

Figure 10.1. *Presentation*

Analysis and Interpretation of Quantitative Data

2. *Awareness of Makes by size of establishment*

Number of employees	Make A 1989 %	1990 %	% Change	Make C 1989 %	1990 %	% Change
1 – 25	27	23	–15	36	45	+25
26 – 50	39	32	–18	21	29	+38
51 – 100	46	36	–22	18	29	+61
101+	47	33	–30	17	33	+94

In 1989, higher levels of awareness of Make A were encountered in the larger establishments with levels reaching 47 per cent at the 101+ employee size. In 1990, however, awareness has fallen across the board, with the greatest drops in awareness among the larger establishments. In contrast, Make C, which experiences comparatively low levels of awareness, especially at the 'top end' of the market, has almost doubled awareness among the 101+ employee size group, and achieved considerable growth in awareness in all size bands. (Their success at the top end gives testament to the wisdom of combining trade press and direct marketing initiatives directed at this sector, in addition to the TV campaign.)

This would all be followed by another table ('3. Changes in awareness by industry') and another narrative, presumably linking industry with size.

This methodical approach is born out of the need to produce a definitive document, largely for the purpose of demonstrating to less-informed management that 'value for money' was obtained. However, there is seldom any direct relationship between the report's volume and its insight, or between number of pages and useful recommendations.

Presentation-led approach

In recent years, two not unrelated developments have taken place. First, the need for a verbal debrief or formal presentation of the survey results has come to precede the need for a fully interpretative report (not least in terms of the timetable of events). Thus top-line results, hot off the laser printer, with bullet point type interpretation and firm (albeit initial) recommendations to provoke thought and discussion, are now the vogue. This trend has been enhanced by a second development, namely that of user-friendly graphics packages for the production of histograms, pie charts, trend lines and so on. These illustrate pictorially the shape of trends, distributions and differences. They can be used in place of numbers, or to complement them. In the same way that numbers, simply expressed, require only a minimum narrative, graphics possibly require even less ('a picture can replace a thousand words'). The illustrations of Figure 10.1 convey much the same message as the more detailed information just developed from Table 10.5.

These changes in presentation have simplified interpretation to a scientific formula:

- Agree the information requirement at the outset.
- Specify analysis in terms of summary output requirements.
- Produce graphical presentations.
- Let the pictures speak for themselves.

In many cases, the presentation material, together with bullet points, a management summary and a technical appendix, now replaces what in the past would have been a weighty tome, just waiting to gather dust. This is not to say that there is no role in the interpretation of quantitative market research information for market or product expertise, or for the drawing on experience from other surveys or secondary data, but there is currently an emphasis on delivering a short sharp blow, possibly with a bit of a blunt instrument, and on getting the hard numbers across in a concise fashion.

11

Analysis and Interpretation of Qualitative Data

Nick Watkins

The gathering of qualitative data is a very subjective process, and usually results in a mass of information. The task of imposing some structure upon it is that of the analyst, and this is almost as subjective as the gathering process, as is described in this Chapter.

Introduction

Qualitative research is essentially unstructured; it is based on a topic list or a very loosely structured questionnaire. In contrast to quantitative research, where the interviewer is trained to read out questions verbatim and to prompt only where instructed, it is by the very nature of qualitative research that the researcher changes the phrasing, sequence and even content of the questions to suit the respondent. This flexibility is essential for qualitative research to fulfil its function of developing hypotheses about market behaviour and providing understanding of the market, rather than measurement of it.

Qualitative research has also been described as an act of discovery and, as with any other exploration, while there is (or certainly should be) a clearly stated goal, the most appropriate route cannot be predetermined and must be changed and adapted as new information or ideas are generated. This shows another critical difference between qualitative and quantitative research. In the latter, data collection and analysis are usually separate and distinct, but in qualitative research they are enmeshed. Data are collected, analysed and the results fed back into the next interview or group discussion; it is an iterative process which generates, tests and refines working hypotheses. The interviewer and analyst are often one and the same.

Another important feature of qualitative research is that it is based on small samples and that sampling is not random but highly purposive. This affects not only how the analysis is conducted, but also how it is interpreted and how it can be validated.

One final observation, at this point, is that qualitative and quantitative research are not two distinct entities but, rather, represent the two ends of a spectrum:

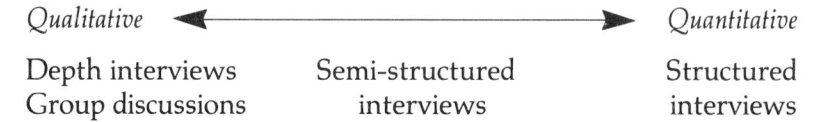

Qualitative ◄─────────────────────►		*Quantitative*
Depth interviews	Semi-structured	Structured
Group discussions	interviews	interviews

This Chapter will concentrate primarily on information derived from groups and depth interviews, but reference will also be made to semi-structured interviewing where relevant.

Sources of qualitative data

As a result of the way in which qualitative research is undertaken, the 'raw' data resulting from it may be in the form of hand-written notes (on a questionnaire form, on a loose-leaf pad, in a notebook or on a scrap of paper), or an audio tape, or a video tape. The written notes will normally have come from a depth (or semi-structured) interview, and the video tape from a group discussion in a studio. Audio recordings may result from an interview or a group discussion, but either form of recording should normally be supported by some written notes, made during or immediately after the event.

The term 'researcher' will be used in this Chapter to describe both the interviewer undertaking a depth interview and the moderator controlling a group discussion. This usage is for the sake of simplicity, and it recognises that the same individual may also undertake the analysis of the data – but the term 'analyst' will be used for that function.

For similar reasons of simplicity, reference will usually be made to the basic data as the result of a series of depth interviews, but this will include the proceedings of group discussions as well.

The characteristics of qualitative business research

All qualitative research seeks to provide an insight into market motivations and attitudes: Why is Brand X used or specified?; What is communicated by this piece of advertising?; What is the image of this company?; How is the market likely to react to this new product? and so on. Even more importantly, all qualitative research aims to discover what is meant rather than just what is said, and all qualitative analysis must ensure that such insight and meaning are revealed.

While it would be naive, indeed foolish, to pretend that corporate decision making is totally rational, the business respondent is forced to operate within the constraints or culture of the organisation. In other words, the extent to which he can impose his own beliefs and attitudes will depend on a host of factors including seniority, the size and complexity of the decision-making unit, the product in question, the size of the organisation, the corporate culture and so on. Conflict between private and corporate beliefs can arise: examples include the Company Secretary who personally supports the National Health Service, but who believes that private medical insurance is a good way of attracting and retaining key staff. Another instance might be the Telecommunications Manager who can see the business argument for cellular telephones, but who privately thinks they are for 'poseurs'. Contrast this with the Sales Manager who craves the particular status symbol but cannot make the business case. It is essential that during both the interviewing and analysis processes these differences are explicitly recognised.

The place of analysis in qualitative research

It has already been stated that a feature of qualitative analysis is its interweaving with the data collection process and the iterative approach. In other words, the analysis starts with the interviewing –

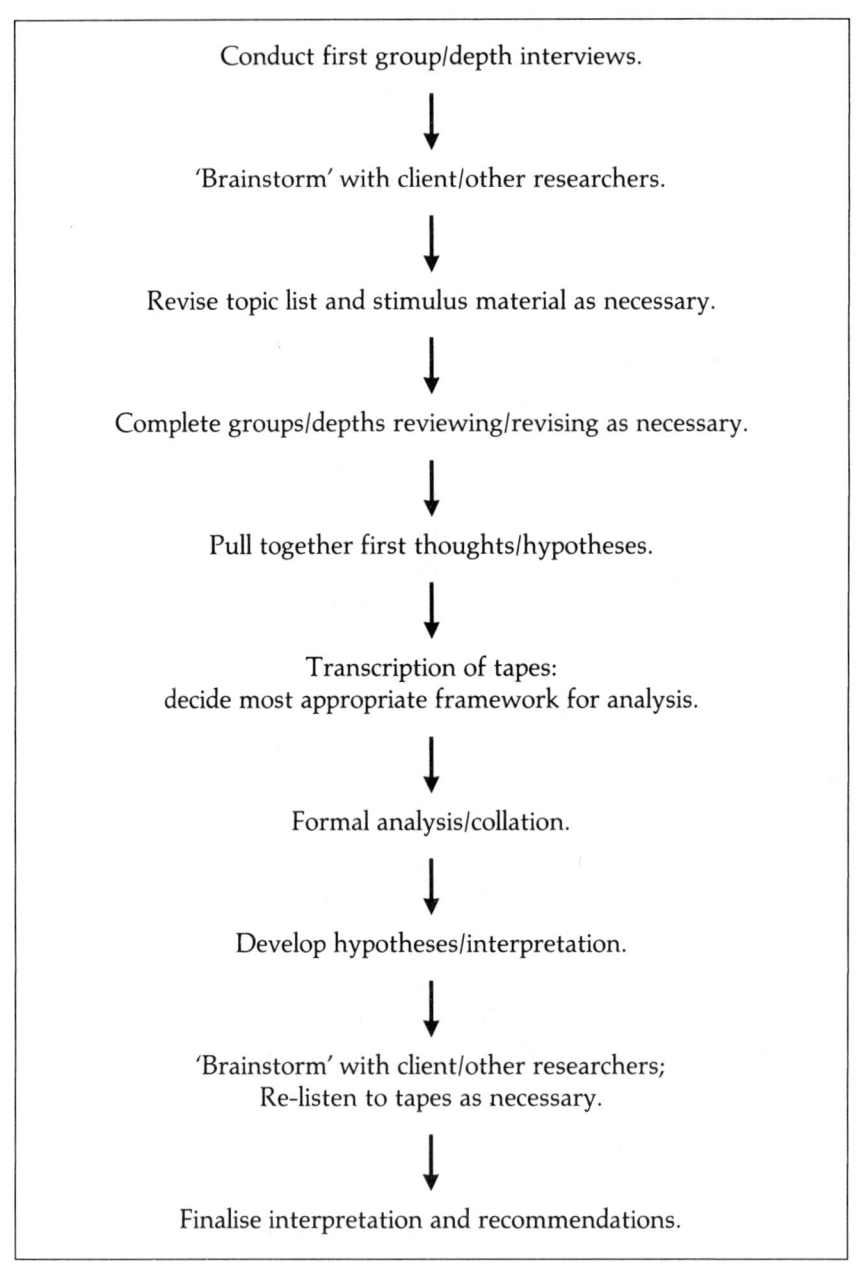

```
Conduct first group/depth interviews.
            ↓
'Brainstorm' with client/other researchers.
            ↓
Revise topic list and stimulus material as necessary.
            ↓
Complete groups/depths reviewing/revising as necessary.
            ↓
Pull together first thoughts/hypotheses.
            ↓
Transcription of tapes:
decide most appropriate framework for analysis.
            ↓
Formal analysis/collation.
            ↓
Develop hypotheses/interpretation.
            ↓
'Brainstorm' with client/other researchers;
Re-listen to tapes as necessary.
            ↓
Finalise interpretation and recommendations.
```

Figure 11.1. *The qualitative research process*

Analysis and Interpretation of Qualitative Data

it is not even at the end of the first group or depth interview but comes earlier as the first responses are assimilated and tested spontaneously against the researcher's implicit hypotheses.

A typical sequence of analysis and interpretation would be as shown in Figure 11.1. This involves three broad stages; an initial overview of the findings, a detailed formal analysis and, finally, the interpretation of those findings.

It can be very beneficial for the researcher to jot down observations, thoughts and ideas immediately after the interview. This is not intended to be a formal or complete analysis, but a record of things said, or unsaid, ideas on what was meant, initial hypotheses and so on, that can be explored in later interviews and put into the subsequent analysis. These can either be recorded on separate sheets of paper or dictated on to the end of the tape recording.

If there is more than one researcher assigned to the project, a 'brainstorming' session at this stage can help to generate hypotheses and establish the most appropriate structure for the next stage.

The analysis process

One of the things that strikes anyone new to qualitative research is the sheer volume of data: hours of tapes, hundreds of pages of interview records, and countless notes and scribbles – there is a huge amorphous mass of words. Perhaps for this reason some practitioners shy away from formal analysis and prefer to rely on 'top-line debriefs' to their clients. This is to be strongly discouraged. Only with a thorough and rigorous analysis can the researcher be sure that all hypotheses have been explored; that the data have not been subconsciously sorted in order to fit with preconceptions; that undue weight has not been given to the most vocal respondents; that essential 'throw-away' lines have not been overlooked.

The analysis process is one of condensing and structuring, translating the mass of data into a form that allows patterns to be identified and hypotheses to be generated and (informally) tested.

So, how is the analysis conducted? Clearly, the start-point is the record of the interviews, which may be written notes, audio tapes, or video tapes. The output from analysis will be some form of analysis pad or chart: the handwritten equivalent of the quantitative researcher's computer tabulations. The process of transferring from one to the other forms this section of the Chapter.

Transcription of recordings

Whether or not the researcher intends to base the analysis on the audio/video tapes, it is essential that a recording be made. For the researcher to rely on memory and handwritten notes is insufficient, and note-taking may be a distraction during the interview (or group). It is rare for a business respondent to refuse to be taped during an interview.

Whatever the nature of the raw data, it is vital that a complete typewritten transcript be made quickly of all of it, even from written records of interviews. Although the essence of qualitative research is its unstructured nature, some kind of structure has to be imposed on it by the researcher. The absence of any kind of structure will considerably diminish the value of the gathered information, and the survey design should provide it as a help also to the analyst. Such structure will be related to the nature of the market under investigation, and will ensure that, for example, every segment of the market is properly represented.

As much order as possible should be imposed on the transcript, reflecting at least the structure of the data but preferably beginning the allocation of the data to analysis categories. All the information known to the researcher about the respondent prior to the interview (or of the members of a group prior to a discussion) should be included at the appropriate place in the transcript. If the researcher himself makes the transcript (as is generally advisable), he should have a notepad at his side as he does so, to record the additional ideas, questions and comments that will arise during the transcription.

The advantage of the researcher's making the transcript is that he can interpret tone of voice and other characteristics of the audio record, that might otherwise be missed. Listening to recordings does allow the researcher to explore tone of voice (irritation, boredom, surprise, hesitation) and the use of silence, while video tapes identify body language. Both also ensure that the researcher knows which respondent made which comment.

Analysis and Interpretation of Qualitative Data

The main benefit of transcripts is that they can be scanned quickly in order to find specific sections. They can be copied and then cut up, so that the findings in different interviews or groups can be compared and contrasted (if each group is copied on to different coloured paper then the source of each is clearly identifiable). The transcriber should type verbatim, identifying the contributions of researcher or respondent (and, in a group, the change of respondent). The researcher can then annotate the transcript to identify individual respondents, and delete any unnecessary text. Notes on tone of voice, prolonged silences or laughter can also be added at this stage.

In all cases, it is important that transcripts alone are not relied on, but that the analyst also listens to the tapes. If the analyst is also the researcher, this serves to refresh the memory; if not, it is essential that all the nuances available from the recording discussed earlier are fully explored and included in the analysis.

Methods of analysis

The vehicle for analysis is a chart, or pad of paper. The precise format varies considerably with the nature of the project and the analyst's individual preferences. However, all methods rely on pulling together all comments relating to a specific topic. These comments are then identified in terms of the individual respondent or the main structural variables (such as user or non-user, large or small) depending on the size and the degree of structure imposed on the project.

The first stage must be for the analyst to read all the way through the transcript and, if relevant, to listen to or watch the whole of the recording, with the aim of gaining a preliminary understanding of the whole subject. Only brief notes would be taken (perhaps on the same pad as used during the transcription process), but these notes will be the key to the selection of the best method of analysis, by identifying the elements of the structure of the responses and by listing the topics actually covered.

The next stage becomes the detailed collation of all the collected data into some sensible order, based on the views obtained during the first stage. The main methods for doing this are now described.

Structured analysis
Where the project is slightly more structured, and certainly where it is

based on, say, 30 or 40 personal interviews, it is usual to create analysis charts for each topic which list the comments on the left-hand side and identify the respondent on the right. These are usually A3, or even A2, sheets of paper and a separate sheet will be created for each topic, each question, or each research objective. A typical example is shown in Figure 11.2

Unlike quantitative research, it is impossible to form long 'banners' with all the possible structural variables. Completing an analysis chart with, for example, company turnover, industry sector, customer status, and the number of products installed as variables, each with three, four or five options would be a leviathan task – it would also leave little or no room for the responses. One of the first tasks facing the analyst, therefore, is to decide which are the key variables. This is one important reason for having previously conducted the initial overview: this process should suggest which variables are the most important. These may, or may not, equate to the variables used to impose a quota on the interviews or to structure the groups.

If one of the quota control variables is not expected to be of great importance, but needs to be clearly identifiable, the analyst can always record those responses in a differently coloured pen.

Clearly, however, other variables may be found to be important as the analysis takes shape. In order to avoid the need to re-analyse the data in terms of these new variables, it is recommended that serial numbers are used for the entries, instead of the traditional five-bar gates. Each questionnaire is given a serial number and this number is written, against the response, under the appropriate column on the right-hand side. Suppose in Figure 11.2 that a favourable comment about Brand X's 'robustness' was made by respondent number 10 who was a 'user' and a 'small' company. The comment would be written under 'favourable' on the left-hand side and the number 10 would be written on the same line in the 'user' and 'small' columns. If it then appears, at a later stage in the analysis, that the length of usage was a possibly important reason for brand loyalty, this fact can be noted. Having classified 'users' into 'established' and 'recent', the analyst simply goes through the analysis papers marking all the 'established' serial numbers in one colour of highlighter pen and all the 'recent' serials in another, and then compares these responses.

Analysis and Interpretation of Qualitative Data

PROJECT:				
TOPIC: Attitudes towards Brand X	USAGE		Co. SIZE	
	USER	NON-USER	SMALL	LARGE
Favourable:				
Non-favourable:				

Figure 11.2. *Structured analysis chart*

In the case of group discussions the same technique can be used by applying the serial either to the individual respondent or to the group as a whole.

The advantage of this approach is that it provides a structured and accessible database from which to work. Extracts from interviews, which the researcher wishes to quote verbatim in the report, can be found easily by writing the page number of the transcript, or the reading on the tape counter, next to the abbreviated response; the serial number of the interview is already recorded.

There is, in this method, the inherent danger that the analyst can become constrained by the structure, and fail to make the associations necessary to identify new ways of looking at the market; a 'journey of discovery' is limited if you never leave the clearly defined roads. It is essential, therefore, that the analyst be alive to this danger and not afraid to change or amend the structure: completeness is much more important than tidiness.

One of the other criticisms is that this process encourages the analyst to record simply what is said. What therefore happens to the thoughts, ideas and associations generated by the analysis process itself? It is for this reason that the researcher should keep a separate 'scratch pad' on which to record any thoughts as he implements the more formal analysis procedures. The bottom of each page of the main analysis is another place for such notes. Typical comments might be:

Perception of the main message seems to be related to seniority (job title)

Why are those in the North more critical of after-sales service?

Does age of respondent affect willingness to accept new concept?

Upon completion of the analysis, these thoughts can be examined and if necessary the tapes replayed and a further analysis conducted by highlighting the serial numbers as described earlier.

Transcript-based analysis
Some researchers prefer to base their analysis around the transcripts themselves. It is perhaps, therefore, more suitable for four or five group discussions than 20 or 30 depth interviews.

Users of this approach annotate the margins of the transcripts with

Analysis and Interpretation of Qualitative Data

thoughts, observations and connections, and also with summaries of each topic. The transcript, as a photocopy, can be cut into segments, each encapsulating one idea or one kind of response, and the segments reordered to fit the required pattern for the analysis. The analyst can then add separate sheets of notes and comment in the appropriate parts of this assemblage.

This method has the advantage that the analyst always keeps close to the original data, and that nothing is lost through abbreviation and transfer. However, it can limit the degree of 'dissection' of the data. It is also more difficult to involve other analysts than is the case with the more formal approach described earlier.

'Free form' chart

The third common vehicle for the formal analysis of qualitative data is the free-form chart. This is a very large sheet of paper such as that from a flip-chart pad; for obvious reasons this is also known as the 'wallpaper' method.

As with the 'structured' approach described earlier, the information is transferred on to the chart in a logical manner. The main difference is that the framework is much less structured. In other words, instead of grids for each topic indicating key variables, such as user/non-user, manufacturing/service and so on, the comments are grouped together in broad topic areas with information about the respondent underneath, perhaps in brackets.

This approach does give the analyst the freedom to expand topics, draw lines to indicate connections and get an overview of the entire project. Proponents of this methodology tend also to use pens of different colours to indicate respondent status or to differentiate quotations from thoughts. They also need a large expanse of wall or floor on which to work – but more sheets can be added as they are needed. It is perhaps appropriate that a 'journey of discovery' produces something that resembles a map of buried treasure. The skill of the analyst is to extract the treasure from that map.

Computerised content analysis

A fourth major method of analysis is to examine the transcript for verbal content. This is a very laborious process if done by hand. The first stage is to select groups of words conveying the required bits of information.

There are now available some free-form database packages which represent a useful tool for this type of qualitative analysis. It must be stressed that they are a tool for the analyst; the software itself cannot possibly conduct the analysis, but it can provide the user with a more efficient way of sorting and interrogating the data.

In essence the free-form database allows any string of words to be remembered, stored in a logical category, identified when needed and associated with other responses. It is important to note that this is not based on the principle of keywording, but involves word and idea associations made by the analyst. As such, the user retains control at all times. It is the user who generates the ideas, the hypotheses, and the method by which they will be tested. The software simply provides a more efficient method of implementing the test. A typical package for this purpose is 'Agenda' by Lotus.

While the use of such packages is at a fairly early stage of development, certain useful observations can be made. It does appear to be more suitable for the rather more structured projects – the 30 depths rather than the four groups. Its greatest value seems to be in replacing with electronic sorting the laborious, time-consuming process of sifting through questionnaires – for example, to see whether respondents with a more technical role or heritage have a more or less negative attitude towards a certain aspect of the new product concept. It must be stressed that control is retained by the analyst: there is no magic, no automatic analysis. Instead, in the example above, the analyst would identify the 'technicality' of each serial-numbered questionnaire. Then attitudes towards the concept, which have been previously input, can be called up and will be presented alongside the 'technicality' data.

The lack of structure in the database is appropriate to qualitative analysis procedures. Also because 'notes' of an almost unlimited length can be added, these can include the analyst's own thoughts and observations (the equivalent of the written 'scratch-pad'), as well as verbatim responses.

Summary

Analysis is seen to be extremely subjective, and one method will suit

Analysis and Interpretation of Qualitative Data

one analyst very well and another not at all. The choice is the analyst's, although to some extent the nature of the project will have an influence. Larger and more structured projects (such as attitudes towards alternative new products) are more suited to the 'structured' approach; small and very unstructured assignments (such as advertising concept development) to the 'free-form chart'.

It may also depend upon who is conducting the analysis. Where the researcher and the analyst are one and the same, a very personal or individual approach can be used, such as annotation of the transcripts. Where several researchers are involved, as might be the case with 30 or 40 depth interviews, it is essential that the analysis be accessible to all. It is the author's opinion that in qualitative research two heads are better than one, and that wherever possible both data collection and analysis should be shared. Letting another researcher analyse 'your' group and then interrogate you on it can be a powerful means of 'getting inside the data'. For the same reason it can be advantageous for a colleague to observe the first group.

Whatever method is selected, certain basic principles apply. The analyst needs to get fully immersed in the detail, and must approach the data with a constantly questioning mind. If, halfway through the analysis, an alternative approach seems better, or the first three groups need to be re-analysed to include additional variables, so be it. It is only an evolving and ruthless interrogation of the data that will provide a sound basis for interpretation and insight.

Interpretation

This is the final part of the procedure, when the researcher moves from the detailed collation and sorting of the information to determining the meaning behind it.

The researcher will have been jotting down thoughts on interpretation as the analysis proceeds, by means of a scratch-pad or similar device. A flash of insight may thus be reached much earlier for one topic than another. As such, as with data collection and analysis, the boundaries between the two are blurred. However, it is important to maintain a distinction between 'analysis' and 'interpretation', because the two are quite profoundly different. Analysis requires the researcher to keep an open mind, to question the data without prejudice. Interpretation, though, demands that the researcher brings all his own experience to bear on that analysis, to make judgements and draw conclusions.

As stated earlier, considerable benefits can be derived from a 'brainstorming' session at this stage. This allows all the members of the research team, including even the client, to bring their different experiences and judgements to bear on the formal analysis. Indeed, it can be a good idea to tape-record these sessions so that they can be revisited later. In some cases, the interpretation process will demand a return to the formal analysis, to re-examine the data in order to validate or challenge the hypotheses generated.

It is important that the research objectives are highly visible at this stage. After all, the focus of the interpretation must be the implications for the objectives determined at the outset.

As an example, suppose that one of the objectives was to consider the likely effect of a new product on existing products already marketed by the client. The analysis will have covered the level of interest in the new and existing product, the image of each and so on. At the interpretative stage, the researcher must pull this together allowing for such factors as tone of voice and level of spontaneity. This must then be viewed in the context of the researcher's experience of other research on that or similar products, and in other markets: for example, what is this market's general attitude to new products – is it cautious or adventurous? How loyal did respondents appear to be to this product versus others? How knowledgeable did they seem to be about new products compared to other markets? How systematic are they expected to be in evaluating new products? Clearly, these questions require not only the thorough analysis of the groups or interviews, but also a level of judgement based on experience. It is very important that the client is always aware of what part of the presentation or report is 'what was said' and what part is 'what I think was meant'. Both are essential for a complete piece of research, and both must be clearly identifiable.

It is especially important for the analyst to clear his own mind of particular attitudes to the subject of research, in order to understand the opinions of respondents. A motor-car may be regarded by the analyst personally as a blessing to mankind, but by a respondent as a

Analysis and Interpretation of Qualitative Data

polluting menace. If the analyst finds a comparison with a motor-car in a response, he must then see it for what it was – unfavourable, rather than the favourable one he himself would have meant. Such judgements can be difficult to make if the researcher has not elicited that aspect of the respondent's views at the time of the interview, but made they must be.

Similarly, the researcher should have asked respondents to explain their bubble diagrams or sentence completions. It is the explanation that is analysed and this can be treated like any other commentary.

Validation of qualitative data

One final question facing the qualitative researcher is the extent to which the findings can be validated since, clearly, there are no statistical tests that can be implemented and exhibited.

On the face of it, validation appears fraught with problems. Sampling is purposive and small-scale, and the process is an inductive rather than a deductive one, ie it does not seek to test hypotheses under strict scientific conditions. Instead, the hypotheses are generated and informally tested by the research process itself.

Much work has been done recently on exploring the viability of validation in qualitative research; in a major review of the literature Sykes[1] concludes that there are five forms of validity:

- apparent validity, ie the data look right;
- internal validity, ie the data are consistent within the research project;
- instrumental validity, ie the data accord with data from other sources;
- theoretical validity, ie the research method can be justified;
- consultative validity, ie the data are justified by those included in the process (interviewers, respondents, client).

It can be seen that the extent to which the findings are internally consistent, to which they accord with previous research (qualitative or quantitative), and to which they generally 'feel right' are important bases for their validation. As such, the interpretation process described earlier, bringing the researcher's collective experience and judgement to the analysis, is clearly essential.

The final point to be made is that the more 'open' the process of analysis and interpretation, the better. Only in that way can those outside the research process understand how the findings have been derived.

Reference

1. W. Sykes, 'Validity and reliability in qualitative market research: a review of the literature'. *Journal of the Market Research Society*, Vol 32, No 3, pp. 289–328, 1990.

12

The Presentation of Survey Results

John Wigzell

The business marketing researcher's final task in a research project is usually to present the results of the project to its sponsor – whether this be the marketing management for work done by an in-house researcher, or the client company for work done by an external researcher. This must be in such a way that the sponsor receives and understands the full value of the survey.

Introduction

Once the analysis and interpretation of the data have been satisfactorily completed, there is the final requirement to communicate the results of the research to the client.

There are three critical words in the previous sentence: *communicate*, *results* and *client*. Communication is perhaps the most important of them. It is not enough simply to report the findings of research; it is necessary to translate those findings into language or images that effectively convey to those who read the report, or listen to the presentation, precisely what the research has taught. Moreover, it is necessary to do this in a way which allows them to understand it, clearly and simply.

The use of the term 'results' is deliberate. Too many researchers seem to think that the purpose of presentation is to show the data that have been generated from the research. On the contrary, data are there to be recorded, analysed and interpreted – not presented. It is the meaning of the data, their message, their relevance to the questions that were originally asked, and their ability to indicate a particular course of action, that need to be presented.

The third critical word is 'client'. This may be an external organisation for those who work in research agencies, but may equally well be a person or a department in the same company for in-house researchers. It has occasionally been suggested that it is somehow a less important task to communicate to colleagues in the same organisation than to outsiders. This is categorically untrue; indeed there may be some justification for believing that it is a more critical task for the in-house researcher to communicate clearly.

The proper completion of any research is when the person or group who initiated the research is in possession of the results, understands how they were derived and what they mean, and what action should be taken as a consequence of it.

Methods of presentation

There are many ways to communicate the results of research studies, but the most common are the written report and the oral presentation. Probably the most usual procedure is to prepare a full written report on the completed study, and then to present it to the sponsor in a personal visit. This latter presentation may be a simple affair, one-to-one between researcher and sponsor, using the written report as the basis, or it may be a major audio-visual event, with special visual aids, presented to an audience of several people. One variant of this procedure has the written report sent ahead of the oral presentation, which then uses visual aids just with the key features of the work – admittedly this detracts from any revelatory impact of the oral presentation, but greatly assists in the main task of communicating the full content to the sponsor. Another variant has the oral presentation first, using special visual aids (and leaving copies of these behind), with the written report completed and despatched only when the sponsor's reaction to the work is seen, and any communication gaps thereby sealed.

The Presentation of Survey Results

It follows that the written and oral forms of reporting, although very different in style and content, are essentially complementary in purpose. Given that point of view, this Chapter will concentrate more on the oral presentation, since its success is vital to the communication process – and much of the technique of the good oral presentation reflects on the written report as well.

The whole point of communication is to take an idea, and to place that idea as exactly as possible in the minds of others. To do so, language is necessary (although a picture can be worth a thousand words). Words are the tools in this process, and must be used in the way that manual craftsmen use their tools – precisely, and with care. Confucius (who may be the world's most quoted man but rarely, one suspects, in the context of market research) said, 'If language is not correct, then what is said is not what is meant; and if what is said is not what is meant, then what ought to be done remains undone.'

The written report

Although much of the philosophy of good presentation comes later in this Chapter, it is obviously sensible that the main elements of the written report should be examined at this stage. A good written report rarely follows the events of the survey in chronological order; rather, it should reflect the needs of the sponsor who commissioned the work and, in particular, the needs (and personality) of the individual who will receive and use it.

Because business marketing research projects vary enormously in type, it is impossible to lay down hard and fast rules as to the 'best' format for a written report, but very likely it will contain:

- a summary;
- a statement of the original problem;
- the terms of reference for the work that was done (probably derived directly from the original research project proposal);
- a brief review of the survey methodology for research and analysis;
- a statement on the limitations and assumptions of the study as they impinge upon the derivation of results from it;

- the minimum of numerical data or summarised opinion to show the bases for the derived results;
- a thorough review of the results of the study – in terms of market size, perhaps, in its various components (such as geographic, end-use, company size, future development) or maybe of perceived company image, or of opinion on an advertisement campaign and so on;
- the conclusions drawn from the study and the marketing recommendations that follow from them.

The report should conclude with appendices containing information relevant to the study, but not essential to the argument of the report: complete sets of data; the mathematical basis of the analysis; blank copies of questionnaires or topic guides; perhaps the sample frame and/or the list of contacts made and so on.

If the report is long, it is worth making a two-volume work, with the appendices in the second volume. In that case, there really should be an index and certainly a detailed table of contents (which should be provided in any report beyond two or three pages in length). Written reports will be read by people other than the intended recipient, and probably at times much later than the date of receipt. It is a courtesy then to guide such readers by means of the table of contents and index.

Some guidelines for report writing (in no particular order of importance) are:

- try to think of the reader at all times that the report is being written: how will *he* read this passage, will *he* understand this table or graph?
- begin with a clear, concise summary of all the main elements of the report, and its main conclusions and recommendations – this is all that some key decision makers will read of the report;
- prefer clarity over a flowery style, but do not take this too far – although not intended as a great work of literature, the report must, nevertheless, be easy (and even pleasant) to read;
- use direct rather than indirect, the active voice rather than the passive, simple construction rather than complex, but it is essential

The Presentation of Survey Results

to be as precise as possible in all statements so that no ambiguity is allowed to enter;

- although there is no need to be over-pedantic, do try not to misspell and do try to avoid glaring grammatical errors – hanging participles are not just bad, they also introduce confusion, and other poor construction may set the reader against you (after all, he may be a pedant where grammar and spelling are concerned);
- make the report look attractive, outside and in, with a good layout, a readable typeface, and using open space freely;
- number sections and paragraphs consistently, to permit ease of cross-reference within the report;
- indent lists for ease of comprehension, rather than putting items all into a paragraph – just as this list is indented;
- use diagrams and graphs where they will definitely help in understanding – not just to show off your word processing software;
- keep data tabulations small in the body of the report, splitting large but unavoidable tabulations into two or more parts, and finally
- revise it – do not be too proud of the first draft to go back over the text, always bearing in mind the intended reader (as well as the longer-term use, and wider readership).

Some of these guidelines do need some expansion, because of their importance.

The reader
Although it is sometimes difficult to do so, it is vital to remember the 'audience' for a written report – not only the intended recipient, but also his colleagues and other personnel in his company. The written report is an impersonal medium, taken in with the eyes only, but it is also a permanent record. This means that with the written record the reader can, rather like using a video recorder, skip certain sections, or 'rewind' to look at them again. Internal consistency is therefore of vital importance. The reader can also revisit the report whenever he chooses and control the pace of his exposure; the listener (to an oral

presentation) must be taken through the story at a convenient and acceptable pace.

The written report is rarely read as a group activity. Each reader brings his own context to it, and makes an individual response. Given the heterogeneity of the readership, it is a difficult task to achieve understanding by everyone, but it must be the writer's aim. To quote Defoe: 'If any man were to ask me what I would suppose to be a perfect style of language, I would answer, that in which a man speaking to five hundred people, of all common and various capacities ... should be understood by them all, and in the same sense which the speaker intended to be understood.'

Clarity

There is a fundamental difference between written English and spoken English. In a written report, we might easily say, 'it does not matter to whom we are referring; this is a universal truth'. Nobody would use a phrase like that in speaking to someone else – how many times does the word 'whom' crop up in spoken English?

It has been said, and not without some element of truth, that there are actually three types of English: the spoken form, the written form, and market research reports. It does seem that a strange affliction creeps over people when they sit before a blank piece of paper (or, in these days, a blank screen) and start to write a report. They become instantly pompous, long-winded, unable to use anything but jargon or long words, and somehow adopt a style of writing that is simply never seen elsewhere.

It is an interesting exercise to calculate the 'fog factor' in research reports. The fog factor is calculated by counting the number of words of three or more syllables in a passage of writing that is about half a page in length, and then dividing by the number of sentences. Consider the following passage:

> After considerable discussion, we have been able to generate a substantial number of alternative scenarios for consideration. Before implementing the actions indicated in these scenarios, it would be advantageous for management to predicate the corresponding activities of competitors in the same market environment.

The Presentation of Survey Results

This passage has a fog factor of 8.5. The same thought could have been equally expressed by: 'There are several options, but whichever course we take, we should try to predict our competitor's response' for a fog factor of 3.

Brevity
A necessary condition for clarity is usually brevity. It is rarely the case that research reports are judged by their length or weight, although many people seem to think that the more expensive the project, the longer the report needs to be. It is important to get to the point; the reader does not want to know how difficult it was to reach the conclusion, but what the conclusion is. As John Cleese says in a Video Arts training film, 'Don't tell me about the labour pains, show me the baby'.

Unnecessary length in the overall report is probably matched by overlong words, sentences and paragraphs. It is much better to err on the side of shortness – short words and short sentences (which will lead to a low fog factor), and paragraphs that restrict themselves to a single concept.

There is, of course, no need to be so short as to be terse, and to make the reader feel that he is being addressed as a child. After all, in the written report the reader has the opportunity to backtrack and read a passage for a second time if it is not clear at first reading. If subsidiary clauses carry the reader away down a side track, he can always refer back to the beginning to see where he departed from the main line – but we do not want to force him to do it too often. Bernard Levin, the noted *Times* (of London) essayist, and traveller, has a very elegant style of writing, which frequently requires the reader to check back to the start of the essay because he uses so many subsidiary clauses. In a research report, such clauses need to be disentangled into separate sentences.

Presentation of data
The written report can (and if it is from quantitative research, should) contain the data from which the conclusions have been drawn. Although a full tabular appendix may accompany the report, it is usual to include some of the data in the text of the report itself. It is therefore like a good road map, in that it allows us to see the detail of the route

by which the conclusions were reached. By contrast, the oral presentation should take an overview; it should show the general direction in which we have come, but not explore every little path. To press the analogy, it should be like a touring map, showing us simply the relationship of one place to another.

This means that in the body of the written report we should not attempt to show the totality of the data. It is our duty to present the numbers in such a way that the reader can see what we are communicating, clearly and simply. If we just put in a mass of numbers, it is unlikely that any but the most diligent will bother to try to unravel it. The data to be shown must be ruthlessly selective, put into an order that makes them easy to read in the order we want them to be seen, clearly labelled, and generally enhanced with headings, lines or boxes so that the message becomes clear. In effect, we are saying to the reader, 'Look at these data and you will see what I have discovered from them'. Under no circumstances should we use tables that say to the reader, 'Here is a mass of data; see if you can discover anything from it'.

Appearance

The report should appeal to the eye, with an attractive cover and a good internal layout. It has occasionally been argued that 'slick' presentations detract from the 'worthiness' of the research itself. In the 1960s, at least one research company deliberately designed covers for its reports that were dull and 'unglossy', on the grounds that its customers would think better of the contents of the report if the covers were not overtly smart. Fortunately, this attitude no longer prevails; researchers now do everything they can to make their output look professional. The advent of desk-top publishing allows us to present our reports with good visual and graphical representation, and has reduced our dependence on tables and the typewriter.

Comparisons of the written and spoken word

Oral presentations are often called 'verbal' presentations, quite incorrectly. 'Verbal' simply means 'with words', and probably describes a written report more accurately than a spoken presentation, which is more accurately described as 'oral'. The written report and the oral

The Presentation of Survey Results

presentation both use words, but use them very differently, and those differences are discussed in this part of the Chapter.

The oral presentation has the opportunity to add sound and movement to vision; it therefore has the opportunity to make much more impact than the report, and to add emphasis in a way that words alone simply cannot do. On the other hand it is transitory, and makes that impact and emphasis just once, to the audience (of one or more) gathered specially to receive it. The audience gets this once-only exposure, and has no chance to 'go back a page', so the oral presentation must carry its audience with it.

The audience hears the oral presentation in the same way that it hears other speech. In written English, we have to ask ourselves whether what is written is clear, concise and grammatical. In spoken English there is a further filter to be applied: is it the sort of thing that someone might actually say in conversation? (although the need to be grammatical is less – as in the earlier comment on the use of 'whom'). Certainly speech is rarely convoluted, but equally certainly it is rarely well structured – very few people complete a spoken sentence, let alone the oral equivalent of a paragraph, without interrupting themselves or being interrupted. This cannot be allowed to happen in an attempt to communicate ideas, so the oral presentation must concentrate on transmitting facts or ideas in short 'packets' of words.

It is not a bad idea to regard the oral presentation as being given in a language that the audience does not understand, for which it needs an interpreter. Under these circumstances, you would make a particular statement, complete in itself, so that by the time the translation is finished, the audience feels that it has got something – yet not so long a statement as to cause the translator to lose his way before the end.

Word order
If the earlier map analogy is extended further, the oral presentation is not just a touring map but is the shortest distance on that map from start to finish. Surplus words, like surplus miles, are counter-productive – the audience is there to see the goal and not to admire the countryside along the way.

A significant difference between the written and spoken language lies in the order in which words and phrases are delivered. An elegant piece of writing, with its opportunity for back-tracking, would be inappropriate as a spoken piece. Speech passes by the listener only once; there is no opportunity to go back to the beginning. As a result, the construction needs to be different.

In a written report, the following passage might be quite acceptable:

> Despite one or two exceptional cases which show contrary policies, and bearing in mind the small size of the sample, which is not unusual in industrial market research, and particularly in a fast growing product field such as this one, it seems likely that most purchasing is done centrally.

In an oral presentation the same words, if they were used, would be more understandable in a different order:

> It seems likely that most purchasing is done centrally, despite one or two exceptional cases which have contrary policies, and bearing in mind the small size of the sample, which is not unusual in industrial market research and particularly in a fast growing product field such as this one.

Neither version is particularly elegant, let alone effective, and both break many of the 'rules' outlined above about brevity and the use of active words. It would be even better expressed as:

> Most companies have a central purchasing policy, although there are exceptions. We have to be aware that this finding is based on a small sample, but this is quite usual in industrial market research, especially in fast growing product fields.

(It would probably have been better in the written report like this, too.)

Signposting
In written English, there are many indicators to the reader showing precisely how the passage should be read, where the stresses come, where to pause, and so on. We use commas, semi-colons, dashes, parentheses, full stops and (perhaps most importantly), paragraphs for this purpose.

In spoken English we do not have that facility. It is therefore more difficult for the listener, than for the reader, to identify where one thought ends and another begins.

The Presentation of Survey Results

To overcome this, a spoken presentation needs to have very good 'signposts'. A simple pause is one kind of signpost. It indicates the end of one thought or one point, but where a series of thoughts follow one another it is helpful to the audience if they can be signposted.
Consider the following passage:

> The data showed that there was a significant difference between the responses of men and women to the idea of having desk-top computers for every employee. In trying to determine the reasons for this difference, several cross analyses were examined, but none of them provided an adequate explanation. There was a slight, though not significant, difference in attitude between higher and lower status employees, however, and a further cross-tabulation showed that female employees with low-status positions were more resistant to the idea than high-status males. This led to the hypothesis that women were concerned not to be seen with a desk-top computer that might be mistaken for a word processor, and thus make them appear to be secretaries.

All this is perfectly logical and reads fairly happily, but it would have to be phrased differently in a presentation, for the audience to follow it:

> Men were much more enthusiastic than women about every employee having a desk-top computer, and the difference was significant. We looked at all the data to try to find an explanation for this phenomenon, without initial success. The only other sub-group analysis that showed a difference was the status analysis. Here, although it wasn't significant, the group with lower status was less keen on the idea than the high-status group. So we ran another analysis, combining status and sex. And this proved to be the key. Lower status females were the group that most objected to the idea; high-status males were the keenest. So we can hypothesize that the explanation lies in the fear of more junior female staff that a personal computer on their desk might be mistaken for a word processor, and thus demean their status to that of a secretary.

The simple addition of the phrase 'this proved to be the key' signposts to the audience that the explanation is coming, and that they had better prick up their ears. The change in the English from 'written' to 'spoken' also helps.

Oral presentations

The remainder of this Chapter is devoted to oral presentations themselves, to some 'rules' for making them more effective, and some 'tips' for anxious presenters. As has already been mentioned, there is much in here also for the writer of a report.

It is necessary, at the start, to remind ourselves why presentations are so important. In the words of the song: 'it's not what you do, it's the way that you do it; that's what gets results'. Whether we like it or not, we are rarely judged as researchers by the elegance of our research design, by the quality of our fieldwork, by the precision of our sampling, by the accuracy of our analysis, or by the skill of our interpretation. All these things will play a part in determining whether or not the research is good research, and each one of them is capable of ruining an otherwise perfect project, but the importance of the presentation overrides all of them.

A presentation, whether it is a research agency presenting to the client, or an in-house researcher presenting to management, is the focus of the project. It is one of the few occasions on which some people – especially senior management people – will be exposed to market research.

Presentations are critical, not only for the individual but also for the business research company and for the business marketing research profession as a whole.

- The *industry*, because, while a substantial effort is currently being made to raise the status of market research as a profession, which effort will continue in the foreseeable future, the industry's public relations effort is all too often spoiled, on a micro level, by poor presentations. When we are given an opportunity to make a good public showing, we often do it rather badly, and this reflects discredit on our colleagues as well as ourselves. It is therefore our duty, as well as good sense, for us to develop our presentation skills. Our presentations must be professional – we owe it to the market research industry, as well as to our companies and to

The Presentation of Survey Results

ourselves, to do the most professional job we can every time we get to our feet.

- The *company*, because the impact of the presentation reflects strongly on the company or the department. Many research presentations are made to senior management and also to staff outside the research area, who may include technical people, research and development teams, financial managers, marketing people and a host of others. The credit for a good presentation will be reflected in the audience's view of the department or the company; the results of a poor performance will similarly rub off on to one's colleagues. Every moment we spend on our feet in front of an audience is, in effect, a commercial for our department, or our company, as well as our profession.

- The *individual*, because what applies to the profession and to the company, also applies to the individual. A presentation is one of the rare opportunities to get exposure to a wide audience, and particularly to get exposure to senior managers in the company. In the same way that a presentation is a commercial for the department, it is also a commercial for the individual. It is the equivalent of the creative man's portfolio, the model's book of photographs, or the actor's chance to show his talent in front of the important director.

These last comments about the individual relate largely to the in-house researcher, making a presentation to his own management, but the impact can still be there for the external researcher, whose good (or bad) performance will probably be reported back to his employers.

A presentation is a major opportunity for researchers to confront senior management. It is very rare that marketing managers take the opportunity to go into the field and watch the interviewing process, it is rare that they study the tabulations or the transcripts and, worst of all, it is rare for a senior manager to read the whole of a research report. They can be guaranteed to read the management summary, but how many of them read the whole report? However, they can nearly always find the time to come to a presentation of the findings. So how do they judge the quality of a research project? All too often, they judge it by the nature of the presentation.

In-house researchers sometimes complain that senior managers treat them as peripheral to the core management of the company, and that there are few career paths from research into senior managerial positions. However, when they are given an opportunity to demonstrate to management, on their feet, how important they are and how central to decision making the research role can be, how many of them – through poor presentation skills – waste the opportunity?

Like it or not, you will be judged not so much by the content of your presentation as by your style. And since it is probably your best opportunity to make your personal mark, it is worth some time and effort.

The major factors in a presentation

A good presenter will be guided by 'a rule of three'. In any presentation, there are three things to consider: them, you, and the message. *Them* means the audience, *you* concerns the presenter, and *the message* is what you want to communicate.

The audience

Just as in a good research project, it is essential in making a presentation to find out all you can about the audience. Do the research: find out how many, who, why are they there, what they will have to do, and what are the politics.

To take each of these in turn, first discover how many people will be in the audience. Obviously you will not want to arrive with 40 35mm slides and carousel projectors for a multi-screen presentation, if you are going to be presenting to one marketing manager and his assistant. Equally, you will not want to turn up with a few scruffy hand-drawn overhead transparencies and suddenly find that there is a sales conference going on, and the whole sales force of 100 representatives is going to make up the audience.

It is not just the number of people that makes a difference to the manner in which you present and the visual aids you use; it is also the nature of the audience. The managing director of one of the largest research agencies, operating in an international group, tells the story of how one man changed the nature of a presentation single handed. It was this group's practice, every year, for the managing directors of

The Presentation of Survey Results

each of the operating companies to meet and discuss their progress. It was a group of about 15 to 20 people and covered large sophisticated operations, such as those in the UK and the USA, down to small units in developing areas. They would report on how their company was going, and what sort of projects they were handling. In particular, they would discuss tricky projects, and seek ideas from their fellow managing directors for overcoming the problems they encountered.

One year, however, the annual meeting coincided with the visit of the chairman of the conglomerate of which the research companies were simply one part. That year each of the managing directors duly presented to the group just like every other year but, strangely, no one had any difficult projects to report on; no one asked his colleagues for their ideas about solving a difficult technical problem; everything in the garden was apparently wonderful. It should have been no surprise. It is simply human nature to want to show the best aspect.

This example serves to illustrate how one man, out of 20, can change the whole nature of a presentation. This is not really surprising – a presentation to a small group of assistant brand managers is likely to have a different tone from a presentation to a board of directors. Unless you have done the research to discover who will be there, you are always likely to take the wrong approach.

The situation is compounded if someone arrives late or leaves early. Nothing is more irritating than the managing director who arrives about 15 minutes after you have started the presentation, apologises for being late but explains that he has been on the telephone to New York or Hong Kong, and asks for a quick reprise of what you have said so far. Alternatively, he will leave about 15 minutes before the end, apologise, and ask if you can just briefly summarise for him before he leaves to catch his flight. If you are forewarned that this is likely to happen (and if the perpetrator is important enough to warrant it) you can at least have a management summary available to hand to him on his arrival or departure, thus causing less disruption to the presentation.

Having discovered how many are going to be present in the audience, and who they are, your next questions are why they are there, what they have come to find out, and why they want to know. Even the best of research presentations is unlikely to draw crowds of eager spectators, unless there is some very good reason for their wanting to hear what the findings are.

It is more than likely that they will all bring a slightly different perspective to the event. For example, in reporting the results of research into a potential new product development, it is likely that the managing director will be present to hear the news, and may well have expansion plans for the company that would be helped by the discovery of latent demand for the new product. Since it will also have obvious financial implications the financial director will be present, and may have a much more cautious outlook. The production director will be present, because a finding that it should be pursued may cause fundamental changes to the current methods of manufacture. The research and development people will be there to hear news of their latest brainchild, and whether any further development work is called for. All these people will be coming with a different set of expectations from the research, and it is easy to upset some of them by failing to take account of their particular angle on the project – the first reaction from people who feel they have been 'short changed' by the research is to dismiss it as incompetent or wrong.

In the same vein, it is useful to know what action will be taken as a result of the research findings, and by whom. If the production manager has to build a whole new line, should the product go ahead, he will want to be very sure that there is a substantial market for the new product before going to all the time and trouble of getting new machines set up. And the financial man will want to know what risks there are if the demand does not materialise. A good presentation will address their concerns, or at least make them feel that their individual worries have been taken into account.

It is a good discipline for presenters to research the homogeneity of the audience. Are they all on the same status level? Are they all from the same discipline? This will often indicate their knowledge of the problem being researched. Do they have an equal level of concern? Do they all have a knowledge of research and research procedures? It seems likely that production people will come into contact with research on a less frequent basis than marketing people, so that if the audience has a good proportion of production staff, it may be necessary to spend slightly more time in talking about the methodology than might be the case with a group of marketing men.

The final piece of audience research is the most often neglected, but

The Presentation of Survey Results

often the most critical. It concerns the politics of the situation. It is absolutely vital, if the presentation is to be a success, that the presenter knows the score – to be forewarned is to be forearmed.

It may well be that the production director is from the 'old school' and does not believe in these new-fangled gadgets that the managing director is proposing they start making. He may be only a few years from retirement and does not want his comfortable life spoiled by having to learn about the computer-aided manufacturing that would be necessary for this new product. He will be most reluctant to give it the green light, and may look to find objections to the research if it suggests a large latent demand. He might ask searching questions about the methodology. The presenter needs to know why those slightly aggressive questions about the technique are coming from someone who knows relatively little about research. If the presenter has found out about the politics, he will understand and will be able to deal with them appropriately.

As another example, in presenting research to advertising agencies on the reaction to a number of proposed new advertisements, it always helps if you know which of the options the agency is recommending, which the client wants to 'win', and whether there is one that the creative department would really like to make. If you know in advance, you can address each of the parties fairly and equally as you present.

The presenter
The first and most important thing to say under this heading is that anyone can be a good presenter. Good market researchers are made, not born; they have to learn their craft and its skills. Good presenters have to learn their craft too – anyone can learn to be a good presenter.

In market research presentations, the presenter starts with one enormous advantage over most of the people present. He knows the subject matter best, and he is perhaps the only person in the room with a thorough knowledge of the data and its interpretation. The assembled group has come to find out what the research has discovered, what it means, and what they have to do about it. Only the presenter has this knowledge, and can therefore guarantee a certain amount of attention.

This is a huge bonus: the presenter does not have to fight for the audience's attention. The whole thing has been set up precisely for the benefit of allowing the presenter to share the results of the research with the audience. The focus of attention, in other words, is already directed at the presenter.

The presenter's own skills and capabilities are, of course, vital to the presentation. The presenter is in the best position to know his strengths and weaknesses, and being aware of one's assets and limitations is crucial to good presenting. It is not always easy to take an objective view of oneself, and it may be necessary to seek the view of colleagues as to one's capabilities as a presenter. Better still is to seek an independent view, such as might be obtained by participation in a training course on presentation and communication. (The Industrial Marketing Research Association runs one such course as part of its education programme, for example.)

Often, those aspects of ourselves which we are most concerned about turn out to be our best assets. For example, everyone has some sort of accent, and some are distinctively regional. People often try to mask it, but a distinctive accent can be a great gift, provided that it does not get in the way of clarity; it identifies and distinguishes a presenter, and is often very pleasant on the ear.

It is necessary to know not only your assets but also your capabilities. Are you better if you write out every word of a presentation beforehand, or working from a loose script, or completely free of notes? It is relatively easy to find out which method you personally find easiest.

There are one or two general rules that may help in this area, but in the end every presenter must work out his own method. It is very difficult, for example, to read a script verbatim and make it sound interesting. Apart from the question of written versus spoken language discussed earlier, it is difficult to pay attention to the audience and read a script at the same time unless you are using an autocue and you have had a great deal of practice with it. Equally, it is very difficult to work convincingly in a totally unscripted manner unless you have a tremendous amount of natural (and organisational) authority. It is asking a great deal of the audience to put up with the inevitable pauses while the presenter searches for the appropriate phrase, and it is asking a great deal of the presenter's brain to tune in to the audience, keep track of the pace of the presentation, and seek out the right word at the same time.

The Presentation of Survey Results

So, as a general rule, it is probably better to work with notes that are sufficient to remind you about the point you want to make. Notes usually need to be slightly fuller than you think when preparing them. In the heat of the moment, and in the full glare of the spotlight, something you have written saying 'attitudes' might not be enough to trigger the memory; 'attitude to Chinese food – positive among triallists, but triallists a minority' will give you much more to work on.

Knowing yourself and your material are the keys to good presentation, not simply because they make you more credible, but also because they allow you to react to the audience. If you know what you want to say and know how best you can say it, you will have some energy left over which will allow you to watch and listen to the audience and, most importantly, to take account of the audience reaction in adjusting your presentation as you go along.

If you can see from the smiles and the body language that the audience is happy and relaxed, you can loosen up the style of presentation slightly. If you see frowns and feel hostility, you can adopt the appropriate posture and manner to defuse it. If you see the audience going to sleep (mentally as well as physically – it may be after lunch on the day the works canteen had a heavy dessert), you can change gear (show a film clip, for example, or play a tape) to liven them up. In any event, you must respond to the audience, and let them know you are responding.

A great deal of communication – perhaps more than half – is not necessarily verbal. We all recognise how easy it is to go into a restaurant and by watching people's behaviour have a pretty good guess at their conversation and even their relationship. The whole of our posture gives clues about how we are feeling; we communicate this in a quite unconscious way. By 'reading' the audience, it is easy for the presenter to see how they are responding to him.

Of course, the same applies to the presenter. The audience will find it easy to tell if a presenter is bored, or feeling supercilious, or consumed with anxiety. The aim of a presenter is to be as animated as he would be in a one-to-one conversation with a very close friend. It is surprising how many lively and animated people, as soon as they have to address an audience of more than five people, become struck with a rigidity bordering on paralysis. The instant they take the stage they become monotonous, dull and boring. The spectre of self-consciousness has got them.

The aim should be to use the same manner, the same gestures and body movements, the same pace and pauses, that you would use if you were talking to a couple of friends over a drink. It is not necessary to learn these, they come naturally; it is necessary to learn to remove the barriers that prevent us from being ourselves.

Perhaps the single best tip about presenting is 'be yourself', but depending on the size of the audience, perhaps you need to be a little larger than life. To project beyond the two people in the bar, perhaps to five people, you would need to be slightly louder, and marginally more expansive with your gestures. To project to an audience of 20, you need to be 'larger' still – but without becoming overpowering.

The message

The objective of a business research presentation is always to inform and sometimes to persuade, but worthy aims such as these do not necessarily have to be achieved in a boring or uninteresting manner. So, as a subsidiary objective, we should always strive to be interesting in whatever we are saying. Of course, it is easy to go too far and produce an entertaining presentation that fails to communicate the main message, but it is often the case that research presentations are dull and boring rather than entertaining. To be interesting to the audience simply means addressing that which they will find of interest.

A presentation should always be clear and concise, as well as interesting. Clarity can be defined as an absence of ambiguity. No one should be in any doubt about what you are saying, or be confused about what you mean.

Concise is the opposite of long-winded; there is no reason to be verbose – it wins no prizes. The ability to summarise the relevant aspects of the research, and present it in a succinct manner, is a rare gift and a much prized one. The irritation engendered among busy managers who have set aside an hour in their diaries to hear the results of the research, and who find that it takes the presenter an hour and three-quarters to tell the story, can usually be seen by the metaphorical steam coming out of the ears of those managers who still remain in the audience at the end of the presentation.

It is worth examining the studies of people's attention span, which point to the fact that, in audiences, it is greatest in the first ten minutes

The Presentation of Survey Results

and drops to its lowest point at 30 to 40 minutes. This must be even more true of people who in their normal daily working lives are not used to spending long periods of time without speaking. A presentation of more than 40 minutes is therefore a risk enterprise. Indeed, if it cannot be adequately summarised in that time, there must be some doubt about the researcher's ability to select the important bits of information from the unimportant. Remember how easy it is to answer a colleague who pops his head round the door to ask, 'What did the research show, then?' It can normally be answered in two and a half minutes.

Making the presentation interesting is not quite as easy as making it clear and concise, but it can be done with a little thought and effort. The next section, on the 'mechanics' of presenting, deals with some of the ways to add interest to the presentation.

With regard to the real 'message' of the presentation, it is largely a matter of the appropriate analysis and interpretation of the data. However, a good presentation will answer Kipling's famous six questions (slightly amended for business marketing researchers):

Why is this research necessary; what problem is addressed?
How was it conducted; what method was used to get answers?
When was it done, and how long will it apply?
Where was it conducted, and among what sample of people?
Who will use the results to take action?
What decisions should be made as a result of the research?

If it answers all these, it is a good presentation.

The presentation format

The format for a marketing research presentation should be very similar to the format for a written research report. It should contain the following elements:

- objectives – the objectives should not simply be a reiteration of the research objectives but should encompass the marketing background, in order to address the questions the audience brings to the presentation and the necessary actions following the report;
- sample and method – we need to explain precisely to whom we

spoke, where, when, and how the questions were asked (if there are non-researchers in the audience it may be helpful to discuss the degree of confidence that can be attributed to the answers);

- notes – this is the point in the presentation when a brief digression is appropriate, in order to set the remainder of the presentation in context; in a qualitative presentation, for example, it may be appropriate to remind the audience that qualitative research addresses attitudes and opinions rather than behaviour, or that it deals with the range of attitudes rather than their extent; it is the appropriate point to tell the audience whether they will be given copies of the presentation at the end or whether they should make notes, and it is the point at which to tell them how you want to handle questions (as they occur, or left until the end).

The presentation must also contain a summary, for use by the sponsor's management, and a set of conclusions and recommendations – but these deserve rather more discussion.

Management summary
The most useful axiom for presentations is another 'rule of three': 'Tell 'em what you're going to tell 'em; tell 'em; then tell 'em what you told 'em'. This is partly about giving the audience signposts, but also a means of communicating effectively. At some point in the presentation, most people will find their attention wandering, however good the presenter. Human nature causes us suddenly to wonder whether we locked the car, or what to have for dinner tonight. It is unreasonable for a presenter to expect 100 per cent attention to every single word. By telling people what we are going to say, and then saying it, and repeating at the end what we have said, most people will get the message.

It is, perhaps, a matter of contention whether the summary and conclusions should be at the beginning or at the end of the presentation. There are arguments for both views, and advocates of both schools. If the 'rule of three' is followed, however, there needs to be no debate, since the summary comes at the beginning and again at the end.

By giving the conclusions first, and then going on to present the

The Presentation of Survey Results

supporting evidence, you prevent people in the audience from selectively listening to the main findings and arriving at their own conclusion. It also helps to deal with those who arrive late or go early. It is easy to reprise for the benefit of the former, without taking up too much time. For the latter, if they have to leave early then at least they know where it was all leading to, and what the results were.

Perhaps the strongest argument for putting the conclusions up front is that there should be no great mystery about research results. Research presentations are not mystery stories, although you might be forgiven for thinking that some of them are, by the way in which presenters hold back the key results until the very last chart by which time everyone's attention may have wandered away and some people have probably left the room to go to their next scheduled meeting. Research is not usually so riveting that people are on the edge of their seats trying to work out what the conclusion is, and to arrive there ahead of the presenter. So why not simply put them out of their misery straight away, and tell them where we are going to arrive on the magical mystery tour. They will be all the happier when they get there.

There are arguments against putting the conclusions first, but they are not strong ones. It is said that if you tell the people the conclusions at the outset of the presentation, they may not stay for the remainder of the presentation because they have heard all they need to hear. If this is the case, and they have indeed heard all they need to hear, then they are quite right to go. It is the presenter's fault for not finding the reason why people had come to the presentation, and addressing it. Such behaviour is disconcerting, but not nearly as bad as people who leave the meeting early when you have not yet arrived at the conclusion.

The principal argument against giving the conclusions first is that it gives the disaffected in the audience the chance to spend the whole presentation dreaming up awkward questions, particularly the unanswerable 'What if . . .?' questions that serve to demean the presenter and the research. This is a much favoured ploy in advertising agency circles, and particularly from creative people who have just seen their great idea demolished. The presenter must prepare for this by asking himself as many as possible of these 'What if . . .?' questions beforehand, and having answers ready.

On balance, the argument for giving a summary of the research results first is very strong.

Conclusions
There is a fundamental difference between the summary and the conclusions of research. It mirrors the difference between the findings and the results. Findings and summaries are simply reportage; these are the answers to the questions that were asked. Results and conclusions assume that some sort of interpretative process has taken place – that someone has given some thought to what those answers actually mean in the context of the original problem. It therefore follows that the section of the presentation called 'Conclusions' is distinct from the opening summary, although a good summary must include a summary of the conclusions.

If the researcher has been properly briefed, it ought to be possible to arrive at some conclusions. The conclusions may not always be taken on board by the sponsor as the researcher sees them, because of information that is not available to him. It may be the conclusion of the research, for example, that there would be tremendous demand for a new product, at the right price, and that the company should press on with a launch at all possible speed. The researcher may not know, however, that a rival company has just announced the launch of a similar product, and the goalposts have therefore moved. This does not matter, nor does it in any way demean the research. The research people were paid to arrive at a conclusion from the facts they were given, and they did so. That was their duty.

As with a written report, the findings should be presented as the evidence from which the conclusions were drawn. They should contain only the detail that is necessary to take the story further. It is not necessary to present every answer to every question that was asked. That is the job of the tabulations in the written report.

Stage managing the presentation

A presentation is a performance, and just like a theatrical performance it needs to be produced, scripted, rehearsed and stage managed. There are several important points to be considered by the presenter.

The Presentation of Survey Results

The audience
Members of the audience are not students listening to a lecture; they are not there for the benefit of the presenter. They are more important than the presenter. If a presentation lasting an hour turns out to be a waste of time, then the presenter has simply wasted an hour. For an audience of ten people, however, it represents a collective waste of ten hours, or a day's working time.

Anything that can be done to make the presentation more interesting for the audience, or more professionally delivered for their benefit, should be done, but it should only be done if it is in the interests of the audience, and not simply for the aggrandisement of the presentation (or it will surely backfire and cause irritation).

Arriving on time
Late arrival is the height of discourtesy. It is also guaranteed to engender hostility in those who have had to wait. There is simply no excuse for it. A theatrical performance always starts when it is billed to start; the performers make sure they are there with enough time to put on their make-up and costumes and be in position before the curtain goes up. So should the presenter.

Appropriate dress and posture
Because a presentation is a performance it should be treated as such, and costume is a part of the preparation. It is a simple courtesy to the audience to dress appropriately. This does not mean that every presentation should be done in a dinner jacket; sometimes it is entirely appropriate to dress in a casual manner, but it should always be considered in relation to the audience. It is not usually sensible to present to an audience of city bankers in an open necked shirt. To do so would destroy the credibility of the presenter. It is nearly always wrong to present in jeans, especially if the wearer then proceeds to slouch in a chair during the presentation.

It is not always necessary to stand to give a presentation but, again, it enhances credibility and authority to do so. It also recognises the relative role of presenter and audience. As Anthony Jay says: 'The speaker addresses his audience respectfully as a subordinate among men of higher status. He cannot demand their attention; the most he can do is deserve it'. Presenting from a sitting position is likely to indicate disrespect for the audience, unless it is a very small audience (say two or three people), the presenter knows them very well, and they are of roughly equal status to the speaker.

Eye contact
It is extremely important to look at the audience, and to look at each member of the audience so far as that is possible. Nothing is more irritating in a one-to-one conversation than the person who will not look you in the eye. It normally leaves you with the impression that he is being deceitful, or simply uninterested. The same is true for a presentation audience.

Many presentations appear to be given to one person in the audience, judging by the eye contact. Of course, if it is the managing director, or the most important person in the meeting, this is not so bad except that it does tend to alienate the others, who inevitably think: 'He is obviously not talking to me'.

The maintenance of good eye contact with everyone in the audience is not only good presentation technique but is also good manners. Communication is a two-way process. In order to establish a channel of communication, there need to be a transmitter and a receiver. If the receiver switches off, then communication stops. As long as you are looking at people, they will be in receiver mode.

One of the most frequent complaints about presenters is that they spend a great deal of their time looking over their shoulder at the screen, to check whether the correct slide has come up or that the overhead transparency is lined up correctly on the screen. Speakers who do this generally succeed in giving an excellent impression of a hunted rabbit, constantly glancing over its shoulder to see who is creeping up on it. The impression created is one of nervousness and anxiety on the part of the presenter. It is also a habit which helps to destroy eye contact with the audience.

Voice modulation
The voice is the speaker's most important tool and, at the same time, the most sensitive instrument. It needs care and attention in the same way that the visual aids need care. In the appropriate place, it can raise a crowd to mutiny or battle, or it can bring them to tears. It can be used to get impact, and not simply by raising the volume and shouting at

people – lowering the volume to a stage whisper will cause people to strain to listen, and can achieve enormous impact. It can be used to emphasise a point and put stress on a particular phrase.

There is one bad voice habit that seems particularly prevalent among market research presenters, namely dropping the voice (pitch, not volume) at the end of a sentence. It has a boring and deadening effect. By comparison, raising the pitch to end a sentence creates a lively, dynamic effect.

Mannerisms

Speakers should not worry too much about mannerisms, since they are for the most part simply a manifestation of the natural personality. Someone who uses his hands a great deal in normal conversation will look stilted and awkward if they are suppressed in presenting. Colleagues can help in spotting those unconscious mannerisms which are frequent enough to distract the audience, so that they are watching for them instead of listening to what the speaker is saying.

Mannerisms can be physical, such as scratching an ear or sniffing. They can also be verbal. We all have our favourite phrases and ways of expression, but there are certain words or phrases that, if repeated, can distract the audience or annoy it. The speaker who says 'actually', or 'in fact', at the beginning of every point or, even more common, the one who uses 'er' or 'um' as a punctuation mark between sentences, can be incredibly irritating to the audience.

Timing

Most people's diaries work in slots of one hour, and one hour should be enough for most presentations. This allows 30 to 40 minutes for the presenter, and 20 to 30 minutes for questions or discussion. There are very few occasions on which the presenter is told, 'We need to have a two-hour presentation'. More often the presenter is asked: 'How long will the presentation take?'

Most research presentations are too long. There seems to be a view that 'we have collected so much information that it will need at least an hour and a half to present it'. However, a presentation should not be designed to show the data that were collected; it should inform people of the results of the research.

Even the best of presentations will sometimes overrun, no matter how carefully rehearsed and timed. In this situation it is essential to have 'pruning points' marked in the script or notes. These are the bits that, when the presentation starts to slip behind its schedule, can be omitted without losing the main thrust of the argument. The presenter should always mark pruning points, for every presentation.

One of the reasons why presentations overrun is that questions or discussions take place in the middle. On the one hand, the presenter must accept that if the audience finds it relevant to start a discussion then its wishes should be respected. On the other hand, it is up to the presenter to control the presentation.

Questions can be controlled to some extent by stating at the outset, 'I will take questions of clarification as and when they occur, but I will be brief in my answers and deal with any complex issues or any discussion at the end of the presentation'. If a discussion which is tangential or disruptive starts in the middle of the presentation, it is up to the presenter to bring the meeting under control and carry on. One good reason for presenting the conclusions at the beginning is that, in these discussion situations, the presentation can be truncated without loss.

Rehearsal

For any presentation, it is important to have prepared it carefully and to run through it with colleagues if possible. The more important the presentation, the more important it is to rehearse. An hour spent in preparation and practice is worth many hours of delivery. Apart from any other consideration it is the only way to time a presentation, but the better you know your material the more confident you will be – and the more confident you are, the better will be the presentation.

The venue

It is particularly important to rehearse a presentation in the place where it will take place 'on the day'. No public performance of a play would ever take place without innumerable rehearsals, in costume and on the actual stage, because it would be unthinkable to expect to get it all right, the first time, in public. Why then do presenters think they will get it right first time? The classic example is the presenter who arrives for the presentation with 35mm slides, only to find that there is no power point in the room.

The Presentation of Survey Results

Unfortunately, few companies are sufficiently enlightened to suggest to presenters that they come along to the venue and rehearse beforehand, but it is always possible to arrive with sufficient time to check everything out and, if necessary, alter the layout of the presentation arena.

It is necessary to establish where to present from, where the visual aids will be projected from, and where the audience will be. If it looks as though you will obscure the screen for some part of the audience (quite common when using overhead projectors), move the seats or block off those where the view will be obscured. Rearrange the room so that everyone can see properly, so that the light is on the presentation dais, and so that you can present from the right side of the screen as the audience sees it (the natural movement is left to right, and will move from the screen to the presenter quite naturally). Check that the projector works, and that you know how to use the remote control, the lights and any other mechanical devices.

Visual aids

In the context of most research presentations, the term 'visual aids' is a misnomer. They are very rarely visual and they are not normally aids. They are usually words (ie verbal, not visual), sometimes scruffily handwritten on acetate, and sometimes typed and therefore too small to be seen beyond the front three rows. They do not normally help communication; quite the reverse – they normally hinder it considerably, especially when the presenter is giving one complex message to the ears of the audience while the screen is giving a slightly different message to their eyes.

There is a great tendency on the part of market researchers to show all the data on screen. Nothing is more boring. Only a few numbers are ever necessary; graphs and histograms are usually much more successful in telling a story – and a research presentation should be telling a story, not acting as a substitute for the written report.

Visual aids have many disadvantages. They take a great deal of time and effort to prepare; they can be expensive; they can divert attention from what is being said to how it is being said; they diminish flexibility; they can result in catastrophe if they go wrong. So why do we use them at all?

Visual aids should be used because a picture is worth a thousand words; because they can communicate things that are quite impossible to communicate verbally. They can add interest, create variety and provide the opportunity to make real impact. A good visual will stay firmly in the mind long after words or numbers have disappeared. The neuro-linguistic programmers tell us that a very large number of people store things in their mind visually (in the equivalent of a huge carousel that brings up the appropriate image when the brain calls it up).

Before starting to create visual aids, the presenter should ask, 'Is it helping communication?' and 'Is it visual?'

There are many types of visual aid, all with their advantages and disadvantages, all with hazards and opportunities. Some of those relevant to research presentations are outlined briefly in the following paragraphs.

Flip charts

Flip charts – pads of large sheets of paper mounted at the top, which can then be 'flipped' over or back – serve to focus the audience's attention, and are excellent for listing the contents of a presentation or acting as signposts. They can be used very flexibly, for words or drawings, and can be used for highlighting in a different colour in the course of the presentation. They should be prepared beforehand – if the presenter does attempt to write or draw during the presentation, it should be brief so that there is not too much time spent facing away from the audience.

Among the disadvantages, however, is the need for flip charts to be very bold and clear, in order for them to be legible. This means that they are not normally very good for showing numerical data, or for large audiences.

Physical objects

Although there are few opportunities to use physical objects in research presentations, they have enormous interest value. The presenter may be familiar with the objects discussed in the presentation, but the audience may not necessarily be so familiar. Any kind of product test, or research involving named products, is always enlivened by showing them.

The Presentation of Survey Results

Perhaps the best example of the use of physical objects is the one quoted by Anthony Jay, of an Army officer lecturing on the value of surprise in war. After announcing the subject he took out a very small squib and placed it on the table in front of him. He then took out a matchbox, and as he began to open it an accomplice detonated a huge thunderflash at the back of the audience. Naturally, they all leapt to their feet – but he succeeded in engraving three points about surprise in their minds forever (deception about time, place and strength).

Overhead projector
The greatest advantage of overhead charts is that they can be prepared relatively quickly, and by anyone with a modern photocopier. Like flip charts, they will take colour and can be drawn on in the course of the presentation. On the other hand, they are perhaps the most abused medium. Often they are lettered by hand which, unless they are prepared by someone with impeccable handwriting or lettering skills, can look scruffy and unprofessional. Sometimes they are typed, which usually means there are far too many words on them for legibility. Sometimes they are typed in capitals in the mistaken belief that this makes them easier to read. Research has shown that most people find a mixture of upper and lower case letters much easier to read. It is, after all, what they are used to in their daily newspapers, books and most other printed media.

Slides
The great advantage of 35mm slides is their complete authority, and their ability to command total attention. They are also the best way of using photographs, and can be changed rapidly to create a great sense of fun while still communicating a point very forcibly. Photographs can have tremendous impact if used carefully. The major disadvantages of slides are that they require a darkened room, giving the audience the opportunity to fall asleep unnoticed, and can create a remoteness about the presentation that causes the audience to feel that they are not involved. They also take time and money to make.

Again, they are much abused. Slides often contain too many words (there should be no more words on a slide than would fit on the front of a tee shirt), are not visual, are too complex, or are irrelevant to the point being made (often because they are left on the screen when the presenter has gone on to the next point). Sometimes they even appear upside down, which is guaranteed to invoke general ridicule and remove any semblance of authority from the presenter.

Tape
Video tape, or even audio tape, is guaranteed to wake up the audience and is greatly under-utilised in research presentations, where the value of seeing (or hearing) a real live respondent can do more to bring the research to life than any amount of anecdotes and reportage from the presenter. It has the advantage of being totally uninterruptable, and can be very persuasive. On the other hand, it is quite expensive to produce well and does carry the risk that the editing may be biased to prove a point.

Computers
The advent of computers has meant that the opportunity to create good visual aids is now widespread. So far, they have not been used very much in presentations, but there seems to be little point in using them to create graphic effects for the overhead transparency, when they can be operated directly (preferably on to a large screen) with stunning effect, particularly for build-up graphs and histograms. One glance at the way in which graphic effects are now used in television news bulletins should clearly show the way forward.

Summary

This summary is at the end, rather than the beginning, but there are some important points on presentation technique and they deserve repeating.

- Presentation of results is an important part of the research process, and it is worth learning to do it well. There are fundamental differences between a written presentation of results and a personal oral presentation.

- Anyone can learn to be a good presenter. The three components of a presentation to remember are the audience, the presenter and the message. Of these, the audience is by far the most important.

The Presentation of Survey Results

- A presentation is a performance. It requires to be properly prepared and stage managed in order to be effective. Visual aids should be visual, not verbal, and must help to communicate the story – which is the most important objective of all presentations.

Part IV:
The Applications of Business Marketing Research

The techniques of business marketing research – how it is done – have now been explored at some length. Equally important to the reader of this Handbook is why it is done – the kinds of purpose for which business research is undertaken.

The simple answer to this second question, of course, is that business marketing research is done to solve a business marketing problem or, more particularly, to help in the taking of a marketing decision. Clearly, this answer is not very helpful since there are probably as many business problems as there are businesses.

Fortunately, these business marketing problems can be grouped into a number of reasonably well-defined applications, which are the subjects of the different chapters in Part IV.

A large proportion of business marketing research work is undertaken to enumerate a market size, as defined by product or service, geographical, and end-user limits. Much of the instruction of Part II was written with this kind of project in mind, so only one chapter in Part IV is devoted to this 'simple' market size assessment.

13

Product Market Size

Tony Dent

This first Chapter in Part IV deals with the problem of assessing the numerical size of a particular market. Although referred to as 'simple' in the preamble to Part IV, such measurement tasks may actually be very complex – they are simple only in so far as the application of the various business marketing research techniques is relatively straightforward.

One of the best ways to illustrate a subject is by example; that is exactly how this Chapter does it – with three examples, in fact.

Introduction

The old cliché question and answer, 'How long is a piece of string?' and, 'Depends whether there's a knot in it' are not inappropriate to the subject of this Chapter. Markets are changing all the time, and the actual definition of a market is subject to variations in:

- political geography (the expansion of 'Europe' at the end of 1989 is a good example);

- types of customer ('we're only interested in the automotive market for steel');

- product ('although we make plastics, our market is actually products A, B and C, whether made from plastic, steel, aluminium or whatever').

Equally important are technological change, economic fluctuation, or even fashion, which may have quite abrupt effects on business markets by compressing or expanding the all-important dimension of time.

Thus companies, which have hitherto been happy to employ annual market size estimates, now frequently require monthly figures. Nevertheless, seasonal variations in some markets are such that it is often inappropriate to use any measure other than the annual market volume. For example, fertiliser usage (and, indeed, that of many other agricultural products) varies significantly from quarter to quarter, and purchasing behaviour may be 'early' or 'late' depending on the farmers' economic circumstances or weather forecasts.

This is, therefore, definitely a case of not trusting one month's figures. Nevertheless, in many of the more innovative business markets for goods and services, monthly figures are required; moreover, when collecting information for a period, it is often more efficient to use a shorter period and accumulate the data.

So, how would we define market size, given that our elements are products, customers and time, in order to be able to measure it?

It is the volume of X (product, or service, or raw material) sold to or delivered to or consumed by Y (the universe of customer types within the geographical area) during the period Z. Before proceeding to discuss methods, however, it is important to consider the degree of accuracy that we are seeking.

As a background to the concept of accuracy, it must be remembered that almost none of the figures we take for granted are in fact precise. No-one knows the exact population of any country in the world at any point in time – for small countries, of course, it can be established subsequently (perhaps). We do not know precisely how many businesses there are in the UK; new registrations and insolvencies always take time to feed through to published figures. In short, almost all the data we use and accept are themselves 'best estimates', and whatever measurement procedure we adopt, it will only ever provide a 'best estimate' qualified by the methodology.

Product Market Size

This point is not a minor one. The accuracy we want for our market size is that needed for our purpose. Therefore, there is little point in establishing an arbitrary requirement such as plus or minus 10 per cent on the estimate when, for example, the purpose requires that a market be at least a certain size, and that provided it is, that is sufficient information.

If our definition is now modified somewhat, to read, 'We wish to estimate the volume of X consumed by Y during the period Z, to an accuracy of... in order to establish...', this now becomes the problem that a business marketing research project would set out to solve. Such a solution is best illustrated by example, of which three typical ones make up the remainder of this Chapter.

A chemical industry market

The problem

A British manufacturer of chemicals has been generating 2,000 tons of by-product each year. The cost of disposal has been £40 per ton, ie £80,000 per annum on average. A new process, mixing the by-product with another material, will produce 4,000 tons of a hardener for epoxy resin. The question is, what is the market size of hardeners for epoxy resin?

Analysis

Following our definition in the introduction, we can assume that the estimate required is for a year.

What, however, is the product? Different formulations of hardener are appropriate for different market segments. It will therefore be necessary to define Y (the customers) according to those segments covered by the appropriate formulation achieved by the process. We shall assume that this is civil engineering and construction, rather than the building industry in general.

More significantly, since this is an entirely new product and market for the company, it is not necessary to obtain accurate figures. A satisfactory conclusion may be arrived at provided that the market volume is at least 10 times the proposed production, on the grounds that a 10 per cent market share would be a reasonable target, given the company's accepted marketing skills. A total market of just 10,000 tons, on the other hand, would require a 40 per cent market share – an unlikely achievement. The accuracy required, therefore, will be order of magnitude, and an accuracy of plus or minus 50 per cent on the estimate could be quite acceptable.

Indeed, of equal importance to market size in tonnage terms will be market value, since critically the company is unlikely to wish to enter the market at a price disadvantage.

Finally, what about the geographical coverage? The company does not wish to restrict the matter to just the UK (unless that market is large enough); it would rather consider a wider market, within which it may expect to be cost-competitive.

The definition statement now becomes:

We wish to estimate in which geographical areas the hardener will be cost-competitive for civil engineering and construction work. Within that area, is the annual market at least 40,000 tons and what is the approximate size and value of the market?

Method

This problem represents a relatively classic industrial market research exercise in so far as, although the answers required are quantitative, one would classify the information gathering process as involving desk research and qualitative in-depth interviews with major users.

The desk research would review all the relevant sources (remembering that estimates of resin usage will equate to usage of hardener). Competitive intelligence will provide price information; the discount structure applied will yield valuable insight into the ordering habits of larger customers – although these last two kinds of information may also have to be sought by field research.

It may be that this research will resolve the problem, but this being an area where Pareto's Law, the 80:20 rule, holds to effect (80 per cent of the business is done by 20 per cent of the customers), it is always worth checking the facts obtained from the desk research with a few of the larger customers – either the buyer or the specifier.

Product Market Size

Questions to be covered would include:

- suppliers/relative importance,
- volume of usage/costs,
- total market estimates/market trends,
- tolerance on specification,
- other major users.

Apart from qualifying the value of the market estimates, such interviews provide valuable insight into the acceptable market approach. Large customers rarely use just the one supplier; if they do, market penetration is likely to prove very difficult for the client. Usually, however, large customers are relatively keen to try a new supplier, if the price is right.

When discussing market size with customers, it is important to employ their time dimension. Thus, although the figure required is annual tonnage (or value), be prepared to collect monthly figures, or whatever time period the respondent uses, and to convert these to annual tonnages. It is also important to emphasise (where necessary) that approximate figures only are required. Many non-responses to volume data are not caused by refusals, but by the respondent believing that you require precise figures which he does not have readily available. (Observe the response differences on postal questionnaires between the question: 'How much do you spend on . . .?' and: 'Please tick the appropriate box which indicates your approximate expenditure on . . .' – nevertheless, for those respondents who take pride in accuracy, it is always worth asking for the actual figure.)

The outcome of such a procedure is a report which provides a best estimate, and a range of estimates for the market size, qualifying the numbers arrived at by the information sources from which they were obtained. Normally, there will be sufficient consistency in broad terms to indicate whether the order of magnitude is appropriate for further action or not. The inclusion of some information on larger customers is very important to provide the sponsor with a feel for the marketplace (which is hitherto unknown to him) as well as providing further qualification to the size estimates.

Comments

This case study represents a project which is normally the domain of the 'in-house' researcher. He will usually have access to colleagues who can easily clarify aspects such as changes in formulation to meet slightly different specifications or, 'Should we consider the Middle East or restrict ourselves in Europe?' It is also easier to borrow the extra week when you realise that you should also include parts of the heavy engineering and manufacturing sectors.

Nevertheless, problems of confidentiality or lack of internal resources may imply the need to use an external research consultancy. Evidently a great deal of cooperation and some flexibility is required to provide a cost-effective answer.

Incidentally, in this example the UK market alone would be unlikely to prove sufficient and, although Europe is large enough (I think), it is probably more sensible to accept the £80,000 cost of disposing of the by-products – or sell the material to someone already in the resin market.

An office equipment market

The problem

A well established manufacturer of plain paper copiers started distributing fax machines three years ago. Sales have been going well and it is considering establishing a manufacturing facility. The question is – what is the market size?

Analysis

Once again, the question needs refining. Is the company concerned with the totality of the fax market or competing within a sector? Is it proposing a fully functioning machine or a basic product?

The company informs us that, at present, it sells a full range of machines and that a volume of sales can already justify a manufacturing facility; however, the proposal is to start production at the low end of the range, and gradually develop across the range. For these

Product Market Size

purposes, it identifies three types of facsimile machine as the range.

It is aware, of course, of the developing market in the consumer marketplace, but the concern is solely with the business sector, including self-employed people working from home.

It is therefore evident that the sponsor is concerned with understanding the business market by sector, in terms of machine functionality and to know the relative growth rates in the market by types of machine, with an accuracy of plus or minus 10 per cent within sector.

With regard to geographical coverage, the company is at present concerned solely with the UK market place.

Our definition of the problem is, therefore:

> We wish to estimate the UK market size for three broad types of facsimile machine, which together form the full range. Estimates of annual sales into business establishments are required for each type, with projected figures for at least three years ahead, to an accuracy of plus or minus 10 per cent on the estimate.

Method

As with every market research study, we begin by asking what information is readily available, and we find that British Telecom publish a fax directory for the UK and have done for a number of years. This source will therefore provide us with an estimate of the growth of the number of users of facsimile transmission in the UK, and we can compare this growth with the company's sales figures to obtain a crude estimate of share. Upon enquiry, however, we find that the source is not, in fact, comprehensive; nor is it up-to-date in a fast moving market; nor does it provide information by type of machine possessed. (However, it may still give reasonably accurate growth rates, by analysis of successive issues.)

Our crude estimate is unlikely to be very reliable, therefore, and we conclude that, to satisfy the research requirement, some form of original data collection will be needed.

A reasonable approach to this problem would be to conduct a major, comprehensive survey of business establishments. The technique would be to select a stratified random sample, with oversampling of larger establishments relative to smaller establishments, and covering questions such as:

- possession of fax machines by type of machine (make and model);
- year of installation of each machine;
- likelihood to acquire (another) machine/by time;
- whether this new acquisition is first, additional or replacement.

To these estimates, we would apply standard grossing-up procedures, to arrive at market size figures by year, then to employ basic econometric techniques to develop a three- to five-year forecast by market sector.

With a relatively mature market such as fax (which has been developing for ten years or more now) a simple forecasting technique based on the S-curve will be reasonably accurate, provided that the installation-by-year estimates are themselves reasonably accurate. The important numbers required for this purpose are estimates of the maximum number of establishments ever likely to have one machine, two machines, or three or more machines, and a reasonable estimate of this may be obtained by taking out those who say never at the third question (above).

It is also necessary, of course, to establish what is the replacement cycle of machines (hence the fourth question).

In simple terms, the S-curve essentially plots penetration growth over time against the maximum expected penetration of the relevant equipment (in this case fax machines) as in Figure 13.1. The estimated growth in establishments during 1990–91 represents the number of first machines acquired that year, while similar curves provide estimates for second machines acquired and three or more machines acquired.

If the information from each curve is added together for each year, and the replacement machine estimates are included, this gives the estimated market size over the period. Note that, eventually, it is assumed that the market settles into a replacement market only. It is therefore important to identify how far away this may be.

Such an approach to the problem, in data collection terms, is relatively costly, particularly since the company is already in this marketplace and, therefore, is likely to possess reasonably accurate figures of its own sales over time. Instead of just using the internal figures as a check on the accuracy of a large-scale survey, we can

Product Market Size

employ them as ratio estimators with a smaller-scale study.

Moreover, at an early stage we identified the fax directory as a useful but inadequate data source. This can also be used as a ratio estimator – but what exactly is a ratio estimator?

If you conduct a random sample of establishments and determine that the market share of a manufacturer is 25 per cent of total sales in 1989, and he sold 25,000 machines during that year, your estimate of the market is 100,000 machines. You have used the manufacturer's sales figure as a ratio estimator for the total market, having determined his market share.

Similarly, if you identify 100 establishments with fax equipment, 85 of which are in the fax directory and there are 150,000 listings in the directory, you can estimate that there are:

$$150,000 \times 100/85$$

establishments with fax equipment in total (ie approximately 176,500).

Given the two sources of data we have available, namely total number of establishments in the directory and the manufacturer's

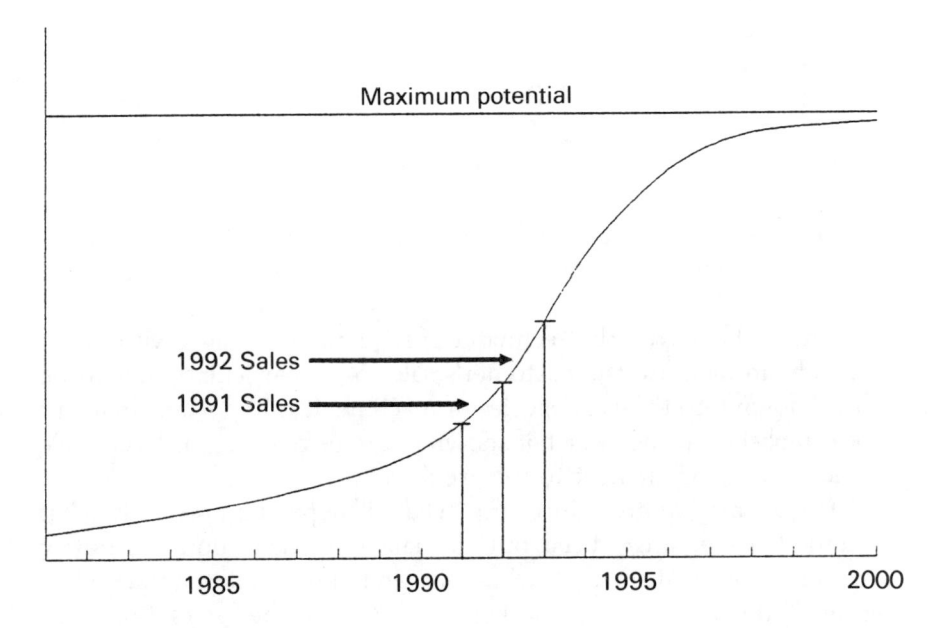

Figure 13.1. *Penetration growth: the S-curve*

own sales figures, we can employ ratio estimators to obtain an accurate market estimate with a smaller sample size than that required for the comprehensive survey discussed earlier.

What, however, is the size and structure of the sample required? Given the fact that we require estimators across the range of equipment, it is sensible to stratify the survey to ensure adequate coverage of each part of the range, and indeed to design the survey as a series of smaller studies to yield a similar degree of accuracy across the range.

Within each stratum, the ideal solution is to employ a sequential sampling procedure, stopping the interviewing when the market share estimate within each sector of the range has been stabilised to within the degree of accuracy required, ie plus or minus 10 per cent. Thus, if the market share stabilises within the band 22.5 to 27.5 per cent, the estimate is 25 per cent.

At the same time, you should be checking, within each stratum, what the proportion is within the fax directory, and whether this has also stabilised. If so, cease interviewing within that stratum; if not, more interviews should be undertaken until it has.

Graphically, the technique of sequential sampling is as shown in Figure 13.2.

The introduction of CATI into business telephone research in recent years has provided improved control procedures, which enable sequential sampling to be employed far more efficiently than in the past.

The questions asked are, of course, the same as those described for the comprehensive survey, and the forecasting procedure is also the same.

One problem with this technique of sequential sampling will be how reliable, in fact, are the customer's sales data, particularly given the breakdown into three categories of machine. It is important that this be established at the outset; if shown not to be reliable, the large-scale study is the only answer to the problem.

The estimation procedure employed will depend on precisely what method of sampling is used, but normally it would be done separately within each stratum of the sample, and the results cumulated to provide the best universe market estimates. For the forecasting stage of the project, it is a valuable exercise to do this for market subsets

Product Market Size

(strata) as well as the total market, in order to cross-check the quality of the estimate.

Comments

It should be noted that sequential sampling is not itself an appropriate technique for market size estimation in its own right – you cannot normally measure a piece of string with elastic. It is appropriate, however, for many instances where market share estimates are the primary requirement, whether for ratio estimation or simply in their own right.

In the case of the above sample we have, in fact, three ratio estimates to employ – one for each year of sales that the company has made. The decision to stop sampling in each stratum is determined when the last of the market share estimates is stable. It should also be noted that the method is only truly accurate for the last three years of sales in the market, whereas the comprehensive survey provides a longer-term theoretical base from which to make growth estimates – 'theoretical',

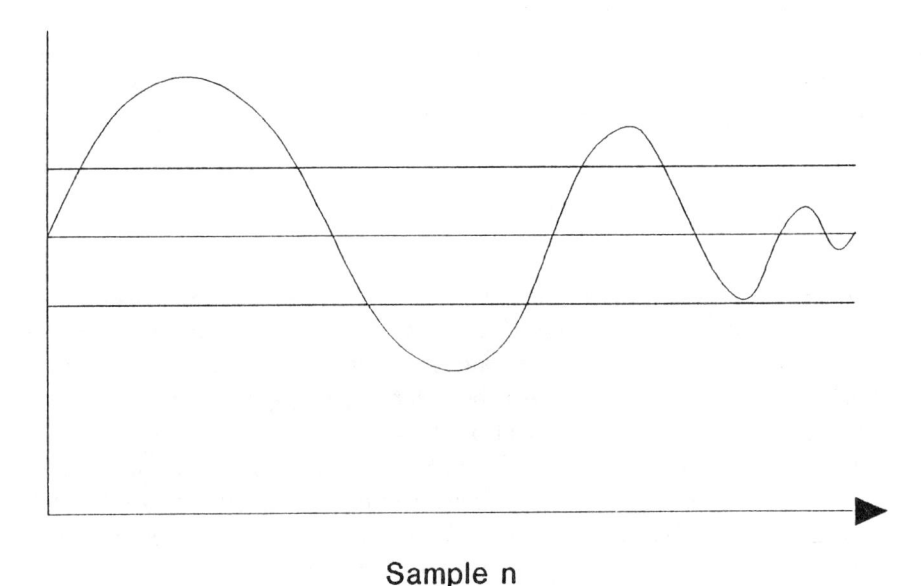

Sample n

Figure 13.2. *Sequential sampling*

since the longer ago the installation the higher the uncertainty in the data anyway.

Finally, given our basic requirements, the emphasis has been on the number of installations each year (as the best indicator of those sold). Obviously, if the requirement were to estimate the volume of paper used in fax machines, the focus would shift to the actual installed figure and the volume of incoming faxes received. In truth this is a significantly more complex problem, although the same principles apply. Nevertheless, the variation in usage over time implies that there will be far greater variance in any estimate achieved.

Parcels service usage

The problem

A major US parcels company wishes to enter the European market and is considering establishing operations in the UK. To evaluate the market potential and the nature of the service it might supply in the first instance, it requires to know the size of the UK market in sufficient detail to understand the proportions of the market represented by international deliveries, urgent deliveries, size of parcel etc. In order to consider distribution requirements, it also requires location data.

Analysis

There are a number of questions to be settled before proceeding with the research. First, what is meant by a parcel? In common sense terms it may be defined as any package requiring special packaging, and include anything inserted into those large envelopes with protective filling. Since desk research will probably prove relatively fruitless at determining any significant information on the market, and it will be necessary to conduct a major survey among customers, the information to be provided must be determined by the sponsor's perceptions and, moreover, by his ability to provide information.

Taking these aspects into account, we might reasonably define the market as:

Product Market Size

- any use of the Royal Mail parcels service (Parcel Force);
- any use of other courier or parcel services.

This definition would, of course, include letters when sent by any medium other than Royal Mail letter post. It would also include, therefore, local despatch services.

Does the sponsor want them included? We shall assume that the answer is 'Yes', but that he wishes to know what proportion of such services represents a high security requirement.

What period is the sponsor concerned with in his estimate of market size? Since he is concerned to create a service, operating daily, he wants to know actually how the market fluctuates on a daily basis. So his actual market requirement is to understand the minimum volume and the maximum volume, as well as how that distribution might vary over time, by day of week and, perhaps, even time of year.

This is becoming quite a complex requirement, although it is simplified somewhat when the sponsor confirms that he is solely concerned with business usage, not domestic.

Method

This problem represents a substantially greater challenge than either of the previous two. There will be significant variances in usage not only by size of business but also by type of business, with companies such as mail order representing thousands of times the usage of a small shop. We therefore need to design our sample to ensure that such organisations are oversampled, in order to obtain reasonable estimates.

If we conduct a preliminary investigation, we shall find that although some of the very large users do keep a record of their usage, the majority of customers – even relatively heavy users – do not. We conclude that we shall have to develop some method of data collection which records the information required, and the most suitable procedure is the use of a 'diary'.

Even so, that will not be the most sensible method for the occasional user; we therefore conclude that our data collection should be divided into a two-phase operation, as follows:

- Stage 1: large-scale screening survey, collecting basic information on a representative sample of all business users,

- Stage 2: follow-up detailed data collection with selected users.

The first phase represents a similar study to the previous example, at least in sample design terms. In both cases, it is reasonable to employ the telephone as a data collection medium, and to employ a comprehensive sample frame such as the *Business Database* (marketed by *Yellow Pages Business Data*), stratifying the sample by category groups to over-sample potentially larger users.

The screening questionnaire should be precise about the market definition, thus:

> ... any usage of Royal Mail parcel post, Red Star, Datapost or other parcels services, and including usage of couriers or despatch services, whether for parcels or mail ....

It should discuss average usage in a week of all such services, dividing usage into broad categories, thus:

- less than one item a week;
- one or two items a week;
- 3-5 items a week;
- 6-10 items a week;
- 11-49 items a week;
- 50 or more items a week.

More precisely, we should also ask about usage *yesterday* (if interviewing on a Monday, then ask about Friday or Saturday). Questions concerning this recent usage can cover more detail in terms of destination, carrier, security or special characteristics. For smaller users, the situation is analogous to newspaper readership surveys, and the techniques used for such surveys are therefore worthy of consideration in this case ('Read yesterday?' is asked to ensure that the occasional reader is included). If *today* is asked for, then the numbers obtained will always be slightly low compared with the actual outcome – there are many people who do not yet know they will be sending an urgent package last thing today.

It may also be appropriate to ask whether usage does vary by the day of the week, and what circumstances affect usage.

Provided that we have a large enough representative sample for this

Product Market Size

phase, adequately distributed by day of week, the screening data will provide a good broad picture of the market volumes by day of week, generated by the smaller users (up to 10 items per week). To achieve this, however, we will need to weight the data to be equal by 'day of week' as well as grossing the data to the universe. The screening also provides an estimate of the numbers of 'larger' users in the universe. The telephone is, however, not an adequate medium for collecting the detailed information from these larger volume users, hence Stage 2.

The second phase would involve a combination of two methods of data collection, both involving personal visits. The variance in usage at the top end means that we will need to over-sample these, and it may be necessary to boost the sample to Stage 2 beyond the number of those actually identified from Stage 1. Either way, although we are collecting information from businesses, our statistic is the parcel or package and we want as many of these in the sample as possible. Thus, as well as over-sampling larger users, we would like to obtain information from them over as long a period as is practical. Thus, one week's data (by day) are better than a day's data, two weeks' are even better and, if the client can wait and the respondents are willing, a month's data are even more appropriate. (Again, we have an analogous situation for media research – this time radio/TV rather than newspaper readership.)

As stated above, a few of the larger clients will keep excellent records of their usage (particularly mail order companies, for example). Thus, a personal visit, spending time transferring their data on to your standardised data collection document, will be appropriate in those cases. Many users will not keep records in a manner adequate for our purpose, however.

In these cases, we will require to recruit respondents to complete a daily diary recording the details of usage in the format required to satisfy the survey objectives. Ideally, as with a TV diary, all respondents should start and finish the diary at the same time. Logistically, this may prove impossible, given that the sample of eligible businesses for this phase may be widely dispersed geographically. In practice, therefore, it may be necessary to start recording data the day after recruitment and go on for an agreed period. That being the case, it would again be necessary to weight the sample by starting day of week, to ensure an even distribution of the basic data.

Researching Business Markets – The IMRA Handbook

The combination of the 'yesterday' data for smaller businesses and the detailed daily data for larger users, grossed up to the universe, provides the range of minimum usage, maximum usage and average usage by day of week – the key information as required by the client.

Comments

Quite obviously this example represents the most complex research project of the three, and one demanding significant resources in terms of professional skills, management, and data collection and processing. It will, therefore, both take some time to complete and cost a significant sum of money.

Moreover, in the event, it may not prove all that useful to the client, other than in strategic budgetary terms. To be of more value in operational terms, relative to the creating of a new business, it would be necessary to analyse the data by area in order to determine where depots and resources would best be established in the first instance. A cost-effective approach might be to over-sample certain key areas to obtain more reliable information accordingly, with relative under-sampling of small towns and rural districts.

Once again, this emphasises the need to design the survey to provide a cost-efficient answer to the problem underlying the client's request for market size data.

Summary

In this Chapter, we have reviewed in broad terms three 'typical' examples of market size data requirements. Different techniques are appropriate for different purposes, and the nature of the estimation problem is not so much defined by the type of market as by the actual reason for wanting the estimate in the first place. Thus, it is perfectly possible to obtain a crude 'order of magnitude' estimate of the parcels market by discussing with a few people who 'know', and analysing the accounts of certain companies and doing a small project among large customers. Similarly, it is possible to do a comprehensive survey

Product Market Size

among resin users to obtain detailed data on their usage.

The 'best estimate' is not a piece of string – it is a measurement fit for a purpose.

14

Researching Competitors

Conrad Brigden

Knowledge of one's competitor(s) is vital to success in business. The methods of business marketing research are the key to the development of this knowledge, which is then used to develop a strategy to counter any moves by the competition, and to make unexpected moves of one's own, to achieve greater profitability.

This Chapter illustrates the appropriate application of the research techniques, and also reflects on the point at which ethical marketing research could cross over into industrial espionage. It is written largely from the viewpoint of the in-house researcher, but much of the technique would apply to an external researcher as well (if perhaps not the same directness of purpose).

Introduction

There are few businesses today who can afford to ignore their competitors. The identification and collection of information on one's competitors, and its subsequent analysis, is essential to the development of an effective product and marketing strategy and for success in today's competitive environment.

By regular monitoring of competitors it is possible, over time, to build up sufficient knowledge to avoid costly mistakes. At the same time much can be learnt about the efficiency of one's own organisation, and practices shown to be successful in competitors can be adopted, where these are applicable. From the information gathered and subsequent careful analysis, those strategies that will maximise one's revenues and build market share can be developed, despite the activities of competitors.

The first task in building a successful strategy should be to find out what your organisation needs to know. Identify the information you will need to provide the answers and prioritise each item. A decision on how then to proceed will depend on the amount of resources available in terms of manpower and money.

Some of the questions that need to be addressed by competitive analysis in order to develop a strategy are:

- How well are our competitors doing? (profits, market share, growth).
- How are they organised? (supplies, production, sales, channels of distribution).
- How do their products compare? (technically, terms of sale, customer satisfaction).
- What are they doing that may impact on our business?
- What can we do to be more effective against the competition?

An important point in developing a successful strategy is the need to monitor the competitors, continuously, and not to treat the subject as a one-off or an annual exercise. Often, key data will not be available just when you need them and the wrong conclusions may then be drawn, with possibly disastrous results.

Identification of competitors

Most organisations are only too well aware of their competitors. However, where there are many, it may be an idea to group them into major, intermediate and minor competitors, as you will find that it is more practical to collect a different level of detail on each group depending on their importance.

Do not neglect those organisations which are not direct competitors at present, but have the potential to become a serious threat. Also, remember to identify those organisations in other countries, particularly in the European Community, who are successful but not yet active in your market, as they may now be looking to expand.

Areas of research

The main areas of investigation and analysis of competitive activity are financial performance, product analysis, marketing analysis, and long-term outlook. We will look at each of these in turn, and at some of the sources of information that are available. We will also consider ways in which each can contribute towards a fuller understanding of our competitors, and can be combined to form a 'scenario' to assist in the development of an effective company strategy.

Financial performance

The financial performance of a competitor company over time is one of the key inputs to understanding it and we are very fortunate that much of the information we require is readily available in the form of the company's annual financial report.

Annual reports
The annual company report provides us with details of turnover, profit, employees and a wealth of other information such as stock value, R&D expenditure and so on – all invaluable to our understanding of the organisation.

Many larger organisations take a great pride in providing their shareholders and employees with such details as where their branch offices and factories are, measurements on the success of new products, customer views on the products and organisation, future development plans, details of their markets and the contribution each makes to the revenue. All this is wonderful material for researchers and analysts.

One area not to be missed is the Chairman's statement at the time of the Annual General Meeting. Often, pearls of information which would be impossible to obtain elsewhere are revealed here.

Remember, he has to convince his shareholders that the company has a wonderful future, and he is often at pains to reveal information that is otherwise hard to get. Many analysts buy a single share in each of the companies of interest and so become a legitimate shareholder. They can then attend the annual shareholders' meetings, learn much which will be useful, and also obtain a copy of the annual report.

The aim of the researcher should be to decide what financial information should be collected, and then to build up that information for the last five or ten years. This will help to identify the effectiveness of past changes made by the company, when the results are correlated against the introduction of new products or changes in key personnel, for instance.

Financial ratios

A very effective tool to help in the analysis is the use of financial performance ratios. You will need to decide which ratios are most applicable for your industry and purpose.

Other ratios can be developed that are more useful for measuring the way the organisation manufactures and markets its products: ratios such as profit per employee, R&D as a percentage of turnover, revenue per salesman, revenue per branch and many more. These ratios tell you a lot, not only about your competitors but also about the performance of your own organisation. Care will need to be taken, when using such figures, to ensure that you are comparing like with like. It is no use looking at turnover per employee, when one company manufactures its own products, while another buys in the finished product.

The ratio information can be laid out and updated regularly as in the simple example on page 311.

As already mentioned, the most useful sources of information from which to build up a picture of your competitors are company reports. These are readily available for both public and private companies (in the UK) from Companies House where, for a small fee, a copy of the last two years' reports are available. Copies of earlier reports, going back ten years, can also be obtained from their Welsh office. Alternatively, you may yourself buy a share in each of your competitors and become a *bona fide* shareholder entitled to a copy of the shareholders' report.

Company A

Year	Turnover £m	Profit £m	No of employees	Turnover per Employee £k	Turnover per Salesman £k	Turnover per Branch £m
1985	5.25	0.5	210	25	525	1.05
1986	5.75	0.8	205	28	575	1.15
1987	6.25	1.1	206	30	625	1.25
1988	6.30	0.2	198	32	630	1.26
1989	7.50	1.7	195	38	750	1.50

A number of British organisations, such as Jordans and Inter Company Comparisons, will carry out Company House searches for you. They also provide regular reports, giving a financial analysis of a range of companies, within an industry sector. These are produced for a wide range of different sectors, one of which may well include your own. Extel cards, available from the Extel Analysts Service, are also a useful source of financial data. They contain a summary covering the last ten years of the key financial data. They cover the public and larger private companies.

Other sources worth considering are stockbrokers. Many of these provide excellent reports on individual companies, and also useful views on the industries in which they operate. As they are frequently quoted in the financial press, their specialisations can relatively easily be identified.

Product analysis

The needs of your organisation under this heading depend largely on your type of business and the products you sell. A manufacturing company producing engines, for instance, may wish to examine the design, production, material specifications, delivery, terms and conditions and customer satisfaction of his competitors. A distributor of car fog lamps may be interested only in the packaging, marketing channels, terms and conditions and the views of the retailer.

Product details

The first point of interest concerns the specifications of your competitors' products. Details of these can normally be obtained from published material, such as sales brochures or maintenance manuals, and by attending demonstrations and exhibitions where they are displayed.

Buying your competitors' products should also be considered where this is practical – it allows a full examination by your technical and production staff. The products can also be used as an aid in the drive for quality, if those involved in the production of your own products can examine the quality of others' and be encouraged to exceed them.

Comparisons of competitive products with those of your own company can usefully be carried out in the areas of design, technical specification, materials used, quality, performance, and methods used in manufacturing. The work of such detailed comparison will need to be carried out by those with the appropriate skills within your organisation. Where the researcher can be of help is by running surveys on users of these products to determine their levels of satisfaction. Such surveys should elicit opinion on the design, performance, operating features, quality, and reliability of the product. Users of your own products should be included in the survey for comparison.

A typical survey question for this type of comparison is normally scalar, and would ask users to rate their satisfaction with product X on a scale of perhaps 1 to 5, where 1 could represent very satisfied and 5 dissatisfied.

Terms and conditions

'Terms and conditions' cover such things as the warranty, discounts, minimum order volumes, delivery, maintenance, training and special offers that may be offered by rival companies.

In many cases your own salesmen are likely to have a great deal of information on these. They are probably the first to know of any changes made by the competition in this area. They should be aware of the researcher's interest in the competition, and encouraged to report any changes. It is good practice to set up regular meetings with

Researching Competitors

them to monitor their views on these points. They have the opportunity of obtaining much of the information on terms and conditions from customers.

Surveys can be carried out on competitors' customers, distributors and retailers, to determine the terms and conditions in use. In most cases, respondents are cooperative and provide the information needed. Obtaining confidential material, such as copies of contracts and orders containing details of the competitors' terms, oversteps the point of what is reasonable ethical behaviour and should not be attempted.

Customer opinions

Many organisations today run some form of survey to monitor their customers' opinions of their products, services and support. Trade magazines in some industries even run their own, in which your products and services are compared to those of your competitors each period, thus saving you the expense. If you decide to conduct such a survey it should be carried out regularly – say once a year – as much of the value to be gained from the results is on the changes in satisfaction recorded from one survey to the next. It is important not only to review the results from the survey with senior members of your organisation, but also to set up a process by which those areas that are below par, or show negative trends of satisfaction, can receive appropriate attention

New developments

A good source of information on new products is the trade magazines for the industry. Many new products are reviewed in such magazines before becoming available on the market. Rumours of new developments also appear in these magazines and in the financial press. It is a good plan to have a systematic review of all the key papers and periodicals covering your industry, on a regular basis, and build up a diary of your competitors, covering opinions on their abilities, financial performance, products and new developments from such sources.

Early warning of new developments can sometimes come from scanning the advertisements for technical personnel. These often describe the job in some detail in order to recruit the best available people. If your key competitor is suddenly looking for two designers, and an expert in robotic production lines, there must be a reason.

Regular discussions with your design and production staff will keep you advised on what to look out for, and how the signs may be interpreted.

Marketing analysis

Marketing analysis is concerned with the way in which our competitors market their products: that is, the channels they use to distribute them, their use of advertising, and the sales and branch organisation, if any.

Sales channels

Details of how competitors sell and distribute their products need to be collected. If they use salesmen, and have branch offices, the details can sometimes be found in the company report or other published material. *Yellow Pages* is another possible source, where retailers and distributors are sometimes grouped together under the banner of the company. Your own sales force is an obvious source, as they are likely to be very familiar with the competing organisations and can provide a great deal of this information. If your competitors use distributors, it is often easy to find a list of these from a simple enquiry as to where one might purchase the products. Sales brochures may contain a list of distributors and major retailers, or sometimes this will appear in advertisements.

If the products are also sold by mail order, the applicable magazines will contain advertisements from mail order companies for the products. You sometimes have to look quite widely to find all the magazines (a rubber manufacturing company has recently had advertisements in a number of gardening magazines for one of its products – butyl sheeting – as liners for ponds). An additional benefit from these sources is that prices are often given.

Use of the media

How does the competition advertise details of its products? By monitoring trade, business and other appropriate magazines, you can record in which magazines and how often they advertise. You may find it useful to build up a folio of each of your major competitor's

Researching Competitors

advertisements, to see if a theme or direction the company is taking can be detected – after all, you would expect some link between advertising and the company's strategy. There are a number of publications giving details of how much each company spends on advertising and the media used. This information can be collected for each one of your competitors. Their attendance at trade exhibitions should also be monitored. Go and visit their stands, and listen to what the other visitors are saying.

Review all this information at regular intervals to see what has changed – whether any competitors show a change of direction or any big increases in advertisement spending, or if new forms of media are being used.

Volume and share

Product volume and market share information is a very important area for the monitoring of competitors. Your organisation may feel it is performing well in the market, but your competitors may be increasing their volumes and share of the market at a greater rate, until one day ... In some industries, such as motor vehicles, the manufacturers submit figures to a third party for publishing on a regular basis. Other industries, such as the computer industry, have a large number of 'industry watchers' who publish numerous reports on volumes, revenue and market shares as a result of surveys which they carry out. Trade associations and magazines sometimes carry out surveys, in which such figures are provided. Another useful source can be research publishers' lists; some commission reports on industries, or publish the results of earlier 'multi-client' reports, which often contain information on the leading suppliers in the industry. Other sources of information include stockbrokers, government statistics and so on. You can, of course, run your own survey, but for this type of information it can be expensive.

Further information to collect on competitors in this area includes monitoring the availability of products and delivery, and trying to build up a picture of their major customers, with the help of the sales force. If you become aware of difficulties experienced by a competitor in supplying his products, from trade reports or dissatisfaction expressed in a survey, here is your chance to demonstrate one of the many benefits of competitor analysis by providing the details and a list of the competitor's customers to the sales force.

Other intelligence to collect is on new product performance. Again, many products are reviewed by trade magazines and newspapers, in which such aspects as design, performance and quality are reviewed. In some industries this has reached a point where comparisons are made with equivalent products from other manufacturers, and a league table is made up of the best to worst (on that journal's criteria, of course). A satisfaction survey carried out on users of the product may, however, be the only way of evaluating the product's acceptance. The difficulty here may lie in finding users to interview, but it is often possible for an independent research company to obtain names from a distributor or retailer, in return for a copy of the survey's findings, of where their customers are.

Long-term outlook

One of the main aims of competitive analysis is to know how competitors conduct their business, and to anticipate what their future intentions may be. Armed with this information, your own organisation should be able to develop an effective marketing strategy and tactics, to allow you to compete on your own terms.

So, what should you be trying to anticipate for the future and what information should be collected to achieve this? Important areas to look at and try to monitor are: personnel, mergers and takeovers, new developments, changes in technology, and marketing.

Personnel changes
Monitor changes of key directors and managers – Where have they come from? How did they and their previous company perform? Were they known to be responsible for any particularly successful operation? If so, how might this apply to your competitor and affect you?

Takeovers and mergers
A takeover or merger can be carried out for many reasons: lack of finance, merging of product lines, removal of competitors, asset stripping, product diversification, a move into a new market by a foreign company and so on. You need to look at the reasons and history of the company making the takeover. Has it carried out this

type of operation before? If so, what were the results? Again, assess the likely outcome, how it might affect your own company, and how long it is likely to be before its effects are felt.

New products and new developments
Some organisations release details of new developments long before the product comes to market. If this is the case in your industry you may be fortunate, but in many industries this is not the case and the available signs need to be read. The previous two sections may contain some of the signs.

A good source of information can be the local papers in the area where your competitor is sited. Advertisements for personnel to 'work on an exciting new development', or to be in the forefront of 'new technology' should be noted. 'Designers required to work on new products, experience of logic chips and micro-actuators an advantage' may only be found in magazines catering for the specialist subject. A talk to your own design department will help you to decide which periodicals need to be monitored, and maybe a helpful person in that department can be encouraged to provide you with a cutting service, to cover both employment and information on new technical developments that are likely to affect the business.

Also look out for small articles in local papers, on such items as requests for planning permission by competitors to develop a new factory or branch office, or others mentioning the retirement at the end of the year of the Sales Director. These are very useful in building up a picture of what is happening in your competitors' organisations.

New geographical markets
With the changes to the marketplace brought about by the developments in the EC, and the opening up of Eastern Europe, we should all be aware of our continental European competitors moving into the UK. They are proceeding by takeovers, mergers, or the setting-up of their own marketing organisations and distribution channels. An early indication can sometimes be found by attending trade shows or exhibitions, where they are showing their products for the first time, and making contact with suitable distributors or retailers. A list of the main competitive organisations in each of the other European countries should be researched, to provide details of product range,

financial details and markets. There are a number of directories covering the major European organisations, and a careful review of these will help you to identify the major threats, and consider a strategy to make their entry expensive or rewarding for your own organisation. Do not neglect the relevant companies in the Americas and the Far East.

A difficult area to judge involves those companies which do not at present compete, but who may decide to do so because of complementary products, expertise in a production method or, more likely, through changes and expertise gained in a technology, such as producing the first electronic version: all these may become major competitors. The last 20 years provide a number of examples of this pattern, the Swiss watch industry being one. This kind of potential competitor is most dangerous if your products are of a more 'traditional' design. Again, if you have an R&D department consult them on the possible trends, and keep a sharp eye on the press for likely clues on tomorrow's world.

Use of surveys

While much of the information discussed so far does not require a special survey, there are some key items that can best be obtained by one. Unless you have a team of in-house researchers, you will need to engage an agency that can provide such a service, controlling the survey yourself, or to hand the whole job over to a consultancy. There are several methods which have proved successful in obtaining information on competitors.

Omnibus surveys

Where a company and its competitors market products which are widely used by consumers or business, omnibus surveys have proved to be a very useful way of obtaining information on the size of a market and the share that you and your competitors have in that market. They have found wide application in consumer research, but could serve just as well in business research. For example, a manufacturer of telephone answering machines may wish to find out the present penetration of the market, future short-term demand, and the shares of his competitors. Using a consumer omnibus he can ask respondents, in their homes, questions on the use of telephone answering machines both at home and in their place of work. Simple questions can be used to filter out those respondents who are not applicable to your products from further relevant questions: 'Do you have a telephone answering machine in your home or place of work?'. By focusing questions on only those who qualify, considerable savings in the cost of the survey can be made. Where the number of 'hits' is likely to be low, it is necessary to enter your questions into the omnibus over a number of runs.

Focus groups (or discussion groups)

Focus groups have been used successfully on groups of users of different products, to understand their views on how they choose their suppliers, on the products and on the importance of their features. Care needs to be taken in the selection of questions and of the members of mixed groups. The sales department will take a dim view if a customer goes away from such an event firmly sold, by a particularly persuasive member of the group, on the merits of a competitor's product.

Video recordings of such groups have proved useful to product developers who do not have the same opportunities of meeting users (provided that the group's members have been told that this will happen). The technique has also proved useful in the development of questionnaires for use in telephone or postal surveys.

Telephone surveys

The telephone survey is now the most common method used to obtain interviews for quantitative research. They have a lot of advantages, such as speed and control of respondent, and in some business areas are often successful in reducing the level of non-response. A typical use of such a survey would be to find market occupancy and market share information.

Face-to-face interviewing

Because of the high cost of face-to-face interviewing, this method is now used mainly in business research for providing qualitative in-depth analysis. It is particularly useful for studies into competitive terms and conditions, and for understanding the differences between satisfaction ratings for different competitors.

Setting up a competitive database

Most of the information you will collect can be held in a database, which will help in providing quick analysis in response to queries, or by giving competitive profiles, while answering queries from other departments over the telephone.

File contents

Typical information held on the database would be:

- company name and HQ address;
- telephone and fax numbers;
- details of other locations;
- key directors, positions and previous history;
- staff numbers (total, office, salesmen, engineers);
- recent staff recruitment;
- financial details (turnover, profit, costs etc);
- ratios (turnover per employee, per salesman etc);
- products and their sales volumes and revenues;
- present year and history;
- market share (present and history);
- sales areas and regions (by salesmen and branches);
- industries or customer-types focused on;

Researching Competitors

- methods of distribution;
- key suppliers;
- key customers;
- advertising campaigns (media used, dates);
- advertising expenditure;
- sales strategy;
- customer satisfaction ratings;
- product strategy and developments;
- recent news items;
- recommendations.

Database software

The choice of software for a database depends largely on the number of competitors, and the amount of information you can collect. In large organisations it will also depend heavily on the advice of your data processing department. For smaller requirements there are several very good database packages on the market for IBM PCs and compatibles, and the advice of the local personal computer dealer or agent should be sought.

Database packages come in the form of 'flat file' or 'relational' databases, and they will need to be set up to meet your requirements. They provide a data entry screen to accept new details or changes to a competitor's record, plus facilities to select and analyse the information held, and others to print out details and construct standard reports. Many databases come with graphics facilities, so that report charts can also be prepared, for any regular presentations to management.

Competitive research – where to start

As can be seen, there is a wide range of information and research connected with competitive analysis. If you have a number of competitors, and wish to provide your company with a comprehensive service, the work involved probably requires one or more full-time employees, and a reasonable research budget.

If your company is considering a formal approach to competitive analysis for the first time, you will be asked what information should be collected to meet your company's need. Faced with this problem, you should map out all the types of information and analysis that would be applicable to your organisation that you could provide. For each of these you should consider the cost of obtaining the information – be it from books, reports, information services, on-line databases or original surveys. Also, consider how often each needs to be carried out and the time each will require. In addition, you should prioritise each piece of information according to what you think its importance is to your company.

Armed with this information, you then need to review it with the Sales, R&D, Manufacturing, and Finance departments, and any others you think are applicable. This discussion should determine what they all consider to be important to their departments, and the intervals at which they require briefing. Finally, a proposal should be prepared and reviewed, to agree what the company can afford to do in terms of time and money.

An alternative and simpler approach might be to collect the basic facts on each competitor – such as employees, locations of premises, products sold, and distribution details. Add to this the financial data, from which you can produce some simple ratios to compare the performance of competitors against that of your own organisation. Analyse this information to produce a report or presentation, comparing competitors with your own company. From the financial histories try to draw some conclusions on the future, by projecting forward each company's performance. Present this competitive pattern to your senior management, who will then be in a better position to advise you on the important competitive issues to be addressed.

Ethics: industrial espionage or legitimate research?

A number of people regard business-to-business market research as another form of industrial espionage. Espionage is the practice of

Researching Competitors

spying, or obtaining secret information. Expressed in these terms, it may appear that conducting surveys on users and buyers, to poll opinions and collect information on competitors, is a form of espionage. Much other material that is used, however, is published and freely available.

The MRS/IMRA Code of Conduct gives some guidance on the subject with regard to surveys, when it says:

> *A.8* Where the use of information that will be contained in the survey report might have an adverse effect directly on the informant's organisation (eg when interviewing a competitor or potential competitor), it is imperative that the nature or sponsor of the survey is revealed before the information is collected.

Section A.2 states that 'no information which could be used to identify people or companies shall be revealed . . . unless the permission of the informant is given'. The Code also requires practitioners of market research to conduct their research 'honestly, objectively, without unwelcome intrusion, and without harm to informants'.

While companies and their competitors may prefer the information discussed in this Chapter to remain confidential, it is nevertheless necessary for all of them to divulge some information to others, if they are to remain in business.

In business research, many of the topics concern the respondent as much as the sponsoring organisation. The respondent is often anxious to obtain further details, to improve his knowledge and his effectiveness in his job. After many a focus group of business people doing similar work, those taking part frequently admit its usefulness, of much the same kind as the benefit derived by members attending IMRA or MRS meetings. Many trade and professional associations consist only of competitors, and a useful source of information they are found to be.

For those intending to conduct research on competitors, the following guidelines are recommended.

- Do not do anything illegal.
- Do not use (or even seek) material belonging to your competitors which is confidential.

- Do not seek a response from a competitor without first revealing your organisation's identity (or, in the case of a separate market research company, that of the sponsor).
- Do not sponsor or hire organisations who offer to provide information that could be deemed to be confidential.
- For the 'grey' areas, try to apply a moral judgement by asking yourself, 'Is this reasonable?' (or 'Would I like it done to me?').
- If in doubt, consult your company's legal department or legal advisers, or contact the IMRA Council or other members for advice (many research agencies are particularly helpful in this respect).

Conclusion

An organisation that collects the information recommended in this Chapter should be able, over a period of time, to construct a complete picture of each of its competitors and, by careful observation and analysis, to develop a successful continuing strategy against them.

While there are other people within an organisation who may well know a considerable amount about the competition as it affects their own area (especially sales), and have strong views on the subject, the marketing researcher will be unique in being able to see the whole range of competitors' activities and their performance. It is most important; indeed, the whole point of the exercise is to be able to summarise the information and make recommendations on the development of a strategy, and to advise on actions that need to be taken. Regular monitoring and reporting is the key to developing a successful competitive strategy.

15

Corporate Image

Peter Hutton

Most companies pay very little attention to their image in the world outside them and yet, in quite a large proportion of cases, the customers of those same companies are quite strongly influenced by their own view – their image – of their suppliers. Where a company does, consciously, consider its external image, very frequently its customers (or, even more seriously, its potential customers) may hold a very different view of it.

It would seem, therefore, that a large number of companies, in the provision of both goods and services, should give some attention to their real image as perceived by their marketplace. The techniques of business marketing research are ideal for the assessment of real image, and this Chapter deals in detail with such assessment.

Introduction

A survey conducted among ICI salesmen found that the vast majority believed that being from ICI 'made it easier to establish new contacts' and 'helped them a great deal' or 'helped them a fair amount'. Why? Because ICI is one of the best-known and most favourably regarded of companies in Britain, both among the general public and among its major commercial target audiences.

The salesmen here are benefiting from the efforts of the company over many decades to ensure that it has a commercially supportive corporate image. Research has shown how companies which have a positive image in one respect such as product quality, will be assumed to have a positive image in many other respects such as profitability, quality of management, and treatment of employees. Thus, the salesman from ICI who approaches a new customer can enter the door with confidence that the new contact will be favourably disposed towards his products, his company, the technical support and other services it can provide, and towards himself.

The company can advertise or use any other communication techniques, making the fairly safe assumption that it does not have to establish its credentials – ie it is known by the target audience and does not have to defend its reputation for product quality or professionalism in servicing the customer. Therefore, it can concentrate on the essential message of its communications.

This is true of many companies, of course, and market research techniques are used to establish the nature of their corporate images as a back-drop to their marketing and corporate communications programmes.

The need for a good image

Companies need a good corporate image to:

- support their marketing and selling efforts;
- aid recruitment of new staff;
- motivate existing staff;
- enhance relationships with investors;
- underpin the credibility of their communications to these and other groups (such as the media and opinion leaders).

Thus, for any corporate communications or research programme, the following become target audiences:

- customers and potential customers;
- employees and potential employees;

Corporate Image

- investors – institutional and private;
- the media and opinion leader groups;
- legislators.

We live in critical times. Each generation produces new criticisms and, with them, new expectations and demands on business and commerce. There is nothing wrong with this – indeed, it is entirely healthy. Businesses thrive and grow strong as they meet the demands placed on them. Too narrow a definition of their role places them in jeopardy of being attacked by pressure groups and other critics, if market forces do not hit them first.

In one sense, the various roles of companies provide the framework within which the corporate image evolves. Each company will be evaluated according to its performance as producer, employer, profit maker, corporate citizen and conserver of the environment. However, performance expectations will vary for each section of the public and for each company. An oil or chemical company is more likely to be judged by its performance with respect to the environment, a bank by its profits and so on.

Each company will create its corporate image through its normal activities – producing and supplying goods to the market, employing people in different roles at different locations, the visible steps it takes to preserve the environment or conserve natural resources.

The modern company has to be aware, as never before, of the changing environment in which it lives and the roles it is required to play. As a producer it is required to meet certain technical standards of production, as well as the standards of quality, design, taste and price expected by the consumer. As an employer it has to conform to legislation designed to protect the rights of the employee, and adjust to a market providing even more attractive packages to attract its employees away. As a business it is required to produce profits for reinvestment and to provide dividends to its shareholders. As a corporate citizen it is required to act within the framework of the law. As a user of natural resources it also needs to be environmentally conscious: a fact which has always been a feature of business and commerce, but one recently brought more to light as the public's attention has turned to focus on the effect of man's behaviour – essentially as consumer and producer – on the natural environment.

Producing the right image

However, without some degree of management it is likely that the business will produce a corporate image which is not as supportive of its activities as it might be. Moreover, as the company changes it is likely that the corporate image will lag some way behind, unless conscious and planned efforts are made to bring it up to date.

The management of a company's corporate image ought to be a key

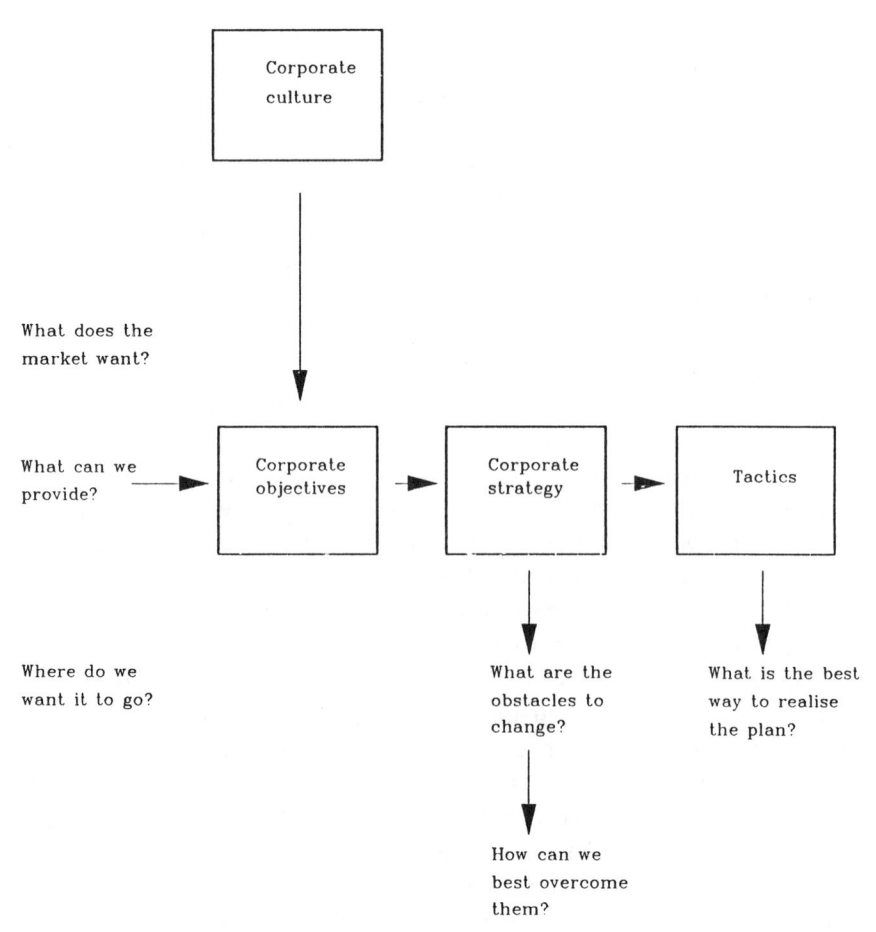

```
                        ┌─────────────┐
                        │  Corporate  │
                        │   culture   │
                        └──────┬──────┘
                               │
What does the                  │
market want?                   ▼
                 ┌───────────────┐     ┌───────────────┐     ┌─────────┐
What can we  ──▶ │   Corporate   │ ──▶ │   Corporate   │ ──▶ │ Tactics │
provide?         │   objectives  │     │    strategy   │     │         │
                 └───────────────┘     └───────┬───────┘     └────┬────┘
                                               │                  │
                                               ▼                  ▼
Where do we                            What are the       What is the best
want it to go?                         obstacles to       way to realise
                                       change?            the plan?
                                               │
                                               ▼
                                       How can we
                                       best overcome
                                       them?
```

Figure 15.1. *Corporate strategy development and execution*

Corporate Image

part of its overall strategy. Corporate strategy is concerned with such questions as 'Where are we trying to get to?' (strategic objectives) and 'How are we trying to get there?' (strategic path). Whatever its strategy, a company will need a corporate image which is supportive, and this, along with the other aspects of the business, needs careful management, as illustrated in Figure 15.1.

Research has an important role to play here. A strategy for corporate image building would start by asking the following questions.

- Which sections of the public are important to us?
- What sort of image do we currently have among each one?
- What sort of image would best enhance our activities and support our attaining our corporate objectives?

Corporate image research would identify whether the company faces a problem of awareness of favourability, and whether perceptions accurately reflect the reality in terms of, for example, range of activities, management quality, profitability and size. Is the image and style of the company professional, reliable, responsive, customer-orientated, progressive and so on?

It could explore the credibility of alternative image concepts and the barriers to their being accepted by key audiences. In this way it helps to evolve the most appropriate messages and style of communication.

In order to establish the effectiveness of the corporate strategy in communications terms, the research would also lay down some baseline measures to be re-evaluated after an appropriate time period, or periods. This repetition of image assessment is illustrated in Figure 15.2, showing it as a continuous cycle.

The appropriate period will depend on the audience and the intended role and intensity of the corporate communications campaign. Some companies, for example, choose to monitor their image every six months among institutional investors in the City (of London, or other financial centres), where the strains in the financial markets feed through to corporate reputations. The 1987 stock market crash saw the images of most quoted companies take a dive, but in this context a relatively small decline was an encouraging trend. Other companies are concerned only with the long-term build up of their

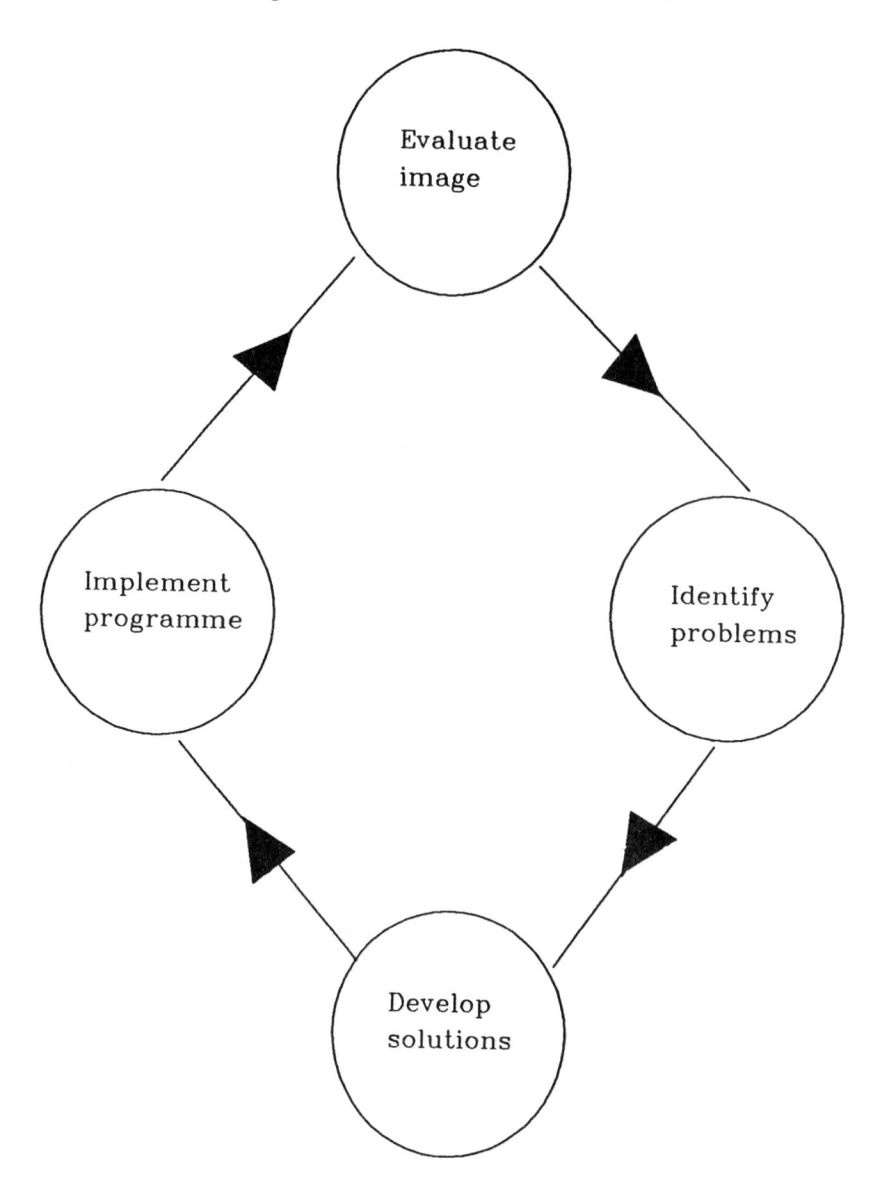

Figure 15.2. *The process of managing the corporate image*

corporate reputations. As with stock market prices, it is generally true that corporate images which move up quickly are liable also to move down quickly, and it is wise to focus on the long term and not over-react to short-term movements.

Among industrial buyers, short-term shifts are harder to obtain and corporate image research is undertaken relatively infrequently and with long-term strategic changes in mind. A five-year gap is a reasonable period over which to assess progress. The base-line research enables priorities to be set, but the execution of these can involve a major reorientation of the business, which is not undertaken lightly.

Levels of corporate image

The corporate image can be thought of as existing at different levels (see Figure 15.3). The *socio-cultural* level is the environment of attitudes and opinions towards business and industry, which are characteristics of the culture. During the 1960s and 1970s, many of the fundamental beliefs upon which private enterprise was based came under fire – the profit motive, private enterprise, the authority of management. Since then, much has changed. Legislation has curtailed the power of trades unions; employees have been given new rights; the government has actively promoted the concept of free enterprise and, through taxation and other policies, has encouraged the accumulation of private wealth, including the extension of shareholding. In other words, much has been done to change the cultural environment in which businesses operate and this is reflected in the attitudes, opinions, behaviour and motivation of managers, employees, customers and opinion formers.

Corporate image research is used to evaluate these cultural values as they relate to the business environment among various audiences.

The next level of corporate image is that of *perceptions towards the business sector* in which a company operates. Whether it be chemicals or insurance, motor manufacturing or mining, each business sector has its own image made up of thousands of impressions, built up over time. Some of these have been directly influenced by the companies within those sectors, others by factors outside their control. The success of the North Sea oil explorations did much to enhance the

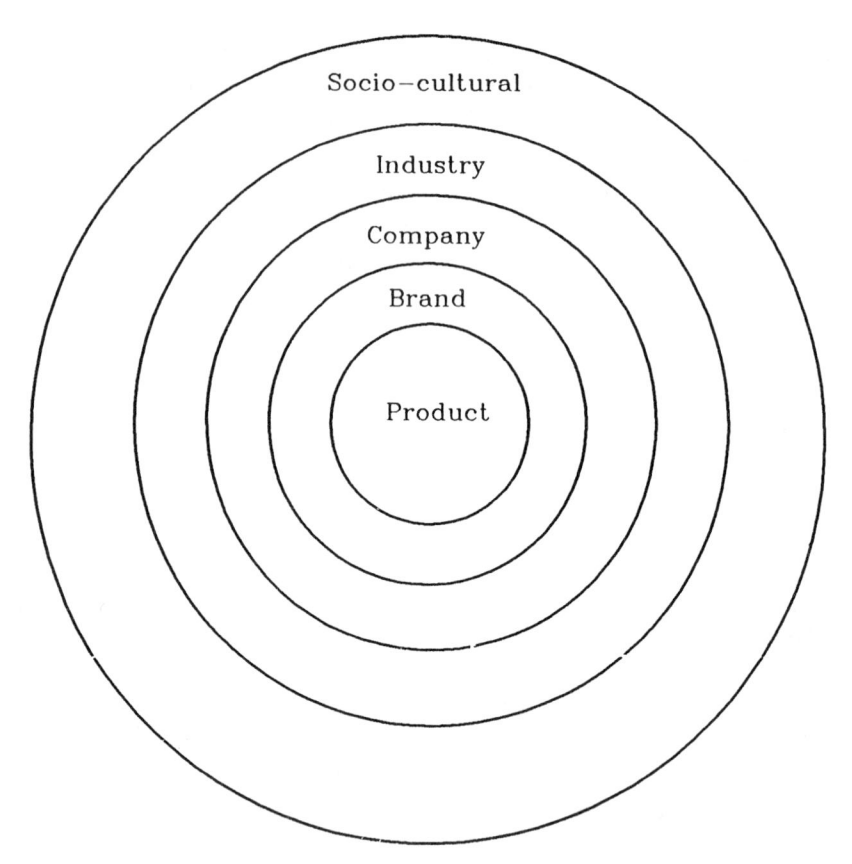

Figure 15.3. *Levels of corporate image*

image of the oil and gas industry during the late 1970s and 1980s, although questions about its safety record have cast a shadow over this industry more recently. Environmental pressure groups have undermined the nuclear generating industry's efforts to trade on the 'high tech' image, which finds favour with the public in relation to North Sea oil. The telecommunications and computer sectors benefit from being associated with advanced electronics, the future and job prospects for this generation's children. The motor industry has benefited from shedding much of its reputation for industrial unrest and low productivity which characterised the 1970s.

Business images are important for individual companies, because

Corporate Image

each company is associated with one or more sectors. For companies in the chemical industry, pharmaceutical manufacture is likely to elicit more positive associations than explosives, but fertiliser manufacture, once laudable, is now under fire from the anti-nitrate lobby. The once innocently perceived CFCs used in refrigerators became the great destroyers of the ozone layer in the upper atmosphere.

All these issues are important and have to be addressed head on by the companies concerned and often as an industry initiative. In the long term, nothing is to be gained from avoiding the very real environmental concerns now being voiced. At the same time, industries have to communicate to the consumer and society at large the very real benefits resulting from their activities. A failure to do so has a detrimental effect on the companies making up each business sector.

The next level is that of *the company itself*. While some companies, such as Ford or Cadbury, have a very high profile through the branding of their products, others, such as Unilever or Proctor and Gamble, have chosen to let their brands carry themselves rather than float on the back of the corporate reputation. This has advantages in markets where new products often fail (or at least have short lives), while it has disadvantages in launching new products, which cannot guarantee a base customer loyalty. Companies such as Heinz or Findus, Rank Xerox or IBM, know that their good track record has established a reputation for quality and reliability, which does not have to be re-established with each new product launch.

The company level is the one to which many key audiences most directly relate – employees, investors, suppliers and competitors. In the case of many industrial products it is also crucial. Buyers are not just buying chemicals, industrial plant or steel. They are also buying the technical support, reliability of delivery, and guarantee of product quality, which the corporate image of the supplier implies.

For many other products bought by industry and commerce, and for the bulk of consumer products, the corporate image is determined largely by the *product and brand images*. A bad experience with a particular product will quickly tarnish the manufacturer's reputation. A product which fails to live up to expectations casts doubt on the company's design capability, quality control, management and integrity.

The level of product and brand images is the level at which a company's commercial success is most vulnerable. Millions of pounds' worth of brand advertising can be undone by the publicity given to motor-car models needing recall to rectify a design fault, or a new brand of petrol having to be withdrawn after it was found to be detrimental to the performance of certain models of car, as Shell found to its detriment with its Formula Shell brand. This is likely to have a serious effect on the corporate image of the company concerned, although much will depend on the way in which that company responds to the problem.

Changes in corporate image

Unless something drastic happens, corporate images change slowly. They are formed by a combination of direct experience of the company's products and services, direct contact with its employees, exposure to advertisements, brochures, leaflets and annual reports, news and features coverage in newspapers and magazines, and conversations with suppliers, competitors or other observers.

Often the company will change while its corporate image remains relatively unchanged. A certain motor manufacturer unfortunately gained a reputation for producing cars which were prone to rust easily. Despite its spending millions of pounds on curing the problem and providing rust-proof working guarantees, the perception remained strong for several years afterwards.

Because of their slow evolution, corporate image problems are rarely tackled effectively by a short-term communications programme. Consequently, effective corporate image building needs a long-term communications strategy, aimed at all audiences of importance to it. Moreover, to be confident that the strategy is working, it is important to monitor change over time.

Corporate advertising is important and is used for a variety of reasons. It provides a clear statement of what the company is about, how it sees itself, or what its priorities are as a business. The Shell corporate campaign which showed the Welsh valleys, after a pipeline had been laid under them, communicated a message of an organisation which placed caring for the environment high on its list of corporate objectives, rather than one which prized short-term profit and

Corporate Image

environmental exploitation ahead of any social responsibility.

Often the fact that the company is advertising is as important as the message of the advertising itself. Research by MORI among institutional investors and stockbroking analysts found that over half believed it to be important for companies to undertake corporate image advertising aimed at the financial community in general. The fact that the company is advertising signals its commitment and resolve to build on past success to take it into the future. This helps to build the confidence necessary for support in the City. It also has an important role in motivating staff and bringing them together behind a single corporate identity. In businesses composed of numerous divisions and operating units, it is important to provide a unifying theme to break down internal barriers, enhance communications and build a sense of teamwork.

Customers and potential customers also appreciate a message and style which corporate advertising can bring to the business, providing an overall identity within which to place their individual experiences.

In its run-up to privatisation, one of the aims of the British Gas corporate advertising was to present the image of its being one major industry. This was important, not only for the City investment community and individual small investors but also for customers and employees who were used to thinking in terms of their own former regional gas boards rather than the national whole.

Image assessment

Corporate images are measured in a variety of ways. One of the most basic, but also most useful, consists of measuring familiarity (how well the company is known) and favourability (how favourably or unfavourably it is regarded). These are, arguably, the two most fundamental measures of corporate image. Familiarity is a precondition for all other corporate image measures; favourability is the overall impression left from a complex range of perceptions and beliefs. The ideal in any audience is to be well known and well regarded. The worst position is to be well known and unfavourably regarded.

Such measures of corporate image mean little in isolation, and have to be evaluated alongside the corporate images of companies of similar

Researching Business Markets – The IMRA Handbook

standing. These might be competitors in the market for its products, or other quoted companies in the market for funds on the Stock Exchange, or other major employers in the job market.

One technique used for measuring familiarity and favourability is to ask respondents to rate companies according to how well known they are. This would be done on a five-point scale, ranging from 'know very well' to 'never heard of'; similarly, those known are then rated on a five-point scale, ranging from 'very favourable' to 'very unfavourable'. By allocating scores to these points (0 to 4 for familiarity, and −2 to +2 for favourability), a researcher can calculate mean scores for each

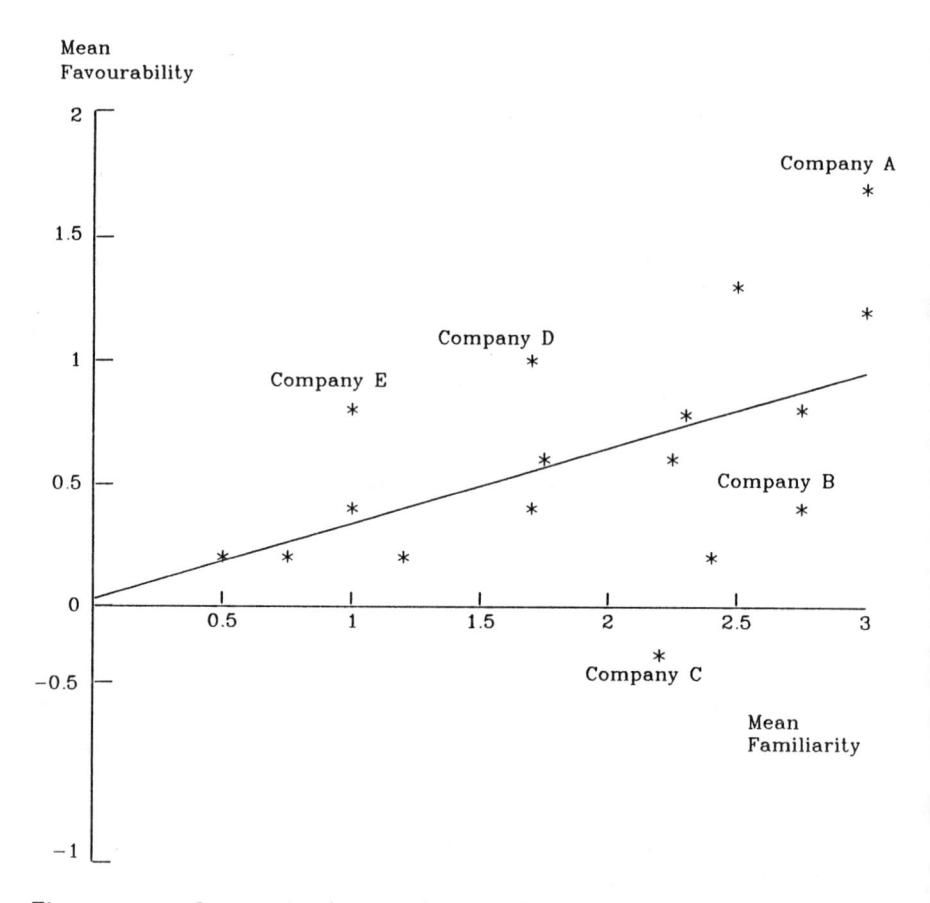

Figure 15.4. *Company familiarity and favourability*

Corporate Image

company asked about. These can then be used to plot companies on a two-dimensional scatter chart according to how well known and how favourably regarded they are.

The familiarity and favourability scatter chart, such as that illustrated in Figure 15.4, provides an overall perspective within which to view a company's relative standing among various audiences, and provides the basic backdrop for a corporate communications strategy. Where purchasing decision makers are the audience, a company such as company A in the top right of Figure 15.4 – well known and well regarded – is likely to be the market leader. Its strong image will enhance all its activities and provide credibility to its communications. Its strategy must be to retain its lead position.

A company to the right of the chart but rather less well regarded, such as company B, is in a vulnerable position. Although well known, it is often known for the wrong reasons. It lags well behind company A and will need a great effort to attain a similar standing and therefore be on an equivalent footing to company A. Its positioning, incidentally, may bear little relationship to its size in terms of turnover, and it may well be many times larger, or smaller, than company A.

Company C is in an even worse position. Being just below the horizontal line means that the target audience is, on balance, more inclined to view it unfavourably than favourably. Its moderate familiarity score means it is probably reasonably well established but has not ingratiated itself over-much with the market.

Company D is reasonably well known and regarded, and will probably move up in familiarity as it communicates. Company E, although little known, is very well regarded by those who know it. Clearly it is doing something right, and a small effort to increase awareness ought to be rewarded also with a highly favourably response.

The diagonal line is the statistical line of best fit. It illustrates how, among this audience, better-known companies tend to be better regarded. Companies above this line are relatively well regarded and those below relatively poorly regarded for their familiarity rating.

Among most general audiences, better-known companies tend to be better regarded, although this starts to break down among more discriminating audiences, such as trade journalists and institutional investors, or audiences, such as MPs, who will take a particular political stance when evaluating certain types of organisation, such as those in the public sector.

Among industrial decision makers, the relationship usually stands up. Companies which are well known and poorly regarded by a substantial number of buyers, tend not to remain in business long. However, there still remains great scope for discrimination between companies which are rated adequately and those rated exceptionally well; in a competitive market it is advantage at the margin which really counts.

Understanding the corporate image

Such research measures are a starting point for understanding a company's corporate image. Others provide a more detailed understanding of its strengths and weaknesses, its character and identity. Often respondents' own verbatim comments provide the best insights into why a company is viewed favourably or unfavourably, why it stands out or where it has failed to live up to expectations. These are best complemented by measures of specific attributes, but need to be carefully chosen as specific to the audience.

An important role for corporate image research is to establish the criteria by which audiences evaluate companies. Those companies which are in a strong position, relative to competitors, will be those which score highly on the factors considered most important. One company found that the reliability of its deliveries was the most important criterion on which it was being evaluated by customers and potential customers. Its low score on this criterion led it to rethink its whole approach to customer relations, in order to establish a competitive edge.

Each audience will have a different set of criteria against which to evaluate a company. Major purchasing decision makers in industry and commerce will often know their suppliers very well and in person. They will probably have a good knowledge of the products they buy and, depending on the type of product, regular direct contact with the firms producing them. The criteria of importance to them are then likely to reflect this detailed knowledge and close relationship with the company. The products will have to meet certain standards and

Corporate Image

specifications, but beyond that there will be a number of aspects of service which are important – such as technical suppport, delivery time, and personal contact with senior management.

Institutional investors will have far less detailed knowledge of the company's products and day-to-day operations, but will have a far greater understanding of its balance sheet. They will evaluate the company in terms of its past financial performance, the quality of its management and, taking into account market considerations, its expected performance in the future.

In the recruitment market, far less esoteric considerations are relevant. Undergraduates, for example, will have impressions about the company as an employer and as a provider of career opportunities, and of its standing in relation to competitors in terms of product quality and competitiveness.

With potential customers it is particularly important to establish an accurate understanding of one's product range. Many companies lose out substantially through assuming that because they know what products they produce, so too does the market. However, as buyers are constantly being bombarded with product information from the whole range of competing companies, and there is no guarantee that feature articles in the press or advertisements get read and the information retained, this is often very far from the truth. Buyers will remember the company for what it has supplied in the past, and many make assumptions about other types of products it is likely to supply; unless steps are taken to ensure effective communication, however, knowledge beyond this is likely to be patchy. A key element of corporate image research among business decision makers is often, therefore, to establish the degree of understanding of the company's product range.

Understanding is also important in other groups. In the City, for example, a very diversified company which is predominantly linked with one sector will find its share price highly vulnerable to changes in that sector's fortunes. A great deal of financial advertising in recent years has been concerned with communicating the range of activities of many of Britain's major companies, in order to avoid this very single sector linkage.

16

New Product Development and Testing

Ken Sutherland

The activities involved in getting a new product successfully to market provide plenty of opportunities for marketing research. There are probably more opportunities to use different kinds of research skill than in almost any other application. The aim of this Chapter is to illustrate these uses, rather than to describe in detail how new products are actually developed and tested.

Introduction

New products are vital to the growth, if not even the survival, of most companies, yet it is amazing how many new products fail and how many new product programmes dwindle away without reaching their goal. If the product and its intended market have been well researched, there is no reason for failure.

There is, however, a great deal more to new product success than just having a good product. Whoever it actually was who said that the maker of a better mouse-trap would cause the world to make a beaten path to his door can have had very little marketing experience. Success in new product marketing involves a combination of many skills, with that of marketing research by no means least among them.

Degrees of novelty

Some understanding must first be reached of what is meant by a new product. There are at least three components to the marketing activity that need to be considered: the product, the supplier, and the marketplace.

To these could also be added the technology involved in the product – important when there is a major change (such as from electronic valves to transistors, or in the introduction of fluidics in control equipment), but considered here to be totally incorporated in the product component. The supplier could be differentiated into original manufacturer and local agent or distributor, but is more simply regarded here as that company seen by the marketplace as the local provider of the product. Finally, the term marketplace has both geographical and end-use sector connotations – but it will be used here to cover both meanings.

If each of these three components is then considered simply as bipolar (either new or not new), there are eight possible degrees of newness, from the one extreme of 'a new product from a newly established supplier to a new market', to the other extreme of 'an existing product from a well-established supplier to an existing market' (which has no novelty element, but still requires marketing research).

To this 'simple' picture can be added the complication already noted – that the market may be either geographical or end-use or both – and the even more diffuse spread in the product itself, which can vary from a slight improvement (in performance, or size, or material of construction) to a completely new design.

Clearly, it will be impossible to discuss all these different degrees of novelty, and this Chapter will concentrate on just one combination: the bringing of a markedly different 'new' product, to a well-known marketplace, by a supplier well established in that market. Mention will also be made, however, of any particular features of interest relating to novelty in the supplier or the market segment.

It should be mentioned that a new product does not have to be a physical object – something that can be picked up (or leaned against). New products in the service industries are equally of interest: the

New Product Development and Testing

banks and insurance companies now talk regularly of new products which they have made available to their customers. The life of computer software is relatively short, so that most products from software suppliers are 'new'.

The new product development path

It is a marketing truism that a new product will succeed if there is an easily established need for it. The ideal new product fulfils an easily demonstrated market need, but the most technically brilliant new product will fail if there is no need for it. A basic business-school philosophy is that development should result from 'market pull' and not from 'product push'.

In an ideal world, need would be paramount in new product development, but in practice this sharp division becomes blurred – needs themselves can be created by good advertising, and novelty is desirable for its own sake, especially where the purchase decision is by and on behalf of the same individual. Some product improvement is 'logical' and so gets done ahead of any demonstrated need for it. Most commonly, a product successful in one market is extended to another 'similar' market, where it is expected to sell just as well. All these divergences from the ideal are quite normal and, with appropriate help from marketing research, all can be successful.

Given an element of ideality, the path followed by a new product from its inception would include:

- identification of need (from incidental input by marketing research staff, or from sales personnel observations);
- development of product concept (by R&D personnel, with inputs from marketing and production);
- detailed design (by engineering personnel);
- manufacture of prototype;
- field testing (in friendly customers' works, and by marketing research techniques);
- design modification (to include results of testing);
- quantity manufacture;

- launch to the chosen market;
- sales, installation and commissioning;
- review of performance and acceptability to customers;
- product improvement.

This series of events is written from the point of view of a machine of some kind, but equivalent stages exist for other kinds of product. There are, of course, many more steps in the path than are shown – no mention is made, for instance, of cost analysis or of initial technical development. The path also has loops in it, to permit the recycle of opinion and consequent modification of any stage.

The events are written, too, from the point of view of a large company, and in that context are reviewed in this Chapter. It must also be realised that some new products reach the market as the result of the determination of an inventive person who has identified a possible market need. Much of this progress will be based on the intuition of the individual – but if he has some marketing awareness there is a greater chance of success.

Characteristics of new product research

The greater part of marketing research is engaged on projects where a great deal of information already exists. The main characteristic of research into new product markets – their novelty – implies that very little factual information may be available. The research may be needed into a concept rather than a physical embodiment, and respondents may require to exercise their imagination rather than reporting on their experience. Under these circumstances, it is vital that the researcher should ensure the absence of ambiguity from questions and responses. The questions should be as simple as possible, and the responses explored for every shade and nuance of meaning.

Although the writer of Ecclesiastes was living in a very different world from today's when he wrote, 'there is nothing new under the sun', a sizeable grain of truth remains in the remark. As human needs have not changed significantly, nothing can ever be completely new in that it satisfies a new human need. It should always be possible to relate a new product to an existing one, even if remotely, in order to make the task of researching it that much easier. Thus, a completely new design of pump may still only achieve the movement of liquid from one place or one pressure to another, and can therefore be compared with existing pumps achieving the same purpose.

The origin of the new product idea

The process by which it becomes apparent that a company should market a new product may be a very complex one. It is rare that the idea bursts forth from a single individual with no input from other sources. The relevant inputs might include:

- realisation that sales overall are falling, and that new products are necessary to return the company to growth;
- rumblings from the sales force that all is not well with the existing product line;
- development of a particular technical capability in the R&D department;
- awareness, from reading in the press, that a new product is making successful inroads into another market segment;
- natural progress in product development as part of a long-standing company programme;
- 'spin-off' of a new product idea from a market research activity of a different kind.

Whatever its source, the idea for a new product, or for the satisfaction of a market need not currently achieved by the existing product range, should eventually reach the attention of the senior management of the company and should lead to the creation of a project team intended to achieve its success.

At this stage in the product's life – its inception – it is vital that all concerned have a clear understanding of what is intended as the goal of the project. It is now that marketing research can be of great help in directing the project along the right lines, and this clarity of perception is extremely important in ensuring that the marketing research is properly directed and will produce the necessary answers.

From inception onwards, it is possible that the new product idea will attract considerable attention, and may acquire a momentum that is difficult to stop. The marketing researcher must not be afraid to give a negative answer, if that is what the research truly shows, simply because everyone else is so keen for the idea to go forward.

To develop or to buy?

Once the germ of the new product idea has formed, an early decision may be whether to develop the new product from scratch within the company or to license the technology from a company already successful in another market. Much of the information necessary to permit the taking of this decision will come from marketing research activities.

The needs of the marketplace may be such as to show that the sponsoring company does have the capability to develop the product or, by contrast, that the technical or marketing requirements put it outside the bounds of possibility, such that buying-in is the only route. In this latter case, marketing research can also be essential in determining the right source, if more than one is available, and the techniques used here will resemble those employed in company acquisitions (as described in Chapter 19).

If the product is to be developed in-house, there is a serious problem concerning timing: the product needs to be launched as soon as possible, to capture the forecast market share, yet enough time must be allowed for full development and testing, or the product could fail to achieve its expected performance and so fail. If, as is probable, the product is being developed to achieve some specific performance characteristics when in use, it will be these characteristics that form the basis of the marketing research investigations necessary at a fairly early stage of the project's life. It is very disappointing to find, as a result of such marketing research activities, that the product would be a world-beater, and then for the actual development programme to fail to achieve the expected performance.

New Product Development and Testing

Research into new products

The main features of the application of marketing research to the development and testing of new products can best be identified by considering them in the context of the various stages along the path to market of a new product, as identified earlier in this Chapter. The methods of research will have a large qualitative content, and the proportion of qualitative research will be higher the earlier the research is in the new product development programme. Even the apparently quantitative aspects will have a strong qualitative element. 'If our product could achieve the following [specified] performance, would you buy one?' may be answerable on a scale of 1 to 5, but the responses will have to be explored in considerable depth to ensure that the interviewer knows the respondent's mind on the matter.

Producing the idea

For all the common sense involved in the earlier comments about 'market pull' being better than 'product push', it is rare that a company will ask its market research department, or engage a consultancy, to 'trawl' the whole marketplace looking for unfulfilled needs. It is not at all uncommon, however, for the question to be put in the form:

> given our particular skills in production and in marketing, given our existing product line, and given our image in our marketplace, what new product (or range of products) would stand the best chance of being successful for us?

In the 1970s and for much of the 1980s, 'diversification' was a key word in company growth. Despite the existence, in business schools' libraries of case histories, of many examples of failure because of lack of understanding of product technology or marketing requirements, companies during this period bought other companies with, it seemed, no concern other than profitability (or realisable assets). There is now evident a much more cautious approach, and many large companies have been forced to 'restructure' (ie cut down in size), and the key phrase has become 'return to our core businesses'. The result has been beneficial in that it has forced companies to discover what, indeed, they are good at, and what avenues they should not venture into, because of a lack of the right business knowledge.

In these circumstances, the more precise question of the last-but-one paragraph can be put sensibly, and the marketing research task can be seen to be a real one, capable of achievement, and an enjoyable job to do. It involves (for an outside consultancy) the need for a very thorough understanding of the company's existing skills and operations. It needs very careful definition by the sponsoring company or it can easily get out of control – but, with that definition, the result can be very rewarding (and, sometimes, surprising).

Researching the concept

Once the idea is established and the need identified, by whatever means, then some research is necessary to establish the precise form of the product. If the idea has come from the kind of research trawl question given in the previous section, that research should have included this kind of information. If the idea has been generated internally, marketing research now can put the idea into its proper market context, and help to define the parameters of product nature and performance.

If, at the other extreme from 'market-pull', the company has a product coming out of a development programme for which a market is to be sought, marketing research is essential at the earliest possible stage in this programme to see if a market can be found, and to see what the needs of that market for such a product would be. The results of such research will save further investment if no market can be determined, or will help to increase the chances of the product's success by identifying those aspects of its nature and performance that are of greatest importance.

Detailed product research

Armed with the specification of the product to suit a market need, to which the preliminary marketing research will have contributed, the product development programme will begin. At the stage where a prototype has been produced and its performance demonstrated, a reasonably firm indication will be needed as to the likely market size for it, and the likely share that the company can expect to take, in order to allow a good budget to be prepared and the likely production facilities to be set up.

This is clearly a task for another marketing research exercise, but now the details of the product are much clearer, some idea of its final performance capabilities can be given, and even a picture of the prototype (or a sample of its product service) can be made available. The research can, and must, now become more quantitative. It is unlikely that a cost to the customer can yet be forecast with any accuracy, and more likely that a range of costs should be one of the desired results from the research exercise.

Because of the novelty of the product it may not be possible to produce much in the way of historical data, but a good researcher should be able to relate this product to something similar, or find another market in which it is already established, or in some way produce some comparative data. Again, because of the novelty, respondents to a research survey at this stage may have very different views of the product's value to them, and a wide range of opinion, with high levels of sample proportion, will be necessary to provide the required answers.

Test marketing

Some kind of preliminary testing of the product in its market will probably be necessary before volume production is begun. In many cases, of course, the product will have been developed with one particular application firmly in mind and, as a result, probably developed in close cooperation with a significant customer for that application. In such a case, much of the test marketing function is achieved by that cooperation.

It is more common, however, for the company to want to seek opinion from several different potential customers, and marketing research skills are valuable in this search. The methods of qualitative research – depth interviews, group discussions, hall tests – are all used for this kind of work, with the product featured and demonstrated as much as possible.

Where a new product can be sold only after a prolonged residence in the customer's works, the marketing researcher's skills can still be employed to control the way in which the customer's opinion is developed during this period.

Product launch

At the point where volume production has begun, the needs of the market should be well understood. However, marketing research still has a part to play – in advising on the best method of launching the product, and on the best ways to promote it once it is launched. These questions are unlikely to form the subject of a separate survey, unless the product is of major significance to the company, but are more likely to be answerable from the combined experience of the in-house marketing researchers or of a consultancy engaged for the purpose.

Continued observation

It is usually essential that, following the launch and promotion of a new product, its performance 'in the field' should be observed quite closely over the first year or two of its life. Modifications to its design may be required, and improvements in its performance may be achievable with little change in the manufacturing process.

Such observation is a simple task for a marketing research unit, either in-house or on contract. A detailed survey at a particular time after the launch, or the use of a regular panel of users, or any other of the researcher's tools can be employed – and should be employed to ensure the product's continued success.

17

Advertising Research

Roy Haworth

A great deal of money is spent on advertising, and a sensible advertiser will try to find out how effective it is. The only way to do this is by some kind of research, and the techniques of business marketing research apply here, too, as this Chapter explains. It also explains how such research should be applied to developing a good advertising campaign, to be effective from the start.

Introduction

Much has been written about advertising research, but it mostly concerns consumer advertising rather than industrial advertising and rightly so, because it is in the consumer area that the larger amounts of money are spent. However, recent years have seen considerable expansion in industrial advertising. It was once rare to see industrial campaigns carried out on television, but nowadays these are quite commonplace.

The problem with researching for industrial advertising is the cost. Seldom are budgets big enough to justify taking all the relevant steps of research in order to ensure that the advertising is salient and effective, and achieving its objectives.

How many industrial companies can spend what Cadbury spent on launching a box of chocolates, ie £10,000,000? Industrial marketing people are normally faced with incredibly small budgets with which to achieve increased sales penetration and profits. In the business arena we, as researchers, are also faced with a marketing and sales community which believes it knows its market, it knows its customers and it knows how to advertise to them.

What we tend to forget is that even business advertising is advertising to people, and it needs to have impact, to be relevant to those people, and to be effective in changing their purchasing decisions. People differ widely, and their roles and their beliefs are changing all the time.

Therefore, we need to identify who those people are who we need to influence, to find out where they are and what their function is, and to understand their motivations. We also need to remember that the marketplace is continuously changing. Nothing is static, and therefore we need to investigate, research and check.

Because of possible budget restrictions, research must be qualitative at most stages in the process. What we are looking for is guidance and understanding – it is not head-counting, although head-counting has its place if justified by expenditure. Research must also be a joint effort with the advertising agency chosen to carry out the campaign. The research is not an end in itself, and guidance should be expected from the experts.

Definition of those to be influenced

One of the problems we have in business-to-business marketing is to understand the people and processes involved in making a buying decision. After all, the advertising is designed to increase sales; therefore it needs to be directed at those people who are going to contribute to the decision to buy our products.

In a typical industrial company we are faced with different levels of decision making. At the top there is the Board of Directors, and reporting to them there will be a tier of general management. Below them there will be engineers, factory managers, foremen – those concerned with the actual production part of the operation. There will then be a level of purchasing people. All these might well have an influence on making a purchase. We must ask: Who initiates the request to purchase a product? Who evaluates that request? Who decides which suppliers should be considered? Who decides on the final selection of a supplier? Who actually places the order? Who liaises with the supplying company? Who sees the company representatives? And who can stop the process at any stage?

Much of this information can be gleaned by talking to sales and marketing people, who are in direct contact with the customers and potential customers. Once this kind of internal research has been done, the researcher can go into the field and talk to a handful of typical customers, to find out for himself whether what he has been told internally is right or not. From this kind of research it can be determined at whom the advertising should be targeted within the type of company to which we wish to sell our products. This also provides information as to whom we should be talking at later stages of research, as we develop our advertising concepts.

How advertising fits into the communications spectrum

At this stage we have probably defined in very broad terms our target market and who the players are within that market who we wish to influence by our advertising.

What we need to know now is the importance of the type of advertising we intend to carry out within the total spectrum of communications received by those people.

This is the time to carry out telephone research. By talking to these specified people within our target market, we can learn what kind of influences are put upon them in the making of any kind of purchasing decision. We need to understand the role of the salesmen, the role of literature, and the type of media read by these people, both general and specific. We need to know how important are visits to exhibitions. We need to know about promotions. We need to understand the importance of the reputation of the companies from whom they buy.

When we put all this information together, we can help marketing to decide what kind of promotional activity they should be carrying out. It might be that advertising is so minimal in its effect in our marketplace that our budget should be spent totally in other areas; for instance, on increasing the sales force, on improving our literatire, on our presence at exhibitions and so on.

However, once we have decided that advertising does have a role to play, we can determine what kind of budget we should be spending on this particular activity.

What to say

Once it has been decided to proceed with an advertising campaign, objectives must be defined very clearly by the marketing department and the advertising agency. Perhaps we are launching a new product; perhaps we just want to tell customers about the company generally and its capabilities. Whatever we want to say, we have to start deciding on the messages that we wish to communicate to our audience.

Marketing research should have an input at this stage. While doing the basic research, such as interviews with people in the buying decision either on the telephone or personally, the researcher can expand the interviews to discuss advertising and the kinds of thing that the respondents want to hear a supplier saying to them. With that information and the objectives of the marketing department, the advertising agency should then put together some concepts, ie the messages to be communicated. These should then be researched with the potential customer. If budgets are tight, we should not fall into the consumer trap of endless focus groups. It is difficult, particularly in the business area, to gather together the right type of person for a focus group, and this procedure might well prove too costly.

Instead, a great deal can be achieved from perhaps a dozen individual face-to-face interviews, at which the concepts created by the advertising agency are looked at by the potential customer. Careful interview techniques can begin to give indications as to which direction the advertising should take.

How to say it

The next stage of development with the advertising agency is to present different ways of communicating the messages that we have decided to create. Our original depth interviews will have already told us what type of media we should use – whether it should be television, or national press, or specialist press, or even direct mail. This stage of research should be carried out again either by group discussion or by a small number of individual interviews, and what we are looking for is the shape of our advertising. Should it be funny? Should it be serious? Should it have a single message, or should it be much broader? Should it be technical, or should it be much lighter and more general? Should it have photographs, drawings and illustrations, or should it be just text? And what should the text be saying?

All these questions can be answered qualitatively by using a small number of interviews, and our final direction can be fed back to the advertising agency. The directive from this stage of research might be 'back to the drawing board', in which case we must repeat the process.

Advertising development

At this stage we have now developed with the advertising agency an advertising campaign which is still fairly rough, but it has pictures, it has words, it has size, and it has shape. We should go back to our potential customers and find from them whether it is communicating what they want to hear. Again, the only way to do this is by face-to-face interviews or by focus group where possible. For this purpose the focus group is more useful because of the cross-fertilisation of ideas that one gets from within such a group, and if this stage of research is done properly then a finished campaign can be developed by the advertising agency.

This stage of research should also provide enough qualitative information for the marketing people and the advertising agency to judge their own final campaign. They will know from the experience gained by participating in or reading all the previous research whether or not they have got it right.

Has it worked?

Of course, we never know whether advertising has worked or not until we see what happens to our sales figures in the coming months.

Even if we are successful in launching our product, or fulfilling other objectives, it is very difficult to define what part the advertising has played in that success story.

However, we do need to keep track of whether our advertising is being noticed, what is thought about it by our potential customers, and whether they are taking the appropriate action. It is easier to carry out tracking these days by means of a business omnibus survey, which is an ideal way of tracking advertising effectiveness.

If we find that there is not an omnibus which is specific enough to cover our marketplace, we need to carry out our own telephone research. It will soon become clear from a fairly simple, straightforward telephone interview survey, whether the advertising is achieving its objectives, even using, say, 20 to 50 telephone interviews.

Conclusion

Remember that we are advertising to people, even in the industrial arena, and always work in partnership with the advertising agency. The various stages of research recommended here are:

- who the people are who are making or influencing the purchasing decision – internal research plus five to ten in-depth personal interviews;
- the importance of advertising in the communications mix, the type of message that should be communicated, and the ideal media to be used – telephone interviews, say 20 to 50;
- whether these are the right messages – two focus groups or ten personal interviews;
- testing rough advertisements – two focus groups or ten personal interviews;
- tracking – omnibus or telephone interviews, say 20 to 50.

All these stages might only be necessary if what you are doing is for the first time. It might already be known who are the people making decisions and to what type of advertising they are responsive. Therefore, the only research exercises that might be needed are those

Advertising Research

concerned with the development of a specific campaign and the tracking.

On the other hand, it might be an enormous industrial campaign for perhaps a new range of personal computers, which might mean a very large amount of money being spent on television. In this type of project, the whole process should be expanded and research carried out at both a quantitative and qualitative level.

The above is a very simple guide to the stages that might be appropriate in your own case. The message is, basically, that advertising costs money, and a small investment in research can ensure the effectiveness of that advertising.

18

The Role of Sales Forecasting in Business Planning

Alan Wolfe

The ultimate goal of business marketing research is to provide the information upon which management decisions can be taken, and to maximise the chances that these decisions will not only be right, but also the best possible ones. The application of marketing research to the decision process is illustrated in this Chapter in the context of business planning – the setting of targets and the means to achieve them. It concentrates on the formulation of the sales forecast and emphasises the importance of accurate data and sound opinion upon its creation.

Business strategy

The tactical decisions of a business are usually made by its line management in production, distribution, sales or finance. To take effective and coordinated decisions, line managers need a strategic plan to guide them. The usual form of such a plan is a short-term (annual) financial budget, operating within a medium-term corporate plan.

The fundamental principle underlying such plans is the management of risk. In order to generate future income from sales, a business has normally to lay out money in advance on resources (such as plant, raw materials, staff, advertising and so on). These costs are more or less certain and controllable, but the sales are less so or may even be non-existent.

The key to profits, and the vital skill of top management in gaining them, lies in management's ability to plan ahead, to balance the certainty of costs against the likelihood of revenue. Business planners make their best contribution to a successful plan by assessing accurately the risks and rewards inherent in the current and future situation of their company.

Risk analysis

Most business events fall within a continuum of uncertainty, illustrated in Figure 18.1, in which the size of profit from low to high is related to the degree of risk, also from low to high.

In the upper-right quadrant of Figure 18.1 are small companies with little to lose and everything to gain, and those operating in markets such as high technology or high fashion. They have to be prepared to accept high-risk operations, but only if the rewards of success are high.

At the other extreme are established businesses, particularly market

Profit margin

High

Rare, eg technological breakthroughs, monopolies	High technology High fashion Small companies Venture management

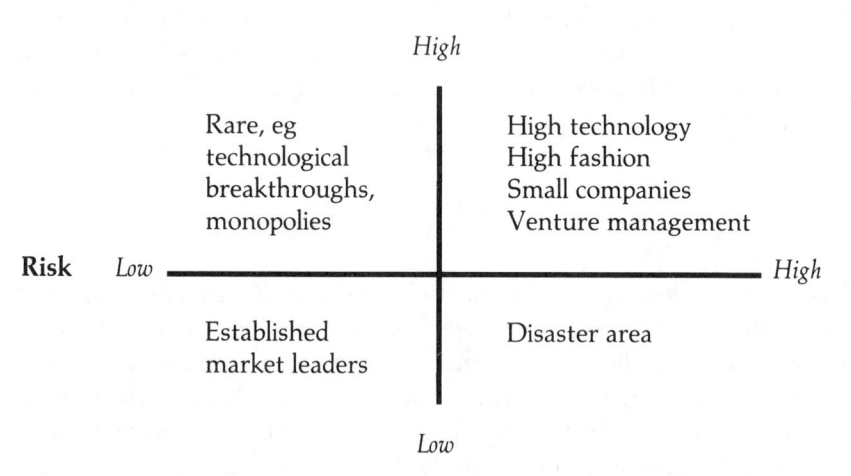

Risk *Low* ─────────────────────────── *High*

Established market leaders	Disaster area

Low

Figure 18.1. *Risk analysis*

leaders. These have very little to gain from the extra 'upside payoff' from a little additional success, but a great deal to lose in 'downside risk' if they get it slightly wrong. So they tend to prefer marketing strategies which minimise their risks even if the resulting profit levels are relatively low.

A major reason for the development by large consumer-goods companies of the discipline of market research in the 1950s and 1960s was because they had grown to dominate post-war markets, and then needed to protect their investment.

High profits at low risk are available only to statutory monopolies or to those with unbreakable patents on technological innovations. In the opposite quadrant, a product portfolio which offers low profits at high risk is a sure qualification for eventual bankruptcy.

Most businesses therefore operate on the diagonal between 'low reward: low risk' and 'high reward: high risk'. The business and marketing strategies appropriate to each end position are considerably different, and decision takers must be aware which game they are playing. A business plan should be based on a good understanding of the likely outcomes of the alternative possibilities inherent in the situation.

The benefits of realism in planning

A realistic view of the future is an essential input to a successful operation. Companies tend to run more smoothly and profitably when sales are on, or better than, target; they tend to run into trouble when sales are below it. Most companies treat a budgeted profit (which is usually set to service capital needs rather than as a residual between revenue and costs) as though it were a fixed cost. Any short-fall of revenue below budget has to be compensated for by immediate cuts in expenditure, even if the achieved revenue is an increase on previous years. Such cuts within a budget year have to be made (irrespective of importance) in items which happen to have short cancellation dates (such as advertising, marketing research, management training and R&D), and in large variable costs such as product specification, plant maintenance and non-union staff.

Making such cuts may or may not solve the problem of short-fall of profit, but it is highly likely that they will leave the company in a worse state – with a product of diminished quality through inadequate plant and reduced specification, lower awareness of weakened brand image among customers, no market data, no replacement products under development, and a shortage of trained managerial staff. Such a company is likely to have a rough ride in subsequent years.

This process of 'eating the seed corn' in order to maintain short-term profits at the expense of long-term growth has bedevilled British industry for decades. It does not happen when a company correctly anticipates a recession year, and plans accordingly – such companies survive, even if temporarily unhappily. It happens whenever a company faces sales lower than expectations, whether the year is one of boom or recession. The most common root cause of business failure is bad planning resulting from over-optimism in the sales forecast.

Such failure is most likely to happen when the sales forecast is developed solely from a company's internal needs: for example when a target profit, set at the level necessary to service the capital, is connected to a sales volume via the previous year's margins and then adopted as a 'forecast', without checking whether or not the marketplace can absorb that volume of sales, or even without investigating anticipated market conditions to determine if a lower volume at higher margins, or a higher volume at lower margins, might not be a potentially better marketing approach. This highly risky forecasting technique is known as 'backing into the strategy', and cannot be recommended.

It is suggested that a realistic forecast of sales is the single most important figure produced by a company during its financial year. Without it, any plan is likely to go seriously astray, thereby at best losing potential profit and at worst putting the survival of the company in doubt. A business planner must have a deep understanding of the nature of a forecast, even if he is not responsible for its generation.

The nature of a forecast

Sales forecasting is not really a matter of foretelling the future – that is a process best left to astrologers and racing tipsters. The basic principle of forecasting is that the future is neither totally known, nor totally unknown: it is uncertain.

The Role of Forecasting in Business Planning

The key process in forecasting is to identify and evaluate the degree of uncertainty about the various elements that affect the future. For example, there is a very high degree of certainty about the time the sun will rise next Derby-day, but a very low degree of certainty about which horse will pass the winning-post first. Any amateur of racing knows that nobody will take bets on a one-horse race, and that the odds quoted depend on the degree of uncertainty involved in picking the winner.

The techniques of forecasting therefore attempt to understand and quantify the degree of uncertainty attaching to various alternative scenarios for the future of a marketplace, as a help to management in balancing risks and pay-offs. Forecasting as a purely statistical exercise, however correct it may turn out to be after the event, does very little to improve the quality of managerial decision-taking.

Some definitions

Forecasting, like any other technical subject, has its own jargon. There are certain ordinary words which have distinctive technical meanings, which are often used casually as synonyms, and confusion can be damaging.

For example, it is important to distinguish among:

- *forecast* – what is believed to be most likely to happen in future (the best and most objective estimate available),
- *budget* – a plan to allocate resources under various headings (budgets are about money, costs, revenues and profits), and
- *target* – what we would most like to happen and will strive to achieve (perhaps irrespective of the realities of life).

It is vital to business planning that the forecast be made first, on the basis of as objective a view as possible of the real world. Budgeted sales can then be set at the forecast level, or preferably slightly below (because the differential leverage on profits, if sales are below budget, produces the dire consequences which have already been discussed). Targets for the sales force and others can be set slightly but achievably above the forecast. This will motivate everyone to strive, as easy targets and self-fulfilling forecasts are not usually a spur to growth.

It is also important to distinguish the meaning of 'forecast' from:

- *projection* – which is an extension of the past forward, with no change in trend (this is, in effect, a forecast made under the single explicit assumption that current trends continue which, in practice, they usually do not), and

- *prediction* – a view of the outcome of a single future event, which implies certainty with no alternative possibilities (the territory especially of the fortune-teller).

A forecast is more complex. It implies uncertainty and a range of possibilities, as a result of explicit assumptions. In a business planning context, to say that 'our sales next year will be 500,000 cases', and to say no more, is to make a prediction. It may or may not turn out to be right; in either case it does nothing to help develop a strategy for achieving it, or to protect the organisation against the unexpected, or to improve the basis of future forecasts.

In contrast, a forecast might be, 'we expect our sales next year to be 500,000 cases, plus or minus 3 per cent, provided that (a) our competitor does not launch another new product, (b) VAT does not change at the next Budget, (c) our new factory comes on stream in August as scheduled and (d) our marketing strategy is in accordance with the agreed plan.' In this case, it is quite clear to those who have to take action (such as scheduling production, budgeting for cash-flow, or setting sales-force targets) what is the natural range of variation to be anticipated, and exactly what the basic assumptions are. If the factory is late, we will not be able to make 500,000 cases. If the competitor launches yet another new line we will not be able to sell that much. If we double our planned price or cut our advertising, sales will be affected.

It is also implied that the forecaster has examined a range of other potential influences, and has concluded that nothing is likely to happen to affect sales to a greater extent than the four items specified. Contingency plans for the likely alternatives can be drawn up, and the environment monitored to make sure of the earliest possible warning of going off-forecast.

To carry out forecasting in this sense may well involve making predictions about events which cannot be properly forecast, and

The Role of Forecasting in Business Planning

certainly the starting point will be to make some projections based on recent trends. However, a balance of statistical and judgemental inputs will be required.

For the purposes of this Chapter, a forecast will be defined as:

> An objective, quantified estimate of what is most likely to happen in the future, based on analysis of the past, with evaluation of the degree of uncertainty, and with any necessary assumptions identified.

Naturally, such a forecast cannot consist of a single figure. It will normally require at least a covering written description, dealing with contingencies surrounding the central forecast.

The dangers of projections

Projections or extrapolations of recent trends on their own are likely to prove misleading as forecasts, because current trends usually do not continue – at least for longer than a few months. Saturation points are reached, and new products, new technologies, or new laws change the business environment. We take action intentionally to try to alter the future. Peter Drucker quotes an example (*Harvard Business Review*, May 1985):

> Around 1909, a statistician at the American Telephone and Telegraph [AT&T] Company projected two curves 15 years out: telephone traffic and American population. Viewed together, they showed that by 1920 or so every single female in the United States would have to work as a switchboard operator. The process need was obvious, and within two years AT&T had developed and installed the automatic switchboard.

Users of computers should be aware that most of the so-called 'forecasting' programs on sales are in fact some variation on projections of the moving average or curve-fitting type, with perhaps exponential smoothing and seasonal factors thrown in. If a program requires no input to make a new forecast other than past sales (ie no price, market or competitive data) then it is almost certainly of this type. It will not provide forecasts in the sense defined above, it will not be capable of anticipating any change in trend, and it is likely to be a long way from reality if used for more than a few months ahead.

Basically, such methods imply: 'if current trends continue and nothing changes, this is where we will end up' – but we (or our competitors, our customers or the government) will do something such as change prices, advertising, suppliers, technologies, or tax rates. It follows that mechanical projection, or any forecasting technique which does not take into account a wide variety of external market factors and which does not require the use of the human brain, is likely to be dangerous for planning.

A sales forecasting sequence for planners

While it may be desirable to update and roll forward the forecast quarterly, or conceivably monthly, during the current financial year, a full re-forecast from scratch is advised at least once a year as part of the budgeting exercise.

The recommended order of events in Figure 18.2 will help to ensure the best and most reliable forecast, and will also ensure that sound actions can follow from it. Steps 1–6 are the tasks to be carried out by the forecaster – if necessary in isolation. Step 1 checks, updates (and expands whenever possible) the company database, and relies on input from marketing research as well as from the sales department.

Step 2 involves analysis of time-series of sales and other relevant variables, with the prime purpose of identifying trends. It must be assumed (until demonstrated otherwise) that the underlying trend is obscured at least by seasonality, other cyclical influences (such as the business cycle, or the baby boom) and random (ie non-cyclical) variations. It is to be advised that any untypical periods in the original database (such as those affected by strikes, public holidays, disasters or other events which are not likely to recur) should be corrected or excluded at this stage.

Step 3 deals with the problem of trying to explain the trend and, most importantly, any past changes in it. The forecaster must examine and try to quantify the possible effects on sales of internal company marketing strategy, competitive activity, and a variety of other external influences.

The first attempt at actual forecast generation, in Step 4, will be to

The Role of Forecasting in Business Planning

> 1. Gather data (monthly or quarterly readings) of sales and related variables for as far back as possible.
> 2. Identify:
>   - seasonality
>   - longer cycles
>   - random variations
>   - trends
>   - discontinuities and other changes in trend.
> 3. Relate the trend to outside influences, and to company marketing strategies.
> 4. Extrapolate the trend (ie assume first that current trends continue).
> 5. Make some assumptions about the future of relevant outside influences, and alternative company marketing strategies.
> 6. Modify the extrapolated trend under alternative assumptions.
> 7. Discuss the assumptions and their implications with all concerned. Play 'what if . . .'.
> 8. Make and publish 'The Forecast':
>   - the agreed best estimate with its assumptions;
>   - a descriptive written scenario;
>   - alternative (contingency) estimates under best and worst assumptions;
>   - action standards for variation of actual from forecast (ie how far can you permit actual to depart from forecast, and for how long, before you change the forecast or re-budget?).

Figure 18.2. *The sales forecasting sequence*

extrapolate the current trend on the deliberately over-simple assumption that it will continue unchanged. This projection should then be modified (Steps 5 and 6) by judgement or more complex methods under the more realistic assumption that there will be uncontrollable changes in the external marketing environment. A range of further modifications should be examined to take account of the potential effects of alternative company marketing strategies and likely counter-action by competitors.

Before proceeding further, the forecaster should take the very important Step 7, by leaving his office and discussing these preliminary forecasts with all who may be concerned with implementing them – production, finance, sales, advertising. It is important that the forecaster should be aware of other people's opinions and plans, and it may be that there are external market or internal company factors of which other people are aware, but the forecaster has not been told. Such events (for example, a scheduled six-month closure of a key plant line for maintenance) could invalidate a whole forecasting exercise.

In its final form, as developed in Step 8 and circulated to all those concerned, the agreed central forecast or 'best estimate' should be stated, with its underlying assumptions. It should be accompanied by a short descriptive written scenario, explaining the viewpoint taken of the economic and marketing climate likely to prevail during the forecast period, and the marketing strategy recommended or assumed to be adopted in consequence.

It is advisable to indicate the degree of sensitivity of the forecast to its assumptions, giving contingency estimates of how sales might vary under the most and least favourable of the likely assumptions. The final document should also specify action standards, in terms of how much natural or random variation can occur in the figures on a month-to-month (or quarter-to-quarter) basis without invalidating the forecast.

The development of climates of opinion in which the users of the forecast are aware of, and lay contingency plans for, all the circumstances most likely to occur, is at least as important a part of the forecaster's tasks as generating the central forecast itself.

Choice of sales forecasting techniques

The choice of the right technique for sales forecasting, in any given case, will vary depending on the nature of the market, the amount of information available about past trends and future developments, the time-scale of the period to be forecast, and the statistical expertise and computer power available to the forecaster.

The Role of Forecasting in Business Planning

In choosing the right technique, the forecaster should bear in mind the following general principles.

- The soundest basis for anticipating the future is a thorough understanding of the past. A good rule of thumb is that three years of back data are needed for every year to be forecast – it is risky to embark on a quantified three-year plan without about ten years of back data.

- Poor quality data lead to unreliable forecasts. No amount of computerised wizardry can turn statistical dross into marketing gold – investment in a high-quality, market-research-based company database will pay off in terms of better estimates of the risks to be faced ahead.

- The timing and context of a forecast should be appropriate to two end-uses:
  - planning – by helping to set objectives and strategies and allocate resources, and
  - control – by providing a basis for evaluating actual performance and making flexible adjustments to tactics.

- Objective analytic methods are to be preferred to the subjective personal and jury methods, unless there are no reliable market data at all. The expertise of those experienced in the market is better used to interpret information than to generate it by guesswork. Surveys of the views of buyers or of company staff should be treated as inputs to the forecast, not as the forecast itself.

- Even though statistical methods are to be recommended, it is best to use the most simple and comprehensible method available. For example, while the more esoteric methods (such as multiple regression) enable the forecaster to take account of a large number of relevant factors at once, all techniques have limitations and can mislead anyone having no knowledge of the underlying statistical theory.

- The most important tools of the forecaster are, in order of importance, the human brain, graph paper and a computer. Nowadays, executives of almost all businesses of significance have access to computers, and there is plenty of software available to carry out any necessary statistical analysis, including graphical reporting. Those still without will be well advised to confine themselves to drawing charts and basing simple calculations on them. However, it is important (whether computing or not) to inspect and test both the input data and the forecast against common sense.

While the required format of the forecast will be of sales in money terms, it is usually advisable to separate this out into its components of volume and price. Volume should also be disaggregated into market size and market share. The reason for this is that the components of price, share and market size will have different trends and be affected by different factors. Much more reliable and comprehensible forecasts of each can be made separately, or at least the greatest source of unpredictability can be identified. This will also facilitate the diagnosis of problems that arise when evaluating sales performance. The importance of standard marketing research input at this stage can readily be seen.

Available techniques

A wide range of sales forecasting techniques is available, the details of most of which lie outside the scope of this Handbook. They are of three broad kinds:

1. the non-statistical, where opinion is vital;
2. the statistical methods involving univariate analysis;
3. the multivariate analytical methods.

The first of these three categories deserves a little expansion here, as its methods of opinion-seeking relate strongly to other marketing research techniques. These methods include:

- the single expert, who can be easily identified as most knowledgeable on the subject;

- the jury, the group of people of comparable expertise gathered together for the purpose of providing opinion (with all the problems of group discussions described elsewhere in this Handbook);

The Role of Forecasting in Business Planning

- the sales force, whose opinion is obviously very relevant but who may not be the best source of unbiased views;

- the 'Delphi' method, in which views are solicited from a set of individuals as numerical estimates (such as, 'What will be our percentage market share in 5 years' time?'); the results of this first round are then summarised and recirculated, with a request for a revised view in the light of the summary, until a reasonable consensus of views is obtained;

- the customers, whose views are perhaps the most important and which represent a major input from marketing research.

Timescales

All companies have to forecast sales for their annual cash budget. As this has to be done several months ahead, and based on available past data, the forecaster in this case usually has to look ahead in time up to two years. Such short-term forecasting can be done, if necessary, by projecting recent trends and then modifying them on judgement in the light of expected market conditions and planned marketing strategy.

Much of a company's activity also affects the longer term. For example, buying plant which is written-down over a period of five or seven years implies that the company will have commercial use for it over that period. It is desirable to make that view explicit and quantitative. However, the longer the look ahead the more changes that must be expected in factors that can affect the market, and these must be taken into account.

Forecasting for the medium term, up to the actual planning horizon of the company, demands more elaborate forecasting techniques – for example, detailed time-series analysis with curve-fitting or, better still, model-building. If such methods are available, they can be used to produce the short-term forecasts as well.

In the period around 1970 there was a vogue for long-range planning, and the corporate planners of many companies commissioned elaborate analyses, from high-flown institutes, to deliver a 'corporate positioning to the year 2000'. Because such scenarios tended to look only at long-term economic, social and technological movements, and neglected the more mundane problems of how the company should arrive there, they usually failed to anticipate the oil crisis of 1973, the subsequent high inflation of raw material prices, the ensuing world recession of 1974-76, and the consequent squeeze on margins. Not surprisingly long-range planning then fell out of favour, and most companies now concentrate on a planning horizon commensurate with the life of their current assets.

The priorities for planning

Business planning is thus usually done to two time horizons: the next financial year, and the period over which capital expenditure is written off. The best help that the forecaster can give to the planner is to make as explicit as possible the degree of risk to which the company is currently exposed, and the circumstances under which the risk will be increased or decreased in the medium term. This is much more important than getting next year's sales figure right or using the latest forecasting technique.

All companies face difficult periods at one time or another. The chance of surviving them depends on the degree to which they can be anticipated, so that offensive and defensive strategies are adopted when they will be most successful.

Companies which gear up to break records every year are in effect using the strategy of the roulette player who exploits a winning streak by doubling the stake every time red comes up, and only one black will wipe out the whole of the earlier winnings. Long-term success lies in distinguishing the years favourable to growth from those best for consolidation, and developing the appropriate strategies for each case. Successful business planning is therefore totally dependent on realistic forecasting of the customers, the competition and the market environment.

19

Acquisition Research

Chris da Costa

Business marketing research is often undertaken on unknown subjects, and one of the greatest unknowns in business is the real nature of an existing company, as it would affect the result of the purchase of it by another company. This Chapter examines the use of research in making known that nature, and it includes a number of examples from practical experience.

Introduction

Market researchers are always asking questions; for acquisitions, however, marketing research is a science in its infancy and so we often find ourselves on the receiving end of questions. So, as we are in the questions business, this Chapter is structured on the questions most often asked in the course of acquisition work. The questions are all from those companies and their advisers seeking to make acquisitions, rather than from those wishing to dispose of a business. It is the acquisitive company which has a much greater need for the services of the market research house.

The questions cover the definition of business marketing research in the context of acquisitions, the importance of research, how research companies differ from the other professions, when to apply research, what specific information is needed, and how the information is obtained. Some of the questions are nice and easy to answer, others are more difficult. I have even included the really nasty ones.

What has market research to do with acquisitions?

Before attempting to answer this question, I first need to put into context the process of company acquisition. The process starts with a company deciding to use acquisition to achieve its growth objectives, which it might do for many reasons and not always to capitalise on the opportunities available – companies also acquire others in order to escape threats. These could include a declining market, competitive pressure, or dependence on one product, one customer, one supplier, one distributor or a small geographical base.

Whatever the reasons for embarking on an acquisition strategy, the company will need to compile a set of acquisition criteria which represents the ideal type of candidate it seeks to purchase. The criteria will normally cover the industry sector, the product range, manufacture or distribution, the degree of control required, the price to pay, profitability, and often the fact that the candidates need to have leading shares in growing markets. There will then be several other parameters specific to the acquisitive company.

The hard task of finding a suitable candidate then commences, and there are two methods. The acquisitive company can either:

- give out its acquisition criteria to a select number of intermediaries – merchant banks, stockbrokers, accountants and other professionals specialising in 'merger broking' – and wait to hear of a company for sale which meets its criteria, or
- compile a list of companies which fulfil the criteria and then directly approach the owners in the hope of opening negotiations.

Although the second method of searching requires more work, it is now generally recognised that the best candidates are not always up for sale and that the proactive approach often achieves the required conclusion more quickly.

Once discussions with the potential vendors commence, the acquisitive company and its financial advisers need to address the subjects of negotiation tactics, the offer, and post-acquisition strategy.

Acquisition Research

Market research has two main functions in the acquisition process:
1. to identify all potential candidates, at an early stage in the process;
2. to evaluate a particular company comprehensively, at a later stage.

The first piece of research is undertaken to ensure that the acquisition criteria are met, and that the candidates representing most opportunity for the acquisitive company are shortlisted. The later research is undertaken to help the acquirer to decide whether to proceed with an offer, the price to pay, and the best negotiating tactics. The research is also used to define the right post-acquisition strategy to adopt, in order to capitalise quickly on opportunities or solve problems as soon as the acquisition is completed.

The two functions of search and evaluation should be viewed as two separate research projects. One might lead to the other, but not necessarily so. For instance, after the identification research, approaches would normally be made by the acquisitive company to the best candidates; it would not be cost-effective also to undertake in-depth evaluation on a number of companies at this stage, only to find that they were not receptive to an approach. Conversely, if an acquisitive company hears of a likely candidate for sale, the evaluation research will obviously be all that is required. This type of research tends to be commissioned just before a public bid, or even during negotiations in many instances; time pressures can be considerable.

In either search or evaluation work, the research can be applied to almost any acquisition criteria, whether they include target companies which are publicly quoted, subsidiaries or privately owned, manufacturers, distributors or service related, operating in the home country or outside it. Whatever the case, to acquire or not to acquire will never be an easy decision. Market research is used to make it a better informed decision.

Why is market research important in making acquisitions?

Illustrated is the sad case where the acquirer gets to know a lot more about the business after he has bought it. Performance is not quite as healthy as he expected. The market looks buoyant – the competitors

Figure 19.1.

Acquisition Research

are doing well – so what has gone wrong for the company just acquired? It could be that the prices are too high, or that the products are of poor quality; certainly the selling efforts need reviewing. This scene poses a lot of unanswered questions. Unfortunately, this is no isolated case.

Over 50 per cent of all acquisitions made in the UK over the last few years are retrospectively judged to have failed, and this 50 per cent figure is generally recognised as being conservative. This may not be a very popular statement to make but it is based on research from the business schools, the management consultants and, perhaps most importantly, the chief executives of companies who have completed acquisitions.

One fundamental reason for this sorry state of affairs is insufficient analysis of acquisition candidates, preceding acquisition. This lack of research is particularly prevalent when concerned with market information. A misunderstanding of a company's markets can cause a complete misreading of the opportunities open to the acquiring company.

Financial analysis is obviously important, but is limited in its ability to understand the reasons for a company's current performance. It is limited in its capacity to forecast a company's potential. Company performance depends critically on the ability to win orders at acceptable margins. This is a function of the market place. If there was a better understanding of how the target companies were performing in their markets, then fewer disastrous decisions would be made.

This might seem obvious, yet many acquiring companies and their financial advisers will undertake a scantier analysis of marketing information when considering the purchase of 100 per cent of a company, than would the stockbroker advising a fund manager in the purchase of 1 per cent of it. Examples abound – here are just two.

- A contracting company decided to broaden its product range by acquiring a company involved in lighting products. Two years later it became evident that the market for that company's products had peaked at about the time of the acquisition; the market's move towards more decorative lighting, sourced from foreign manufacturers, reduced the customer base to such an extent that a significant part of the operation had to be closed down.

- An office furniture manufacturer heard of an opportunity to acquire a loss making upholstery manufacturer. The acquirer identified problems in production – problems he was well able to solve; the business was bought 'cheaply'. It transpired, however, that although there were production problems the prime cause for the company's poor financial state lay in the marketplace. The new owners, not understanding the competitive environment or what policies were needed to be successful in a market unfamiliar to them, suffered greatly.

These two particular acquisitions proved to be very expensive mistakes. A better understanding of the target companies' businesses, before the takeovers were concluded, should have resulted in a lower price being paid or withdrawing altogether. The biggest problem is that the majority of those involved in making acquisitions still know very little about business marketing research, and are completely unaware of its value to them. There are still too many who think that market research is limited to being stopped in the street to be asked, 'How many cigarettes do you smoke?'.

Can I do some of the market research myself?

The answer to this question must be 'Yes', but there will be some major obstacles the acquisitive company needs to overcome in obtaining the information required. The ease of the task is obviously dependent on the skills and the time available in-house.

Among the problems that the acquisitive team can encounter are:

- out-of-date information: in industries where market structure and trends change rapidly, published information can soon become misleading;
- insufficient detail: often the only published information available relates to macro markets whereas companies can operate in specific market niches, which perform differently from the market as a whole;
- bias: at times the information generated may be slanted to support a case by those with a vested interest in its conclusions;

Acquisition Research

- wrong source: too often information is sourced from a few personal contacts at the wrong level in the wrong companies, or from the vendors of the target company;

- negligible company information: particularly if the target company is unquoted, the amount of published information available could be almost non-existent;

- confidentiality: obviously the need for secrecy will constrain the amount of information the acquisitive company can itself obtain; the independent research house is able to move freely among its sources while maintaining strict confidentiality.

These problems confronting the acquisitive company all stress the importance of obtaining information which is accurate and reliable. The lack of reliable information can dog the acquirer from the first stage of attempting to identify candidates, often right through to completing the acquisition. The only alternative to proper research is guesswork.

To take an example, let us go back to the start of the acquisition process. A target company has been identified; the company's filed accounts reveal a little of the past financial record, and other published information in the press gives just a bit of gossip. However, despite this information gap, our acquisitive company decides to proceed, in the hope that all the information required will be available from the vendor.

Once negotiations are under way, the acquisitive company does normally get the facts on the target's resources, the past financial record, and perhaps a breakdown of activities. But it is very unlikely to get information on how the target is currently performing in its markets, whether it is losing market share, whether competition is squeezing prices, whether major customers are increasingly unhappy with its products, whether the markets for these products are starting to decline – in short, whether the target has a whole host of problems or in fact is an excellent acquisition opportunity.

For this type of information, the acquirer is dependent largely on the views of the vendor. However, unless the vendor himself has just had some market research completed, which is unlikely, these views will at best be unreliable, and at worst downright misleading. Even if the vendor is aware of major problems, he is unlikely to be explicit about them.

So, the acquisitive company and the financial advisers are now left to confront the final decisions: 'Do we make an offer?' and 'How much should we pay?' These decisions still depend on a large amount of guesswork. They are decisions in a high-risk area, and normally of considerable strategic importance to the future of the acquisitive company, but how can you calculate the value you can add by solving the problems in the acquired company, when you have not been able to identify these problems? How can you plan to capitalise on the opportunities in the target company when you are unaware of them? Not by guesswork.

What information is needed to improve acquisition decisions?

Although the depth of research required will obviously vary in each case, I would strongly advocate that the following checklist be fully covered well before an acquisition is concluded.

- *The market.* This will include the size of the market in which the candidate or candidates operate, the structure, trends, both past and present, by sector, by product, and by application, the main suppliers, pricing strategies to estimate the current and future ability to earn acceptable or premium margins, and channels of distribution.

- *The candidate's activities and resources.* These will include a breakdown of products and services, by market, by country, the customer base, the competitors, the brands if any, distributors used, marketing methods employed, location of factories, employee numbers split by activity, the style of management, and ownership, including the individual to approach to enter negotiations.

- *The candidate's financial performance.* This will include sales, pre-tax profits, debt, shareholders' funds and the respective financial ratios, how these compare with the competitors' financial records, and also brief stock market statistics for quoted companies such as share price, stock market capitalisation, and price earnings ratios.

Acquisition Research

- *The candidate's market performance.* This will include its position and share of the markets it serves, the trends in market shares, pricing policies, the extent to which the candidate fulfils the criteria by which customers evaluate their suppliers compared to the competition, company strengths and weaknesses, an explanation of past performance and the likelihood of increasing or decreasing sales in future.

- *The preferences and practices in the candidate's industries.* These will include the key factors required to be successful in the industry, the constraints to market entry, regulations influencing the market, and future changes in technology, materials, new products or suppliers, or threats and opportunities which might impact on the market.

Diversifying companies who are seeking to make acquisitions in unfamiliar markets might need research to cover all the above five sections. Companies expanding by acquisition in their own markets will obviously already have sufficient knowledge on many points in the checklist, but there will still be large gaps.

A company considering acquiring a competitor, for instance, will obviously be (or should be) fully aware of the structure of the target's market, channels of distribution, market positions and a lot more. However, the acquisitive company is unlikely to be reliably informed of the target's strengths and weaknesses, the threats and opportunities in that business, how the target is currently performing in its market, and whether it is likely to experience profitable growth in future, or not.

Remember, for information to lead us to the best opportunities, to the right decisions, it needs above all else to be reliable. A few conversations with friends in the industry, or bits of information that the sales reps have gleaned, are unlikely to amount to a sufficient level of knowledge on the target company.

Isn't this industrial espionage?

There might be some readers who will recognise the value of having answers to the points covered under the previous question, but who will disregard the principle on the grounds that most of the information would be unobtainable. I should stress that all the information is available if the right research techniques are applied. I should also stress that these techniques do not include snagging your trousers from climbing over barbed wire on factory gates with binoculars and camera at the ready.

Acquisition research is a combination of field research, financial analysis, and desk research – normally in that order of importance. We have taken the business marketing research techniques which have traditionally been used to help the marketing manager's decisions, and applied these same techniques to the field of corporate strategy. So research, which until recently was used only to test a new product or help a company to win new business, is now being used to identify and evaluate acquisition opportunities.

The field research is so much more important than desk research because every acquisition criterion, or every acquisition candidate, is a special case: even for research on large quoted companies, there is rarely sufficient published information from all sources to fulfil much more than a third of the information requirements. All acquisition research relies heavily on the techniques of the interview. They will include both personal and telephone interviews with suppliers, distributors, customers, competitors, and all others whose knowledge and views of the marketplace and the candidate are worth obtaining. These interviews have to be structured so as to maintain confidentiality, which is normally an essential requirement in all acquisition research.

At various stages during the research process, the market research findings must be combined and coordinated with the financial analysis – the two techniques cannot be easily split, for if you do not compare a company's marketing information with its financial record, something tends to get missed and the research will suffer. Moreover, the acquisition criteria will normally include financial parameters which need to be met relating to the ideal candidates, such as the level of profitability, their potential purchase values, stock market information, and ownership details. So the report and accounts of the candidate or candidates, the subsidiaries and competitors, must be analysed to enhance or confirm the market research findings, or even redirect a further programme of interviews.

Acquisition Research

It is not surprising that the few research houses specialising in acquisitions have either developed from a financial base, or had close ties with the City. Research staff will normally include those from a financial background as well as those from marketing research.

It might be helpful to illustrate how the techniques of marketing research and financial analysis interrelate in the same project by an example. The brief for an American multinational was to analyse in depth a particular French food manufacturer. The research objectives were to establish its merits as an acquisition candidate, devise an approach strategy, help to value the business, and establish what changes would need to be made if the acquisition was concluded. The research required that five main types of information be obtained.

1. The scope of the group's activities, broken down by sales of product type, by activity and by country. Published information showed the group to have both manufacturing and distribution facilities, and to have a number of brands selling throughout most of the major European countries. Through a combination of financial analysis of the subsidiary accounts, and market research where financial information was unobtainable, the relative importance of each component part was established. It was a very different picture from what the group report and accounts implied.
2. The resources and operations of the group. Desk research revealed the relative importance of the shareholders, the split of personnel between manufacturing and distribution, the numbers of factories and distribution outlets by size and location, the type of plant and equipment being used, and the size of its transport fleet.
3. The size and trends of the markets being served. Again desk research showed the various market sizes by product and country and the market shares of the major suppliers, including the target's position in its major markets.
4. The performance of the group's major activities. Through a programme of interviews with the group's customers, competitors, and suppliers in its major markets, which happened to be based in France, Germany and the UK, it was revealed how the group was perceived in the market place, its strengths and

weaknesses by activity, whether it was currently meeting the needs of its customers, whether it would continue to increase its market share in the future, and the level of future demand for its products and services. The fieldwork combined with analysis of the accounts of the main competitors updated the market shares originally sourced from the desk research, and helped to confirm the level of profit margins being generated in the market place.

5. The group's long-term strategy. Once the research had confirmed the suitability of the group as an acquisition target for the American multinational, it was important to develop the right approach strategy. The research revealed that, because of the substantial market shares its brands held in Europe, entry into the American market was essential to maintain the rate of growth. The American company's distribution network was the 'trump card' in bringing the two parties together.

Don't the merchant banks do this sort of work?

The marketing research houses specialising in acquisitions are closest in activity to the corporate finance departments of the merchant banks and the larger accountants and, to a slightly lesser extent, to the management consultants specialising in corporate planning. Although there are some aspects of common ground, the services offered by these organisations in the main complement rather than compete with each other.

The emergence of the large accountancy firms and overseas banks as providers of acquisition advice has resulted in a highly competitive environment in corporate finance generally. In their desire to compete effectively, a few corporate finance departments are now offering market research as part of their acquisition service, in association with the research houses specialising in this area. This trend will probably continue.

The research houses do not compete with the management consultants by advising on corporate strategy: the researcher will get called in at the acquisition search stage, once the client's strategy for expansion has been defined. With regard to the merchant banks and accountants, the research house will not give financial advice or get involved in transacting the acquisition. Once the research is complete, the client or the corporate finance adviser will take over.

Conversely, the other advisers involved in acquisitions will all undertake financial analysis, and to various degrees provide some research service based on publicly available information, either published or online. However, it would be very unusual for this research to incorporate business marketing research as described in this Handbook. The other advisers will not have their own field force for programmes of interviews in the home country, let alone the multi-lingual field force required for cross-border acquisition research.

What about cross-border acquisition research?

Some time ago a well-known UK engineering group decided to diversify by introducing a range of specialist pump equipment. The group board were assured by their engineers that the equipment was a 'world beater'. This was particularly important as it became evident that the domestic market was too small to absorb sufficient capacity of the plant, which had already been constructed.

The group looked overseas for a way out of their problem. They decided to launch the new product in continental Europe, particularly in the heavily industrialised countries, where they felt there would be strong demand for the equipment they had designed.

At about the time the board was considering the best means of entering the European market, they heard that the owners of a West German valve manufacturer wanted to sell their business. This acquisition candidate appeared to offer the UK group a number of advantages:

- most of its valve sales were derived from the process industry, where there was thought to be most application for the UK group's new pump equipment;
- the German company had a strong distribution network in other European countries;
- the company's financial record showed reasonable profit growth, and the price the vendors were seeking was 'not expensive';

- besides offering their new pump equipment a distribution route the UK group could control, the candidate also appeared to have the potential of becoming the German base from which the UK group could expand into other product lines.

The deal was completed. The acquisition proved to be a disaster – the European sales budgeted for the new pump equipment never materialised, and the acquired business started making losses. Despite its lateness, market research was commissioned.

The survey showed that although the UK group's pump equipment was acceptable in the UK market, the more advanced sectors of the main European markets regarded the equipment as obsolete; it was being displaced by designs which had not even been considered by the UK group. The result was to limit the new product's sales to a number of specialist sectors of the market. However, although the market as a whole for pump equipment was growing in Europe, the problems for the UK group were compounded because a number of potential applications in the specialist sectors were being supplied by in-house production facilities.

The market research also found that the future for the West German valve company was just as gloomy. The markets were changing; high profit margins had attracted foreign competition, particularly in France, which was the company's second most important market. Prices were being reduced in an attempt to maintain market share, at a time when new production capacity had been created to meet increased demand, now being absorbed by the competition.

Regrettably, this UK engineering group's experience of making acquisitions in Europe is not unique. Acquiring foreign companies represents a far greater risk than a domestic acquisition. Much of the industry structure and marketing conditions which are taken for granted at home prove to be major unknowns in a foreign acquisition. Language, culture, customer preferences, local regulations, plain xenophobia, and sometimes even climate conspire against the acquisition of a foreign company (see Figure 19.2).

However, although the risks are high the rewards from foreign acquisitions are also potentially high, particularly in Europe. What is of fundamental importance, particularly when considering acquisitions in

Acquisition Research

Figure 19.2.

unfamiliar territory, is to seek ways of reducing the risk of buying the wrong company. Here are some guidelines for the acquisitive company, some of which specifically relate to the foreign acquisition.

- Buy profitable companies: 'turn-round' situations in unfamiliar territory increase risk.

- Buy companies which have leading positions in their markets: market leaders tend to demonstrate greater profit stability by having most influence over prices.

- Buy companies which are operating in markets which are growing strongly.

- Buy companies which offer some degree of synergy: seek to capitalise on combined strengths and resources.

- Buy companies whose main markets are based in European countries, where there is a degree of familiarity: export markets will already have helped to reduce the 'psychological distance'.

- Understand the markets in each country and the candidate's performance in those markets.

- Undertake the market research before the acquisition is concluded: this will prevent your missing the good acquisition opportunities, as well as your buying a poor company.

- If the research needs to cover markets in a number of countries, appoint one research house, with multi-lingual capabilities, to undertake the whole project: company comparisons, which are an important part of acquisition research, will be impossible if several local research firms are involved.

At what stage does marketing research become involved?

Although the information requirements centre on the stages relating to the identification of candidates and company evaluations during negotiations, the marketing research house may get involved at almost any stage up to and, indeed, after completion of the purchase. Here are some examples.

Example 1. An early-stage example was a project for a manufacturer of branded knitwear, who wished to diversify by acquiring leading brands in other consumer markets. The brief was to identify leading suppliers in a whole range of markets which had strong growth potential, and which also offered the client some degree of synergy in distribution and marketing. Market sizes, market shares, growth trends, threats and opportunities in some 20 product groups, ranging from luggage to adhesives, were all analysed and then profiles were compiled on a short-list of candidates which offered the client most

Acquisition Research

potential. Also, by discovering the main strengths and weaknesses in the target companies it was possible to compile an approach strategy for each target. The client then approached the owners of the target companies direct; all of them were private or group subsidiaries. Negotiations commenced, and a successful acquisition resulted.

This example shows how market research identified a target company representing the right potential for the acquisitive company. It also shows that with the acquirer being well-informed on each candidate's activities and performance, there was a greater likelihood of the owners' being responsive to an approach.

Example 2. An example which was further along in the process involved research for an engineering component manufacturer who had already identified a market in which to expand. The brief was to recommend the best method of entering a market for the distribution of programmable controllers. This project involved both market analysis and quite detailed company analysis. The research showed that although the sector was experiencing very high rates of growth with sound long-term potential, the current suppliers were financially weak and not fulfilling customers' requirements. In this project, the client, with considerable resources at its disposal, was advised to start a new operation rather than make an acquisition.

Example 3. A snack food manufacturer, having already commenced negotiations with an acquisition candidate in the health food market, required a 'marketing audit' on the candidate's business. The sales and profit record was impressive, and the vendors were seeking quite a high price although there was little asset backing. Research revealed that the candidate's market share in its key product area was nearly 80 per cent but, contrary to the views of the vendors, the market was static and starting to decline. The candidate was using only one channel of distribution, supplying the independent health food shops. A major customer was about to stop ordering, and growth at historic rates would not be maintained. Having had the major problems identified, the acquirer established that it had the resources to solve these problems by using its own export skills and customer base to open new markets for the vendor's products. The acquirer also used the research findings to negotiate a much lower price for the business than the vendors originally demanded.

Market research can thus be successfully applied to fulfil a number of requirements for information, at various stages in the process:

- to identify all potential candidates offering opportunity, and not just those known to be for sale;
- to increase the likelihood of a successful approach to the owners of the target, by understanding the target company's markets and talking the same language;
- to confirm that acquisition is indeed a necessary strategy, or to identify a more cost-effective means of market entry;
- comprehensively to evaluate companies identified either before the approach stage or during negotiations;
- to benefit negotiations, particularly relating to price;
- to base post-acquisition strategy more soundly, by identifying the real problems and weaknesses, and helping to realise the opportunities.

What costs are involved in research?

The costs of acquisition research are a direct reflection of the number of man-days required to complete the project. Obviously projects vary: an acquisition costing, say, £2 million, of a company based in the same market as the acquirer, might need only a small programme of customer interviews to confirm reputation, quality of performance, and market developments. The cost should be well below the £5,000 mark.

At the other end of the scale could be the proposed takeover of a quoted company valued at £250 million, operating in several industries and in a number of overseas markets. This research is likely to require a large programme of face-to-face and telephone interviews, financial analysis and desk research; it is also likely to need to be completed very quickly, say within two weeks, for a project which under normal circumstances would take two months to complete. The cost of the research is likely to be around the £20,000 mark. It is not reasonable to expect acquisition research to be paid for on a contingency ('success-

Acquisition Research

fee') basis. If it is not in the client's interest to proceed with an acquisition, there should be total freedom to say so.

As it happens, the term 'success-fee' is often a complete misnomer. It might be a success for those professional advisers working solely on a contingency basis but, too often, the acquisition for the acquiring company proves to be far from a success.

Summary

Not until acquiring companies become better informed about what they are buying can completion of the deal equate to success. To be better informed, the information needs to be relevant and reliable: more often than not, as I have tried to portray in this Chapter, that is impossible without market research.

So I would like to conclude with the following suggestions:

- Be active in identifying acquisition opportunities: too many good candidates are missed because market research was not used at the identification stage.

- Seek to reduce the risk of acquiring the wrong company: whether before the approach, or during the negotiations, get your marketing audit done.

- Ensure that you obtain reliable information on which to base your acquisition decisions: unreliable, irrelevant or inaccurate information is worse than none at all.

- To develop your post-acquisition strategy, try to ensure that the real problems and the real opportunities for the target company have been identified before completion: it could affect your offer.

- Use the professionals: the techniques of marketing research do enhance acquisition analysis, but only if the skills are well applied.

Part V: International Research

Not surprisingly, in a Handbook sponsored by a British Association and written by British authors working in Great Britain, there may be a feeling that it is biased towards conditions in the United Kingdom. This is most definitely not the case. The techniques of business marketing research are almost universal, and the text of the Handbook so far can apply as much to Americans working in the USA or, with suitable adaptations to allow for different languages, to Germans working in Germany.

Once you step outside your own country, however, there are some changes in method and attitude that need to be taken into consideration. These matters are considered in Part V which, of necessity, has rather more of a flavour of UK-orientation. Even so, as far as techniques are concerned, much written here can apply just as easily to Americans working outside the USA, or Germans outside Germany.

20
International Research
Denis Pirie

Introduction

The subject of international research is a vast one, which could be described in one page yet not be covered adequately in a whole encyclopedia. It covers research in countries other than the UK, and as a look at any atlas will confirm, the UK occupies but a small part of the globe. Similarly, international research spans many needs, from a cursory overview of whole regions to the most detailed of product market research in a specific foreign country. Last, but not least, the organisation requiring the research could range from a large multi-national corporation with access to ample financial, technical and personnel resources, down to the small business with a highly specific product, seeking to export for the first time.

This Chapter on international research seeks to examine some of the issues, problems and decisions that researchers will probably have to face in the international field, from helping to decide whether or not to undertake international marketing research at all, through to conducting or commissioning any ensuing project in a manner that will help their company or client to make useful business decisions about foreign markets. It will examine similarities and differences between home and international research, show how to do desk and field research, discuss who should conduct the research, and show what further help is available.

International and home market research

If research into one's home market requires empathy and commitment, how much more of both qualities is required in a foreign market of which one has less tangible experience? When a company starts trading, its management quickly learns to identify the market and understand its needs in order to satisfy them better. If the company succeeds in doing these things, it will probably survive and thrive. If it does not do these things, that company will almost certainly cease to function. However, the company invariably starts trading in its home country, where it was formed and is located. While it is true that certain facts about the company's home market will need to be consciously learned, many other aspects of that home market will not need to be learned, such as language, political and economic environment, cultural aspects, business practices etc. It is because this whole business environment will be considered as natural by the entrepreneurs forming the company, that they will not find it necessary consciously to study it.

When the company has grown sufficiently to give serious consideration to expanding into an export or international trading situation, the specific peculiarities of that company's market in a foreign country will need to be consciously learned, together with all of these hitherto taken-for-granted 'environmental' factors, if the company is to know its new foreign market as well as it knows its home market. After all, why should potential customers in a foreign country expect from what is, to them, an as yet unknown foreign supplier, less understanding and commitment than they would from their known and reputable local suppliers? Indeed, one could reasonably assume that most customers in any country might expect foreign suppliers to have to try that much harder than local suppliers to convince customers that they are serious about the market and, in turn, have earned the right to be treated equally seriously by the customer.

Clearly there are ways in which international research is very similar to that conducted in one's home market, and other ways in which there are great differences between them.

International Research

Similarities between home and international research

Marketing research is not an exercise carried out in a vacuum. It is a systematic means of collecting, collating, analysing and presenting data to help answer pre-identified questions about a defined market. Regardless of whether the market to be researched lies at home or in a foreign country, the questions that need to be answered about that market are equally important to the decision maker. So, too, are the consequences that stem from the decisions taken. Therefore the research needed to help in making those decisions is also equally important, regardless of market.

For a manufacturer wishing to introduce a new product into one or more new market sectors within its home country, and another manufacturer in the same country wishing to introduce a new product into one or more sectors of a new country, the situations may seem very different. However, the fundamental questions that need to be answered by the decision makers in either company about either market are probably very similar.

In both cases, the basic question that the decision makers must answer is whether or not they enter a given market, as defined by its geography, the product to be researched and the sectors to be considered for market entry. Following that, there are further questions to be considered.

- Which optimal product variant, to which optimal market sectors, in which order?
- To what standards (whether determined by law or by market requirements)?
- At which optimal price (for both supplier and end user)?
- Against which competition (indigenous and imported)?
- Via which optimal marketing method, and to which potential customers?
- By which optimal distribution channel (agent, distributor)?
- With what likely degree of success, over what period and at what cost?

The final 'go or no-go' decision, regardless of the market, could just as easily be (and often unfortunately is) made by guesswork, as by the use of a properly executed piece of systematic marketing research. The decision, by either method, could be equally emphatic, but the consequences of that decision, depending on the methods used to reach it, could be as successful or as catastrophic for the decision makers whether the market is in one's home country or a foreign one. Likewise, the marketing researchers' skills at locating and communicating with the appropriate respondents and data sources are just as vital to the quality of the research in either market.

Differences between home and international research

The differences between home and international marketing research lie not so much in where the research is to end, as in what information is available at the point the research begins.

What will now be termed the basic 'marketing environment' of any foreign country being researched is the critical factor – and the critical difference between home and foreign marketing research. The marketing environment of any country covers a number of aspects that will be described in more detail below, but the vital difference between a home and a foreign environment is that the former does not need to be consciously studied whereas the latter does.

Over and above these 'environmental' differences between home and foreign countries, there are also market-specific differences relating to the role of the particular product market within the marketing environment of the foreign country being studied. The following notes describe, first, the environmental differences, and then the market-specific ones.

Language

Language is an obvious factor. Language is a medium of communication, and the deeper the researcher needs to probe to understand a foreign respondent's needs and views, the more thoroughly that researcher will need to understand the different language.

The problem of discovering precisely what it is that the respondent wants to communicate can occur even when the language used for

International Research

communication is English. Thus, American, African or Asian English speakers could be using similar sounding language to communicate quite different concepts. Of course, this does not mean that a foreign market should not be tackled by a researcher who is not totally fluent, to mother-tongue standards, in that country's language. It does mean, however, that even those researchers who would claim some fluency in the foreign languages concerned should be constantly aware of the need to ensure that foreign respondents have the same understanding as the researcher of the real meaning of the question.

The researcher, in turn, should properly understand the real meaning of the respondent's answer, whether by use of translators or other bilingual support. When foreign language questionnaires are used, these should always be translated by a person whose mother tongue is the language into which the questionnaire is to be translated. In that way, the researcher will avoid some of those hideous gaffes sometimes made by foreign manufacturers in mis-translating their product brochures into English. Correct translation, more importantly, will ensure that the sense of the question as meant by the researcher will be identically perceived by the foreign respondent. Similarly, researchers having reports prepared for them by foreign nationals would be well advised to have such reports checked by an English mother-tongue speaker to ensure that the report will be both understood and taken seriously by those to whom it is to be presented.

Culture
Culture is another important environmental factor. Whether for reasons of religion, history or social custom, different countries – or even parts of countries – will have evolved different customs and attitudes. It is the function of the researcher in a foreign market to recognise and appreciate these differences in behaviour as facts which may have an important bearing on the research. It is not the researcher's role to criticise or make value judgements about cultural differences, but he must explain their existence to the sponsors of the research and what, if any, impact these will have on marketing in and to that culture. In that role, researchers will need to be emphatic both to the culture of the respondents and to that of the research sponsors, to whom the culture of the former will need to be explained when the final report is presented.

Economic differences
Economic criteria form a very important environmental factor. These relate to a country's degree of development, the complexity of its infrastructure, its financial mechanisms and structure, income distribution, exchange controls and import restrictions. These economic aspects are of particular importance to the researcher, because the inevitable purpose of researching a foreign market is to increase profits from the sales of goods or services to that market. It is not enough to know that there is a thriving market for those goods and services that the sponsor of the research would like to produce. Profitability can only stem from receiving payment for goods or services actually sold, rather than merely knowing of the existence of a desire to buy them. It will be economic considerations that will heavily determine the likely profitability of any particular market.

Political and legal factors
The political and legal framework of the country is another important environmental factor. The nature of a country's form of government is determined by its political structure and political philosophy. The government in turn determines the legal framework of that country, so the politico-philosophical decision as to whether that country has a 'planned' or 'market' economy or what degree of either will govern – among other things – the degree to which international trade is possible and, if so, via which channels (for example, by having to sell to a state-controlled purchasing authority or being free to sell to an individual trading purchaser) and with what degree of ease.

It would be true to say that central state purchasing bodies are often slower and more bureaucratic than their more flexible and responsive free-market equivalents in other countries. However, it is equally true that while the central state purchasing body takes a time to make up its mind in the first place, it takes an equally long time to change from its original decision once it has been made. It is for the researcher to gather all the facts to help in making the decision as to whether trade with such a country can be mutually beneficial and profitable.

Climate and geography
Climate and geography are very obvious and important environmental factors. Yes, refrigerators have been sold to Eskimos and sand has been sold to the Gulf States, but that was precisely for climatic and

geographical reasons (in the first case to keep products cool but not frozen, and in the second because round-grained desert sand was not suitable for cement, whereas imported irregular grained sand was ideal). More mundanely, climate and geography can affect such decisions as how well a product may need to be 'ruggedised' or specifically adapted to survive either weather or rough geographic conditions, or even to survive the extra time spent in transit on long journeys over geographically vast distances. Finally, the cost of such long journeys must affect either profit margins or sales prices.

Business practices
Business behaviour and practices are yet other environmental differences between countries. Japan is probably the world's most consummately successful trading nation, yet many of its business practices are totally different from those applying in Europe or America. Some of these concern business etiquette, as any foreign business visitor to Japan will confirm (and it is always worth asking one before visiting Japan). Other behaviour and practices stem from Japanese industry's perceived role in relation to Japanese society as a whole, which will differ from the more individualistic perception the English or American company has of its role within its own society. Researchers should not be deterred by what might appear to be the inscrutability of foreign business behaviour and practices, but should strive to know, understand and be able to interpret them. It is worth bearing in mind that for all the 'uniqueness' of the business behaviour and practices of the Japanese, they have managed to penetrate other countries' markets so well only by themselves learning business behaviour and practices that are totally alien to them. So it can be done.

Other foreign business behaviour or practices may prove more ethically difficult to accept. One country's view of 'commission' may be another country's definition of 'corruption'. The decision as to whether to trade under such circumstances is one that the sponsors of the research must take, but the fact that such circumstances exist, and may well be essential to doing business in that market at all, is one that should be objectively recognised and reported by the researcher.

Standards
Finally, standards are also an environmental consideration, referring,

in this context, to legally enforceable product standards. Researchers must find out whether there are current standards for the product or country being researched, and to what degree these are legally enforceable. Some countries, such as the USA and Germany, are extremely strict on the product standards they set and the degree to which these are enforced, while other countries are less exacting on both points.

Checking the 'importability' of the product into the country being researched should be one of the first tasks of the researcher. If the product does not meet existing standards for the country to be researched, a decision must quickly be made on what to do next. The research sponsors will have to determine whether that country should be excluded from the research plan, or whether they are prepared to accept that modification of the product to meet different standards will be necessary and justifiable, should the subsequent research indicate a market worth entering.

Market-specific differences
The above points represent aspects of the ways in which the marketing environment differs between countries. Obviously, these aspects are not mutually exclusive. They are intertwined in a manner and to a degree that make each country's environment distinctive, but they have been mentioned separately, as different dimensions of a country's uniqueness, to help the researcher begin to unravel the mystery of the country in which a given market is to be researched.

In addition to these market environment differences, the researcher must consider the ways in which the market for the particular product, or service, behaves differently in the foreign country being researched from the way it does in the home market. These market-specific differences form the crux of the entire research project.

All the above-mentioned environmental factors will influence the shaping of the size, structure, trends, share, distribution, standards and so on of a product market in a given country. However, within the constraints set by those environmental factors, the respondents forming the mix of end users, wholesalers, dealers, importers, competitors, standards or governmental officials, trade press or trade associations that together make up that country's product market, will all have market- or industry-related attitudes, views, needs and information that must be collected, collated, analysed and presented by the researcher.

Here, too, standards are important; however, these are not the legally enforceable product standards referred to above as environmental, but standards or norms set and enforced by the market as a whole, by some discrete sector of it, or even by individual key decision makers. These are standards of market acceptability relating to price, quality, delivery, design, durability and service. They may not have any recognition in law, but they will be the key determinants in the decision to buy, and in the final analysis that decision is what the whole of the research is about.

In general (and there will be exceptions) environmental research is largely secondary research, determined from published sources or desk research, while market-specific research is largely primary and therefore the subject of field research.

Making the decision to export

The first – and most important – decision to be faced in foreign marketing is whether or not to export at all. There are, as will be seen, many excellent reasons for exporting, but it will be for each individual would-be exporting company to decide whether exporting is the right course for that company to embark upon at that time. If exports produce benefits they most certainly incur costs, and while every company will appreciate the benefits, not all will be willing – or able – to accept the concomitant costs.

In the final analysis, exporting, like any other aspect of business, is about profitable trading; if one cannot conduct export trade profitably then it is best not to be in that aspect of business at all. However, those who, having objectively examined both the pros and cons of exporting, conclude that exporting is both advisable and profitable and have systematically set out to export successfully, will be rewarded with profit and a great deal of satisfaction.

Reasons for exporting

There are a number of very good reasons for exporting:

- increasing earning power – at its simplest, more money can be made by selling more products to more customers, beyond the limits of the home market; whether or not net margins exceed these at home (and in many cases they do), companies with successful export markets can certainly increase production, obtain economies of scale and spread their initial investments over a greater volume;

- spreading business risk – keeping one's eggs in more than one basket obviously limits vulnerability to fluctuations in the home market economy; lessening any risk increases the chances of profitable operation;

- sharpening business competitiveness – learning from the home market only is a weakness; foreign sales bring contact with new ideas, trends and applications, as well as developments in packaging, selling techniques and customer preferences; the more that is learned, the better is likely to be the ensuing product and its marketing;

- meeting competition on its home ground – all successful products will face competition sooner or later; to sell in foreign competitors' home markets is the best way of assessing their plans and prospects, and getting early warning of new products and techniques – attack can be the best means of defence;

- improving home market reputation – a company's home market customers may well hold it in higher regard when it becomes known that the company's products are successful on its competitors' home ground.

While it is true that the bulk of UK export trade is in the hands of large firms, many smaller companies are among the most successful and profitable exporters. Smaller companies have their own advantages, in that they are often quicker and more responsive in decision making and opportunity taking, more flexible and more personal in their dealings with customers, and can more easily generate and maintain staff enthusiasm and commitment.

Should a company export?

If a company sells successfully in its home market, it is almost inevitable that someone, somewhere outside the country, would also be interested in buying. However, can that company compete and win that business, once it is identified? That is the key question which only the company concerned can decide for itself, on a harshly realistic basis. Exporting is only one way in which a company can grow. Export business will take time to develop, and the development of it can strain the resources of a small company.

Active exporting is not a marginal activity, to be given second-rate priority in terms of urgency and resources, and to be reliant on the vagaries of home market performance. It will be – certainly at the beginning – less straightforward than home selling, for as has been shown earlier in this Chapter, there is more to learn. To be successful, exporting needs top priority commitment and top priority resource allocation.

Commitment is a critical factor:

- from the top of the company through the whole of the staff;
- at the beginning of overseas selling and equally strongly thereafter;
- (and, especially) of the necessary resources in terms of money, time and personnel.

The resources needed will be considerable. Research will cost time and money. Servicing foreign markets is likely to cost more than servicing the home market. Adaptations of products or packaging may be necessary. New equipment may be required, and good promotion in a new market will also cost money. To serve a new foreign market as reliably as an existing home market will entail giving preference to its needs – certainly in the initial stages. The company must ask itself whether or not it is prepared to give this kind of resource commitment to foreign marketing.

What, where and how to export

Having decided in principle that the company wishes to pledge the commitment and resources to foreign marketing, it is now faced with three new questions: What is it going to sell? Where is the selling to be done? How (and when) is such selling best done?

What is to be sold to foreign customers may well have to be adapted to meet local needs, laws and perceptions. For example, Rolls Royce would not expect to sell a 'Silver Mist' in Germany, where the word 'mist' means what in England would be politely called 'dung'. Similarly a 'gift' would be less than welcome in Germany, where the word means 'poison'. Coca-Cola, in the 1920s, had its name translated into Chinese characters, only to discover that it read as 'bite the wax tadpole'. Amusing, maybe, but a very expensive joke for those who do not conduct research properly.

Where a product is to be sold is a vital question, especially for a first-time exporter. With so many countries to choose from, it makes sense to develop a set of criteria to screen potential export markets, based on the producing company's ability to service the foreign market properly in the short and medium term. From the company's viewpoint, language, proximity, previous knowledge of a country and ease of getting paid will form some of the criteria to be weighted for consideration. Unless the company is intending to target a 'niche' (or specialist) market, a large market size might not be a key factor if servicing it properly is beyond the company's ability. The weighting of these factors is purely subjective at this stage and can only be done by the company itself. It is intended to produce a very small list of potential foreign markets ranked in order of attraction to the exporting company. The top markets on this priority list can then be the subject of desk research in greater depth.

How (and to whom) will the selling best be done will begin to emerge from the desk research just referred to. As has been seen, foreign markets may differ in many respects from the home market, but to know where to start looking in any foreign market it might be helpful for the company to analyse its home market. It would then discover in what market sectors it has been most successful, and then look to see whether a similar sector exists, what it comprises, and how it is serviced in the foreign market being studied. How it is serviced will involve examining channels of distribution and selling methods in the country concerned.

Behind all these questions lie both the resource commitment

International Research

necessary for foreign marketing success and the real need not to waste these scarce resources unnecessarily or impractically.

Desk research

To quote the special leaflet on International Desk Research, published jointly by IMRA and MRS:

> When you need to research an international market, it is tempting to jump on a plane . . . but you may be able to learn as much as you need to know in Britain. And even if an overseas trip is needed, there is a lot of useful background research you can do before you go. There is a wealth of information available in the UK, much of it for free, so make the most of it.

This is equally true of many other countries, where good stores of information are available for the sorts of desk research described in this section.

Some of the following categories of information are likely to be required in any project a researcher is undertaking:

- Demographic: size and age structure of the population, socio-economic groups, ethnic minorities, extent of urbanisation, present and forecast growth rates;

- Economic: gross national product, inflation, economic growth rates;

- Political: structure of government, political stability, attitude to foreign investments/imports, legal requirements for foreign investment/imports;

- Trade: import penetration, import restrictions, import/export trade patterns;

- Product markets: size (by volume and value) with trends, market segmentation, local production, concentration/fragmentation of the market, supplies, distribution patterns, companies involved;

- Media influences: extent of main media – press, television, radio.

The objective of desk research is to obtain as much useful information, under whichever of the information categories mentioned above is relevant to one's specific project, within the researcher's home country before embarking (if necessary) on fieldwork in the foreign country. The sources mentioned below – including government ones – are those available to UK-based desk researchers. Researchers whose home market is not the UK will, in various degrees, find equivalent organisations and facilities available to them locally. The principles, and to a large extent the sources, will be the same.

In-company data

Unless the country or market to be studied is one totally new to the company, there will often be some evidence of previous contact between the company and the foreign market to be researched. This is particularly the case when research is needed by the company in order to transform existing passive exports to that market into active exporting. The in-house researcher should start by examining all previous correspondence, reports, enquiries or orders (whether successful or not) from the country concerned, as well as questioning any other staff members who have visited that country on company business. The amount of useful data held within the researcher's own company – generally in a highly unorganised way – is often underestimated. Because no one has previously bothered to collect such data systematically, there is a tendency to believe that it does not exist.

National and international statistics

Most countries, with various degrees of reliability and fineness of classification, publish statistics relating to production, imports and exports, as well as much other economic and financial statistical data. In addition, similar data are also published by international or supranational bodies such as the United Nations, the European Community (EC), the International Monetary Fund (IMF), and the Organisation for Economic Cooperation and Development (OECD). EC-like bodies exist for other regional areas, such as the Economic Commission for Africa (ECA), the Economic Commission for Asia and the Far East (ECAFE), and the Economic Commission for Latin America (ECLA). Similarly, worldwide international bodies specialis-

International Research

ing in particular subjects also publish statistics on their own subject, such as the Food and Agriculture Organisation (FAO), the International Air Transport Association (IATA), the International Bank for Reconstruction and Development (BRD), the International Civil Aviation Association (ICAO), the International Telecommunications Union (ITU), the International Union of Railways (UICF), the Universal Postal Union (UPU) and the World Health Organisation (WHO).

Research in national statistics can provide valuable data, but can be very frustrating when the trade statistics (import and export figures) are not collected under the same categories as are those for production (or even when import categories do not quite match export categories). Again, these can be problems when attempting time series analysis and it is discovered that the basis of collecting the statistics has changed in the interim period. The most frustrating discovery is that the precise product category required is buried under that sad epitaph of desk researchers' hopes, NES (Not Elsewhere Specified). Finally, there are often problems in comparing national statistics of different countries – thus country A's recorded exports of a product to country B seldom tally with country B's recorded imports from country A (even when allowance is made for the fob/cif differences).

The existence of such problems should not deter the researcher from using national statistics, as they remain the skeleton around which subsequent research will flesh a true model of the market. Indeed, some of the very causes of frustration, such as changing tariff codes, are the result of international efforts to harmonise coding and thereby improve intercountry statistical comparability. As for the NES problem, look on the bright side: at least there is an upper limit of measurement of the product buried within the NES heading, and one which other research will help to identify more closely.

The main sources of national or international statistical information, which provide some market size data, are listed in Appendix D.

General and trade press

Newspapers and periodicals can be a useful source of information on foreign markets. The *Financial Times* and *The Times* produce detailed supplements on specific countries or markets, while publications such as *The Economist* are also good sources of background information.

Directories such as *Benn's Press Directory*, *Willings Press Guide* and *Ulrich's International Periodicals* detail both the general and the specialist trade press worldwide.

Clearly, poring through back numbers of newspapers, periodicals and trade journals can be very time consuming, so it may be more cost-effective to examine press monitors such as the Predicast F & S Index, which categorises information under US Standard Industrial Classification codes, by country (there are three volumes: Europe, USA and Rest of the World), date and source of publication. The series can be seen at the Export Market Information Centre and other reference libraries, and will point the researcher towards a page-referenced and dated source in a named periodical. The same service is also available in online format from its producers.

Where trade journals are concerned, the researcher will seek articles in his home country's trade journals about the target country, as well as in that country's own appropriate trade journal for articles on its home market, and other useful data such as competitive advertising. In some 'high-tech' industries, it is also a good idea to scan the relevant US trade journals, as some of these take on almost a worldwide dimension and are in any event often useful to indicate possible product developments.

Where a particularly useful article has been identified, try – although it may not always be possible – to locate the author for more detailed background, as it is invariably the case that the author has far more information on the subject than was ever published in the article.

Banks

In order to promote their involvement in international trade, most UK and foreign banks publish free reports on individual countries. These provide very useful financial and economic data, but are less informative about specific product markets within the country concerned. As London is a major financial centre where most of the world's important foreign banks maintain a base, it is useful to approach the London branch of banks native to the country being researched, to see what home market data they can provide.

Trade associations

Trade associations in the UK and overseas are a useful source of information about foreign markets. Some UK trade associations maintain libraries or information centres about their own specific market sector in the UK, and often about that market in different overseas countries. However, where these libraries exist they are not always available to non-members of the trade association. UK trade associations can also be helpful in providing contacts with their counterparts in other countries.

It is worth bearing in mind that, in foreign countries, trade associations sometimes play a more important and official part in the activities of their industry than do their sister assocations in the UK. In some countries trade associations have an almost statutory role in collecting industry statistics and can therefore be a very important source for researchers.

UK trade associations are listed in the *CBD Directory of UK Associations*; a similar directory, the *CBD Directory of European Associations*, lists, under industry headings, trade associations covering similar interests throughout Europe. Both of these publications can be found in major UK reference libraries.

Online databases

A wealth of data is increasingly available on electronic databases which are accessible online. UK and OECD statistics can be accessed in this way, as well as market information and journal abstracts on a worldwide basis. Use of online databases can be extremely cost-effective, especially for the in-house researcher.

Access to these databases can be made via organisations that subscribe direct to the individual databases concerned, or via some of the main libraries. ASLIB's Information Resource Centre (telephone: 071-430 2671) can assist, and the *Directory of Online Databases*, published by Cuadra Associates, will help to determine which database should best be accessed.

Published market research

Published marketing research (PMR) differs from *ad hoc* studies in that the former are both commissioned by and remain the copyright of the publishers, whereas *ad hoc* studies invariably remain confidential to the company commissioning them. In general, PMRs are broader in scope than *ad hoc* studies: the former will present a detailed picture of a given market while the latter, being tailored for use by its specific company sponsor, will concentrate in greater detail, down to specific products. However, by definition, PMR studies are available to be used by a researcher wishing to purchase them, whereas *ad hoc* studies are not.

PMRs can often be quite expensive to purchase but, if a suitable one is available, it could well be worth the expense of purchasing it, compared to the time and cost that would otherwise be incurred in trying to replicate its data.

Details of available PMRs, their prices and publishers, are given in *Market Search* (the International Directory of Published Market Research) published by Arlington Management Systems. This directory is also available at some major reference libraries.

Company information

Company information – mainly on larger companies – is available from Extel and, especially in the USA, from Investors Service and Frost & Sullivan; in France there is DAFSA *Informations Internationales* of Paris for Europe, and in Germany *Handbuch der Deutschen Aktiengesellschaften*.

DTI sources

One of the best possible sources for UK researchers of foreign markets is the Department of Trade and Industry. The Export Market Information Centre (EMIC) library is open to the general public and provides the following facilities:

- statistics – world-wide statistics are available showing patterns of trade, production, prices, employment and transport;
- market research reports – a selection of overseas market reports supplements the statistics collection;

International Research

- directories – overseas trade and telephone directories are available;
- development plans – these economic plans for selected countries are available on loan to exporters;
- online databases – a search service is available to selected commercial online databases.

As well as the library, EMIC's Product Data Service (PDS), a mass of mostly unpublished market data, is available for examination. It is held on microfilm, and classified by country and product or industry. Trained staff are available to assist.

Within the DTI there are market branches covering the main regions of the world, with desks covering every individual country. These desks are in constant contact with commercial officers in each of Britain's 200 or so overseas posts. Country desks provide tariff information and issue Country Profiles, as well as *Hints to Exporters*, an invaluable series of booklets for any field researcher planning to visit the country concerned. Country desks and market branches can be accessed through the DTI's seven regional offices in England and its equivalent offices in Wales, Scotland and Northern Ireland.

The DTI maintains a special unit providing information on the European Single Market up to and after 1992, as well as supporting the British Standards Institute (BSI) in the provision of a special unit, Technical Help for Exporters (THE), which holds information on foreign technical standards and legal requirements.

Finally, for British manufacturing or service exporting companies there is the Export Marketing Research Scheme. This scheme, provided by the DTI and managed on its behalf by the Association of British Chambers of Commerce, offers professional advice and financial support to British companies undertaking approved overseas marketing research. Further details of EMRS are given in Appendix F.

Field research

Depending on the nature of the study being undertaken, desk research alone may provide sufficient information on which the sponsor of that research can base reliable marketing decisions. However, the more product-specific the scope of the project is, the more likely it will be that fieldwork will prove to be necessary. In such cases the desk research could be compared to a skeleton, while the ensuing fieldwork will provide the fleshing out needed to provide the full detailed picture of that market.

In looking at foreign field research, it is not intended to go over again the techniques already covered in Chapter 6. These techniques and methods in themselves are universally applicable, but if they are to be effective their specific application in foreign countries will have to take into account environmental and market-specific differences between the home market and other countries.

Getting the 'feel' of these environmental and market-specific differences is a prime purpose of desk research, which is why empathy has to be one of the major attributes of the successful international field researcher. Without that 'feel' or understanding, the field researcher cannot select those techniques most likely to produce suitably reliable data. For example, telephone interviewing may be a more useful technique in European or US markets than in certain Third World countries. Telephone networks in such countries may not be so well developed, or their use, when available, may not be considered acceptable to the respondent.

As no country is identical to any other in all aspects of environmental and marketing behaviour, clearly it would be impossible in one small Chapter to describe each different factor in each different country. Suffice it to say that the differences exist, and desk researchers planning to undertake their own field research will need to identify them.

It is probable that the most difficult task lies with the researcher in a smaller company, researching a foreign market in which that company has had little or no previous experience. This means that there are no company-related sources to help the researcher, such as export sales staff, previous customer records, nor are there overseas representatives such as agents or distributors. However, home-based desk research will have identified lists of companies, organisations or individuals within each of the categories of involvement in the manufacture, development, approval, distribution and consumption of the product or service under study in the country and market concerned.

Having determined which interview method, or mix of methods, is most appropriate to obtain the information required, the researcher must select how many of which respondents in each category need to be interviewed in order to produce data to the degree of reliability required.

There is a considerable element of skill involved in targeting the correct number and type of potential interviewees in each category. This skill is even more critical in the case of foreign research than it is in home research. Less than the optimal number of the right respondents in each category will damage the validity of the information on which the research sponsor plans to make strategic decisions. More than the optimal number of interviews can make the costs of the research rise rapidly and unnecessarily, and might even jeopardise the continuation of the study. Foreign research costs will inevitably be much higher than those for home country research, and to them must be added the likelihood of the researcher's lesser familiarity with both the foreign country itself and the practices of the respondents.

Once the researcher has determined the optimal mix of interview methods and the ideal number and type of potential respondents, he must contact those selected for personal interviewing, with a view to obtaining their willingness and establishing a mutually convenient time, date and place. On receipt of confirmation the researcher can now plan a visit itinerary, or organise replacements should respondents be unwilling or unavailable to be interviewed. The researcher must plan as much as possible before departure, because afterwards there will just not be time.

The incidence of Murphy's Law (if it can go wrong, it will) seems to rise in direct proportion to the difference and distance between the market being researched and the researcher's home market. However, when they arise, these problems relate more to the logistics of travel than they do to research matters. By good desk research and proper planning, the occurrence of those unforeseen but inevitable problems which will occur – such as missed travel connections, strikes, bad weather, hotel misbookings and so on – need not disrupt a schedule of planned interviews excessively.

Of course, Murphy's Law provides opportunities as well as threats to planned field research. However well an overseas market is desk researched, a programme of field interviews always seems to identify an extra, potentially invaluable source, who perhaps could not possibly have been identified at the desk research stage but who might be available for contact. The foreign researcher can be sure that this is likely to occur, but not where and when on the fieldwork visit. So, while the number of interviews should be planned to make the best use of time spent overseas, it should not be planned so tightly as to prevent taking up the opportunity of an added valuable interview if one should present itself. Good planning includes taking into account the unforeseeable as far as possible.

British researchers making overseas field trips would be advised to make their first port of call the British Embassy, High Commission or Consulate, details of which are listed in the *Hints to Exporters* booklets for each country (without which no researcher should venture overseas at all). The purpose of this call is not to ask how the research should be conducted, or to ask the British representative to fix up interviews, but rather to inform the representative of the researcher's presence in the country and of what the researcher is planning to do. At very least, the researcher can obtain a confirmation of desk work undertaken, but equally this could be an occasion for the researcher to discover that a potentially valuable source may have been overlooked. Researchers of other nationalities will undoubtedly find officials of their own Embassies overseas ready to provide a similar service.

Finally, the researcher should travel as light as possible. Brochures, pamphlets, books and articles will inevitably be collected on a field trip. Unless the researcher wishes to trust postal services, or risk heavy excess baggage charges on the return journey, this extra material will have to be carried – so room should be left for it.

In-house or consultant?

The previous section looked at some aspects of a company's conducting foreign research using its own in-house researcher. While the difficulties facing the in-house researcher – especially one conducting overseas fieldwork for the first time – are not to be ignored, there are clearly benefits for a company in using its own researchers to conduct studies in foreign countries.

The first of these usually thought of is cost, although this benefit is less important than it would at first appear to be. The costs of an in-

International Research

house researcher's time, even including overheads, will invariably be below those charged by even the most inexpensive consultancies, so at face value there are clearly large savings to be made by companies in using their own researchers. What should then be taken into account is the fact that the in-house researcher will not be available for any other company work while engaged on this foreign project. However, some cost savings will be made by using in-house researchers, and this could enable a company with a tight research budget to stretch limited resources further.

Companies using their own researchers for foreign projects will, of course, improve their own and their researchers' first-hand knowledge of the foreign market researched. Such added 'hands-on' experience is itself a beneficial acquisition for the company, especially in the early days of post-research marketing development. Unlike a consultant, who will by then be working on another project for another client, the in-house researcher will still be available to the company for reference, interpretation or advisory purposes.

The in-house researcher will almost certainly have a greater knowledge of the company, its products, its existing markets and its aspirations than will an external consultant. Consequently there must be savings to be made in the time necessarily spent on briefing consultants on company and product background.

The use of external consultants, on the other hand, also has benefits, especially when conducting foreign research. The first of these is objectivity. Companies may attach more weight to an objective view from an independent external consultant. This may be somewhat unfair to in-house researchers, whose professional objectivity is thereby slighted, but such companies might equate the added weight in direct proportion to the added cost of the study. After all, the more one pays for advice the more likely one is to take note of it. In addition, there may be in-company 'political' reasons for using external, and therefore neutral, consultants.

Anonymity is another benefit to be derived from using consultants. The company commissioning the foreign research may have reasons for not wishing to alert foreign respondents in overseas markets to its interest. A consultant conducting a closed (ie client-anonymous) study is in a much better position to do this, than is the in-house researcher of the company that wishes to remain anonymous. Respondents, too, may be prepared to assist in the study only on condition that their identity is not disclosed. While compliance with this wish is an obligation under the IMRA/MRS Code of Conduct for all researchers, whether in-house or consultant, it would be reasonable to assume that respondents wishing non-disclosure would be more likely to impart information to a consultant, who can filter out references which might identify the respondent.

Without wishing to impugn the skill of in-house researchers, the breadth of techniques available to and used by marketing research consultants could be wider, possibly enabling more appropriate techniques to be used than might be available to the in-house researcher. It is certainly likely that the consultant will have a greater knowledge of the local conditions and language(s) relating to the foreign country under study, probably for the reason that this market expertise was one of the key criteria for selecting the consultant in the first place.

Finally, an important advantage of using consultants for overseas research is the saving of time to the sponsoring company. This is as true for smaller companies as for larger ones because, in smaller companies, skilled management resources (and this includes in-house researchers) are likely to be scarce and have heavy demands on their available time.

So, a company seeking foreign business marketing research in order to make better and more reliable foreign marketing decisions could have a choice, if it has competent in-house research staff, as to how that research is conducted. Either route – in-house or external consultant – has its advantages, but whichever route is chosen by the company it is important that the research be done and to a standard which will provide the company with firm facts on which to base reliable decisions. It might be held that some research is better than no research, but there are greater dangers to the company's future profitability in taking decisions based on inadequate research, which it believes to be solid research, than there are in basing its decisions on acknowledged guesswork.

Part VI:
The Management of Business Marketing Research

The bulk of this Handbook is concerned with data, their gathering, organising and general management. Although much of this information is gathered by people, from people, it is the information itself that has held the centre of the stage so far.

Now it is the turn of the practitioners themselves, and especially their management (including self-management), to be examined. This part of the Handbook deals with business marketing research projects as activities involving people, and looks at the problems of such involvement.

The reader should note that this is not an attempt to write a text on personal and business management in general, although these are important skills for many people involved in business marketing research (and some key texts on the subject are included in Appendix E)). Rather, it is a look, once again, at the stages of a business marketing research project, this time highlighting the personnel and management aspects.

The first Chapter describes that most common of research activities – the commissioned survey – and examines how it is set up and controlled by the sponsoring researcher, but is also helpful to the implementing organisation.

The second Chapter deals with the various kinds of business marketing research organisation, and looks at the management problems of research service companies (consultancies and field service agencies); it also discusses the activities of the freelance consultant or researcher.

21
The Management of Commissioned Research
Keith Bailey

The majority of business marketing research projects of any size will incorporate a survey of some kind. This may be done by the staff of the sponsor's company, but is more often undertaken by an independent organisation, under the direct control of the sponsor, or under a separate contract. This Chapter is concerned with the selection of such a contractor, and the control of the resultant contract – although much of the latter part would relate also to a survey conducted by in-house staff.

The role of the researcher

Most of you reading this Chapter will be researchers, although the precise nature of your job will vary widely. Within a manufacturing or service company, you may have a job which encompasses market research as one small part of your responsibilities; or you may be engaged full-time in marketing research – in a manufacturing or service company or in a research or marketing consultancy or as a freelance consultant or researcher. Your position will govern your approach to a business research project. In a research consultancy you will generally be responding to a client's brief and designing a research programme for him. If you are on the client side yourself then the time available to you, and your own skills and experience, are likely to dictate whether you undertake research yourself or instruct others to perform the task on your behalf.

It is important to remember that business marketing research is not only concerned with commissioned surveys: there is much to be gained from the analysis of statistics, through desk research and in consulting published market surveys and reports. These individual techniques are addressed earlier in this Handbook; in this Chapter we shall concentrate on the commissioning and management of surveys – whether they are full sample surveys, censuses or more qualitative investigations – looking at them mostly from the point of view of the researcher commissioning them.

The research brief

The starting point for any research has to be the research brief. Despite earlier references to it, the brief is such a vital part of any research that no apologies are made for referring to it again. It must be the researcher's first task to prepare it.

A well written research brief establishes everyone's terms of reference; it ensures that all parties are thinking along similar lines; it forms a reference point against which to measure the progress of a project, and indeed to judge the worth of a particular research approach. Time spent in preparing the research brief properly is time soundly invested in ensuring a well thought-out project, and in increasing its value to its sponsors.

The first priority in drawing up a research brief is to define the marketing problem – what the question is that you are supposed to be answering. Try to understand as much as you can about your company's or your client's position, what is known and what is not. Challenge any assumptions; are they sound or are they, too, an unknown? The more you ask, the more you will understand and the better informed you will be in designing an appropriate research programme and in interpreting its findings.

Agreeing the objectives

A prime purpose of the research brief is to establish the objectives of the research project and to agree them, beforehand, with the sponsor.

Set down on paper your knowledge of the sponsor's needs as the background to the project and then list the objectives in conducting the research as you see them. Agree with the sponsor what it is you want to discover – which questions have to be answered. If you set realistic objectives, and are sure you know what you will do with the information you plan to collect, if you are in agreement on the objectives that you will work to then there can be no question as to your response when challenged: 'Why didn't you ask . . .?'. If it was not covered by the objectives, you cannot be expected to have thought of it.

Agreeing the objectives with the sponsor is your first opportunity to contribute to the research. You can use your knowledge and experience to question and challenge; you can show that you want to ensure that only necessary and worthwhile research is undertaken and that that research correctly addresses issues and delivers findings upon which decisions can be taken.

Do you need a survey?

Once the objectives are agreed, you can now ask yourself if a research survey is needed. Is a survey actually required to meet these objectives?

Perhaps the answers to the questions already exist elsewhere in the organisation; maybe the requirement is just for a few man-days to blow the dust off a few files, extract any relevant information and write it up as a short report.

Perhaps the information exists or might be expected to exist in published sources; maybe the requirement is for a visit to a commercial library or a telephone call to the appropriate trade association.

Perhaps the same, or very similar, survey has already been undertaken; maybe a telephone call can obtain its prospectus from the publisher, and all that then needs to be done is to submit a purchase order.

Who will do it?

The detail of the research programme – methodology, sample, timing, budget and so on – should follow from the agreed objectives as part of the brief. From this brief as the basis for development, you, as an in-house researcher, may devise your own research programme and plan to conduct it yourself. Alternatively:

- recognising that, for whatever reason (size, timing, technical content), it is beyond your internal resources, you may write a detailed research specification which becomes the basis for asking freelance researchers or a consultancy to undertake the work, or
- you may decide to invite research proposals from a research agency or consultancy, thus benefiting from their examination of your problem and their suggestions for a research programme.

The decision on how to proceed with a survey involves a number of factors:

- in-house resources,
- other in-house commitments,
- sample size,
- interviewing level,
- technical content,
- timing requirement,
- geographical location.

Do you, as the in-house researcher, have the time and resources to devote to the project? Are you a competent interviewer, capable of interviewing senior businessmen or of absorbing a highly technical subject, or should outside help be sought?

Then again, rather than wait several months for a single in-house researcher to conduct an extensive interviewing programme, should some or all of the interviewing be sub-contracted? Is it cost-effective to send an in-house researcher on a tour of Europe, the USA, the Far East, or would it be preferable to engage a local researcher in those countries?

If a research agency or consultancy is engaged, its proposal document should be seen as forming an integral part of the research brief. If one of a number of proposed options is accepted or, after discussion, modifications are agreed, the final format of the programme should be set down on paper for reference.

Once the decision to use outside help has been taken, a proper brief is even more vital, representing, as it does, the basis for the work and the justification for some expenditure. With it, you and your research contractor will both know where you are going. If difficulties occur, reference back to the research brief should enable you to take sensible action without straying from the original objectives.

Selecting a research contractor

You are seldom faced with a total vacuum when selecting a research contractor; your colleagues or predecessors will have had experience of commissioning research, or your organisation will have found its way on to the marketing lists of a number of research agencies. However, how can you be certain that an agency is the best one for the job? The 'household names' in marketing research, which are regularly quoted in media opinion polls, while generally happy to offer business marketing research services may not necessarily have the most appropriate skills or experience for your particular project.

The selection of a research agency should be treated as a desk research exercise in its own right. Various sources of information on research contractors may be consulted. The IMRA *Membership Directory* can be of value, both for its classified sections and advertising. However, of much greater benefit, in that it provides broader details about companies and their areas of expertise, product fields and techniques, is IMRA's *European Guide to Industrial Marketing Consultancy*.

The Market Research Society Yearbook and the ESOMAR (European Society for Opinion and Marketing Research) annual *Directory*, both also provide summary details of research organisations in the UK and overseas respectively. For researchers with a keen interest in export and international market research, the *International Directory of Market Research Organisations*, published jointly by the Market Research Society and the British Overseas Trade Board, should be a valuable acquisition.

What to look for

Whatever the source, your first action should be to flag the research agencies which might be of interest.

- Do they have experience of your product or market?
- Do they offer the techniques required?
- Are they large enough for the job in hand?
- Do they cover the countries concerned?
- Are they members of the appropriate professional association(s)?

It may take several 'trawls' through the directories to refine this list to a manageable size. If, as will frequently be the case, it is not possible on the basis of the information given to produce a short-list of, say, three agencies to be briefed, a useful step is to request further details from possible contenders.

A short note to the contact named in the directory entry should request:

- a copy of the agency's literature,
- details of experience in specified product fields or markets if appropriate,
- a list of current clients,
- other relevant information.

For overseas agencies, a fax or (getting rarer these days) a telex will elicit a quicker response. If the agency can offer neither of these facilities, and a telephone call confirms that this is the case, you should consider the wisdom of continuing with this contact. Are you prepared to rely on the vagaries of the international mail, particularly to countries such as Italy, for communications between you and the agency? Are you prepared to pay courier costs for draft questionnaires, reports etc? Is a fax bureau service a viable alternative?

As a client, I was frequently astonished by the tardiness of many research organisations in sending the requested details; I might have reached the briefing stage with my short-listed agencies before all brochures had landed on my desk. If an agency does not respond promptly to a possible sales opportunity, how are they going to respond to communications during the course of a project?

The standard of presentation of the information requested may say a lot about the various companies; certainly the content of the responses will enable a short-list to be constructed. Experience in your product field or market, or a related area, can be a major advantage in that it may indicate a degree of understanding of market structure, sampling problems, sources of published data and so on.

If a contractor has just the right experience this may be a warning sign, indicating that the agency has your major competitor among its clients. In consumer markets, clients can be paranoid about their agencies not working for their competitors. In the more restricted business markets, such an attitude is frequently not practical and is only rarely of concern. If you want to employ the services of a research company that is an expert in your particular area then it has to be accepted that that expertise has almost certainly been acquired by working for your competitors. In any event, no reputable, professional research agency is going to compromise its own position through indiscreet handling of confidential information.

By ensuring that your agency contacts are members of IMRA, the MRS and/or ESOMAR you will get the additional protection of the industry's codes of conduct. For researchers earning their living by selling research services, the threat of censure or expulsion from the professional bodies is likely to carry far more weight than an imposing 'confidentiality agreement' prepared by the sponsor's legal department.

From the contractor's point of view, if such an agreement is imposed, whether or not it is legally enforceable, the more complex kind may warrant inspection by the contractor's own legal advisers. This is partiularly so if the agreement gives the particular sponsor 'exclusivity' for a defined product field. Before accepting such a restriction, a research contractor should assure itself that the volume of business from that sponsor warrants the exclusion of others, and that it is protected (perhaps by the payment of a retainer) should the sponsor and agency 'fall out' or otherwise cease to work together.

As a final point regarding information from short-listed agencies, their lists of clients can be quite illuminating. Do you recognise some respected names amongst the list? Do the clients' activities confirm claimed expertise in a certain area? Is there synergy or conflict with your own business? If you are particularly concerned about the credentials of an agency, reference to the IMRA *Membership Directory* may give you the name of a contact within a quoted client company; a short telephone call may be sufficient to obtain reassurance or may suggest that you try elsewhere.

Briefing research contractors

In order for you to obtain a sensible proposal from a contractor, he must be briefed on your intentions and requirements. From a shortlist of 'eligible' research agencies, it is standard practice to brief no more than three. Your initial communications or, if necessary, a few additional questions should enable you to select three capable candidates.

It is a waste of everybody's time to approach more than three agencies; as a client you will not endear yourself to your research agencies if you depart from this norm. Certainly, research agencies are unlikely to give of their best if they know or suspect that they are but one of a whole host competing for a job. Of course, if you know to whom you expect to award the job, it is probably neither fair nor necessary to seek competitive proposals.

Research contractors will not normally charge for producing a proposal; clearly such a policy is only practicable if they stand a reasonable chance of winning the job in a competitive situation. To charge for proposals would decrease the number of frivolous requests, and especially the tendency to request proposals merely as ammunition to reduce the fee of a favoured agency, but commercial reality would seem to mean that such a move is unlikely.

Nevertheless, circumstances may dictate that a fee would be charged – if so, this should be stated clearly and agreed in advance. If you are inviting an agency over from Paris to be briefed you may consider it reasonable to pay the air fares. If the topic or market under investigation is unknown to both client and agency, it may be sensible for the agency to spend some time researching available sources; if this extends beyond what one might normally expect (say, half a day) then it would be appropriate to agree a suitable fee.

The Management of Commissioned Research

There is no substitute for a personal briefing of research contractors by the client; this enables an understanding and rapport to build up between the parties, and facilitates discussion and agreement of relevant issues. However, any personal briefing should be supported by the written research brief. There is much to be said for supplying the written brief in advance to allow the contractors time to consider it and its implications. They can then come to a meeting with a list of questions prepared in advance, thus ensuring the fullest discussion.

A written brief ensures that all potential research contractors receive the same basic information. In evaluating their proposals you know that each has been given the same facts from which to draw their conclusions. It will often be the case that new facts – perhaps a potential problem area – emerge during one of the personal briefings. This may lead to an agreement with that particular agency to vary a part of the brief. In such circumstances it is sensible to communicate this change to the other agencies, even if they have already been briefed, to maintain the comparability among briefings and their resultant proposals.

After the personal briefing, research agencies will frequently telephone with supplementary questions while preparing their proposal. This is usually a sensible step, but in replying you should consider whether the question should have been anticipated earlier or whether the agency is looking to force you to make decisions in an area where you actually want the agency to make recommendations.

Whether or not to reveal the allocated budget for a given project is a dilemma. If you wish to spend no more than is necessary, the temptation is to say nothing and see which proposal offers the most information for the least cost. For the research agency, however, it is frustrating to submit a £20,000 proposal for a comprehensive personal interviewing programme only to find that only £5,000 is available and that a telephone survey covering key objectives is the only option. While such a difference should have been resolved during a briefing, some clients genuinely have no idea of the cost of a research project and therefore such differences do occur.

Unless the sponsor commissions a substantial number of projects, has a good feel for the current cost of research, and can agree to a detailed research specification (covering method and number of interviews), it is probably best for the approximate budget size to be indicated. Research agencies want to win business; they would rather propose creative techniques to make the most of a £5,000 budget than put forward elegant designs, statistically highly reliable, but costing four times as much and which lose them the job.

When briefing research agencies, you should agree a date for receipt of proposals. This date should allow a realistic time for the preparation of the document; since human nature ensures that proposals are in any case written only just before the deadline, however, it need not be too generous. You should bear in mind what the research agency has to do. If preliminary desk research has to be undertaken, or if quotes have to be obtained for sub-contracted fieldwork overseas, for example, this should be reflected in the time allowed.

It is also beneficial to the research agency to indicate how long you anticipate it will take to decide among the proposals. This detail needs to be borne in mind in laying out a proposed time-scale for the research; it can be crucial if a tight deadline is set for completion of the project.

Choosing a research proposal

You have done all your preparatory work; you have selected reputable, well-qualified research agencies; you have given a comprehensive, fair briefing; the research proposals have arrived. If they do not all arrive on time, perhaps you have the first criterion in choosing among potential research contractors.

Unless you have specified the precise methodology and sample-size, and are basically only seeking a competitive tender, then a major priority in assessing proposals must be the research design proposed and its ability to meet your objectives. The research agency will have justified the design with appropriate arguments. If any element remains unclear then clarification should be sought.

It is quite common that, given three proposals, one eliminates itself and the difficulty rests in choosing between the other two. If the briefing process has been undertaken conscientiously there should be sufficient information on which to make a decision. On occasions, it may be necessary to telephone or to meet with the agency for further discussion, or even for them to make a formal presentation of their proposals. The latter situation may be particularly appropriate if the

The Management of Commissioned Research

choice is not yours but that of your own 'clients' – the internal users of the research.

In reading proposals you should check the following.

- Does the agency show a good understanding of the research problem?
- Has the proposal addressed the points listed in the brief?
- Will the research meet the specified objectives?
- Are you satisfied with the credentials of both the agency and the researchers?
- Have time or other constraints been met?
- Is the cost acceptable?

Remember that you will be working closely with the agency for a number of weeks or months. Are you happy to deal with the personnel you have met? Are these, in fact, the people who will be working on your project?

Cost alone should never be the sole basis for evaluating proposals. If you can resist the temptation, do not look at that last page until you have formed a view on the research design proposed. Consider carefully what is being offered for different costs before finally deciding. If one proposal looks particularly cheap or particularly expensive, you should ask yourself the reasons. Is like being compared with like? Is there a flaw in one agency's understanding? Is it underestimating the cost of a particular element?

Serious fee discrepancies should be challenged, low ones just as much as high ones – it is better to have the agency revise its fee before commissioning, than to find it asking for additional cash subsequently or perhaps being forced to take short-cuts once it becomes apparent that the budget is insufficient. Similarly, if you prefer elements of a particular proposal, but it is more expensive, put this to the agency. At worst the company can insist that that is indeed the fee, but if they want your business they will want to see what accommodations can be made, for example: Do you need that second presentation to your Board? Would a slightly smaller sample compromise the reliability of the results?

Where an apparently high fee is drawn to a contractor's attention, it is not unknown for the company to discover mistakes in the costings (either genuine or 'invented'): perhaps the contingency allowance is too cautious; perhaps, knowing that you are seriously interested or that there is a drop in business intake looming, a 'commercial decision' may be taken to drop the fee to win the business. This sort of situation should be approached with great care. If you force a low fee on a contractor, you may both live to regret the decision.

Of course, if you are seeking funding under the Export Marketing Research Scheme (see Appendix F) you will need your three proposals for submission, together with your application to the EMRS administrators for their decision. It is important that you do not commission the work before this is received.

Controlling a research project

Once an agreement is in place between a sponsor and the chosen research contractor, then the project can begin in earnest. It may only be for desk research, but is more likely to involve a survey of some kind; the remainder of this Chapter considers how the sponsor's researcher should relate to the contractor's activities. It is difficult to separate the control of the contract from the control of the commissioned project by the contractor, since the sponsor needs the assurance that the control of the project is being done effectively. This review thus includes comment on the control process, partly as a help to the contractor's personnel, and partly as a help to the sponsor, who should ensure that such a process is covered by the research proposal.

Commissioning the project

Most research contractors will insist on written confirmation of an order; if not, it is certainly good practice to write a letter of confirmation. This can serve to avoid confusion, or indeed argument, at a later date and can clarify any alterations to the proposal which have been verbally agreed between you.

If the proposal offered a variety of options, the letter should set down the one(s) selected. If methodology, interview content etc, were

The Management of Commissioned Research

altered, the letter should give a formal record of these changes. If you have received reassurances from the contractor on a point of some concern to you, it is an opportunity to put these in writing.

The confirmation letter could well include a brief specification for the research: the number and type of interviews; interview length and basic coverage; sample nature and size; specific tasks for the research contractor; level of reporting (data tables, presentation, interpretative written report); fee; time-table.

At the same time as the commissioning letter, a note of regret to the unsuccessful agencies is polite, and spares you telephone calls from them asking what the decision is. They will generally welcome a few words of explanation as to why they have been refused the job; if you might still consider them for future projects, your note can ensure that your points of view are taken into consideration the next time around.

With the project commissioned, you can expect to receive an invoice from the contractor. Either the research proposal or the associated terms of business will set out the basis for payment which, typically, will be 50 per cent on commissioning and 50 per cent on delivery of the final report. A normal alternative would be one-third on commissioning, one-third at a mid-way point, such as on completion of interviewing, and one-third upon delivery of the report.

The advance payment both gives a sign of your commitment to the project and provides your contractor (typically operating with very little working capital) with funds to pay the expenses of the project – in particular, interviewers' fees. On a particularly large project, especially if it consists of various phases, you might consider stage payments based on the different phases of the research. A three-stage project, consisting of desk research, and qualitative depth interviews followed by a telephone survey, might warrant five or six payments:

- on commissioning,
- on completion of the desk research,
- on commencement of the depth interviews,
- on completion of the depth interviews,
- on commencement of the telephone survey,
- on final completion of the project.

This ensures that the contractor is provided with sufficient funds and is recompensed for work done, while still providing safeguards for the client.

At any point it may be decided to alter the precise scope of the project; stage payments enable such changes to be reflected in invoices with the minimum of disruption. In some instances the project may be abandoned before completion of all phases; stage payments avoid the need for complicated refunds. Whatever the method adopted, keeping the final payment until the report is delivered gives the client the ultimate sanction of withholding partial payment if dissatisfied with the work. Fortunately this should not be necessary if the project is correctly managed, and should be used only as a last resort.

Project administration

The detailed administration of a project should be undertaken by the contractor, and the sponsor need be involved, if at all, only at key points in the research. You should, of course, be aware of all the component parts from the details in the proposal.

Project briefing

A 'kick-off' meeting will often be in order to agree the final planning of the project. You may have decided which contractor to use, but still wish to elaborate on parts of the proposal or on your objectives. It may well be necessary to provide further background on your organisation's products or services, possibly involving a factory visit or product demonstration. Your own personnel may wish to brief the contractor you have selected, to ensure that the objectives are reliably communicated.

A briefing meeting may see the introduction of agency research executives to the job, where previously only a director or partner has been involved. In any event, and particularly if some time has elapsed since the original briefing, a meeting serves to concentrate everybody's minds on the problems in hand, and to stimulate and motivate all involved.

One point to be considered early on is the sampling frame. Whether the sponsor is to provide a customer list, or the agency to purchase a list from, say, *Yellow Pages* or a similar source, this can often be a cause of delay and frustration. Early agreement on the exact requirement, and resultant placement of a purchase order, can considerably ease matters. From the contractor's point of view, one of the most common causes of difficulty in project execution is the client's failure to deliver a promised list on time or in agreed detail – or even at all.

Questionnaires
In a typical project the questionnaire now becomes a priority. If not detailed in the preliminary briefing or the proposal, the kick-off meeting should agree the coverage of any interviews, to enable the contractor to draft a questionnaire. If you have your own ready-prepared questionnaire, the contractor may wish to adapt it to a format which is familiar to his interviewers and/or suited to his data processing procedures. At the same time, he may have observations as to the practicality of asking questions of the type, or in the manner, suggested.

It is reasonable for the sponsor to expect to see a draft of the questionnaire for comment and approval. In some instances, the agency may require guidance with technical terms, industry expressions, jargon etc. It is the contractor's task to produce a questionnaire which will enable him to meet your research objectives. Reference to the research brief and the stated objectives as a check may indicate some areas of potential omission, and you can ask for an explanation as to how the questionnaire will meet the objective concerned.

It may be useful for you to 'pilot' the questionnaire on colleagues or even target respondents. While this is no substitute for a true pilot by the contractor, it may point to areas of ambiguity or misunderstanding which can then be corrected.

If the research is to be conducted in another country it may be necessary to have the questionnaire translated, and your guidance may be sought for this. Translations are best done by a researcher who should be fluent in the language in question, to ensure the questionnaire design factors are adhered to. The sponsor's local offices can be a useful source for local industry terms, jargon etc, which no researcher can be expected to know.

Where visual aids are to be used as stimulus material in interviews, your guidance may again be sought to ensure that they properly represent your company's products or views. You should ensure that you have a full set of the final versions of all interview materials for future reference.

Interviewer briefing
For a project involving personal or telephone surveys, the interviewers must be instructed as to the nature of their task. Depending on the complexity of a job, the research budget and the abilities of the individual interviewers, the interview briefing may be conducted in person, by telephone or in writing. Personal or telephone briefings should in any event be supported by written interviewer instructions.

Personal briefings can be a costly exercise, but in business marketing research it is usually essential that the interviewers and consultants are brought together. The complexity of a product or market can best be communicated in this way; it also allows the interviewers to ask questions of the consultants, and thus ensure their comprehension.

The sponsor can play a useful part in the briefing by communicating the relevant aspects of his business; the briefing can also serve to reassure you as to the suitability of the interviewers selected. It is not a pleasant matter for sponsor or agency, let alone the interviewer, if an interviewer is rejected on the basis of the briefing; nevertheless this can be preferable to having poor-quality work carried out, or to leaving the sponsor with a potential reason for questioning or rejecting the interviewer's work at a later stage.

Briefings can serve to motivate and get considerable commitment from interviewers. They allow interviewers to become conversant with the basis of the market under study and with the relevant industry terms; this leads to greater confidence in carrying out the work and ultimately to better quality work. Nevertheless, care must be taken not to provide too much detail or to confuse the interviewer. In few cases does the interviewer need to be a PhD to carry out the work; the briefing should simply make him conversant with aspects of the research, and enable him to appear knowledgeable across the table from a respondent. Certainly it should ensure that he is never obviously out of his depth.

If a pilot has already been conducted, it can be enormously reassuring to interviewers on the main stage of the survey to have a short debrief from the pilot interviewer(s). This can show what aspects are difficult (and how to handle them), what are relatively easy

The Management of Commissioned Research

(despite looking difficult), and what was impossible (and so has been changed in the final version).

Fieldwork monitoring
For a time now there is relatively little for the client to do. During fieldwork and data analysis, so long as things are going well, there is little need for contact between client and contractor. However, it can still be of benefit to agree a regular process of liaison; depending on the particular needs of a project this might be weekly, fortnightly, or even monthly.

At best, the agency may only have to report that everything is on course. Otherwise, there may be questions from interviewers to be answered; there may be sampling difficulties to be overcome; there may be problems in contacting respondents and consequent delays to fieldwork; the client may find his internal deadlines have moved, and that there is a need to 'squeeze' a day or two at some point in the research timetable. The liaison should certainly serve to keep everybody up to date and to cement relationships further.

An occasional problem arises when the sponsor's list of contacts or sample frame proves to be inadequate for the research survey purposes. This will have happened for a variety of reasons, but the result is that the contractor cannot complete the survey. Such a situation must be discussed quickly between client and contractor, and methods of rectification decided. The client may have to accept an addition to the fee, to cover the extra work that the contractor will now have to do. To avoid this situation, it is vital that the client should ensure that the original lists are indeed as good as expected (by the methods outlined earlier in this Handbook), or give the job to the contractor as part of the project.

Analysis
Most of the effort of data analysis can safely be left to the research contractor. Nevertheless, the analysis specification should be agreed in advance. This should be in the original research brief, and reflected in the contractor's proposal. Certainly analysis requirements need to be borne in mind in designing the questionnaire and the sampling procedure.

If the data are to be analysed by computer, the contractor will prepare an analysis specification. Unless you feel confident with research procedures and computer processes, this is probably best left to the contractor, but a sight of the analysis specification will show you how the tabulated data are to be laid out, and you can than be sure that the presentation will match your needs.

In business marketing research the client's assistance may be needed in grossing-up and weighting procedures. Despite the researchers' best efforts, respondents will frequently answer questions in value terms rather than volume, or in obscure units. The client may be able to help in agreeing conversion factors (eg average prices to convert value to volume) or judging whether exceptional data are at all possible or totally out of court. (Naturally, care must be taken in such situations to abide by the Code of Conduct and not reveal individual informants' identities.)

Presentation and report

The techniques of presentation, both orally and in the written form, have been explored from the research contractor's point of view in Part III. You, as the intended recipient of the report, may well have your own views as to how you wish this to be done. Unless all your own personnel with an interest in the results can be sure to have read a pre-submitted written report, the preferable approach is that the contractor should first make an oral presentation of the findings (with appropriate visual aids, and hard copies of the same for those present). This should then be followed by a full interpretative report.

This procedure has a number of advantages, among which are:

- speed in getting the main findings to you;
- the opportunity to discuss aspects of the research and their interpretation before a comment is committed to print;
- the written report then taking account of issues raised at the presentation, answering queries and developing upon areas of particular interest to the client.

The oral presentation
The research presentation may be the only exposure some of your

The Management of Commissioned Research

personnel get to the research. It has to be well planned and prepared, the contribution of the client being to provide the facilities: agreed date, convenient venue, and specified audience, described in Chapter 12 as being necessary to make the contractor's presentation effective.

If a large audience is expected, you, from the client's side, may wish to review the presentation in advance of its being given. This might involve a full-scale 'dress rehearsal', a separate presentation at an earlier date, or simply being given an advance copy of the charts to be presented. Whichever the case, the matter should be agreed well in advance, preferably before the work is commissioned.

It should also be agreed in advance between you and the research contractor who is to say what by way of introduction. This avoids an embarrassed silence while everybody waits for somebody to start, and also avoids presentation by both sides of (possibly contradictory) research objectives.

The written report

If the written report is to follow on from the presentation, it should be attended to as soon as possible. You may wish that a draft report be submitted for approval. As with an advance copy of the presentation, this permits errors in content or interpretation to be corrected.

If you take issue with some aspects of the research, or wish to expand upon the interpretation, this is best done in a separate note circulated with the report. You may wish, in any case, to take the report, condense it, draw conclusions from it, and formulate recommendations which are then circulated (or presented) to your senior management or other 'internal' personnel.

Afterwards

Your involvement will not, it is hoped, end with the project report. The conclusions and implications of the research findings will be debated and should be turned into action. You can contribute to this debate; the in-house researcher is perhaps better positioned here, although clients should not waste the knowledge and expertise that an agency researcher will have accumulated during the course of a project. Some dialogue following presentation and report is to be expected, but if it is clear that considerable further commitment from the contractor is desirable, a consultancy agreement is probably the fairest way to proceed.

If a client knows his market, then good research should confirm his expectations more often than not; seen positively, this is justification for the research. If the objectives call for confirmation of a given view or theory, they have been answered. It is also probably an indication that the research has been well designed and conducted. In these circumstances, what needs to happen is to look beyond that initial feeling of confirmation, to see what detail the research has uncovered; there are bound to be one or two areas revealed by close scrutiny of the report which give rise to questions. If it is not in the basic findings, then it may, for example, be in the specific answers of certain sample sub-groups, or lurking in the list of 'others', which the research contractor has thought were not key answers to a given question and has lumped together at the bottom of a summary table. Close scrutiny always pays dividends.

On the other hand, if the market is thought to be well known and yet the results are painting a very different picture, the results must first be checked with the contractor. If data are weighted or grossed-up, has the calculation been properly worked out? Is the sample correct? Are there any odd features about any one respondent or any group of them? Have the questions been interpreted by respondents in the way that was originally envisaged?

Once you are certain of the research method and results, and a discrepancy remains, you then have to examine your own company's expectations and why there is a discrepancy between them and the research findings. Careful attention to detail will reveal the common ground and point to explanations for some discrepancies. Others may be left unresolved, and point to the need for further research. Close study of sales and marketing experience may well show that the original expectations were erroneous, and that the research findings are in fact nearer to the truth.

Where the research is into a market unfamiliar to the client, the results must share the trust put into the contractor in the first place. This is not to say that the results should then be forgotten. If a decision to develop a new market is based on them, the research findings should be tested against the experience gained in the development – and the market should be surveyed again within five years.

The Management of Commissioned Research

If all has gone well, both client and contractor are pleased, and your function as the link between the two will have been shown to be a major one. The rapport which can develop among all the parties to a good survey is important, and may lead to an even better job next time.

22

Personal and Corporate Organisation

Ken Sutherland

The management of business marketing research involves some features that are peculiar to the profession and are worthy of note in this Handbook. Not least among these is the high proportion of individuals who operate on a freelance basis, while many a company involved in business marketing research is quite small. The particular problems of management – of self and company – in business marketing research are reviewed in this Chapter.

Introduction

Business marketing research involves its practitioners in a number of personal skills, which have themselves been discussed at length in previous Chapters in this Handbook. The discipline itself is still more art than science, although its exact scientific content increases each year. To practise that art requires a great deal of management skill, even if only self-management, and it is that particular skill which is to be examined here, from the points of view of both the individual and the company manager.

The organisations involved in business marketing research vary widely in size – from a freelance worker to quite large full-service agencies or consultancies, with separate departments to match the various stages of a business marketing research project. This variation is just as true for the in-house marketing research capability, which ranges from part of the time of one person, employed also on other things, to a fully-fledged marketing research department of some considerable size and employing researchers, interviewers, analysts and technical experts.

Regrettably, it is true that for most manufacturers of industrial products, marketing research is not a continuous operation and, for some, it is both irregular and infrequent. Under these circumstances an in-house marketing research capability is uneconomic (and would be most unsatisfactory to work in). Only for large companies, with a good range of products, or products whose nature is changing quite rapidly, can there be the justification for a full-time department devoted to marketing research. For other potential users of marketing research, it is necessary to engage the services of a specialist marketing research consultancy or agency when the need arises.

Managing the in-house department

Most of the problems of managing an in-house marketing research department are those of general management — personnel relations, budgeting, career progression, communications and so on — and, as such, are not the subject of this Handbook. The present Chapter is concerned only with the special features of management imposed by the character of the work.

The first such feature, as already mentioned, is that of irregularity in demand. Even in a large company it will not be possible to create a steady work load, and there are bound to be peaks and troughs in the need for marketing research by the other parts of the company. The best way to deal with this situation is to staff the department in sufficient numbers to handle comfortably the minimum demand upon it, and then to put peak loads out to external contractors, retaining control of the projects within the department.

The minimum staffing level should include at least one experienced researcher, who is knowledgeable of the company's activities and able to communicate with the other parts of the company sufficiently well to define their research requirements. If that researcher can also analyse and interpret research results, the minimum requirement would be completed by a good interviewer who is able to handle telephone interviewing, with perhaps one of these staff members, or both, undertaking interviews in the field. The skills necessary to manage externally placed research contracts are then as described in Chapter 21.

Part of the 'base-load' of work for such a department would be to review and store information in newspapers and the trade and professional press related to the company's activities, to maintain awareness of the company's competitors (as described in Chapter 14), and to keep track of any advertisement campaign (as in Chapter 17). The in-house workers will also ensure that internal company information of relevance to marketing research work, such as regular sales reports, will be provided to them.

Business marketing research services

The provision of business marketing research services to user companies is undertaken by a wide range of organisations. These include:

- the individual consultant, freelance researcher or interviewer, or recruiter or moderator for groups;

- an agency providing a particular fieldwork service (interviewing by telephone or face-to-face, or organising groups, hall tests or clinics), and doing so with its own staff, or by the use of freelance personnel, or by a combination of the two – since varying load affects agencies just as much as user companies;

- a consultancy specialising in particular marketing research techniques, or in particular end-user sectors, which may also cover the relevant fieldwork, or contract it out to a fieldwork agency.

The division betwen the freelance individual and the company (even one as small as a partnership of two people) is the most fundamental, and the following notes pay regard to that difference. However, many of the comments about the activities of the freelance worker apply as well to the individual within a company, and so can be read with equal interest by a marketing manager.

The individual worker

The most important characteristic of self-management for the individual worker (in any occupation, not just business marketing research) is that of efficient management of working time – if an individual is not actually working on fee-paid work, revenue is probably not accruing. This means that non-paid time has to be reviewed very carefully for its benefit to the worker's goals. These may involve improved skills or wider end-user industry knowledge, which will require attendance at seminars or conferences, or taking part in study courses or distance-learning programmes. Such demands must be examined very carefully as to their potential benefit when balanced against the loss of working time.

A vital activity for the individual worker is the need to generate business, ie to market himself. This work, by definition, is unpaid but without it there may be no paid work. A 'rule of thumb' suggests that as much as 25 per cent of the available time should be spent in marketing the individual's skills. This can seem to be a high figure, and may result in the actual paid days lasting a great deal longer than eight hours, to make up for the time 'lost' in getting the business.

The balance between paid and unpaid time has a marked effect on the fee that the individual needs to charge for his services. A fee can be simply calculated by dividing the required annual revenue by the expected number of working days. The revenue has to be calculated to include all the expenses (including net salary) that cannot be charged back to the client: travel, communications, secretarial services, professional society memberships, pension and health care payments, tax and social security, stationery and printing, equipment and so on. The time component then has to allow for non-earning days – there are 233 available days per year, with 8 national holidays and 4 weeks' vacation – and if the one-quarter unpaid rule is followed this gives approximately 175 days per year in which to earn the required revenue. A turnover of £50,000 would thus require a daily fee of around £285, or an hourly rate of about £35.

The efficient use of time

Another element of time that greatly concerns the individual worker

Personal and Corporate Organisation

is to use that time which is available in the most efficient way. Some of the tried and tested techniques for this include:

- making a list of jobs to be done in a particular time period (a day or a week), assigning priorities to each (usually in terms of required finishing times), and then sticking to the resultant programme, only allowing a new entrant to the list if it really does have high priority;
- carrying an 'interruptions folder' of work that can be done when even the best organised timetable goes astray;
- organising a visit programme so as to maximise the amount of interviewing that can be done in the time available;
- setting aside a specific time each day or week to do those routine jobs, such as reading of journals, that would otherwise never get to the top of the priority list;
- doing small jobs at once – it can take as long to fit them into a priority schedule as it does to do them, but there must be a time slot in the schedule for this purpose;
- if a time efficiency programme is just being started, keeping an honest time-use diary for at least one month, to see where the time really does go (and the results will probably surprise you).

The efficient use of time is vital for a productive life as an individual worker in business marketing research. It has often been demonstrated that even those who seem most efficient in their job may be wasting as much as 50 per cent of their time – when you work for yourself, it is *your* time that you are wasting.

Getting started
To establish oneself as a freelance operator in some field of business marketing research is not easy. It cannot sensibly be done without experience – partly because you will have nothing to offer to a prospective client, and partly because you will not know anything about the market into which you will be trying to sell your services. It is obvious that the ideal entry into the freelance marketplace should be a well-planned move, but it is a regrettable fact of life that hard

economic times produce a number of individuals without a job, who look at marketing research as a way of earning a living.

The characteristics required of a freelance worker, researcher, interviewer or consultant, are reasonably obvious: a need to be able to work with and among people and yet to be happy to accept periods of working in isolation; the capability of presenting information clearly, orally and in a written form; a reasonable degree of numeracy; an ability to absorb and understand technical matters, which may be quite complicated; the ability to cope with adversity in the business context.

To set up in business as a freelance as part of a planned career move should be done only with some assurance of immediate work – from a previous employer, or from a friend in the required business sector. It is very difficult to start as an unknown quantity and then to seek business for yourself, to produce revenue quickly.

As a new freelance, you should take on only that work which you can do easily and well – leave the difficult and unfamiliar jobs until you are established. For the same reason, start with small and simple jobs – leave the large and complicated ones until later.

If at all possible, you should have some specialisation to offer your marketplace – in language, or marketing research skill, or knowledge of the technology in your preferred end-user market.

Finally, you should know your intended marketplace well in terms of its component entities and to whom you will have to market your services – and then do this, hard.

Other considerations

There are some other factors of relevance to the individual worker's position in business marketing research, besides time and how to start. These include:

- being soundly advised on your business operations, especially in relation to your income tax and VAT liabilities;

- being absolutely sure of the contractual relationship with your client (for example, avoid a contract that offers to pay you 'on approval of your report' – By whom will the approval be given? Will it be over the telephone or in writing? How long will it take? Can you have a maximum time for this approval to be given? and so on);

Personal and Corporate Organisation

- getting some payment at the start of the job, to help you through its early stages and to pay for services that you may need in order to get the job done – cash flow is always a problem for the individual worker;
- getting to know the best and nearest sources for data that you will need in your work, and the types of data that they offer – you will regularly have to decide whether to do your own desk research, or to get someone else to do it for you, or to buy the information in the form of a published directory or access to an online database.

Whatever your level of expertise at the start of a freelance career, you must maintain your existing skills in as up-to-date a condition as possible; you should try to extend your business marketing research skills beyond your original specialisation; you should remain continuously aware of progress in those end-user sectors of interest to you and your potential clients. It is not surprising that much of the freelance worker's actual earning time tends to occur in the evenings and at weekends.

The business marketing research services company

It is less easy to generalise about the companies providing business marketing research services, because of the diversity in their nature – from a two-person partnership as consultancy or service agency, to a large company able to provide all kinds of service from within its own resources. Nevertheless, there are some common features, in addition to the basic problems of general company management.

For most such companies, there will be the same variation in work load that afflicts the in-house business marketing research department. The impact of this kind of variation will depend very much on the size of the company – a variation of 10 per cent for a large agency might represent a trebling of the load for a small one. This problem has to be solved by the use of external freelance workers recruited for the duration of the job, probably from a pool of such people held on the company's books for just that purpose.

Variations in work load also occur in its nature – 6 groups to be recruited one week, 500 telephone interviews to be organised the next, and 12 depth interviews in the next – or in the country within which the work has to be done, requiring fluent speakers of different languages in successive weeks. Here again, the successful agency deals with the matter by having the necessary expertise available in its own skills register, which is then recruited as it is needed.

As will have become apparent from earlier parts of this Handbook, a consultancy company is one that can undertake the full responsibility for a business marketing research project, working to no more than a project brief, while an agency will normally take on only specific fieldwork tasks, working for an in-house department or a consultancy. Although this is not a sharp division of type, the consultancy may specialise in a limited range of end-user sectors whereas an agency's specialisation would normally be in the fieldwork tasks themselves.

Specialisation is, indeed, an advantage for smaller companies. An agency might offer a studio for group research, perhaps with video recording facilities, or an array of telephone booths for supervised telephone interviewing, perhaps with a CATI system, or a strong capability to undertake interviews in a range of foreign languages. A well defined specialisation is much easier to market to potential clients than a generalised 'we can do anything' approach.

It is also important, however, not to invest too heavily in expensive equipment or computer software systems until it is certain that they will be fully used. Under-usage of such investments will add to what is always a problem – the cash flow – which affects small companies as much as individuals.

Some other points needing attention by the service company include:

- the choice between having either a permanent field force of interviewers, whose wide geographical scattering may make their management difficult, or recruiting locally on a short-term basis, which then needs the maintenance of a good skills register and of good relations with its members so that they will respond quickly when the need arises;

- the requirement for a good field-force manager on the staff who is able to manage the permanent or temporary workers, and is able to see where confidence can be placed in the results and where the occasional contact verification may be needed;

Personal and Corporate Organisation

- the requirement for information sources to make desk research easier, which will involve the choice from sending one's own researchers out to libraries, or establishing a good in-house library, or using online databases – this can be made easier if a member of staff can take on the function of information manager;

- the importance of good staff management, providing career progression where possible, and taking great care in the initial selection of staff to ensure good internal relations and a reasonable length of stay once appointed.

It is, of course, vital for the company's future that a good marketing programme is instituted. The managers should know their marketplace well, sell to it hard, only take on work that they know they can do, and try to balance the work load as much as possible. It is fatal for a marketing services company to fall into the very traps that they may be advising their clients to avoid.

Non-exclusive research

The bulk of the content of this Handbook has been concerned with the work involved in carrying out specific business marketing research projects for a single client. This is, indeed, where the bulk of the effort expended on business marketing research goes, but for the sake of completeness it is necessary to make reference to the existence of two other types of research project: multi-client research and published research.

Multi-client research is still confidential, but now to a small group of clients rather than to just one. It comes about where a consultancy (or a service agency) develops an idea that it considers to be of value to several potential clients, and persuades them all to sponsor it – in full recognition that after its completion the work will be available to all. One major benefit of this way of working is that each client gets the results of what may be a large, expensive study at only a fraction of its total cost. The service company may thereby be able to do a rewarding job, that none of the individual end-users would have considered doing on its own.

There are offsetting difficulties, of course, and these relate to the multiplicity of interests involved. The preparation of the original research brief will involve the melding of several different inputs, while the preparation of the results of the research will be similarly complicated and will almost certainly require different types of presentation. This complication must be allowed for in the job costings.

The idea for such research may come from an end-user company, but is more likely to arise from the experience of the consultants and is a good way to capitalise on this experience.

Published research is undertaken by a number of research publishing houses, who issue for general sale a report on a particular market segment. The report will be prepared in a format that the publisher has found to be successful, so that while the work involved in the research may be little different from that of a single-client study, the final preparation of the study report will be to the commissioning publisher's standards, and there can be no thought of writing with a particular client in mind.

Such work can be very rewarding, especially to individual workers, and it can be found from personal contact or by responding to advertisements in the business press or the marketing research journals.

Part VII: Appendices

The remaining pages of the Handbook contain a number of Appendices, each providing useful information for the reader. They cover some organisational aspects of business marketing research, and then give some sources of information for the researcher.

Appendix A

IMRA – its Aims, Functions and Membership Grades

The Industrial Marketing Research Association is the recognised UK professional association for people engaged in generating, analysing and using information for business-to-business marketing of goods and services.

A distinctive feature of the Association is the wide spectrum of members, representing researchers employed by companies in most manufacturing and service industries; specialists in government departments and other official bodies; teachers and researchers in universities, polytechnics and colleges; employees of market research and marketing consultancy firms.

Services

Contact and information

The annual directory, available only to members, offers direct individual contact with other professionals in the field. The monthly newsletter provides information about IMRA activities and news of other events relevant to business marketing research. Regular meetings of regional sections and specific industry groups give opportunities for discussion and the development of personal contacts.

Courses, conferences and seminars

IMRA runs an annual programme of training courses open to both members and non-members. These range from basic training courses for new entrants to the profession to residential seminars for established researchers and one-day courses on specific topics or techniques.

The IMRA annual conference offers professional papers on a business marketing research theme. Each year several *ad hoc* conferences or seminars are organised.

Publications

Conference and seminar proceedings are generally available in published form. Publications of the Association include the comprehensive *Researching Business Markets - The IMRA Handbook*, a number of monographs on particular topics, and a *European Guide to Industrial Marketing Consultancy*.

Appointments service

The Association runs an appointments mailing service, distributing notices of vacancies to all members on behalf of employing firms. *IMRA News* also carries advertisements for business marketing research appointments.

Professional Support

IMRA represents the interests of business marketing researchers to providers of information and works towards engendering confidence among respondents from whom members wish to obtain information in the course of their research. The membership card issued to each member draws attention to the Association's published Code of Conduct, to which all members formally subscribe and against which any complaint about their activity can be objectively assessed.

Membership

Associate membership is open to any person wholly or largely engaged in business marketing research.

Full membership is available to those with at least three years' experience in business marketing research and who have been Associate members for at least one year. Only Full members are entitled to vote at general meetings of the Association or in postal ballots and only Full members may be elected as officers of the Association or as Council members.

Affiliate membership is designed for people with experience of or interest in business marketing research but who are not wholly or largely engaged in practising it. Overseas membership is open to any person resident outside the UK who qualifies for membership of any of the above grades. Student membership is available to students following full-time courses in management and business studies in the UK.

Enquiries about membership, or any other aspect of the Association's activities, should be addressed to:

The Membership Secretary
IMRA
11 Bird Street
Lichfield
Staffs WS13 6PW
Tel: 0543 263448   Fax: 0543 250929

Appendix B

Qualifications and Training in Business Marketing Research

There are, as yet, no formal qualifications in business marketing research. The Market Research Society offers a Diploma in Market Research, within which there is one industrial case study, but the remainder of the Diploma is strongly consumer-market orientated.

IMRA offers a series of training courses which, each year, include at least one residential course, lasting four days, covering all aspects of business marketing research. IMRA also arranges, each year, a series of short (half- or one-day) courses dealing with an individual practical skill involved in such research. In addition to these, both centrally and through its Regions and Subject Groups, IMRA arranges courses, seminars and symposia on subjects of topical interest.

Some coverage of marketing research is given by courses offered by universities, polytechnics and other further education bodies under the general heading of 'marketing' but, here again, there is a low business content.

It should be noted, however, that increasing attention is being given to marketing in MBA courses, and that some of these courses refer to market research although with only minor coverage of business research.

Appendix C

Summary of the Code of Conduct

The joint IMRA/MRS Code of Conduct is intended to regulate the activities of practitioners of market research, to safeguard the legitimate interests of both users and of informants to market research and the public and business community at large, and to preserve the good name and standing of market research as a discipline and a profession.

The Code has been operated in various revisions since 1954 – the current revision was introduced in 1983. Both rules of conduct and guidance on good practice are included; however, although good practice is not mandatory on members, a breach of the guidelines laid down may be regarded by the Association as a serious matter.

The Code deals with the various aspects of the practice of market research in a number of sections, as outlined below.

Conditions of membership

Membership is conditional on the Association being satisfied as to the good standing of the applicant or member. Action may be taken up to and including withdrawal of membership from any person breaching the Code of Conduct, or otherwise bringing the Association or the profession into disrepute. It is a condition of membership that the Code be accepted.

Responsibilities to informants

This section lays a duty on members to protect the interests of informants. The Code requires that members should preserve the anonymity of informants and that no information should be attributable to themselves or their organisations without a specific waiver, and this requirement extends to disclosure of identity by indirect as well as direct means. The Code also respects the informant's right to refuse to cooperate or to withdraw from cooperation at any time – even to retract any information already given. It is also required that an informant should be able to check the credentials of a member conducting an interview. Members are urged to be as open as possible with informants, and informants should be made aware of their rights under the Code.

The interaction between suppliers and users of market research

This section lays down rules and procedures governing the relationship between the supplier and the user of market research information; however, these may be varied by mutual agreement between the parties, possibly in the form of a contract. The Code here identifies areas which should be explicitly dealt with in the relationship between supplier and client, and requires a member supplying information to draw attention to any area where the relationship between supplier and client departs from the model given in the Code. The section does not give licence to depart from any other part of the Code.

Responsibilities to outside contractors and field workers

Members of the Association are under a duty to ensure that persons undertaking work for them abide by the Code of Conduct, and that they are not discouraged or precluded from doing so whether or not they are members of the Association. Interviewers must be provided with information and guidance to enable them to fulfil the requirements of the Code to informants.

Summary of the Code of Conduct

Responsibilities to the general public, the business community and other institutions

This section deals with public and business perception of market research. The Code requires that members shall not abuse general confidence in the profession, its practitioners and its standards, and shall attempt to prevent non-members from bringing disrepute to the profession. Members shall not misrepresent or allow to be misrepresented other activities, especially sales approaches and anything which might be construed as industrial espionage, as market research.

Professional responsibilities

Under this section it is the duty of members to ensure that all persons working for them, whether within or outside their own organisation, abide by the Code in work connected with market research. Members are expected to behave in a professional manner towards one another and in their dealings with the Association, and a special responsibility is laid on the senior members of organisations.

Note: The preceding pages have provided a guide to the IMRA/MRS Code of Conduct, and a summary of its main features. Like all summaries it omits much and glosses over detail. Specifically it should be noted that, as the summary is prepared for IMRA use, much of the more consumer-orientated content of the Code has been ignored.

The summary is intended to give the flavour of the Code, and it is hoped that in this it is successful. However, no responsibility can be accepted by IMRA for any omissions or errors – conduct remains governed by the Code alone, and its operation and interpretation remain the prerogative of the two UK professional bodies: IMRA and the MRS.

Appendix D

List of Information Sources

This Appendix contains a number of sources of data, useful directly or indirectly in marketing research work. These are relatively specialised, and the reader must not forget:

- his local Borough or District, and County reference libraries, which can have a surprisingly good array of directories, and

- the libraries of professional bodies (the RSC for books on chemistry and chemicals, the IMechE for books on machinery, energy and waste processing, and so on), and of trade associations – although these may be rather more restricting in their accessibility.

The listed sources relate only to the United Kingdom, although equivalent bodies can be found in most Western European countries.

Business Statistics Office
Cardiff Road, Newport, Gwent NPT 1XG

City Business Library
55 Basinghall Street, London EC2V 5BX

Companies House
55 City Road, London EC1Y 1AY

Companies House (Registrar of Companies)
Crown Way, Maindy, Cardiff CF4 3UZ

Export Market Information Centre (EMIC)
1 Victoria Street (entrance on Abbey Orchard Street) London SW1 0ET.

Government Bookshop (HMSO)
49 High Holborn, London WC1

Science Reference and Information Service (part of the British Library)
25 Southampton Buildings, Chancery Lane, London WC2A 1AW

University of Warwick
Business Information Service, Gibbet Hill Road, Coventry CV4 7AL

Appendix E

Bibliography of Major Relevant Texts

The list of books in this Appendix is intended to offer the user of the Manual an extended reading list on the subject of business marketing research, and related topics. They are not necessarily the latest or the best on their subject, but are included as a help to the reader seeking further enlightenment.

Industrial marketing research

The Industrial Market Research Handbook
 Paul Hague
 Kogan Page, Second Edition, 1987

Handbook of Industrial Marketing and Research
 Ian MacLean (ed)
 Kluwer-Harrap, 1976

Market research in general (mainly consumer orientated)

The Effective Use of Market Research: A Guide for Management
 Robin Birn
 Kogan Page, Second Edition, 1990

Researching Business Markets – The IMRA Handbook

A Handbook of Market Research Techniques
Robin Birn, Paul Hague and Phyllis Vangelder (eds)
Kogan Page, 1991

Applied Marketing and Social Research
Ute Bradley (ed)
John Wiley, Second Edition, 1987

Marketing Research
Peter M Chisnall
McGraw-Hill, Third Edition, 1986

The Marketing Research Process
Margaret Crimp
Prentice Hall, Second Edition, 1985

Qualitative Market Research
Wendy Gordon and Roy Langmaid
Gower, 1988

Low-Cost Marketing Research
Keith Gorton and Isobel Doole
John Wiley, Second Edition, 1989

Do Your Own Market Research
P N Hague and P Jackson
Kogan Page, 1990

How to do Marketing Research
P N Hague and P Jackson
Kogan Page, 1990

Marketing Research
A Paraswaman
Addison-Wesley, 1986

Applied Qualitative Research
R Walker (ed)
Gower, 1985

Consumer Market Research Handbook
R M Worcester and J Downham (eds)
Elsevier, Third Edition, 1986

Bibliography of Major Relevant Texts

Marketing management

International Marketing Management
 Subbash C Jain
 PWS-Kent (Chapman and Hall), Third Edition, 1990

Marketing Management
 Philip Kotler
 Prentice Hall, Fourth Edition, 1980

Handbook of Sales and Marketing Management
 Len Rogers
 Kogan Page, 1988

Behavioural Aspects of Marketing
 Keith Williams
 Heinemann, 1981

Economics

Economics: An Introduction for Students of Business and Marketing
 Frank Livesey
 Heinemann, Third Edition, 1990

Economics
 Paul Samuelson (and William Nordhaus, for this edition)
 McGraw-Hill, Twelfth Edition, 1986

Statistical Analysis

Introductory Statistics for Business and Economics
 T H and R J Wonnacott
 John Wiley, 1977

Appendix F

The Export Marketing Research Scheme

[For UK companies wishing to undertake marketing research outside the UK, the Export Marketing Research Scheme can be a valuable source of financial help. The following notes on the Scheme have been supplied for inclusion here by the Association of British Chambers of Commerce, the operators of the Scheme.]

The EMRS is administered by the ABCC on behalf of the Department of Trade and Industry. It is designed to encourage the use of marketing research as an integral part of export strategy, by facilitating the systematic collection, collating, evaluation and presentation of information on which marketing decisions can be based.

Companies (but not Divisions within Companies) who have less than 200 employees are eligible to apply for the Scheme's support, if their products or services are mainly of UK origin and are exportable from the UK. UK trade associations conducting research on behalf of their members are also eligible to apply.

Our Export Marketing Research Advisers can offer free professional advice on how to set about export marketing research and on all stages of the project – from preparing the research brief to writing a report following overseas fieldwork.

The Scheme also offers financial help to companies undertaking an export marketing research project. Support may take one of four forms.

1. If a member of your staff has the ability and experience to carry

out marketing research to a satisfactory standard, we will support marketing research studies conducted in-house by paying up to half of essential travel costs and interpreter's fees, plus a daily allowance towards hotel and meal costs incurred by one researcher during overseas field work. (*Note:* This support does not extend to research relating to European Community countries.)
2. If you commission professional consultants to undertake marketing research for you overseas, we will pay up to half the cost,
3. If you purchase published market research, we will pay up to one-third of the cost,
4. If you are a trade association, and commission research or carry it out in-house on behalf of your members, up to 75 per cent of the project costs can be supported.

There are a few specific areas where financial support cannot be granted. These include:

- general background research which is not part of a specific project;
- overseas visits where marketing research is not the primary objective;
- sales or promotional trips;
- attendance at trade fairs or exhibitions;
- research conducted wholly or mainly on a group visit or trade mission (whether or not a subvention is made available);
- research carried out wholly in the UK;
- market development;
- omnibus studies.

Support *cannot* be given for marketing research projects already commissioned, under way, or completed. Similarly, support cannot be given for published market research already purchased.

Companies wishing to apply for assistance are advised to contact the ABCC at the following address to obtain further details about the Scheme, and should allow at least 28 days for an application to be processed:

The Export Marketing Research Scheme

Export Marketing Research Scheme
Association of British Chambers of Commerce
4 Westwood House
Westwood Business Park
Coventry CV4 8HS
Tel: 0203 694484
Fax: 0203 694690

Index

accuracy *see* precision
acquisition research 373ff
  cross-border 385
  information requirement 380
  in-house vs contractor 378ff
advertising
  as part of corporate image creation 334
  research 351ff
  tracking 355
'agenda' analysis software 248
ALA (American Libraries Association) 92
AMA (American Marketing Association) 92
AMSO (Association of Market Survey Organisations) 41
analysis of qualitative data 237ff
  as iterative process 238, 239
  charts 244, 247
  problem of large volume of data 241
  techniques 241ff
analysis of quantitative data 64, 219ff
  techniques 222ff
analysis methods 217ff

as part of original brief 221, 437
importance in questionnaire design 198
Annual Abstract of Statistics (UK-HMSO) 91
annual reports, use in competitor research 309
anonymity
  as means of increasing response rates 122
  as means of improving responses 114
applied research, marketing research as 32
Aslib (Association of Special Libraries) 92, 411
attitudinal questions 189, 191
Aucamp, J 110, 128
authors, list of 15

Baker Library (Harvard) 91
banks, as source of international data 410
BARB (Broadcasters' Audience Research Board) 128
behavioural questions 189, 190
Benn's Media Directory 91, 410

Index

bibliography of relevant texts 467ff
body language, importance in interviews 55, 172
brainstorming
  as problem definition technique 49
  in qualitative data analysis 241
British Library Document Supply Centre 87
British Technology Index 90
British Telecom Fax Directory 295
business 36
Business Line business omnibus surveys 137
business market characteristics 142, 239
business marketing research 36
  change from 'industrial' 35
  comparison with consumer research 37
  international 395ff
  management 443ff
  qualifications and training 459
  variability among respondents 180
Business Periodicals Index 90
business planning, sales forecasting in 359ff
Business Statistics Office 465
business strategy 359

CAPI (computer-assisted personal interviewing) 97, 101, 112, 114, 135
CATI (computer-assisted telephone interviewing) 56, 57, 103–105, 114, 298
CD-ROM storage 92
censuses, as forerunners of marketing research 33
central location interviewing 134ff
  see also: clinics, hall tests
  recruitment problems 136
City Business Library 48, 86, 91, 465
clarity in written reports 258
classification questions 190, 192
clinics 134ff
client lists, as sample frame 146
clustering of interviews 56, 57, 59, 63, 101, 106, 115
Code of Conduct (IMRA/MRS) 41, 42, 81, 110, 117, 125, 133, 134, 170, 323, 418, 456, 461ff
coding of quesionnaires 57, 182
commissioning of research project 432
Companies House 92, 310, 465
competitor research 307ff
  identification of competitors 308
  information available 309ff
  marketing analysis 314
computers
  use in data analysis 223, 247
  use in desk research 87ff
  use in oral presentations 284
  use in questionnaire design 203
concept research as part of new product research 348
consultants in business marketing research 445, 449ff
Cooper, A J 117
cross-tabulations 64, 227

Dafsa 91, 412
databases
  as source of information 83, 411
  in competitor research 320
data analysis *see:* analysis
data collection techniques 95ff
  see also: qualitative/quantitative data collection

475

Index

Datastream 91
Datastar 88
Delphi method for sales forecasting 371
depth interviews 50, 130, 166, 168
  see also: face-to-face interviews
  analysis and interpretation 238
  limitations 51
  skills 163ff
  use of instructured quesionnaires in 189
desk research 79, 83ff
  as part of problem definition 48
  in international research 407ff
Dialog 88
Directory of European Associations (CBD) 411
Directory of Online Databases (Cuadra) 92, 411
Directory of UK Associations (CBD) 411
Dun & Bradstreet 91

Economic Commission for Africa 408
Economic Commission for Asia and the Far East 408
Economic Commission for Latin America 408
Economist (The) 409
Education Year Book 167
eligibility for inclusion in samples 151, 157
  individual selection from several eligible 153
EMIC (UK–DTI Export Marketing Intelligence Centre) 86, 410, 412, 466
EMRS (Export Marketing Research Scheme) 413, 432, 471ff
errors in research results 160, 440

ESOMAR (European Society for Opinion and Marketing Research) 427
  Directory 425
ethical standards and practices 41ff, 307, 322ff, 381ff, 401
European Community 408
exporting, as business decision 403ff
Extel cards 91, 311

face-to-face interviews 51
  advantages 54, 97
  as data collection method 54ff, 96ff
  combined with other data collection methods 96
  duration 99
  for competitor research 319
  limitations 55, 100
  questionnaire design 208ff
  skills 163ff
fax, postal questionnaires sent by 113, 117
field research 79, 95ff
  agencies 445, 449ff
  in international research 413ff
filtering
  in questionnaires 60
  in tabulations 225, 227
Financial Times 85, 409
Findex 90
focus groups see: group discussions
fog factor in written reports 258
Food and Agricultural Organisation 409
forecast
  in business planning 362
  of market size growth 296
freelance workers 445, 446ff
'free text' search of databases 88

476

Index

government publications 91, 466
Green, P E 30, 31, 32
grossing-up 155, 157ff
   dealing with incomplete data 159
group discussions (focus groups) 52, 129, 130ff
   analysis and interpretation 238
   in competitor research 319
   limitations 52
   observation 133
   problems of recruitment 132
   recording 52, 130
group dynamics 131
Guide to Official Statistics 91

Hague, P N 125, 126, 136
hall tests 134
Handbuch der Deutschen Aktiengesellschaften 412
Hints to Exporters (UK–DTI) 413, 416
Hoppenstedt 91
Hospital and Health Services Year Book 146

ICC (Inter Company Comparisons) 91, 311
image assessment 325ff
   in competitor analysis 313
   levels of corporate image 331
   need for a good image 326
   producing a good image 328
   techniques 335ff
IMRA (Industrial Marketing Research Association) 9, 35, 39, 41, 92, 270, 323, 324, 407, 427, 455ff, 459, 461, 463
   European Guide to Industrial Marketing Consultancy 425
   Membership Directory 425, 428, 455, 456
incentives 123, 136, 212

individuals
   as research contractors 446ff
   selection from a number eligible 153
industrial espionage *see:* ethical standards and practices
industrial market research, origins 35
Industrial Outlook (US Dept of Commerce)) 85
information services
   specialist companies 84
   specialist employee 89
in-house information sources 85, 408
in-house researchers 10
   choice between external contractor and 81, 416ff, 423ff
   management 44
International Air Transport Association 408
International Bank for Reconstruction and Development 409
international business marketing research 395ff
   choice between contractor and in-house researchers 416ff
   home vs international research – differences 398ff
   similarities 397
International Business Reply service (Royal Mail) 123
International Civil Aviation Organisation 409
International Directory of Market Research Organisations (BOTB/mrs) 425
International Monetary Fund 408
International Telecommunications Union 409

Index

International Union of Railways 409
interpretation
 of qualitative data 249ff
 of quantitative data 219, 231ff
interviewer bias 56, 101, 114
interviewer briefing 207
 client involvement in 436
interviewer card 98, 110
interviewing
 managing the interview 168
 planning the interview 164
 quality 174
 setting up the interview 173, 174
 skills of 163ff
 structure of the interview 163
Investors Service 412

jargon 75, 180, 200
Jordans 311
jury, as used in sales forecasting 370

Key British Enterprises (Dun & Bradstreet) 145
Key Directors business omnibus surveys 137
Kompass 67, 91, 92, 145

language, as problem in international research 398
letters, importance of cover letter in postal research 213
libraries 86
library co-operative 87
Library of Congress 87
listening, vital importance in interviewing 172

mailing lists 146
 as base of sample for postal surveys 119

quality 120
updating 121
Manual of Industrial Marketing Research 9
marketing 31
 definition 30
Marketing File (Dun & Bradstreet) 145
Marketing Pocket Book (UK Advertising Association) 85
marketing problem
 as basis for research 73ff
 definition 45, 46, 48
 prioritising objectives 47
marketing research 31, 33
 definition 31
 history 34
 role in corporate acquisition 374ff, 388
Market Research Development Fund 97, 99, 107, 109
Market Search (Arlington) 412
market size (*see also* grossing-up)
 definition 290
 estimation 154ff, 289ff
'Marquis' questionnaire design software 203
McCarthy's press cutting service 90
MCI Mail 88
membership lists as sample frame 146
Mintel report on Sports Sponsorship 48
moderator in group discussions 52, 53, 130, 133
MRS (Market Research Society) 39, 41, 98, 110, 323, 407, 427, 459, 461, 463
 Newsletter 137
 Yearbook 425
MSI (*Marketing Surveys Index*) 90

478

Index

multi client research 451
multivariate analysis 64
Municipal Year Book 146

Nathan, L 139
new product research 341ff
　characteristics 344fff
　development of new products 343
　techniques 347ff
New York Public Library 87
Nielsen Retail Index 128
non-exclusive research 451ff

observation
　as part of face-to-face interviews 97, 100
　as problem definition technique 49
　of group discussions 52, 133
observation techniques for data collection 124ff
　advantages 125
　limitations 126
　used in combination with other techniques 125
OECD 408
omnibus surveys 137ff
　in advertising research 356
　in computer analysis 318
online databases 84, 87ff, 411
　advantages 87
　disadvantages 88
　hardware 88
　software 89
oral presentation of research results 254, 264ff, 438
　comparison with written reports 260
　format 273ff
　major factors 266ff

management of the presentation 276ff
　position of the summary 274
oversampling 149, 295

panels 128ff
　problem of conditioning 129
　'rolling' panel 130
Parcel Force (Royal Mail parcel service) 301
Pareto's law 292
Pergamon Infoline 88
piloting
　of postal survey 122
　of questionnaires 182, 202
policy analysis 36
polls, of public opinion 34, 110
postal research
　advantages 58, 113
　as data collection method 58ff, 112ff
　as part of mix of data collection techniques 59, 113
　limitations 59, 115
　methods for improving response rate 60, 118, 212
　questionnaire design 211ff
　response rate as problem 60, 115
precision
　of data analysis 64
　of data collection 14, 128, 143
　of information requirement 76
Predicast F&S Index 90, 410
presentation
　of postal questionnaires 122
　of research results 253ff, 438ff
　of results as basis for interpretation 234
Prestel Viewdata 88
probabililty sampling 61, 148ff

Index

Product Data Service (UK-DTI) 413
projecting and enabling techniques 131, 166
projection of trends, as part of business planning 364, 365
prompts and probes in interviewing 171
public sector research 34
published information, as source for desk research 83, 85
published market research 412, 452

qualitative data analysis *see:* analysis
qualitative data collection 50ff
qualitative research 49
  definition 50
quality of research data 58, 59, 97, 101, 105, 108, 114, 129
quantitative data analysis *see:* analysis
quantitative data collection 53ff
questionnaires 177ff
  as basis of postal research 112
  characteristics 178
  classification of questions 189
  design 194ff
  draft agreed with client 435
  importance of analysis requirements in design 222
  length important in postal research 60, 121
  roles in business marketing research 177
  types 181
quotas 62
  design 143
quota sampling 62, 150

random numbers in sample selection 152

Rawnsley, Allan 9
recording of interviews
  audio (tape) recordings 51, 98, 170, 242
  audio/video recording of group discussions 52, 130, 134
reminder mailings in postal research 123
research brief 46, 73ff, 422
  as basis for interpretation of research results 231
research contractors (consultants/fieldwork agencies)
  briefing by client 428
  choice between in-house personnel and 81, 416ff, 423ff
  management 449ff
  selection by client 425, 430
  types 445
research project
  control 82, 432ff
  costing 79
  definition of objectives 422
  management by client 421ff, 432ff
  management by contractor 443ff
research proposal 77ff
  costing 80
research survey design 143
respondents
  benefits from research for 41
  role in interviews 179
  role in questionnaire design 194
  wearout of 129, 130
response rates
  effective 116
  for postal research 115
  for telephone interviews 109
  overall 116
responses
  costs of 113

Index

dealing with non-response 123, 153
risk analysis in business planning 360
Robson, S 134
routeing in questionnaire design 182

sales forecasting 359ff
  techniques 366ff
sample design 141ff
  importance of analysis requirements in 222
sample frame 61, 103
  definition 144
  evaluation 146ff
  screening 147, 148, 151
sample matching 129, 130
sample selection 148ff, 152
sample size 63, 150
sampling
  as core discipline of marketing research 33
  theory 40
  types 60ff
Schlackman, W 129
scope of research, definition 76
S-curve for forecasting 296
self-administered questionnaires
  as data collection method 58ff, 112ff
  combined with other data collection methods 96
  see also: Postal research/questionnaires
semi-structured questions/questionnaires 181, 184
sensitive issues 51, 59, 98, 132
sequential sampling 298
show-cards 54, 99

signposting in presentation of research results 262
Smith, E 138
sorting techniques in interviews 99
spreadsheets, downloading information to 88
SRIS (British Library Science Reference and Information Service) 48, 86, 466
standard break, in data tabulations 224
statistics 71
  as part of marketing research 33
  dealing with 'outliers' 158
  importance in sampling 61, 142
stratification 40, 63, 149
structured questions/questionnaires 181, 182
studios for group discussions 133
sugging ('selling under the guise of market research') 110
survey research, as forerunner of market research 33
Sykes, W 251
systematic error 143

tabulations 64
  components 223
  for quantitative data analysis 222ff
  specifications 225
  see also: cross-tabulations
technical matters in research brief 76
Telecom Gold 88
teleconferencing 103, 131
telemarketing 110
telephone interviewing
  advantages 56, 104
  as data collection method 56ff, 103ff

Index

as part of mix of data collection techniques 57, 96, 104
  duration 107
  for screening of sample frames/mailing lists 103, 104
  in competitor research 319
  limitations 57, 107
  questionnaire design 205ff
  skills 163ff
test marketing
  as part of new product development 349
  central location interviewing to simulate 135, 136
time, efficient use of 446
Times, The 409
topic guides 51, 96, 132, 189
tracking (over time) 128, 355
trade associations 86, 411
transcriptions
  as basis for analysis 243, 246
  of interviews as vital part of data analysis 242, 243
trust, as vital component of successful interviews 167
Tull, D S 30, 31, 32

Ulrich's International Periodicals 91, 410
United Nations 408
Universal Postal Union 409
universe, to be sampled 141
  definition 143, 145
unstructured questions/questionnaires 181, 187

see also: Topic guides

validation of interviews 96, 98, 104, 110
validity of qualitative research 50, 238, 251
videoconferencing 103, 131
videodisks 93
visual aids
  in interviews 54, 99, 109, 115, 210
  in presentations 281ff

Wardle, J 134
Warwick University Business Information Service 466
weighting of research results 154ff
Whitley, E W 115, 119
Willing's Press Guide 91, 410
Wilson, Aubrey 35
World Health Organisation 409
WORM disks 93
written reports for results presentation 254, 255ff, 439
  comparison with oral presentation 260ff
  guidelines 256ff

Yates, Frank 33
Yearbook of World Electronics Data (Elsevier) 85
Yellow Pages 144, 148, 434
  Business Database 302